# Perspectives on the Economics of Aging

Ali Gökhan Gölçek
*Niğde Ömer Halisdemir University, Turkey*

**IGI Global**
Scientific Publishing
Publishing Tomorrow's Research Today

| Vice President of Editorial | Melissa Wagner |
| Managing Editor of Acquisitions | Mikaela Felty |
| Managing Editor of Book Development | Jocelynn Hessler |
| Production Manager | Mike Brehm |
| Cover Design | Phillip Shickler |

Published in the United States of America by
  IGI Global Scientific Publishing
  701 East Chocolate Avenue
  Hershey, PA, 17033, USA
  Tel: 717-533-8845
  Fax: 717-533-8661
  E-mail: cust@igi-global.com
  Website: https://www.igi-global.com

Library of Congress Cataloging-in-Publication Data


CIP PENDING

ISBN13: 979-8-3693-7753-6
Isbn13Softcover: 979-8-3693-7754-3
EISBN13: 979-8-3693-7755-0


British Cataloguing in Publication Data
A Cataloguing in Publication record for this book is available from the British Library.

# Table of Contents

# Detailed Table of Contents

In this chapter, I discuss the economic effects of population aging and the potential that it offers for public sector management, social justice, and economic development. As the population continues to age, public spending for social security and health care increases, but the so called "Silver Economy," which is based on the increasing demand of goods and services for seniors, remains underexplored. The chapter focuses on intergenerational equity, resource allocation and economic transitions and provides a roadmap on how the 'problems' of aging societies can be addressed in a way that unleash the potential of such societies. Using both international and Asian examples, it analyses the complex interconnections between demographic change, public expenditure, social justice and consumer cultures, and proposes new ways of thinking to support sustainable and equitable growth. Thus, this chapter unfolds a multilayered approach to understand the various economic and social changes that occur due to the presence of aging populations.

**Chapter 2**

*Tabassum Bashir, Aligarh Muslim University, India*
*Deoshree Akhouri, Aligarh Muslim University, India*
*Salma Afroj, Aligarh Muslim University, India*
*Kalim Ahamd Khan, Aligarh Muslim University, India*
*Akanksha, Aligarh Muslim University, India*
*Hamza Hamza, Aligarh Muslim University, India*

This chapter examines lifelong learning among older people and highlights the relationship between lifelong learning, economic participation, and demographic trends. Through an analysis of the theoretical underpinnings, demographic developments, and practical ramifications, it seeks to improve the conversation on older adult education. To support older adults in their ongoing learning endeavors, regardless of their self-identification as learners, the chapter redefines traditional educational concepts by promoting a broader understanding of learning as a lifelong process and emphasizing the integration of emerging learning theories, research, and policies. In cognition, emotion, and behavior, psychological theories are examined and emphasize how aging impacts mental processes and emotional experiences. Lifelong learning is essential for improving employability in a labor market that is constantly changing and for adjusting to the workforce's needs, which benefits both individuals and the economy. The chapter promotes the removal of obstacles to lifelong learning and development.

**Chapter 3**

*Salma Afroj, Aligarh Muslim University, India*
*Tabassum Bashir, Aligarh Muslim University, India*
*Pallav Vishnu, Aligarh Muslim University, India*
*Kalim Ahmad Khan, Aligarh Muslim University, India*

An extensive review of digital inclusion among seniors is given in this chapter, with particular attention on social integration promoted by digital technology, economic engagement, and the effects of post-COVID-19 digital inclusion. It seeks to make a significant contribution to the current conversation on digital inclusion by examining the tactics and obstacles that go along with it. Technology continues to influence how we obtain health information, maintain relationships with loved ones, and participate in society as our living environments grow more digitally connected. This pattern has been highlighted by the COVID-19 pandemic, proving internet access a crucial socioeconomic factor that influences health. The usage of digital technologies by older individuals has a direct impact on their quality of life and health outcomes more than ever before. It draws attention to the expanding significance of digital technology for daily activities, social communication, and healthcare access, with digital access emerging as a major social determinant of health.

**Chapter 4**

*Lakshmi R. Nair, Christ University, India*

The Chapter is the fruit of research undertaken by the author who shows light to the last phases of human life. The chapter provides the cultural backdrop on growing up. The title: Ring out "Ageing Miserably;" Ring in "Growing Gracefully" suggests the author's skeptical reading of the common meanings of "ageing". At the same time the author with critical arguments revises the meaning of ageing. The researcher reaches a remedy to the problem. The research is centered on Economics of Ageing. "Heaven on Earth" a Proposed Indian Model in every Taluk numbering 6057 units located at the most healthy, hygienic, environmentally fit chosen part of the Taluk. Each center with 10 acres of land instituted legally through constitutional litigation. No other financial commitment is on the part of the state. The Indian Model means for grownup citizens aged above 60 joining institution as per rules. There will be an economic design for the running of the project.

    *S. Srinivasan, Department of Humanities and Social Sciences, Graphic*
       *Era University, Dehradun, India*
    *N. Rajavel, Department of Social Work, Bharathidasan University,*
       *Khajamalai Campus, Trichy, India*

The study focused on how technology improves the lives of elderly people. The study emphasizes life satisfaction, quality of life, social support, subjective well-being, life satisfaction among older adults, and social networks. Technology can improve the lives of elderly people. How the Theories of Specialization in Old Age can enhance the quality of life. The research study was conducted in Trichy District, Tamil Nadu, India. The research design used cross-sectional analysis. The study selected 75 rural and 75 urban samples, totaling 150 samples collected in the research. The researcher used multi-stage sampling. The findings of the study are aimed at understanding the impact of quality of life on older adults. To identify the subjective well-being and how technology usage helps older adults cope with situations.

    *Tiago Manuel Horta Reis da Silva, King's College London, UK*

This article explores the intersection of age-friendly housing and urban planning within the broader context of the economics of aging. As populations worldwide continue to age, there is a growing need to adapt housing and urban environments to meet the specific needs of older adults. This chapter examines the economic implications of age-friendly housing initiatives and the role of urban planning in creating sustainable, inclusive environments for the elderly. By analysing current trends, policies, and economic models, the chapter aims to provide a comprehensive understanding of how age-friendly urban planning can contribute to the well-being of older adults while also benefiting society at large. The discussion includes case studies from various global contexts, highlighting best practices and innovative solutions. The chapter concludes by offering policy recommendations and identifying areas for future research.

Old age is one of the life stages that every living being will encounter if they live a normal life course. Thanks to the opportunities provided by developing technology and economic development, the average life expectancy is gradually increasing and the number of people who manage to reach the old age stage is increasing day by day. In old age, people's employment opportunities decrease and this may cause economic bottlenecks for the elderly. It is becoming more and more likely that elderly people who try to survive in old age by relying solely on public resources will experience economic difficulties. The relationship between the elderly population and GDP per capita and health expenditures is tested with Johansen cointegration test and toda yamamoto causality test. A cointegration relationship was found between the variables. According to the model results, a causality relationship was found between the elderly population and GDP per capita and health expenditures.

Priya S. Dev, Department of Social Work, Bharathidasan University,
Trichy, India
J. O. Jeryda Gnanajane Eljo, Department of Social Work,
Bharathidasan University, Trichy, India
S. Srinivasan, Department of Humanities and Social Sciences, Graphic
Era University, Dehradun, India

In contemporary society, parents strive to provide a better life for their children by pursuing job opportunities. There is a significant increase in parents entrusting the duty of baby care to their own parents or in-laws. Taking care of grandchildren is a herculean task for some, while for others; it brings happiness and enjoyment during their retirement life. In these circumstances, they have their own concerns regarding health, family, children, as well as the grandchildren in their care. The findings of the study reveals that, the positive, as well as negative, aspects of intergenerational caregiving have substantial importance in the area of policy making. The study conclude with a statement regarding the need of Social support policies, that can play a pivotal role in identifying the needs of grandparents during the caregiving process and the essentiality to establish intergenerational bonding between grandparents and young adults.

# Preface

In an era characterized by rapid demographic transitions, the phenomenon of aging populations has emerged as a defining global challenge and opportunity. Across the world, societies are experiencing unprecedented shifts in age demographics with increasing life expectancy and decreasing fertility rates. While these changes present large economic, social and health care challenges, they also present new opportunities for reimagining the role of older adults in developing resilient and inclusive economies. This book, *Perspectives on the Economics of Aging* provides crucial insights into the complex interrelationship between the demographic process of aging and the structures of the world economy as well as potential economic consequences of this major process.

Typically speaking, aging is viewed as a burden as worries about increases in healthcare costs, maintaining a workable pension system, and diminishing labor forces continue to grow. But this view overlooks the huge potential for older people to add value to economic and social development. By embracing the silver economy, fostering digital and economic inclusion, and rethinking intergenerational equity, societies can transform the challenges of aging into opportunities for innovation, growth, and solidarity. This volume brings together contributions from scholars and practitioners, offering interdisciplinary analyses that blend theoretical insights with empirical data and case studies.

Aging is not an academic subject only; it is a moral and practical imperative. Adaptive systems facing this challenge require policymakers, researchers, and other stakeholders to come up with solutions that maximize equity and sustainability and recognize the value to all members of society for all age groups. This book offers a framework to make sense of the nuances of aging economies and identifies tangible pathways to foster well-being, resilience, and inclusion.

# ORGANIZATION OF THE BOOK

The book opens with *The Economics of Aging: Global Trends and Perspectives* provides the background for understanding global trends that underlie population aging. In this chapter we look at the many ways in which aging impacts economies, from changes in labor force participation to healthcare spending to social security systems. Setting the stage for a more detailed discussion of the challenges and opportunities that an aging society offers, it provides an overview of demographic data and its place with regard to economics.

*Lifelong Learning: Demographic Trends and Economic Participation in Older Adults* emphasizes the potential of education to effect a real transformation in opportunities for adults in their later years. This chapter looks into the role of lifelong learning in promoting active economic and social participation, skills enhancement and mental health of ageing populations. It also highlights education as a way to open up traditional views of aging and with it a life of economic empowerment, and contribution to society.

*Digital Inclusion and Economic Participation of the Elderly Challenges and Strategies*: Digital literacy plays a significant role in closing the gap between the haves and the have nots, but also in creating the divide between generations. Critical barriers to digital inclusion for older people, including barriers of accessibility, affordability and lack of training, are identified in the chapter. It presents innovative strategies and case studies on how technology can enable older individuals to participate economically, socially connect and collectively strengthen intergenerational cohesion.

The fourth chapter, *Ring out "Ageing Miserably;" Ring in "Growing Gracefully"* reimagines ageing from cultural and philosophical perspectives. But its main ingredients are challenging the stigmas of society about old age and calling for a paradigm flick to be concerned about dignity, personal development and a positive approach to aging. The chapter blends cultural, economic and psychological perspectives to offer a full life quality support framework for older adults to overcome aging as a chance for renewal and self-expression.

*Technology Improves the Quality of Life for Elderly People: Quality of Life for the Elderly People* considers how gerontechnology transforms the lives of aging citizens. It shows how wearables, smart homes and telemedicine can increase independence, health and connections. This chapter stresses that advancing technologies should be brought into aging strategies to manage disparities in health and enhance overall well-being.

The sixth chapter, *Designing for Longevity: Economic Perspectives on Age-Friendly Housing and Urban Development* addresses the defining importance of the built environment in the support of aging populations and includes a literature review and case studies. This chapter focuses on innovative ways of urban planning and housing design that boost accessibility, safety and inclusivity. It presents how economic and architectural perspective can be integrated to develop age friendly environment to improve the quality of life of older adults while reconciling social cohesion and sustainability.

The seventh chapter, *The Effects of Türkiye's Ageing Problem on the Elderly*, addresses the multi-faceted relation between the aging population in Türkiye and its socio-economic structures, outlining the issues and policy responses. The economic dimensions of ageing are examined, such as health expenditure, pension systems and the relationship between demographic shifts and GDP per capita. The study finds cointegration between aging demographics, health spending, and economic growth using empirical analyses. Financial sustainability, income diversification for the elderly and promotion of intergenerational solidarity in the context of demographic change are identified as policy recommendations.

*Intergenerational Caregiving on Grandparents Health: A Case Study* investigates the health implications of caregiving relationship for older adults. The chapter examines the effects of intergenerational caregiving on grandparents' physical and mental health using an empirical case study, and how it affects other family structures and support systems. This reveals the significance of intergenerational dynamics in developing policies and interventions to promote well-being among people of all ages.

These eight chapters together offer a full exploration of the issues and potential associated with demographic aging. This volume examines this phenomenon through a variety of different perspectives and thereby prepares the reader to understand this key global phenomenon in the 21st century as well as to contribute to the resolution of the problem.

**Ali Gökhan Gölçek**
*Nigde Ömer Halisdemir University, Turkey*

# Acknowledgments

This book, *Perspectives on the Economics of Aging*, has been both an enjoyable and difficult journey to create. First, I would like to thank the IGI Global team for their professional support towards this publication to completion. Even as we challenged ourselves to a particularly ambitious publication timeline, they've been there for us with their commitment to excellence. This project was completed successfully under the tight schedule to a great extent, although it presented a great challenge, a result of the resilience and cooperation of everyone involved.

First of all, I am deeply indebted to the chapter contributors who were able to deliver their chapters with academic rigor under the constrained time frame. They have proven to balance quality with urgency.

It also goes to the peer reviewers who, at a more timely speed, provided helpful reviews about the chapters. Their expertise did more than enrich the scholarly depth for this book, but it also helped ensure that this book meets the highest of academic standards.

Finally, I wish to express my thanks to my wife, family and colleagues for their constant encouragement and understanding. Their support helped keep the effort going until we could bring this book to completion.

My hope is that this volume will be a useful resource in the research, practice and policy of the economic dimensions of ageing. I want to thank all those people who helped to real possible, especially in such an extremely difficult situation.

# Introduction: On The Trail of Aging

Aging, what does it signify in human life? Is it an end or a new beginning? Do societies perceive aging as a process where individuals lose their productivity and importance, or is it valued as a period when experience and knowledge become most precious? And how do we, as individuals, perceive aging? These questions are fundamental for anyone seeking to understand and discuss the phenomenon of aging. However, these questions do not remain solely at the individual level; aging is a complex phenomenon with profound effects on societies' socio-economic structures, policies, and futures.

The world's population is aging rapidly. The World Health Organization (WHO) predicts that by 2050, approximately 22% of the global population will be 60 years or older. However, it's crucial to recognize that these statistics are not merely numbers; they signify profound transformations that resonate across a wide spectrum, from the global economy and social security systems to healthcare policies and individuals' quality of life. The critical question is: Is this transformation solely a challenge? Or is it a process that harbors opportunities?

Of course, aging is not just an individual experience; it's also a collective phenomenon. For example, why are the economic contributions of older individuals in society still overlooked? Why isn't the "*silver economy*," which highlights the economic impact of older adults, discussed enough? Perhaps we are asking the wrong questions when we contemplate aging. This book is an invitation to understand the multifaceted impacts of aging and to reframe the questions that arise from these impacts.

## RETHINKING AGING

Aging is often approached as a "*problem*." The burden on social security systems, the increase in healthcare expenditures, the shrinking workforce, and the rise of the dependent population... Each of these problems demonstrates the pressure that aging exerts on economic and social mechanisms. Yet, we must still ask: Is aging truly a problem, despite all this? Or is this merely the result of an incorrect perspective?

Consider this: We live in a world where older individuals are more visible in society. Even though the media constantly emphasizes the aesthetic concerns of aging, this visibility presents an opportunity to address the role of older individuals in society within a broader context. Could aging cease to be a process where individuals solely represent the "*past*" and instead transform into an era where they shape the future with their knowledge, experience, and stories?

## A JOURNEY THAT BEGINS WITH QUESTIONS

The purpose of this book is to address aging in individual, societal, and global contexts. However, it aims to avoid stereotypical approaches while doing so. Each chapter of the book attempts to address the following questions from a different perspective:

o   Should we perceive aging solely as an economic burden, or as a phenomenon that opens doors to new opportunities?
o   For instance, is it possible to increase the labor force participation of older individuals?
o   How can technology be used to improve the quality of life for older adults?
o   How can aging transform inequalities in the social structure of societies?

Aging is not just an economic phenomenon, but a social one as well. In fact, societies' perceptions of aging shape the roles of older individuals within those societies. For example, while older individuals are seen as sources of wisdom and guidance in some societies, they are perceived as a "*burden*" in others. These perceptions directly impact social policies, access to healthcare services, and the quality of life for older adults.

Another critical point is intergenerational interaction. The relationships that younger generations build with older individuals form the foundation of social solidarity. However, in modern societies, intergenerational bonds are progressively weakening. This situation affects not only the social and emotional well-being of older individuals but also that of younger generations. So, is it possible to rebuild these bonds?

On the other hand, demographic aging shapes not only individual lives but also policies. Social security systems, healthcare services, and retirement policies are areas directly influenced by aging. However, these policies are often based on short-term solutions. Developing a long-term and sustainable approach is inevitable for addressing the challenges posed by demographic aging.

For example, the sustainability of social security systems plays a critical role in meeting the basic needs of the aging population. However, these systems should not be solely based on financial balance; they must also consider social equality and justice. In this context, the political implications of aging should involve not only reforming existing systems but also developing a new social contract.

## WHY THIS BOOK?

This book aims to address aging as a multifaceted phenomenon. It intends to offer a guide to understanding the impacts of aging through its economic, social, and political dimensions, and to managing these impacts. However, this guidance is not limited to simply answering questions; it is also built upon asking new questions and inviting readers to rethink aging.

Each chapter tackles the phenomenon of aging from a different perspective. It discusses the impacts of aging across a broad spectrum, from economic effects to the design of social policies, from intergenerational relationships to the role of technology. The purpose of this book is to offer readers a new perspective on aging and to help them understand the transformative effects of this phenomenon on societal structures.

In conclusion, aging is not just an individual process, but also a societal phenomenon. Understanding the multifaceted impacts of this phenomenon is a critical step towards building a more just, sustainable, and inclusive society. This book serves as a small starting point for anyone who wishes to take this step.

**Ali Gökhan Gölçek**
*Nigde Ömer Halisdemir University, Turkey*

# Chapter 1
# The Economics of Aging:
## Global Trends and Perspectives

**Ali Gökhan Gölçek**
https://orcid.org/0000-0002-7948-7688
*Niğde Ömer Halisdemir University, Turkey*

## ABSTRACT

*In this chapter, I discuss the economic effects of population aging and the potential that it offers for public sector management, social justice, and economic development. As the population continues to age, public spending for social security and health care increases, but the so called "Silver Economy," which is based on the increasing demand of goods and services for seniors, remains underexplored. The chapter focuses on intergenerational equity, resource allocation and economic transitions and provides a roadmap on how the 'problems' of aging societies can be addressed in a way that unleash the potential of such societies. Using both international and Asian examples, it analyses the complex interconnections between demographic change, public expenditure, social justice and consumer cultures, and proposes new ways of thinking to support sustainable and equitable growth. Thus, this chapter unfolds a multilayered approach to understand the various economic and social changes that occur due to the presence of aging populations.*

## INTRODUCTION

"*The world is changing.*" The changing demographics and dynamics of the modern age could not be better described than those described by J.R.R. Tolkien's (2004) words. Today, aging, has become the phenomenon which shapes these demographic

DOI: 10.4018/979-8-3693-7753-6.ch001

shifts. Yet, this global phenomenon foretells an imminent and possibly disruptive ending (as an early warning) to societies all over the world.

The proportion of the world's population above the age of 60 is increasing at an accelerating pace because of decreasing fertility rates and because of growing life expectancy. In 2023, according to United Nations data, people over the age of 65 make up over 10 per cent of the world's population, and that is set to grow to 16 per cent by 2050. This demographic transformation forces the occurrence of profound and lasting changes both in economic systems and resource management as well as in social structures.

One of the most substantial macrolevel dimensions of aging is economics. The importance and consequences of aging have economic implications that range from individuals' living standards to macroeconomic policy. In particular, problems for both individuals and households stem from falls in elderly income, growth in healthcare outlays, the sustainability of national pension systems, and shrinking labor markets.

The disruption of actuarial balance is a primary economic consequence of aging. Actuarial balance is the mathematical relationship between what contributions are collected in a social security system and what benefits are paid out. This balance is adversely impacted by growing older versus a shrinking working age population. Actuarial imbalances seem to go along with the system of taking in fewer contributions from active workers and paying out to more retirees.

But aging should not be evaluated just in terms of economics. The growth of the elderly population has helped create a new economic sector – the "*silver economy*", which includes goods and services targeting them. In this case, the rising demand of an aging population represents new market opportunities and inspires new innovation.

This means that assessing economic impacts of aging should not be treated in isolation from existing challenges. Given the scope and magnitude of the demographic change occurring, it is essential to dissect the multidimensional dynamics of aging to fully manage potential difficulties and leverage the opportunities. Within this framework, the reshaping of sustainable economic development strategies is critically important in order to coincide with the changing demographic structures.

## AGING POPULATION: GLOBAL TRENDS AND AGING FUTURE

Aging is a phenomenon of globalization, one of the most important demographic indicators of the times. However, the most striking manifestation of this demographic change is the large rise in the share of the global population aged 65 years and over. By 2050, the global population of people in this age group is projected to double from 761 million to 1.6 billion. A particularly sharp increase is observed in the segment aged 80 and above. This trend is indicative of a broader demographic transition characterized by declining fertility rates and increasing longevity, evident in both developed and developing countries (Kiri, 2023). In other words, population aging emerges as an inevitable outcome of demographic transition, driven by factors such as rising life expectancy and shrinking family structures. This demographic shift is becoming apparent even in societies with relatively young populations, taking on an irreversible character. Indeed, according to 2021 data, 10% of the global population was aged 65 and over; by 2050, this figure is expected to rise to one in six people (United Nations, 2023).

*Figure 1. Global birth and death trends (1950-2100): Historical data and projections*

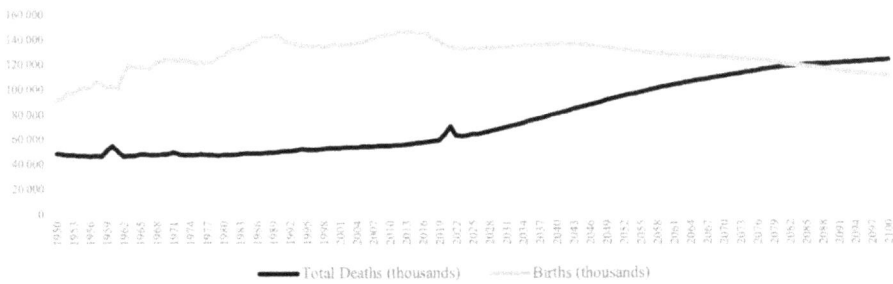

*(United Nations, 2024)*

Examining the historical trajectory of global demographic trends reveals that, since the 1950s, birth rates have significantly exceeded death rates, driving a marked increase in world population during the second half of the 20th century. However, demographic projections for the 21st century anticipate a systematic decline in birth rates and a gradual rise in death rates, culminating in a turning point in the 2070s when death rates are expected to surpass birth rates.

Such profound demographic shifts lead to paradigmatic changes in societies' socio-economic and political dynamics. This transition, driven by changes in fertility and mortality rates, affects not only the quantitative dimension of populations but also their age composition. In this context, the notable increase in the population aged 65 and over has multidimensional implications for the sustainability of social security systems, the structuring of healthcare services, and the dynamics of labor markets. Therefore, analyzing the historical trends in total population and the pro-portion of elderly population becomes a methodological necessity to understand the broader societal impacts of aging.

*Figure 2. Global population dynamics: Total population vs. aging demographics (1950–2023)*

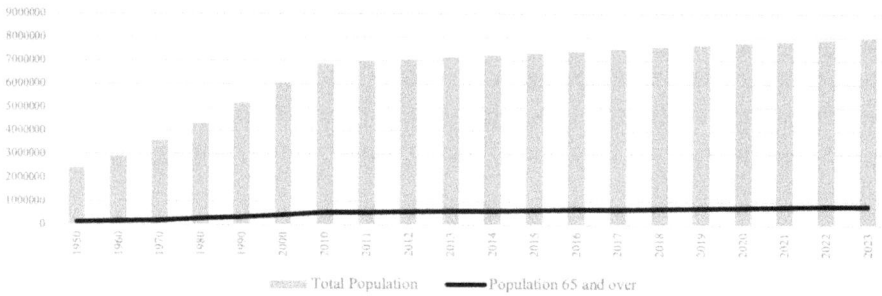

Total Population ▬▬ Population 65 and over

*(United Nations, 2024)*

As illustrated in Figure 2, demographic data reveal a steady increase in total population alongside a continuous upward trend in the population aged 65 and over. This demographic shift can be explained by structural factors such as rising life expectancy and declining fertility rates. Notably, in recent periods, the growth rate of the elderly population segment has significantly outpaced the overall population growth rate. This trend underscores the prominence of aging as a dominant parameter of global demographic transition and highlights the necessity for societies to develop comprehensive socio-economic policies to adapt to this new demographic reality.

This situation brings about a significant increase in dependency ratios. The dependency ratio reflects the burden on the working-age population (15–64 years) to support the needs of the elderly population (Sanderson & Scherbov, 2015). Figure 3 demonstrates the historical trajectory and future projections of dependency ratios, revealing a striking pattern of transformation. Since the 1950s, the composition of total dependency ratios has been dominated by child dependency ratios. However, due to declining fertility rates and increasing life expectancy during the demographic transition, the old-age dependency ratio has gradually gained prominence within the total dependency ratio.

*Figure 3. Projected dependency ratios: Child, old-age, and total trends (1950–2100)*

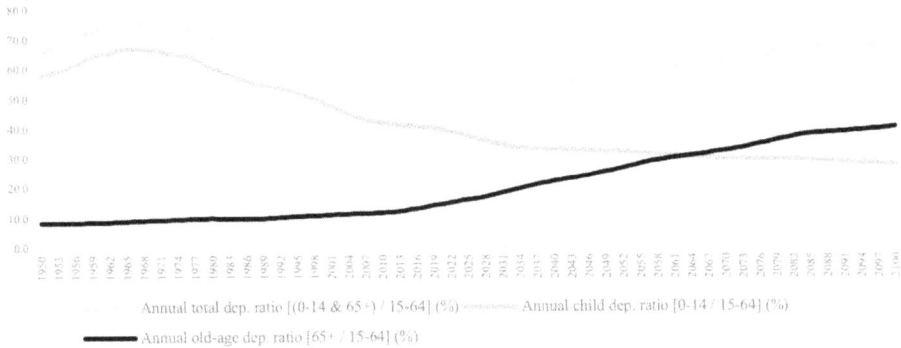

Annual total dep. ratio [(0-14 & 65+) / 15-64] (%) ———— Annual child dep. ratio [0-14 / 15-64] (%)
——— Annual old-age dep. ratio [65+ / 15-64] (%)

*(United Nations, 2024)*

From the 2020s onward, a notable upward trend in the old-age dependency ratio is projected to persist systematically until 2100. Conversely, a continuous decline in the child dependency ratio is observed. This demographic shift has multifaceted impacts on socio-economic systems, presenting structural challenges such as the financing of social security expenditures, the actuarial balance of pension systems, and the growing demand for healthcare services. The cumulative impact of child and old-age dependency ratios on the total dependency ratio suggests that the economic burden on the working-age population will increasingly intensify. At this juncture, the economic implications of an aging population are profound and multifaceted, significantly disrupting actuarial balance.

## ECONOMIC IMPACTS OF AGING

Analyzing the potential impacts of aging on economic systems is of critical importance from the perspective of the sustainability of future economic structures. The demographic aging process creates structural effects not only by placing pressure on social security systems and pension funds but also by influencing labor market dynamics, productivity parameters, and growth trends. This demographic transformation has multidimensional consequences, such as shifts in public expenditures favoring healthcare and social services, contraction in labor supply, and changes in consumption patterns. Understanding the economic implications of an aging population provides an analytical framework for policymakers to implement mitigating interventions and enhance the resilience of economic systems. Furthermore, aging should not only be viewed as a challenge but also as a domain where potential opportunities, as exemplified by the "silver economy," emerge. In this context, analyzing the economic impacts of aging establishes a methodological foundation for both alleviating economic pressures and ensuring sustainable socio-economic development.

*Figure 4. Dynamic relationships of the economic impacts of aging*

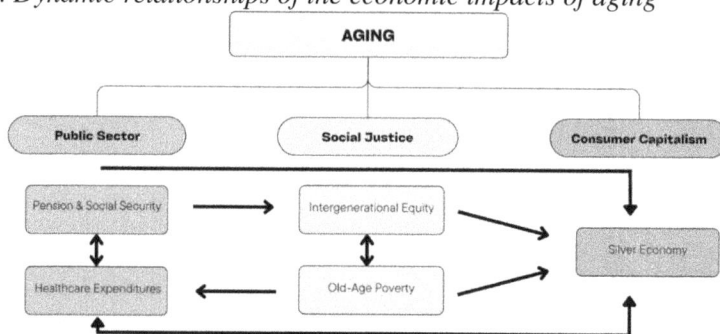

Figure 4 systematically visualizes the economic impacts of aging and the complex structure of interactions between various concepts. At the center of the analysis is the *"Aging"* phenomenon, connected through a multidimensional network of risk and opportunity parameters. In the context of risk factors, key variables such as *"Old-Age Poverty," "Healthcare Expenditures," "Pension and Social Security,"* and *"Intergenerational Equity"* are highlighted, while the *"Silver Economy"* is identified as a potential area of economic opportunity. This interconnected network indicates that while aging imposes economic burdens, it also offers avenues for innovation and growth. The vector representations in the figure illustrate the directions of interactions and their potential outcomes for economic systems.

Among the areas most influenced by population aging are the public sector. This impact is particularly evident in two key areas: health and pension systems. Healthcare costs increase with population of older people and pressures the social security system. This shift can result in less spending on other serious areas like education and infrastructure. These pressures throw the actuarial balance of traditional social security systems off balance, putting them at risk for long term sustainability, and depend on contributions from current workers to fund retirees. However, these challenges also create opportunities: The public sector's introduction of innovations in addressing issues related to aging can make the sector better and more efficient in the healthcare space thus lessening the deficit in the social security systems.

Aging generates a biderivean relationship between intergenerational equity and the risk of poverty in old age from a social justice perspective. The competing economic and physical burdens of an aging population's withdrawal from the production process onto a younger generation's back. Because younger individuals are forced to contribute more, and receive less social security in the future, this creates an imbalance. Beyond its impact on the individual quality of life, old age poverty itself adds to societal economic resilience and turns existing inequalities deeper. However, there are some solutions for these challenges. For instance, developing new models for intergenerational resource sharing and mobilizing inclusive policies for all societal segments may mitigate these adverse effects.

From a consumer capitalist perspective, the silver economy is one of the positive economic outcomes from population aging. Their consumption power is to be enhanced by the increasing average lifespan of the elderly population and by the longer participation of the elderly population in economic activities in general, which together open up new areas of economic growth. This development is particularly evident in three sectors: Housing solutions for the elderly that meet their needs; healthcare technologies and services for the elderly. The silver economy grows in these areas. But full exploitation of such opportunities requires some caveats, such as the income levels of the elderly population and their ability to get social support. However, full realization of the silver economy potential may not be conceivable if these conditions are not adequately met, and economic contributions of the elderly population may remain limited.

## Old-Age Poverty: Multidimensional Dynamics and Global Risks

Old age poverty as a phenomenon is beyond the simple dimensions of economic deprivation and actually takes sight of many multidimensional parameters referring to access to healthcare and social support mechanisms and various structural inequalities. Systemic risk factors, including economic recessions, global health crises and demographic transitions, further amplify the dynamics of this phenomenon. Old age poverty, in this context, is conceived of as a domain to address the system vulnerabilities characteristic of socio-economic systems and call for policy action.

Traditionally, poverty among the elderly is defined by a single parameter: income insufficiency. Nevertheless, this one-dimensional approach is not sufficient to represent the complex phenomenon. Older people's experience of poverty should be analyzed in terms of other multiple factors combining conditions of accommodation, lack of health care accessibility and social isolation, as emphasized by the Gordon et al. (2000). According to the OECD (2023), prolonged low-income levels and precarious employment conditions throughout the life cycle manifest as economic insecurity in later life.

Globally, old-age poverty prevalence is observed to be higher in low-income economies compared to developed economies.

*Figure 5. Old-age poverty rates across selected countries (2010–2021)*

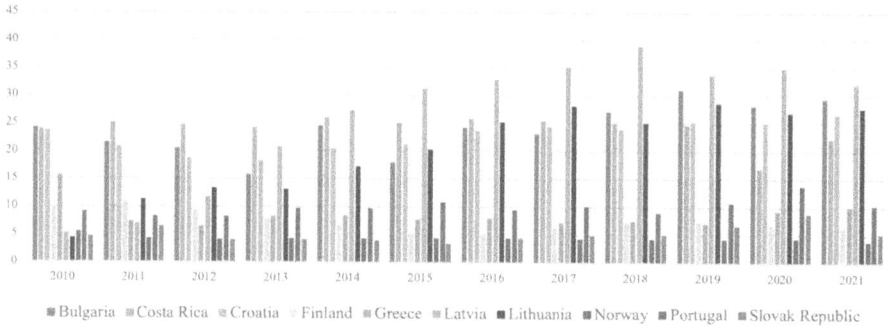

(OECD, 2024)

Figure 5 visualizes the temporal trend of old-age poverty rates in selected countries between 2010 and 2021. It reveals that while old-age poverty is more prevalent in low-income economies, it tends to remain at relatively low levels in developed economies. Notably, countries like Bulgaria, Greece, and Latvia exhibit persistently high levels of old-age poverty. In contrast with advanced welfare states like Norway and Finland, the poverty rates among the elderly in such states are considerably lower and become more stabilized. The existence of such determinants as the extent of coverage of social security, accessibility to health care and macro economic stability on old age poverty, is confirmed in these findings. Although there are some cyclical fluctuations in some countries over time, the sole trend implies that the problem of old-age poverty is much more pronounced in low-income countries.

Economic vulnerability of the elderly population is accentuated by the high cost of healthcare and absent of social security mechanism (Arai & Khan, 2023). While social security systems in developed economies has a critical role in diminishing old age poverty Esping-Andersen (1999) argued that these systems are facing sustainability challenges arising from demographic transitions. The emergence of this reality demands that social policies should be revised to better fight poverty.

## Healthcare Expenditures: The Rising Costs of Aging

With respect to the face of global demographic aging trends, research on the interplay between aging and healthcare expenditures is a vital area for work. A large body of empirical literature evidences that health care spending appreciably increases with aging, especially in the 65 years and older population segment (Fledsberg et al., 2023; Hou et al., 2022; Kallestrup-Lamb et al., 2024; Lorenz et al., 2020; Yang et al., 2003). Nevertheless, socio-economic inequalities of access to health services are intensified by the difficulties faced by elderly persons in low income groups to fund their expenses on health care (Hao et al., 2020; Kola & Owumi, 2019; Mohd et al., 2018; Park, 2012). The quality of life then becomes determined in large part by accessibility to healthcare for the elderly population.

Studies of empirical expenditures in healthcare for aging populations suggest that shallowness of this relationship is not limited to chronological age progression. However, this dynamic is shaped, to a determinant degree, by factors such as the differential health needs of age cohorts and morbidity levels. It is imperative for the healthcare accessibility does not only for the individual's quality of life but also for the stability of macroeconomic health policies. Moreover, the study of how healthcare spending varies across different age group categories and the factors that change this spending pattern is more holistic. The heterogeneous composition of age groups as well as determinants such as morbidity warrants a deeper understanding of how demographic aging is related to healthcare expenditures.

Many of the elderly suffer from chronic diseases, which also have a great prevalence, and these chronic diseases produce catastrophic healthcare expenditures that are the principal cause of recipient poverty among the elderly. Disadvantaged elderly people are caught in a vicious circularity, where poverty on the one hand depresses economic resources, and on the other squelches health outcomes, perpetuating economic hardship, as Zeng et al. (2020, 2022) suggest. This cycle sensitizes on the impediment to meeting elderly populations with adequate healthcare services. In addition, as Ma et al. (2022) comment, the intergenerational transmission of poverty is a serious problem, because following health related financial burdens might discourage investments in education and health for younger generations and perpetuate cycle of disadvantage.

## Intergenerational Equity: Resource Management and Justice

The issue of intergenerational equity again is to be discussed in the context of demographic aging. Public resources allocation to the elderly population's needs like health care and pension payments can restrict investment in education and employment opportunities for the younger generations. Policymakers are thus confronted by a complex decision problem in choosing among alternative distributions of public resources in such a conflicting situation.

Insofar as aging populations matter, the concept of intergenerational equity is of special importance because it deals with resource management, and fairness. Demographic changes, such as increased life expectancy and falling birth rates - in other words, aging societies - are placing new constraints on the allocation of resources and on social justice worldwide. Normative intergenerational equity gives a norm about an equitable delivery/resources and opportunities to current and future generations. This concept stems from an ethical right that future generations must be allowed to inherit a world uninhabited by the negative consequences that resource depletion and opportunity constraints resulting from the actions of the present generation Bessant et al. (2011). As such, this conceptual framework has played a critical role in debates over sustainability, in particular within the climate change and environmental rehabilitation conversation, and the poverty and socio-economic inequalities conversation (Hendlin, 2014).

From the intergenerational equity perspective, demographic aging brings new challenges. As a part of the society, increasing elderly population constitutes faster growth in demand for the resources such as healthcare services, pension system and social welfare. This increasing demand complicates the optimal allocation of public resource and may create a situation of potential conflict between the needs of elderly people and younger generations (Wade-Benzoni et al., 2010). For example, the allocation of healthcare resources over time through the asymmetrical process was on parity with the elderly to the detriment of younger populations' access to essential services.

Multidimensional implications of intergenerational equity extend to the economic systems. According to the needs of aging populations, industrial public policies such as social security, pension setting, and making expenditure on healthcare are subjected to ongoing restructuring. However, all this transformation will exacerbate financially the existing generation while reducing resource accessibility for the ones who will come next. At the same time, expenditures on public goods exclusively adapted to the needs of the elderly may hinder the investment in other (future-oriented) areas, for example to education and infrastructure, and, consequently, lower economic opportunities available for the younger generations, which will be reflected on strong negative impact on the economic growth performance in the long run.

An intergenerational equity also includes a critical reflection of such social security systems. Structural reforms in these systems are needed for intergenerational equity. According to Esping-Andersen & Myles (2009), the design and implementation of social security systems requires multidimensional strategies for equality optimization. In this setting, the potential to reduce the intergenerational gaps in the distribution of financial resources supporting social security systems is enormous.

## Pension and Social Security Systems: Sustainability and Reform

Demographic variables – specifically process of demographic aging, increasing trend of life expectancy and transformations in employment patterns – have come to be core areas needing urgent intervention in the area of sustainability and reform of pension and social security systems on a global scale. Its implications are such that if traditional pay-as-you-go (PAYGO) social security systems are to resist these financial pressures, their structural characteristics and financing mechanisms will need to be reevaluated first. The sustainability of social security systems is contingent on these economic conditions, demographic trend, and policy choices that determine both the relative effectiveness and equity of these systems.

Demographic transition, usually characterized by population aging, one of the biggest challenges to social security systems. Rising dependency ratios reflecting the falling ratio of working-age individuals to retirees constitute the manifestation of this demographic transformation, which is likely to menace the financial viability of PAYGO systems. Social security systems serve as basic insurance mechanisms shielding from mortality and income risk and do so in a way that may unintentionally crowd out private saving and capital formation and this crowding out effect may lead to a downgrading of future generations real wage levels (Sen, 2016). This exclusionary effect is particularly concerning because the reliance on public pension systems could inadvertently weaken the economic fundamentals essential for sustainable growth.

The role of employment policies in ensuring the sustainability of social security systems is also critical. As reflected in reforms that raise the standard retirement age, increasing the labor force participation rate of older adults is vital for bolstering the payment capacity of social security systems (Neumark & Song, 2011). These policy choices, beyond merely extending individuals' working lives, contribute to the creation of a more robust financial infrastructure for social security systems. In this regard, the integration of anti-age discrimination regulations supports the development of an inclusive employment environment that encourages the participation of older workers in the labor market.

*Figure 6. Projected changes in pension age across OECD countries*

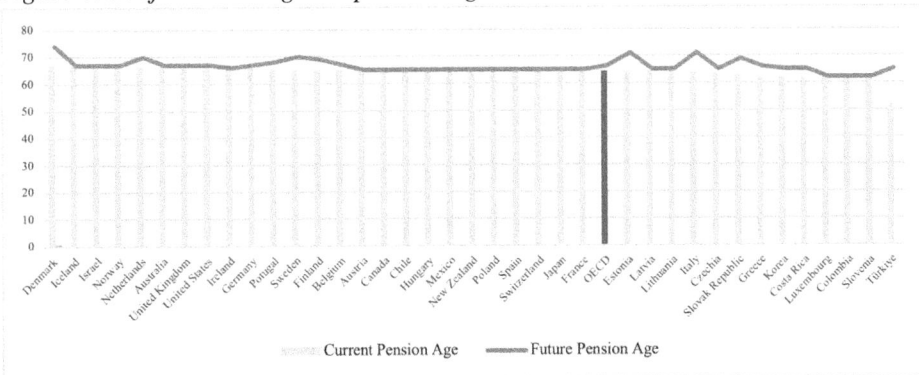

(OECD, 2023)

Figure 6 presents a comparative view of current and projected pension ages in OECD countries. The data indicate that many countries plan to raise the standard pension age in the coming years. This upward trend reflects measures adopted to address societal aging and the financial burdens on social security systems.

Current pension ages have already exceeded the OECD average in Denmark and Iceland and are predicted to go even higher in countries with longer life expectancies. By contrast, countries, such as Türkiye whose current pension ages are lower, attempt to gradually increase them over time. This is a global strategy to protect the economic resilience of social security systems, whilst balancing the strain that this large aging population will place on the system.

Yet, also for most countries, the social security systems tend to perform with lower operational efficiency, as actuarial deficits are deepening in these systems because the retiree population is increasing. A study of the actuarial balances of social security systems is necessary in order to address the challenges of these social security systems.

Demographic changes play a major role in determining whether pension systems are actuarial or not. Moreover, the actuarial balance is under strain in regions with higher aging rates, such as Europe or East Asia (Zhang et al., 2023). The result is unsustainable financial pressures on social security systems as a result of having higher pension payouts than contributions.

Measures taken to fix the problems of pension and social security systems to make them sustainable tend to be short-lived. Nevertheless, the increasing speed of aging and changes in the world economic and demographic processes indicate that it is necessary to go deeper and wider with the changes. Reforms should therefore not only concentrate on fiscal assessments of the actuarial equilibrium, but also on the re-organization of social security in relation to social rights and justice between generations. These measures are important to ensure that full scale systemic crises do not occur in the future. Improving the efficiency of these systems is a process that demands changes that can respond to present difficulties and at the same time to future requirements of the economy and society. According to this understanding, the sustainability principles of pension and social security policies should be the top goals of any actions taken in this area.

## Silver Economy: Unlocking the Positive Potential of Aging

The concept of the silver economy has appeared in the literature as a useful approach that focuses on the effects of ageing populations and their potential for generating positive change with regard to economic, social, and cultural development. Instead of focusing on the issues of aging, which are mostly considered negative, this approach focuses on the positives of the process. With growing population aging rates across the globe, and the silver economy, there are many possibilities for both economic prosperity and the provision of new products and services that are relevant to the older population. This transformation yields two critical outcomes: On the one hand, it creates new markets resulting from the growth of the demand for products that are targeted at older consumers, and, on the other hand, it produces numerous problems that call for business and policy solutions.

Certain needs of the ageing populations are escalating the growth rate in demand of products and services targeted for the elderly population. For example, Guo et al. (2023) estimated that the size of China's silver market will be worth 17 trillion RMB ($2.6 trillion) by 2025, which suggests great market opportunities for new products aimed at the elderly. Such tendencies are not unique to the Chinese market; analogous trends are noticeable globally. There is a growing emphasis on creation of goods and services including mobility products, health management equipment, and accessible homes for the elderly.

Age friendly environments go beyond the physical products to include services that strive to enhance the quality of life for older persons. A good example of this is the Decade of Healthy Ageing (2011-2020) plan developed by the United Nations. This is why this initiative should involve different stakeholders including the private sector to develop age-friendly services (Vera-Sanso, 2023). This is because, older people need to be in a position to get the necessary support in order to be healthy and or live a comfortable life.

The tourism industry has also shown increasing concern in the creation of age related products. According to the study by Liew et al. (2021), there is the need for the development of tourism experiences that can suit the older travelers. These are accessible rooms and transportation, tailored holiday packages, and programs that enhance social interactions and physical movement within the elderly.

Silver economy has implications for many industries, including healthcare, housing, entertainment, and technology. According to Maj-Waśniowska et al. (2018) the same societies that are threatened by poverty and social exclusion due to aging also has the potential to generate new jobs and growth through the silver economy. This dual dynamic points to the need to make careful and deliberate investments in age friendly interventions.

Likewise, Klimczuk (2016) comparative analysis of the silver economy models in the European Union shows a growing concern with technology solutions for the elderly. This development therefore afford new business opportunities for those who can well harness and market such technologies. The silver economy also boosts the total economic stability by opening up new employment in health care, social services as well as technological industries.

Consequently, the silver economy presents promise in the consumption of age-appropriate goods as well as the growth of economies. With the aging of societies, demand for targeted approaches will increase, opening up a profitable market that will contribute to the economy and help overcome problems connected with population aging. In order to unleash this full potential, it is crucial for the policies to be developed in cooperation with the representatives of the business sector to guarantee the positive impact of the silver economy on the society and older people in particular.

## CONCLUSION AND EVALUATION

Population ageing is one of the most important demographic trends of the 21st century. This change affects every aspect of the economic, social and political systems of the world and the lives of people and the shape of societies and the economic prospects of countries.

Population ageing is a demographic process that results in the change of population structures worldwide and within specific countries. This paper also establishes that the population of the elderly is growing at a fast pace, which is an economic concern globally. Several critical issues arise in this process: These are, increasing the dependent population as compared to the working population, decrease in the labor force, and decrease in output. These challenges are detrimental to economic development and lead to the regulation of the future of social security systems. The problem is worse in the developing countries; therefore, such countries need to involve themselves with the other countries of the world to share their experiences.

A clear example of this is old age poverty which has been increase due to this process. The absence of financial independence among the elderly people worsens the income inequalities and frays social connections. This issue grows due to two primary factors: high costs of health care and the growing reliance on social security. Thus, elderly poverty becomes a problem which concerns not only separate persons but also certain layers of population. Hence, specific economic and social rules and measures with regard to the aging population should be comprehensive and creative.

But demographic change also offers new prospects: societies are growing older. Most importantly this segment or the silver economy, that is, the economic models designed for the elderly can foster new markets and jobs. Technological advancements and innovative solutions for elderly individuals provide dual benefits: enhancing their standards of living and at the same be productive workers in the economy and employment. Concretely, technological advancement in the healthcare of the elderly increases the effectiveness of the healthcare delivery systems with tremendous outcome in the general society.

This work reveals that population aging has dire economic and social implications. These effects thus demand broad strategic interventions from the policy makers and societies. Three key areas emerge as priorities in managing an aging population: Increasing health care expenditure, sustainability of social security systems, and future of intergenerational income distribution. To address these challenges, policymakers must pursue two primary goals: maintaining the efficiency of the current systems and enhancing positive economic development while increasing social cohesion. These goals can therefore only be met through the use of new and inclusive strategies.

Consequently, the challenge of the aging societies of the world should be tackled with due respect to social equity. This problem cannot be addressed by the internal regulation of individual countries; international cooperation and best practices are just as important. This is especially crucial for countries having a high rate of population aging. This paper also argues that incorporating development plans with age-friendly policies will be paramount in achieving sustainable development in the long-run.

Therefore, demography – the aging of societies – is both an economic and a social phenomenon. To achieve this, successful management of this process will improve on economic development and social wellbeing of the people as well as the relations between the generations and social equity. To treat the economic effects of ageing population as a potential in terms of development and prepare strategies according to it will allow societies to get the best results from this process. Thus, the balanced approach should be pursued in the decision-making processes that involve the evaluation of the aging population's needs and the impact on the present and future generations.

As this study concludes, it seems fitting to recall another simple yet meaningful quote from Tolkien's (2004) introduction: *"There is always hope."* By shaping the future with social solidarity, innovative approaches, and solutions centered on human dignity, it appears possible to meet the needs of aging societies and manage this transformation successfully.

# REFERENCES

Arai, Y., & Khan, I. A. (2023). *Silver Hues: Building Age-Ready Cities*. World Bank, EAP Regional Paper.

Bessant, J. C., Emslie, M., & Watts, R. (2011). Accounting for Future Generations: Intergenerational Equity in Australia 1. *Australian Journal of Public Administration*, 70(2), 143–155. DOI: 10.1111/j.1467-8500.2011.00723.x

Esping-Andersen, G. (1999). *Social Foundation of Postindustrial Economies*. Oxford University Press. DOI: 10.1093/0198742002.001.0001

Esping-Andersen, G., & Myles, J. (2009). Sustainable and Equitable Retirement in a Life Course Perspective. In Clark, G., Munnell, A. H., & Orszag, M. (Eds.), *The Oxford Handbook of Pensions and Retirement Income* (pp. 839–858). Oxford University Press., DOI: 10.1093/oxfordhb/9780199272464.003.0042

Fledsberg, S., Svensson, M., & Johansson, N. (2023). Lifetime healthcare expenditures across socioeconomic groups in Sweden. *European Journal of Public Health*, 33(6), 994–1000. DOI: 10.1093/eurpub/ckad140 PMID: 37649353

Gordon, D., Levitas, R., Pantazis, C., Patsios, D., Payne, S., Townsend, P., Adelman, L., Ashworth, K., Middleton, S., Bradshaw, J., & Williams, J. (2000). *Poverty and Social Exclusion in Britain*.

Guo, Y., Liu, M., Wang, J., Xia, Y., & Zhao, D. (2023). Demographic Challenge: The Rise of the Silver Economy in China. *Advances in Economics. Management and Political Sciences*, 34(1), 120–125. DOI: 10.54254/2754-1169/34/20231688

Hao, L., Xu, X., Dupre, M. E., Guo, A., Zhang, X., Qiu, L., Zhao, Y., & Gu, D. (2020). Adequate access to healthcare and added life expectancy among older adults in China. *BMC Geriatrics*, 20(1), 129. DOI: 10.1186/s12877-020-01524-9 PMID: 32272883

Hendlin, Y. H. (2014). The Threshold Problem in Intergenerational Justice. *Ethics and the Environment*, 19(2), 1–38. DOI: 10.2979/ethicsenviro.19.2.1

Hou, X., Liu, L., & Cain, J. (2022). Can higher spending on primary healthcare mitigate the impact of ageing and non-communicable diseases on health expenditure? *BMJ Global Health*, 7(12), e010513. DOI: 10.1136/bmjgh-2022-010513 PMID: 36564087

Kallestrup-Lamb, M., Marin, A. O. K., Menon, S., & Søgaard, J. (2024). Aging populations and expenditures on health. *The Journal of the Economics of Ageing*, 29, 100518. DOI: 10.1016/j.jeoa.2024.100518

Kiri, L. (2023). Demographic transition - Global population patterns and trends: The case of Albania. *Academic Journal of Business, Administration. Law and Social Sciences*, 9(2), 29–36. DOI: 10.2478/ajbals-2023-0004

Klimczuk, A. (2016). Comparative analysis of national and regional models of the silver economy in the European Union. *International Journal of Ageing and Later Life*, 10(2), 31–59. DOI: 10.3384/ijal.1652-8670.15286

Kola, L., & Owumi, B. (2019). Causes of Poverty in Old Age, Not a Structural Failing? *Journal of Aging & Social Policy*, 31(5), 467–485. DOI: 10.1080/08959420.2019.1642692 PMID: 31328675

Liew, S. L., Hussin, S. R., & Abdullah, N. H. (2021). Attributes of Senior-Friendly Tourism Destinations for Current and Future Senior Tourists: An Importance-Performance Analysis Approach. *SAGE Open*, 11(1), 2158244021998658. Advance online publication. DOI: 10.1177/2158244021998658

Lorenz, N., Ihle, P., & Breyer, F. (2020). Aging and Health Care Expenditures: A Non-Parametric Approach. SSRN *Electronic Journal*. DOI: 10.2139/ssrn.3576293

Ma, Y., Xiang, Q., Yan, C., Liao, H., & Wang, J. (2022). Poverty Vulnerability and Health Risk Action Path of Families of Rural Elderly With Chronic Diseases: Empirical Analysis of 1,852 Families in Central and Western China. *Frontiers in Public Health*, 10, 776901. Advance online publication. DOI: 10.3389/fpubh.2022.776901 PMID: 35237547

Maj-Waśniowska, K., Wałęga, A., & Wałęga, G. (2018). Silver Economy, Poverty and Social Exclusion in the European Union Countries. *Proceedings of the 10th Economics & Finance Conference,* Rome, 341–353. DOI: 10.20472/EFC.2018.010.023

Mohd, S., Senadjki, A., & Mansor, N. (2018). Trend of Poverty among Elderly: Evidence from Household Income Surveys. *Journal of Poverty*, 22(2), 89–107. DOI: 10.1080/10875549.2016.1186779

Neumark, D., & Song, J. (2011). *Do Stronger Age Discrimination Laws Make Social Security Reforms More Effective?* DOI: 10.3386/w17467

OECD. (2023). *Pension at a Glance 2023.* https://www.oecd.org/en/publications/pensions-at-a-glance-2023_678055dd-en.html

OECD. (2024). *OECD Data Explorer*. https://data-explorer.oecd.org/vis?fs[0]= Topic%2C1%7CSociety%23SOC%23%7CInequality%23SOC_INE%23&pg=0&fc =Topic&bp=true&snb=2&df[ds]=dsDisseminateFinalDMZ&df[id]=DSD_WISE _IDD%40DF_IDD&df[ag]=OECD.WISE.INE&df[vs]=1.0&pd=2010%2C&dq= .A.PR_INC_DISP%2BINC_DISP_GINI...Y_GT65%2B_T.METH2012.D_CUR.& to[TIME_PERIOD]=false&ly[cl]=TIME_PERIOD&ly[rs]=COMBINED_UNIT _MEASURE&ly[rw]=REF_AREA%2CAGE%2CCOMBINED_MEASURE& vw=tb

Park, J. M. (2012). Equity of Access to Primary Care Among Older Adults in Incheon, South Korea. *Asia-Pacific Journal of Public Health*, 24(6), 953–960. DOI: 10.1177/1010539511409392 PMID: 21653609

Sanderson, W. C., & Scherbov, S. (2015). Are We Overly Dependent on Conventional Dependency Ratios? *Population and Development Review*, 41(4), 687–708. DOI: 10.1111/j.1728-4457.2015.00091.x

Sen, P. (2016). Anyone for Social Security Reform? SSRN *Electronic Journal*. DOI: 10.2139/ssrn.2844652

Tolkien, J. R. R. (2004). *The Return of the King: Being the third part of The Lord of the Rings*. HarperCollins Publisher.

United Nations. (2023). *World Social Report 2023: Leaving No One Behind in an Ageing World*. https://desapublications.un.org/publications/world-social-report-2023 -leaving-no-one-behind-ageing-world

United Nations. (2024). *Population Division: World Population Prospects 2024, Online Edition*. https://population.un.org/wpp/Download/Standard/Population/

Vera-Sanso, P. (2023). Will the SDGs and the UN Decade of Healthy Ageing Leave Older People Behind? *Progress in Development Studies*, 23(4), 391–407. DOI: 10.1177/14649934231193808

Wade-Benzoni, K. A., Sondak, H., & Galinsky, A. D. (2010). Leaving a Legacy: Intergenerational Allocations of Benefits and Burdens. *Business Ethics Quarterly*, 20(1), 7–34. DOI: 10.5840/beq20102013

Yang, Z., Norton, E. C., & Stearns, S. C. (2003). Longevity and Health Care Expenditures: The Real Reasons Older People Spend More. *The Journals of Gerontology. Series B, Psychological Sciences and Social Sciences*, 58(1), S2–S10. DOI: 10.1093/ geronb/58.1.S2 PMID: 12496303

Zeng, Y., Xu, W., Luo, B., & Fang, Y. (2020). *Study on the Demand and Utilization of Health Services for the Poor Elderly in China*. DOI: 10.21203/rs.3.rs-46192/v1

Zeng, Y., Xu, W., & Tao, X. (2022). What factors are associated with utilisation of health services for the poor elderly? Evidence from a nationally representative longitudinal survey in China. *BMJ Open*, 12(6), e059758. DOI: 10.1136/bmjopen-2021-059758 PMID: 35760535

Zhang, M., You, S., Zhang, L., Zhang, H., & Wang, Y. (2023). Dynamic Analysis of the Effects of Aging on China's Sustainable Economic Growth. *Sustainability (Basel)*, 15(6), 5076. DOI: 10.3390/su15065076

# Chapter 2
# Lifelong Learning:
## Demographic Trends and Economic Participation in Older Adults

**Tabassum Bashir**
https://orcid.org/0000-0001-9944-5648
*Aligarh Muslim University, India*

**Deoshree Akhouri**
*Aligarh Muslim University, India*

**Salma Afroj**
https://orcid.org/0009-0001-8420-5462
*Aligarh Muslim University, India*

**Kalim Ahamd Khan**
*Aligarh Muslim University, India*

**Akanksha**
https://orcid.org/0009-0008-7217-1278
*Aligarh Muslim University, India*

**Hamza Hamza**
https://orcid.org/0000-0003-2569-2165
*Aligarh Muslim University, India*

## ABSTRACT

*This chapter examines lifelong learning among older people and highlights the relationship between lifelong learning, economic participation, and demographic trends. Through an analysis of the theoretical underpinnings, demographic developments, and practical ramifications, it seeks to improve the conversation on older adult education. To support older adults in their ongoing learning endeavors, regardless of their self-identification as learners, the chapter redefines traditional educational concepts by promoting a broader understanding of learning as a lifelong process and emphasizing the integration of emerging learning theories, research, and policies. In cognition, emotion, and behavior, psychological theories are examined and emphasize how aging impacts mental processes and emotional experiences. Lifelong learning is essential for improving employability in a labor market that is constantly changing and for adjusting to the workforce's needs, which benefits both individuals and the economy. The chapter promotes the removal of obstacles*

DOI: 10.4018/979-8-3693-7753-6.ch002

*to lifelong learning and development.*

## INTRODUCTION

This chapter will delve into the multifaceted realm of lifelong learning processes, examining how they intersect with demographic trends and economic participation among older adults. The aim is to offer a targeted and insightful contribution to the ongoing discourse on older adult learning, informed by a critical analysis of its philosophical underpinnings, demographic shifts, and practical implications. Demographic trends encompass the evolving characteristics of a population over time. These include birth rates, mortality rates, migration patterns, and age distribution. Understanding these trends provides crucial insights into how populations expand or contract and how they can shape social, economic, and political dynamics. This chapter also aims to deliver a comprehensive overview of the concept of older adult learning, focusing on integrating emergent learning theories, research findings, and policy considerations. People are keenly aware of the evolving discourse around lifelong education, lifelong learning, and learning societies, and we believe it is essential to reframe the field of educational gerontology. This reframing involves shifting the discussion away from mere 'education' and towards a deeper exploration of how older adults - regardless of their self-identification as learners - can be integrated into ongoing learning revolutions.

Ultimately, the author intends to not only offer insights into the current practices of older adult learning but also to construct a forward-looking agenda for the future of this field. As people move into the 21st century, demographic patterns are anticipated to show decreasing birth rates, a stable population size, and a progressively older global population. The age distribution worldwide is expected to transform, with median ages on the rise and a gradual shift from a younger to an older demographic. As of 2000, Europe already had more individuals over the age of 60 than under the age of 15. North America is projected to have a similar demographic makeup by 2030, followed by Latin America and Asia by 2040. In terms of sheer numbers, the Asian/Pacific region currently has the highest proportion of elderly individuals. It is expected to be home to two-thirds of the world's 2 billion elders (60 years or above) by the middle of the century. The global population of those aged 80 and above is also expected to increase significantly from 69 million to 379 million by 2050. At that point, almost 10% of the developed world's population will be over 80 (WHO, 2020, 2021,2022,2023).

Many people agree that one of the best seniors can do for their psychological, mental, physical, and cognitive health is to pursue lifelong learning. Seniors must pursue lifelong learning to cope with practical life skills and adapt to shifting living conditions. Lifelong learning has been viewed as an essential tool for involving education, business, public organizations, and youth in educational work with senior citizens, developing and implementing innovative projects for senior citizens' learning, and creating a system of work with senior citizens to study their needs. Building on these points, the current study discusses the demands of older adults in India about lifelong learning and explores the options for addressing these needs. This chapter will also delve into psychological theories of aging through the lens of the three traditional psychology domains: cognition, emotion, and behavior. The chapter will focus on how aging impacts individuals' mental processes, emotional experiences, and behavioral patterns. Examining these domains in tandem can better understand how aging affects individuals from multiple psychological perspectives. As a result, a large portion of India's population is elderly. It is commonly accepted that seniors become more socially isolated and disconnected as they age and that this disengagement is the leading cause of their cognitive deterioration and other health problems. Additionally, it has been noted that senior citizens who withdraw from everyday activities, including going to work, experience a variety of psycho-social issues. Anxiety, sadness, delirium, dementia, personality disorders, and substance misuse are among the most prevalent psychological problems that older adults face. Loss of autonomy, sadness, anxiety, loneliness, financial limitations, and a lack of social networks are common social and emotional problems. The complex psycho-social problems that older adults face are frequently entangled with physical illnesses.

## MEANING AND CONCEPT OF OLDER ADULT

Few people lived to old age even before the dawn of recorded history, and most of those fulfilled vital roles in their communities. Elders have been portrayed as seers, saints, tribal leaders, healers, and sources of wisdom and concern for the general good in religious writings, mythology, and folklore. There is, then, a certain irony to the worry and concern that permeates national and international conversations regarding the impending problems imposed by aging societies. However, there is more to this than irony in a state of readiness that exists only to prepare for a disaster. It guarantees the arrival of the crisis. Assume we understand the potential benefits older adults can provide (World et al., 2012; Formosa, 2019).

The term "productive aging," first used in 1982, is typically connected to working actively. However, over time, it has come to refer to various aspects of work, including volunteering, providing care for others, and other endeavors that "produce good/service for society, whether paid or unpaid" (Caro et al., 1993, p. 6). From the perspective of baby boomers in Singapore, researchers want to investigate the relationships between lifelong learning and the concepts of productive aging. They first examine the grounded meanings of productive aging as expressed through lifetime learning, using data from the qualitative study of lifetime Learning among Older Adults in Singapore, which included 64 interviews with learners and non-learners of the baby-boomer generation (age 50-64). Next, they look at the advantages of lifelong learning as viewed by baby boomers, emphasizing how it might improve overall wellness and promote productive aging. A section analyzing obstacles to lifetime learning follows to provide light on learning deterrents (Bjorklund et al., 2011; Cocquyt, 2017). They aim to rethink what it means to be productive in later life by exploring older people's perspectives on lifelong learning and their involvement or lack thereof in formal and informal learning. Lastly, they contend that lifelong learning should be acknowledged as more than just an additional factor in productive aging; instead, it should be recognized as a facilitator that helps to strengthen the capacities of the other factors such as family care, economic output, and volunteer work that improves productive aging (Thang et al., 2018 Aug 23).

If so, we must recognize how older people interpret their experiences and the social milieu in which a given cohort understands aging. We must proactively establish policies, practices, and infrastructure that leverage the potential contributions of the elderly population to our communities. It is untrue that life has suddenly become more extended than necessary for individuals to lead healthy, fulfilling lives. There is no reason to think that over evolutionary history, the human life span, or the amount of time the species may live has altered significantly, if at all. People lived short lives on average up to the 20th century. Less than half of born individuals lived to be fifty years old (World Economic Forum, 2012; Sokolec, 2016; Formosa, 2019).

## LIFELONG LEARNING: CONCEPT AND DEFINITION

For people of all ages, lifelong learning (LLL) is essential and has many advantages for the individual and society. It encourages their full engagement in the economy and society, makes it possible for them to become more knowledgeable and engaged citizens, enhances their sense of fulfillment and well-being, fosters their creativity and invention, and boosts their productivity as employees and volunteers. We all learn throughout our lives since learning is innate. According to some authors, knowing for older adults is fusing environmental and personal experiences to influence personal enrichment through acquiring or modifying knowledge, skills, values, attitudes, behavior, and worldviews (Formosa, 2019; Spulber, 2019).

The implementation of a behavior functional to manage the external and internal (thoughts) demands of stressful situations is made possible by the need for a high level of cognitive and behavioral efforts to cope with the demands of a dynamic society and, concurrently, psycho-physical abilities impairment (Folkman &

Moskowitz, 2004; Sung, 2023). We refer to these mental and physical endeavors as psychological coping. Two categories of psychological coping are defined by Lazarus and Folkman (1984): passive coping, also known as emotion-focused coping, which helps control the emotional reaction to the problem and active coping, also known as problem-focused coping, which enables the person to handle or fix the situation that is causing them distress. Requests to deal directly with stressful circumstances positively impact adaptation, mental health, or well-being, making active coping more successful. Passive coping is less effective because there is no direct coping with the conflictive occurrence, only avoidance and denial behavior and no confrontation. The ability to control one's emotional experiences improves with age (Meléndeza et al., 2018). Elderly individuals may have the highest level of passive coping compared to active ones since they are skilled at controlling their emotional states. Psychological coping is essential in how older adults deal with day-to-day issues. Resilience is another feature that can affect how well older adults adjust to social situations (UNESCO, 2022).

## Lifelong Learning as Social Capital

The new but expanding reaction to adult aging is described in this chapter, along with strategies for releasing the social capital that comes with having more people live longer. To fully benefit from the social capital, learning, and innovation sparked by aging populations, society must first address two significant challenges: first, how to access a source of accumulated social investment that is underutilized mainly at the moment, and second, how to acknowledge that the process of adaptation, which is a hallmark of the aging process, is in and of itself a significant source of innovation and business opportunity (Withnall, 2012).

Even though older people's social capital is sometimes underappreciated, it nonetheless constitutes an untapped source of saved money. The survival and proliferation of this type of capital are contingent upon the interplay of lifelong learning, social innovation, and adaptation. It also necessitates identifying the domains in which senior citizens excel. A crucial factor to consider would be how unfavorable social views hinder the use of accumulated capital and the understanding that effective use necessitates intergenerational cooperation (Field, 2005; Cocquyt, 2017). Learning to live in an age-diverse environment is one of the most significant social advances, and it would have many positive effects on design, retail, workforce engagement, cultural adaptability, and striking the correct balance between continuity and change (Balatti et al., 2002). If given the proper conditions, such as access to age-friendly workplaces and updated skills through lifelong learning, older people can contribute to innovations that will be required as societies learn to adapt. These talents are crucial in a world where seemingly unrelated aspects of an issue are interconnected, even though they are frequently different from younger people in terms of degree rather than value (Zunzunegui et al., 2007; Del Ser & Otero, 2003).

## Lifelong Learning Process to Change and Adapt

The impact of continuous education and active economic engagement in the lives of older adults is invaluable. A multitude of compelling evidence, from personal experiences to extensive research, highlights the profound benefits of pursuing learning opportunities during the later stages of adulthood. The positive effects extend beyond personal development, with implications for reduced reliance on government-funded social services and individual and community well-being enhancements. Field's (2009) report titled "Well-being and Happiness: Inquiry into the Future of Lifelong Learning" provides significant insight into the intricate link between adult education and overall well-being. While the economic advantages of adult learning are commonly underscored, Field's thorough exploration of existing evidence emphasizes the substantial impact of learning on promoting well-being. Through a comprehensive analysis of various studies, Field's findings consistently point to the modest yet tangible positive influence of adult learning on overall well-being.

Moreover, the report underscores the notably influential role of adult education in enhancing the well-being of vulnerable demographics, particularly older individuals (London, 2011). The increasing demand for ongoing skill improvement in an ever-evolving labor market has led to a steady rise in the popularity of lifelong learning in India. This change in society is a result of the quick development of technology and the general availability of the Internet, which have increased the use of online learning environments for developing professional skills, fostering personal growth, and improving skill sets (Horsley, 2010; Withnall, 2012). Lifelong learning is essential to promoting economic participation, particularly when the nature of employment and the demographics of the workforce change.

On the one hand, the flow of knowledge and competencies fosters an environment suitable for personal enrichment; on the other hand, it necessitates skill upgrades and updates. Meanwhile, every aspect of life is becoming more and more digitalized. In today's English, terms that begin with "e-," such as "e-banking" and "e-govern," are becoming increasingly common. Considering all these facts, we can affirm that today is an IT and knowledge society. This chapter explores the relationship between lifelong learning and economic participation and explains why it is critical for both people and economies:

a. **Skill Development and Adaptability**: Maintaining mental clarity, social involvement, and quality of life in older adults requires skill growth and adaptation. Many cities provide specialized workshops that appeal to various interests and skill levels, ranging from technology to creative arts, as part of their education programs for older individuals. Furthermore, seniors have the freedom and accessibility to learn new skills and seek information at their speed, thanks to online platforms like Coursera, Udemy, and Khan Academy. These learning experiences improve intellectual development, flexibility, fulfillment, and growth (Nguyen, 2020).

b. **Technology Use**: Digital literacy training helps older people stay informed and connected in an increasingly digital world by providing basic computer skills, social media knowledge, and online safety knowledge. One way to promote digital health technology is to encourage older people to use the Internet and apply it to their care. This study looks at the existing situation of older people's Internet use, the social, psychological, and physical variables that affect it, and the need for intelligent services among older people (Sun, 2020). Furthermore, assistive technologies like smart home automation, health monitoring devices, and hearing aids are essential for boosting independence because they let seniors live more independently and manage their lives more skillfully. When taken as a whole, these technological developments help older individuals live longer and more engaged lives (Horsley, 2010).

c. **Cognitive Skills**: Playing memory games, solving puzzles, and doing strategy-based tasks are good mental workouts to maintain mental agility. Acquiring new abilities, like picking up a musical instrument or learning a new language, also offers engaging challenges that can improve cognitive function and overall well-being. These pursuits enhance mental sharpness and provide rewarding experiences that promote growth and a sense of achievement (Spulber, 2019; Di Nuovo et al., 2020). A zone of feasible functioning that considers age-related limitations and individual endowments is shaped by normal aging. People's ability to function in this zone can be affected by their choice to partake in or abstain from healthy intellectual, physical, and social activities (Hertzog, 2008; Guarino et al., 2020).

d. **Physical Activity:** Programs for customized physical activity, like yoga or tai chi, benefit older persons because they enhance mobility, balance, and general health. Moreover, adaptive sports like swimming or walking clubs offer beneficial social interaction and physical activity, improving overall well-being and building community. These exercises encourage a more active, involved lifestyle and support physical health (Horsley, 2010). Consistent physical exercise has been shown to improve health outcomes and quality of life in the populations it studies, yet age is the most physically inactive demographic. The physical and psychological aspects of health relate to role-playing physical functioning, general health, role-emotional functioning, vitality, psychological health, and social functioning (Bashkireva et al., 2018).

e. **Social Engagement**: Based on comparable patterns of social interaction, older individuals may be divided into smaller groups. Older persons can contribute meaningfully to their communities and feel connected by volunteering for causes or organizations. Similarly, participating in group activities like clubs, discussion groups, or classes encourages social contact and mental stimulation, giving them rich experiences and dependable relationships to enhance their life. These social interaction activities foster a lively and contented lifestyle and im-prove emotional well-being. (Croezen, 2009; Rainer, 2014). Numerous scholars attempted to define aging in the most advantageous way possible, considering various elements such as the environment, economics, the digitalized society, and biological and psychological aspects. The research aims to improve older adults' social involvement while also figuring out how to maintain their health and self-sufficiency for as long as possible. The benefits of cognitive remediation have been demonstrated by physical activity and social interaction (Harmell et al., 2014). We have seen that several factors contribute to successful, active, and joyful aging, including environmental control, personal development, physical activity, social interaction, and finding a new purpose in life (Zunzunegui et al., 2003; Spulber, 2019).

f. **Emotional Adaptability**: For older individuals, counseling and therapy are vital sources of support that help them develop resilience while navigating big life transitions like retirement or loss. Furthermore, mindfulness and meditation are beneficial practices that promote a good outlook and effective stress management, which enhance emotional flexibility and general well-being. With the help of these strategies, senior citizens may manage life's changes and lead balanced, satisfying lives. Lazarus and Folkman defined two categories of psychological coping in 1984: active coping, also known as problem-focused coping, which enables the individual to control or alter the issue causing them discomfort, and passive coping, also known as emotion-focused coping, which assists in maintaining their emotional reaction to the problem. Requests to deal directly with stressful circumstances positively impact adaptation, mental health, or well-being, making active coping more successful. According to Meléndeza, Satorresa, Redondoa, Escuderob, and Pitarquec (2018), elderly individuals better manage their emotional experiences. They may also be skilled at controlling their emotional moods. Maximum degree of passive coping compared to active coping.

g.  **Practical Skills:** Keeping stability and well-being as we age requires health management and financial awareness. A strong foundation for economic security can be established by learning about budgeting, investing, and retirement planning. This will enable older people to live comfortably and stress-free during their later years. Maintaining health and quality of life simultaneously depends on efficient health management, which includes understanding prescription schedules, managing chronic diseases, and navigating complicated healthcare options. A more secure and satisfying existence can be attained by older persons who master these areas, giving them more power and freedom (Horsley, 2010). A course such as Financial Literacy enables senior citizens to understand better how to use bank products and to develop theoretical and practical knowledge in social protection and pension law. The venerable age that this course allows people to feel appropriately aged and independent in their financial judgments (Spulber, 2019).

h.  **Community Resources**: The lives of senior citizens can be significantly improved by using community resources. Senior centers offer Numerous options, such as social activities, health treatments tailored to the requirements of older people, and educational programs. Furthermore, interacting with loved ones, friends, and neighborhood organizations creates solid support systems that provide practical and emotional help. When used in tandem, these resources create a wealthier, more connected, and more supportive environment, enabling older people to live happy, supported lives. In today's quickly evolving employment market, where new technologies, industry practices, and job needs often emerge, skill upgrading through lifelong learning is crucial (Spulber, 2019). By continuously learning new skills, people improve their career flexibility and stay relevant, which makes it simpler to move into alternative professions or industries when their interests or the needs of the market change. In a fast-paced workplace, this proactive approach to education guarantees flexibility and ongoing professional development. Older adults have fewer resources to adjust to a stressful and quick socioeconomic shift. According to Harada et al. (2013) and Glisky (2007), the average physic-cognitive decline, impairment of working and long-term memory, attention impairment, slower information processing speed, and age-related influences on problem-solving activity can all account for the low level of social adaptation.

## Lifelong Learning Strategies for Economic Participation

Economic participation is changing significantly due to trends in the demographics of the senior population. Lifelong learning and adaptability are essential for preserving economic participation and stability as life expectancy rises and conventional retirement patterns change (UNESCO, 2022). By addressing obstacles, including health-related issues and age discrimination, and by putting supportive legislation in place and fostering inclusive work settings, older persons can maintain their economic contributions and enjoy a higher quality of life. Comprehending and capitalizing on these patterns can enhance approaches for assimilating senior citizens into the labor force and optimizing their financial possibilities (Balatti et al., 2002; Sung, 2023).

Lifelong learning fosters social relationships, promotes personal growth, and builds a more cohesive and resilient community. People who adopt an attitude of constant learning are better able to deal with the challenges of contemporary life, form deep connections, and make valuable contributions to society (Morris et al., 2019). Below are a few strategies; we will look at each one by one;

a. **Formal Education and Training**: Formal education and training are essential for professional development and career advancement. Advanced degrees or certifications can boost earning potential and open new employment options. Participating in professional development events like conferences, workshops, and seminars also helps people stay current on developments in their sector, which keeps their skills competitive in a labor market that is changing quickly (Boström et al., 2002).

b. **Informal and Self-Directed Learning**: Informal and self-directed learning offers flexible and individualized options for skill acquisition and professional improvement. People can learn at their own pace and convenience using a variety of courses provided by online platforms such as Coursera, edX, and Udemy. In addition, self-study through reading books, articles, and research papers on industry-related topics keeps people informed and advances their expertise. These methods enable continuing to learn and grow professionally outside conventional educational environments (Boström et al., 2002).

c. **Employment Opportunities among Adults**: Continuous learning dramatically improves employability and increases competitiveness in the labor market by giving people access to current information and skills. Additionally, by giving people the knowledge and abilities needed to launch enterprises or provide specialized services, lifelong learning enables people to consider freelancing or entrepreneurial endeavors. This continuous learning creates a variety of chances that support professional growth and business success. By giving people up-to-date information and skills, continuous learning increases employability and makes them more competitive in the labor market (Petner-Arrey, 2016). Additionally, by equipping people with the fundamental knowledge and abilities required for entrepreneurial endeavors, lifelong learning can enable people to launch their own companies or engage in freelancing employment. Continued education enhances employment possibilities and creates new avenues for career advancement.

d. **Economic Benefits of Lifelong Learning**: Lifelong learning can result in substantial financial advantages for an individual, including increased earning potential and increased employment stability. People with improved credentials and abilities frequently have more access to better jobs and higher pay. On the other hand, ongoing skill improvement lowers the likelihood of job obsolescence and enables them to adjust to shifting demands. More broadly, increased productivity from a trained labor force propels economic growth and competitiveness (Dorsett, 2010). Furthermore, lifelong learning encourages innovation by giving people the skills to create novel concepts and technological advancements, stimulating entrepreneurship, and boosting the economy.

## CHALLENGES AND BARRIES TO LIFELONG LEARNING

Age-related stereotypes and technological difficulties can prevent older adults from fully participating in educational and professional growth opportunities. Age discrimination also limits older adults' access to training and skill development, making it challenging to pursue career advancement (UNESCO, 2022). Health and care needs also impact older adults' economic participation. Increasing healthcare costs can strain their financial stability, making it difficult for them to continue working or engaging in economic activities. Long-term care needs further complicate their situation by reducing work capacity or consuming significant financial resources (Chiţiba et al., 2012).

a. **Accessibility Issues**: Significant obstacles to educational opportunities exist because of accessibility concerns, especially for people in underprivileged communities. Participation in online learning may need to be improved by the digital divide, characterized by restricted access to technology and internet connectivity. Financial barriers, such as the price of schooling and training programs, can also keep people from pursuing additional education and skill development. These difficulties underline the necessity of more extensive initiatives to guarantee fair access to educational opportunities and resources. The digital divide and financial limitations significantly hamper access to educational possibilities (Rawas, 2024). Online learning can be hindered by limited technology availability and internet connectivity, particularly in underprivileged areas. However, the high expense of training and educational programs may make it more difficult for some people to seek lifelong learning. These difficulties highlight the need for more excellent work to close the gaps in technological access, lower the cost, and expand the accessibility of educational resources.

b. **Motivation and Engagement**: It can be challenging to motivate people to pursue lifelong learning when they are reluctant because they fear failing, lack confidence, or believe the content is irrelevant. Making sure that learning opportunities are relevant and valuable by carefully matching them with people's career goals and personal interests is crucial to overcoming these obstacles. Addressing these elements can make learning experiences more stimulating and engaging, promoting continued involvement and growth (Spulber, 2019). Encouraging someone to continue lifelong learning might be complex if they fear failing, lack confidence, or think the material is unimportant. The key to overcoming these challenges is ensuring that learning opportunities are carefully matched with people's interests and career aspirations to ensure they are both relevant and valuable. By addressing these factors, learning experiences can be more engaging and exciting, encouraging ongoing participation and development (Rainer, 2014).

c. **Role of Employers and Policymakers**: Employer efforts are essential for the development and contentment of employees. Providing employees with on-the-job training and development programs helps them grow in their professions and learn new skills. It also boosts their capacities, encourages loyalty, and offers financial support for additional schooling or certifications. These programs improve individual performance and help the organization become more competitive and successful. Enacting policies is essential for encouraging economic engagement and lifelong learning (Nagarajan et al., 2023). The government's support of easily accessible and reasonably priced training and education initiatives motivates people never to stop learning. Providing incentives or subsidies to encourage people and companies to invest in learning and development can also help to promote skill development and career advancement. Together, these actions contribute to establishing a culture that values and allows people to continue learning and growing (Quinn et al., 2002).

## FUTURE TRENDS AND OPPORTUNITIES

Workplace accommodation is essential for integrating older workers and fostering an inclusive environment. Employers can promote age diversity by implementing policies that accommodate the needs of older employees and provide opportunities for skill development. Lifelong learning helps these workers stay relevant in a rapidly evolving job market. Similarly, social support systems enhance older adults' economic participation and well-being. Community-based programs offer valuable support and engagement opportunities, reducing isolation and boosting involvement. Access to affordable, comprehensive healthcare supports older adults' economic participation and overall health (Hult et al., 2020; Halicka et al., 2021).

Future-focused technological developments will be essential. Increasing older individuals' digital literacy is necessary for their full engagement in the modern economy, which includes online work and education. The progression of assistive technologies will bolster individuals' capacity to oversee medical issues and preserve mobility, thereby enabling sustained economic participation. The "silver economy," which refers to the economic development prospects brought about by the aging population, offers new potential for businesses catering to senior citizens' needs. In addition to increasing worker productivity and creativity, intergenerational collaboration can use the experiences and strengths of younger and older generations (Czaja et al., 1994). Below are a few criteria that will enlighten us in detail.

a. **Technological Advancements**: Due to technological developments like automation and artificial intelligence, lifelong learning is crucial for adjusting to new tools and systems and changing job positions. Continuing education will be essential for acquiring the skills required to prosper in a tech-driven economy as these innovations transform the workforce. Improving one's digital literacy via lifelong learning will guarantee that people can contribute and stay competitive in this quickly evolving environment (Heinz et al., 2013).

1. **Evolving Job Markets**: To succeed in changing employment markets and take advantage of chances in cutting-edge sectors like digital media, biotech, and green technology, one must pursue lifelong learning. Learning to manage virtual collaboration and remote work environments will also be crucial as remote work becomes increasingly common. By continuing their education, people can adjust to these changes and participate in the economy in a dynamic, more digital workforce (Honey et al., 2014).

b. **Workforce Participation**: Due to financial need, a desire for ongoing involvement, or personal fulfillment, many older persons continue working past the customary retirement age. Part-time, freelancing, or consulting jobs, which provide more flexibility and can accommodate different personal demands and energy levels, are frequently used to facilitate this move. With these arrangements, senior citizens can maintain their economic ties and balance other facets of their lives while contributing their expertise to the workforce (Dantas et al., 2017).

c. **Retirement Trends**: As people live longer and postpone retirement to maintain financial security, retirement trends are changing. The requirement to prolong working lives to ensure adequate resources for later years is reflected in this trend. Moreover, phased retirement is becoming more popular, enabling older persons to ease into retirement by cutting back on their working hours or assuming less demanding positions. This strategy facilitates the transition from full-time employment to retirement while preserving motivation and involvement (Quinn et al., 2002).

2. **Senior Entrepreneurship**: A growing proportion of senior citizens pursue entrepreneurship, launch their own companies, or participate in entrepreneurial endeavors. They frequently use their wealth of knowledge and experience to launch businesses that reflect their interests and expertise (Honey et al., 2014). This trend offers a rewarding means of staying involved and active, and by introducing experienced viewpoints and abilities to the business sector, it promotes economic variety and creativity.

## DEMOGRAPHIC TRENDS AND LEARNING PROCESS

The current demographic changes are taking place in the context of profound social and technical change. These changes are marked by a quick evolution of many elements of daily life, significantly impacted by changes in society's structure and technological advancements. Because of this, even seemingly simple tasks become more complex and require new abilities. Take grocery stores and self-checkout systems, for example. These days, this straightforward activity entails using different payment methods, navigating digital interfaces, and fixing technological issues. Comparably, real-time worldwide communication is made possible by platforms like Skype, which is very different from more conventional means of communication. These instances show how the advancement of technology is transforming our daily lives at a rapid and fundamental pace (Dantas et al., 2017; Brewster et al., 2014).

Learning itself is a dynamic idea that changes with this dynamic environment. Education was traditionally thought to occur mainly in childhood and early adulthood, preparing people for their everyday lives and vocations. However, it is evident from the world's current rate of change that education cannot be limited to these formative years. Learning must be a lifelong, ongoing activity instead. Field's study highlights the variety of advantages of lifelong learning. Lifelong learning has substantial effects on social capital that go beyond simply picking up new information and abilities. Social capital is the networks, social norms, and social trust that promote cooperation and coordination for mutual gain. There are various ways that lifelong learning improves social capital; we will look at each one by one:

a. **Expanding Social Networks Competencies**: Learning exercises significantly improve social competencies by fostering the development of interpersonal skills, problem-solving techniques, and adaptability, all of which are necessary for productive cooperation and communication in various social settings. Furthermore, learning frequently entails social interaction with new people through workshops, online courses, formal educational settings, or community events. This helps one's social network grow and creates essential connections for both personal and professional life (Biggs et al., 2012).

b. **Fostering Common Norms and Tolerance**: Continuous learning exposes people to various viewpoints and ideas, fostering tolerance and understanding. It promotes an awareness of common standards and values and aids in appreciating multiple points of view. The senior population's demographic patterns substantially impact economic involvement, affecting people and larger economic systems. To shape practices and policies that promote financial stability and growth, it is imperative to comprehend these trends and their consequences for economic involvement as the number of older persons worldwide rises.

c. **Increasing Longevity**: Life expectancy has improved dramatically due to improvements in healthcare, nutrition, and living conditions, which has led to a more extensive and expanding older population. Particularly in many industrialized nations, the percentage of older adults, generally defined as those aged 65 and older, is quickly increasing due to individuals living longer. This change in the population emphasizes the need for specialized policies and initiatives to meet the exceptional opportunities and problems faced by the aging population.

d. **Changing Family Structures**: As family dynamics change, so do the living situations and caring obligations of the elderly. The care and support services for the elderly are impacted by the trend toward nuclear families and smaller residences, which typically leads to more independent living arrangements. Moreover, it has been demonstrated that smaller families and geographically dispersed family members worsen older adults' feelings of social isolation and loneliness. To combat these problems, more social support systems and community engagement initiatives are needed.

e. **Health and Mobility**: The inability of older persons to work and participate in economic activities is primarily impacted by health and mobility issues. Older adults frequently suffer from chronic health concerns, which might hinder their ability to participate in numerous duties and obligations fully. Mobility problems also make participating in social and professional activities challenging. However, these difficulties are becoming less severe because of developments in assistive technologies, allowing older persons to continue being active members of their communities and maintaining a higher level of independence despite physical restrictions (Biggs et al., 2012).

# AGE AND INTELLIGENCE: THE CLASSIC AGING PATTERN

Multidirectional age profiles in intellectual performance are a hallmark of the typical pattern of intellectual aging that has been repeatedly found in research. While age-sensitive talents show a moderate to significant loss with age, age-irrelevant abilities remain broadly consistent throughout maturity. The research study sought to ascertain whether adult assessments of test familiarity and difficulty varied depending on whether the exam was age-sensitive or age-irrelevant and whether these assessments were associated with the evaluators' ages (Cornelius, 1984; Gajewski et al., 2020).

One of the psychological phenomena that is investigated the most in-depth is intelligence, despite disagreements over its definition and assessment. Though they are different, intelligence and cognition are closely related. To become "intelligently" understood, one must acquire cognitive functions like thinking, working memory, and attention. Raymond Cattell first distinguished between fluid and crystallized intelligence in the 1960s.

## Language Learning in Older Adults

Studies have shown that bilingualism has cognitive benefits for older persons, with bilinguals performing mentally better than their monolingual counterparts. On the other hand, further research is required to determine the long-term effects of language learning on cognition. This study compared older adults' behavioral and fMRI responses to a Stroop task before and after a language-learning intervention (Wrigley et al., 2003). On the Stroop task, accuracy and reaction time were improved following the language acquisition intervention. Using the neuroimaging data, we found significant differences in activity between congruent and incongruent trials in key prefrontal and parietal brain areas. These results are consistent with previous research using the Stroop paradigm.

More research is needed to determine the optimal circumstances for language acquisition as an effective cognitive intervention for older adults. When language learning is sufficiently involved, it can enhance executive functioning, among other mental functions. By advancing our understanding of cognitive reserve and how to improve it through targeted therapies, their findings set the stage for future research (Schultz et al., 2024 Aug 7). Variability (= intra-individual variation within tasks in individual time-serial data of repeated observations), inconsistency (= intra-individual variation across trials within tasks at one measurement), and inter-learner dispersion are three examples of variations in learning across different types of functions within a single session. A deeper understanding of differences in the amount of a developmental variable within and among older L2 learners' sensitivity to intervention analysis will allow future interventions based on meditation to be more precisely suited to the third age.

By comparing the effects of late-life second language learning versus lifelong bilingualism, researchers hope to shed light on the mechanisms underlying the benefits of bilingualism as a life experience, particularly about cognitive reserve in older adulthood and the ability to differentiate between healthy older adults and those experiencing late-life cognitive impairment and depression.

## Psychological Perspective and Theories

Lifelong learning is intricately linked to numerous psychological theories and concepts that elucidate human growth, motivation, and social interaction. Before delving further into psychological theories of aging, it is critical to weigh the ramifications of this concept. Or do psychological theories of aging contribute to our understanding of how individuals cope with age-related losses? Do psychological theories of aging relate to biological theories of aging in the same way that theories of physiological changes associated with aging are related to psychological changes commonly associated with aging?

Psychological theories of aging cover the age-related psychological changes and adaptive psychological mechanisms or lack thereof to counteract the losses brought on by physical deterioration. The body of research indicates that both theories are valid. For example, cognitive psychology studies age-related changes in compensatory mechanisms and mental performance. The conceptual muddle is exacerbated by the difficulty in distinguishing psychology from social or psychosocial theories of aging, which may be more advantageous theoretically than practically. Just as it is impossible to study a person's "psyche" in isolation, judgments on people should not be formed without considering their immediate and more significant social, cultural, and historical context (Fisher, J. C., 1993; Richeson et al.; J. N., 2006; Wernher et al.; M. S., 2015;). The following critical psychological theories and viewpoints shed light on the significance of continuous learning and its effects on people:

*Table 1. Psychological theories and viewpoints*

| **1. Development Theories** |
| --- |
| **a. The Theory of Childhood Development by Sigmund Freud**: For much of the twentieth century, many perceived aging as a one-dimensional deterioration process. This idea makes it unsurprising that most eminent scholars' research has focused on changes in human development in childhood and adolescence. One well-known example is Sigmund Freud, who stressed the significance of a child's early years in shaping their personality and believed that psychological development is a process that happens in stages (Colarusso et al., 1992). |
| **b. Stages of Psychosocial Development Proposed by Erik Erikson**: Erikson postulated eight phases of psychosocial development that many perceived aging that people go through. Every stage has a unique struggle or obstacle, like integrity vs hopelessness in old age or identity versus role confusion in youth. By encouraging personal development and adaptability at every step, lifelong learning can assist people in overcoming these obstacles (Development Through Life: A Psychosocial Approach" by Barbara M. Newman and Philip R. Newman, 11th ed., 2022; Orenstein et al., 2022). |
| **c. Jean Piaget's Theory of Cognitive Development**: Theory focuses on the maturation of cognitive capacities from childhood to adulthood. Although lifelong learning is consistent with the notion that cognitive growth continues throughout life, his theory of learning ends in adolescence. Adults might benefit from fresh experiences and educational opportunities to further improve their mental skills (Handbook of Child Psychology and Developmental Science" edited by Richard M. Lerner, n.d.; Piaget, 1976); Barrouillet, 2015). |
| **2. Motivational Theories** |
| **a. Self-Determination Theory (SDT)**: Developed by Deci and Ryan, SDT asserts that the need for relatedness, competence, and autonomy drives motivation. By enabling people to interact with others, feel competent in new abilities, and exercise autonomy in selecting what they wish to study, lifelong learning helps to meet these requirements (Ryan et al., 2000). Individuals' well-being is said to be facilitated when their basic psychological needs (autonomy, competence, and relatedness) are met, according to Ryan and Deci in Self-determination Theory: Basic Psychological Needs in Motivation, development, and Wellness (Guilford et al., 2017; Behzadnia et al., 2020). |
| **b. Growth Mindset**: Two mindsets are distinguished by Carol S. Dweck's (2006) mindset theory: fixed and growth. A fixed mindset is the conviction that one's skills are inherent and unalterable, which pushes people to take calculated chances and demonstrate their value repeatedly. On the other hand, a growth mindset emphasizes personal development and sees obstacles as chances for advancement. It maintains that skills can be acquired through work and education (Mindset: The New Psychology of Success", 2006; Liu et al., 2022, January). This idea, popularized by Carol Dweck, highlights that intellect and aptitude can be acquired with commitment and hard work. It promotes lifelong learning by viewing obstacles as chances for personal development rather than immovable barriers. |
| **3. Learning Theories** |
| **a. Constructivist Learning Theory**: Based on the research of Piaget and expanded upon by Lev Vygotsky, this theory holds that learners build their knowledge and understanding of the world through experiences and reflection. Lifelong learning is consistent with this theory since it constantly adds to and reassesses knowledge through new experiences (Vygotsky, 2018). |
| **b. Experiential Learning Theory:** David Kolb's experiential learning theory emphasizes learning through experience, reflection, and application. This model is well-suited to lifelong learning since it frequently entails acquiring new experiences, thinking critically about them, and applying what is learned to real-world situations. The four stages of the learning cycle—Concrete Experience, Reflective Observation, Abstract Conceptualization, and Active Experimentation—are the foundation of this theory (The Kolb Learning Style Inventory: A Comprehensive Guide to the Theory and Applications", 1985). |
| **4. Social and Behavioral Theories** |

continued on following page

*Table 1. Continued*

| |
|---|
| **a. Social Learning Theory**: Albert Bandura's Social Learning Theory emphasizes the importance of modeling, imitation, and observation in the learning process. Interacting with others, monitoring their behaviors, and modifying them in response to social feedback all enhance lifelong learning. This method promotes lifelong learning because it emphasizes the value of continuous social contacts and observational experiences in professional and personal development (Chen et al., 2015). |
| **b. The Theory of Planned Behavior:** According to Icek Ajzen's theory, attitudes, subjective norms, and perceived behavior control all impact intentions, which drive behavior. Through this perspective, lifelong learning can be comprehended, as people's intentions to learn are influenced by their attitudes toward learning, societal expectations, and learning capacity (Chen et al., 2015). |
| **5. Well-Being and Psychological Growth** |
| **a. Positive Psychology**: A field founded by Martin Seligman and others that emphasizes values, strengths, and a happy life to increase happiness and well-being. This psychological approach encourages people to cultivate positive qualities, such as resilience, gratitude, and significance, to increase general happiness and life satisfaction. Because these qualities are essential to well-being, such as engagement, personal success, and a sense of purpose, lifelong learning is consistent with positive psychology (Authentic Happiness: Using the New Positive Psychology to Realize Your Potential for Lasting Fulfillment" by Martin Seligman, 2002). |
| **b. Flow Theory**: The idea of being completely absorbed and involved in an activity that frequently results in a sensation of timelessness and high satisfaction is explored in Mihaly Csikszentmihalyi's Flow Theory. Experiences that strike a balance between difficulty and competence can create a state of flow in the context of lifelong learning, which improves the enjoyment and efficiency of the learning process ("Flow: The Psychology of Optimal Experience" by Mihaly Csikszentmihalyi, 1990). |

# ECONOMIC WELLBEING IN OLDER ADULTS

A community's overall well-being is the result of numerous elements cooperating to provide the best possible standard of living for every one of its members. Here, it is stated that encouraging older people to pursue lifelong learning can significantly impact the community's wellness. The global phenomenon of an aging population offers opportunities and challenges for communities' well-being (Levasseur M., 2009). According to research, older people who are healthier, more active, and more educated tend to use fewer resources and services from their families and communities. Simultaneously, healthy, active seniors enhance communal well-being by offering their life experience, knowledge, and assistance. From the standpoint of social capital, the connection between community wellness and lifelong learning is argued. According to this concept, older persons' formal, informal, and nonformal learning activities encourage an engaged, active lifestyle that contributes to the development and maintenance of communities. Access and opportunity issues are also covered (Merriam & Kee, 2014).

Older adults' financial security is essential to their and society's well-being. The proportion of elderly individuals in the US who live in poverty has significantly declined during the last thirty years. The existence of vital support systems like

Medicare, Social Security, and private pensions is primarily responsible for this improvement. Though there has been progress, financial anxieties still significantly impact many older people's general quality of life. Getting proper medical care might be especially difficult for older people if they need more money or their current resources are insufficient (Sung, 2023).

In addition to improving health and well-being, volunteering and lifelong learning help older people feel more integrated into society and more cohesive. However, more is needed to know about the possible advantages of lifetime learning and volunteering. Volunteering results from lifelong learning and vice versa, creating a healthy circle of later-life social interaction. Initiatives and programs that engage senior citizens in constructive endeavors should promote and ease participation in other activities (Sung et al., 2023).

## CONCLUSION

In a dynamic and changing labor market, lifelong learning is essential to economic participation. People who update their skills regularly become more employable, can adjust to changing job demands, and take advantage of new opportunities. This benefits the individual and boosts the economy through increased productivity, innovation, and entrepreneurship. Removing obstacles to lifelong learning and developing a culture of continuous education will be crucial to optimizing economic participation and guaranteeing that people and economies can prosper in the future. Renowned psychologist Erik Erikson proposed that the last phase of the human life cycle involves the development of a sense of integrity or despair. As people age, they reflect deeply on their lives and their experiences. Those who have successfully handled their affairs, overcome obstacles in life, and accepted successes and failures can reflect on their past with great fulfillment and little regret. They can find serenity and acceptance in their older years because of their integrity, which keeps them from giving in to terror when faced with disease and death.

Numerous psychological theories stress that continued growth, motivation, and well-being favor lifelong learning. These ideas offer a framework for understanding why lifelong learning is crucial for social interaction, personal development, and happiness. Despite the changes that come with aging, older persons can continue to grow, adapt, and experience a whole life by concentrating on these areas. This chapter provides a psychological perspective on aging, emphasizing essential theories and concepts concerning cognition, emotions, and behavior changes. These succinct explanations are meant to help practitioners comprehend the mechanisms that influence their older patients' cognition, emotions, and behavior, even though there is a wealth of literature on psychological theories and aging.

This chapter aims to equip practitioners with the fundamental knowledge they need to help their senior clients more efficiently and knowledgeably. Emotional functioning and the importance of social integration are largely steady as we age, much like personality qualities. Even if how we perceive emotions changes over time, they still impact our mental and physical health. For example, experiencing negative emotions as we age still affects physiological functioning and, in turn, physical health, just as it did in earlier life stages. On the other hand, those who perceive their life as a sequence of lost chances or personal adversities could feel extraordinarily hopeless and obsessed over what might have been in a different situation. These people struggle with unmet expectations and unhealed scars, making death a frightening possibility that makes them feel empty and inadequate.

# REFERENCES

(1985). The Kolb Learning Style Inventory: A Comprehensive Guide to the Theory and Applications"

Balatti, J., & Falk, I. (2002). Socioeconomic contributions of adult learning to community: A social capital perspective. *Adult Education Quarterly*, 52(4), 281–298. DOI: 10.1177/074171302400448618

Barrouillet, P. (2015). Theories of cognitive development: From Piaget to today. *Developmental Review*, 38, 1–12. DOI: 10.1016/j.dr.2015.07.004

Bashkireva, A. S., Bogdanova, D. Y., Bilyk, A. Y., Shishko, A. V., Kachan, E. Y., & Arutyunov, V. A. (2018). Quality of life and physical activity among elderly and old people. *Advances in gerontology=. Uspekhi Gerontologii*, 31(5), 743–750. PMID: 30638330

Behzadnia, B., Deci, E. L., & DeHaan, C. R. (2020). Predicting relations among life goals, physical activity, health, and well-being in elderly adults: a self-determination theory perspective on healthy aging. *Self-determination theory and healthy aging: Comparative contexts on physical and mental well-being*, 47-71.

Berglund, G. (2007). Adapt or you're toast?–Remodelling the individual in lifelong learning. *Nordic Studies in Education*, 27(2), 120–129. DOI: 10.18261/ISSN1891-5949-2007-02-02

Biggs, S., Carstensen, L., & Hogan, P. (2012). Social capital, lifelong learning and social Innovation. In World Economic Forum, Global Population Ageing: Peril or Promise? (pp. 39–41). Retrieved November 16, 2013, from http://www3.weforum .org/docs/WEF_ GAC_GlobalPopulationAgeing_Report_2012.pdf

Bjorklund, B. R. (2011). *The journey of adulthood* (7th ed.). Prentice Hall.

Boström, A. K. (2002). Informal learning in a formal context: Problematizing the concept of social capital in a contemporary Swedish context. *International Journal of Lifelong Education*, 21(6), 510–524. DOI: 10.1080/02601370220000016730

Brewster, P. W., Melrose, R. J., Marquine, M. J., Johnson, J. K., Napoles, A., MacKay-Brandt, A., Farias, S., Reed, B., & Mungas, D. (2014). Life experience and demographic influences on cognitive function in older adults. *Neuropsychology*, 28(6), 846–858. DOI: 10.1037/neu0000098 PMID: 24933483

Brookfield, S. (2012). The impact of lifelong learning on communities. In Aspin, D. N., Chapman, J., Evans, K., & Bagnall, R. (Eds.), *Second international handbook of lifelong learning*. Part 2 (pp. 875–886). Springer. DOI: 10.1007/978-94-007-2360-3_53

Butler, R. N., & Gleason, H. P. (1985). *Productive aging*. Springer.

Chen, M. F., Wang, R. H., & Hung, S. L. (2015). Predicting health-promoting self-care behaviors in people with pre-diabetes by applying Bandura social learning theory. *Applied Nursing Research*, 28(4), 299–304. DOI: 10.1016/j.apnr.2015.01.001 PMID: 26608429

Chiţiba, C. A. (2012). Lifelong learning challenges and opportunities for traditional universities. *Procedia: Social and Behavioral Sciences*, 46, 1943–1947. DOI: 10.1016/j.sbspro.2012.05.408

Cocquyt, C., Diep, N. A., Zhu, C., De Greef, M., & Vanwing, T. (2017). Examining social inclusion and social capital among adult learners in blended and online learning environments. *European journal for Research on the Education and Learning of Adults, 8*(1), 77-101

Colarusso, C. A. (1992). *Child and adult development: A psychoanalytic introduction for clinicians*. Springer Science & Business Media. DOI: 10.1007/978-1-4757-9673-5

Cornelius, S. W. (1984, March). The classic pattern of intellectual aging: Test familiarity, difficulty, and performance. *Journal of Gerontology*, 39(2), 201–206. DOI: 10.1093/geronj/39.2.201 PMID: 6699376

Croezen, S., Haveman-Nies, A., Alvarado, V. J., Van't Veer, P., & De Groot, C. P. G. M. (2009). Characterization of different groups of elderly according to social engagement activity patterns. *JNHA-The Journal of Nutrition. Health and Aging*, 13, 776–781. PMID: 19812867

Cumming, E., & Henry, W. E. (1961). *Growing old: The process of disengagement*. Basic Books.

Czaja, S. J. (1994). Employment opportunities for older adults: Engineering design and research issues. *Experimental Aging Research*, 20(4), 265–273. DOI: 10.1080/03610739408253976 PMID: 7843213

Dantas, R. G., Perracini, M. R., Guerra, R. O., Ferriolli, E., Dias, R. C., & Padula, R. S. (2017). What are the sociodemographic and health determinants for older adults continue to participate in work? *Archives of Gerontology and Geriatrics*, 71, 136–141. DOI: 10.1016/j.archger.2017.04.005 PMID: 28458105

Dench, S., & Regan, J. (2000, February). Learning in later life: Motivation and impact (Research Brief No. 183). Retrieved November 16, 2013, from https://www.employment-studies.co.uk/pubs/summary.php?id=rr183

Development Through Life. (2022). *A Psychosocial Approach" by Barbara M* (11th ed.). Newman and Philip R. Newman.

Di Nuovo, S., De Beni, R., Borella, E., Marková, H., Laczó, J., & Vyhnálek, M. (2020). Cognitive impairment in old age: Is the shift from healthy to pathological aging responsive to prevention? *European Psychologist*, 25(3), 174–185. DOI: 10.1027/1016-9040/a000391

Diggs, J. (2008). Activity theory of aging. In Loue, S., & Sajatovie, M. (Eds.), *Encyclopedia of Aging and Public Health* (pp. 79–81). Springer. DOI: 10.1007/978-0-387-33754-8_9

Dorsett, R., Lui, S., & Weale, M. (2010). *Economic benefits of lifelong learning*. Centre for Learning and Life Chances in Knowledge Economies and Societies.

Field, J. (2005). *Social capital and lifelong learning*. Policy Press.

Field, J. (2009). *Well-being and happiness: Inquiry into the future of lifelong learning (Thematic paper 4)*. National Institute of Adult Continuing Education.

Formosa, M. (Ed.). (2019). *The University of the third age and active aging: European and Asian-Pacific perspectives*. Springer. DOI: 10.1007/978-3-030-21515-6

Gajewski, P. D., Falkenstein, M., Thönes, S., & Wascher, E. (2020). Stroop task performance across the lifespan: High cognitive reserve in older age is associated with enhanced proactive and reactive interference control. *NeuroImage*, 207, 116430. DOI: 10.1016/j.neuroimage.2019.116430 PMID: 31805383

Golding, B. G. (2011). Social, local, and situated: Recent findings about the effectiveness of older men's informal learning in community contexts. *Adult Education Quarterly*, 61(2), 103–120. DOI: 10.1177/0741713610380437

Guarino, A., Forte, G., Giovannoli, J., & Casagrande, M. (2020). Executive functions in older people with mild cognitive impairment: A systematic review on motor and cognitive inhibition, conflict control and cognitive flexibility. *Aging & Mental Health*, 24(7), 1028–1045. DOI: 10.1080/13607863.2019.1584785 PMID: 30938193

Halicka, K., & Surel, D. (2021). Gerontechnology—New opportunities in the service of older adults. *Engineering Management in Production and Services*, 13(3), 114–126. DOI: 10.2478/emj-2021-0025

Havighurst, R. J. (1961). Successful aging. *The Gerontologist*, 1(1), 8–13. DOI: 10.1093/geront/1.1.8

Heinz, M., Martin, P., Margrett, J. A., Yearns, M., Franke, W., Yang, H. I., Wong, J., & Chang, C. K. (2013). Perceptions of technology among older adults. *Journal of Gerontological Nursing*, 39(1), 42–51. DOI: 10.3928/00989134-20121204-04 PMID: 23244061

Hertzog, C., Kramer, A. F., Wilson, R. S., & Lindenberger, U. (2008). Enrichment effects on adult cognitive development: Can the functional capacity of older adults be preserved and enhanced? *Psychological Science in the Public Interest*, 9(1), 1–65. DOI: 10.1111/j.1539-6053.2009.01034.x PMID: 26162004

Herzog, A. R., Ofstedal, M. B., & Wheeler, L. M. (2002). Social engagement and its relationship to health. *Clinics in Geriatric Medicine*, 18(3), 595–609. DOI: 10.1016/S0749-0690(02)00025-3 PMID: 12424874

Honey, A., Kariuki, M., Emerson, E., & Llewellyn, G. (2014). Employment status transitions among young adults, with and without disability. *The Australian Journal of Social Issues*, 49(2), 151–170. DOI: 10.1002/j.1839-4655.2014.tb00306.x

Horsley, T., Grimshaw, J., & Campbell, C. (2010). *How to create conditions for adapting physicians' skills to new needs and lifelong learning*. WHO Regional Office for Europe.

Hult, M., Pietilä, A. M., & Saaranen, T. (2020). Improving employment opportunities for the unemployed through health and workability promotion in Finland. *Health Promotion International*, 35(3), 518–526. DOI: 10.1093/heapro/daz048 PMID: 31132120

Janssens, J. (2002). *Innovations in Lifelong Learning: Capitalising on ADAPT. CEDEFOP Panorama Series*. CEDEFOP, PO Box 22427, Thessaloniki, GR-55102 Greece

Lerner, R. M. (Ed.), *Handbook of Child Psychology and Developmental Science*. DOI: 10.1002/9781118963418

Levasseur, , MTribble, , D. S. CDesrosiers, , J. (2009). Meaning of quality of life for older adults: importance of human functioning components. *Archives of Gerontology and Geriatrics, 49*(2), e91–e100.

London, M. (2011). Lifelong learning: introduction. *The Oxford handbook of lifelong learning*, 3-11.

Merriam, S. B., & Bierema, L. L. (2014). *Adult learning: Linking theory and practice*. Jossey-Bass.

Merriam, S. B., & Kee, Y. (2014). Promoting community wellbeing: The case for lifelong learning for older adults. *Adult Education Quarterly*, 64(2), 128–144. DOI: 10.1177/0741713613513633

Merriam and Kee (2014). *Promoting Community Wellbeing: The Case for Lifelong Learning for Older Adults.*

Mihaly Csikszentmihalyi, (1990). "Flow: The Psychology of Optimal Experience"

Morris, T. H. (2019). Adaptivity through self-directed learning to meet the challenges of our ever-changing world. *Adult Learning*, 30(2), 56–66. DOI: 10.1177/1045159518814486

Nagarajan, N. R., & Sixsmith, A. (2023). Policy initiatives to address the challenges of an older population in the workforce. *Ageing International*, 48(1), 41–77. DOI: 10.1007/s12126-021-09442-w PMID: 34465930

Nguyen, C., Leanos, S., Natsuaki, M. N., Rebok, G. W., & Wu, R. (2020). Adaptation for growth via learning new skills as a means to long-term functional independence in older adulthood: Insights from emerging adulthood. *The Gerontologist*, 60(1), 4–11. PMID: 30321326

Orenstein, G. A., & Lewis, L. (2022). Eriksons stages of psychosocial development. In *StatPearls* [Internet]. StatPearls Publishing.

Petner-Arrey, J., Howell-Moneta, A., & Lysaght, R. (2016). Facilitating employment opportunities for adults with an intellectual and developmental disability through parents and social networks. *Disability and Rehabilitation*, 38(8), 789–795. DOI: 10.3109/09638288.2015.1061605 PMID: 26114628

Piaget, J. (1976). Piaget's theory.

Quinn, J. F. (2002). Changing Retirement Trends and Their. *Policies for an aging society*, 293.

Rainer, S. (2014). Social participation and social engagement of elderly people. *Procedia: Social and Behavioral Sciences*, 116, 780–785. DOI: 10.1016/j.sbspro.2014.01.297

Rawas, S. (2024). ChatGPT: Empowering lifelong learning in the digital age of higher education. *Education and Information Technologies*, 29(6), 6895–6908. DOI: 10.1007/s10639-023-12114-8

Richeson, J. A., & Shelton, J. N. (2006). A social psychological perspective on the stigmatization of older adults. *When I'm, 64*, 174-208.

Rowe, J. W., & Kahn, R. L. (1997). Successful aging. *The Gerontologist*, 37(4), 433–440. DOI: 10.1093/geront/37.4.433 PMID: 9279031

Rowe, J. W., & Kahn, R. L. (1998). *Successful aging*. Dell/Random House.

Ryan, R. M., & Deci, E. L. (2000). Self-Determination Theory and the Facilitation of Intrinsic Motivation, Social Development, and Well-Being. *The American Psychologist*, 55(1), 68–78. DOI: 10.1037/0003-066X.55.1.68 PMID: 11392867

Schultz, D. H., Gansemer, A., Allgood, K., Gentz, M., Secilmis, L., Deldar, Z., Savage, C. R., & Ghazi Saidi, L. (2024, August 7). Second language learning in older adults modulates Stroop task performance and brain activation. *Frontiers in Aging Neuroscience*, 16, 1398015. DOI: 10.3389/fnagi.2024.1398015 PMID: 39170898

Sokolec, J. (2016). The meaning of "place" to older adults. *Clinical Social Work Journal*, 44(2), 160–169. DOI: 10.1007/s10615-015-0545-2

Spulber, D. (2019). Coping and resilience in life-long learning and ageing: New challenges. *Geopolitical. Social Security and Freedom Journal*, 2(1), 93–103. DOI: 10.2478/gssfj-2019-0009

Sun, X., Yan, W., Zhou, H., Wang, Z., Zhang, X., Huang, S., & Li, L. (2020). Internet use and need for digital health technology among the elderly: A cross-sectional survey in China. *BMC Public Health*, 20(1), 1–8. DOI: 10.1186/s12889-020-09448-0 PMID: 32917171

Sung, P., Chia, A., Chan, A., & Malhotra, R. (2023, May 11). Reciprocal Relationship Between Lifelong Learning and Volunteering Among Older Adults. *The Journals of Gerontology. Series B, Psychological Sciences and Social Sciences*, 78(5), 902–912. DOI: 10.1093/geronb/gbad003 PMID: 36626304

Tornstam, L. (2005). *Gerotranscendence: A developmental theory of positive aging*. Springer.

UNESCO. (2022). *5th global report on adult learning and education. Citizenship education: Empowering adults for change*. UNESCO Institute for Lifelong Learning. Hamburg: UIL.

Vygotsky, L. (2018). Lev Vygotsky. *La psicología en la Revolución Rusa. Colombia: Ediciones desde abajo*.

Wernher, I., & Lipsky, M. S. (2015). Psychological theories of aging. *Disease-a-Month*, 61(11), 480–488. DOI: 10.1016/j.disamonth.2015.09.004 PMID: 26603197

WHO. (World Health Organization), (2020). Decade of Healthy Ageing 2020-2030. Geneva: WHO.

Withnall, A. (2012). Lifelong or longlife? Learning in the later years. In Aspin, D. N., Chapman, J., Evans, K., & Bagnall, R. (Eds.), *Second international handbook of lifelong learning*. Part 2 (pp. 649–664). Springer. DOI: 10.1007/978-94-007-2360-3_39

Wolf, M. A., & Brady, E. M. (2010). Adult and continuing education for an aging society. In Kasworm, C. E., Rose, A. D., & Ross-Gordon, J. M. (Eds.), *The handbook of adult and continuing education* (2010 edition, pp. 369–378). Sage.

Wrigley, H. S., Richer, E., Martinson, K., Kubo, H., & Strawn, J. (2003). The language of opportunity: Expanding employment prospects for adults with limited English skills.

Zunzunegui, M. V., Alvarado, B. E., Del Ser, T., & Otero, A. (2003). Social networks, social integration, and social engagement determine cognitive decline in community-dwelling Spanish older adults—. *Journal of Gerontology*, 58B(2), S93–S100. DOI: 10.1093/geronb/58.2.S93 PMID: 12646598

# Chapter 3
# Digital Inclusion and Economic Participation of the Elderly:
## Challenges and Strategies

**Salma Afroj**
https://orcid.org/0009-0001-8420-5462
*Aligarh Muslim University, India*

**Tabassum Bashir**
https://orcid.org/0000-0001-9944-5648
*Aligarh Muslim University, India*

**Pallav Vishnu**
https://orcid.org/0009-0007-3674-5871
*Aligarh Muslim University, India*

**Kalim Ahmad Khan**
*Aligarh Muslim University, India*

## ABSTRACT

*An extensive review of digital inclusion among seniors is given in this chapter, with particular attention on social integration promoted by digital technology, economic engagement, and the effects of post-COVID-19 digital inclusion. It seeks to make a significant contribution to the current conversation on digital inclusion by examining the tactics and obstacles that go along with it. Technology continues to influence how we obtain health information, maintain relationships with loved ones, and participate in society as our living environments grow more digitally connected. This pattern has been highlighted by the COVID-19 pandemic, proving internet access a crucial*

DOI: 10.4018/979-8-3693-7753-6.ch003

*socioeconomic factor that influences health. The usage of digital technologies by older individuals has a direct impact on their quality of life and health outcomes more than ever before. It draws attention to the expanding significance of digital technology for daily activities, social communication, and healthcare access, with digital access emerging as a major social determinant of health.*

## INTRODUCTION

The World Health Organization (WHO) generally defines older adults as 60. However, this can vary by region due to differences in life expectancy and socio-economic conditions. In some global health contexts, they use 65 years as a standard threshold, particularly in higher-income countries. The WHO developed a definition of healthy aging. Attaining and preserving functional ability makes aging well possible (Fallon & Karlawish, 2019; Michel & Sadana, 2017). Older people are a valuable resource for any society. Aging is a natural phenomenon with opportunities and challenges (Ageing and Health India, n.d.)—the gradual, continuous process of natural change known as aging begins in early adulthood. Early middle age is when several body functions begin to decline gradually. People do not become "older" or "elderly" at a certain age. Being 65 or older is the traditional definition of older age. However, the explanation's foundation was history rather than biology. Germany was the first nation to establish a retirement program, and they determined many years ago that 65 was the right retirement age. 1965, the United States set 65 as the minimum age to qualify for Medicare insurance. This age is close to when most people retire in most developed economies (G. et al.).

The National Digital Inclusion Alliance (2017) states that digital inclusion is "necessary to ensure that all individuals and communities, including the most disadvantaged, have access to and use of Information and Communication Technologies." This includes content, apps, and software "designed to facilitate and encourage self-sufficiency, participation, and collaboration," reliable internet connectivity at adequate speeds, digital devices that meet users' requirements, access to technological skills training, and technical assistance. Digital inclusion refers to ensuring that all individuals and communities, regardless of their socio-economic status, have access to and can effectively use information and communication technologies (ICTs). It goes beyond just access to technology. It encompasses the skills, infrastructure, and opportunities to participate fully in the digital world. Digital inclusion is essential in various spheres of life, including education, healthcare, employment, governance, and social participation (Holgersson et al., 2019).

No nation or community should be denied access to digital tools and technologies since digital inclusion is vital to shared economic and social growth. Acknowledging this, "From Access to Empowerment: Digital Inclusion in a Dynamic World" offers a comprehensive, multistakeholder approach to digital inclusion that is action-oriented and sensitive to changing global trends. It does this by moving beyond the traditional focus on access and skills. This report emphasizes the following:

A. The significance of a dynamic and holistic approach to digital inclusion and toward deeper exploration of digital foundations, enablers, and the comparative advantages of each sector and stakeholder. It draws on ideas, innovations, strategies, and case studies from the worldwide public sector, business, and civil society. This entails acknowledging the interaction between digital inclusion and developing worldwide trends, ranging from the changing face of poverty to the increasing complexity and difficulties brought on by new tools and methods of operation.

B. Complete, significant, and widespread engagement in political, social, or economic digital activities must be shaped. The cornerstones of digital inclusion are learning and skill development, hardware and connectivity accessibility and affordability, and building other iterative, mutually reinforcing dimensions such as engagement in civic and political life, participation in the digital economy, and confidence and trust in the digital environment.

C. The government plays a critical and catalytic role, with "public sector enablers" as the cornerstone of effective policies and initiatives for digital inclusion. These are a few developments of digital skills within government agencies: cross-government architecture and collaboration, lifetime development of digital skills and capabilities, and a clear national vision, strategy, and commitment.

D. Acknowledging that digital inclusion is a collaborative endeavor involving the entire society is essential. Leveraging the potential of this collaboration is crucial in addressing the various interconnected facets of digital inclusion, such as encouraging individuals to engage, participate, and co-solve problems, utilizing businesses and public-private partnerships, and collaborating with civil society organizations.

## ELDERLY POPULATION: MEANING AND DEFINITION

The group of people 65 and older is commonly called the "elderly population" (United Nations). This age threshold is commonly used in demographic studies and social policies to categorize individuals as elderly, though in some contexts, the age may vary slightly. As per the World Health Organization (WHO), to guarantee the elderly population's well-being and facilitate their successful integration into society, it is imperative to recognize and cater to their needs. Due to rising life expectancy and falling birth rates, the senior population is expanding quickly in many nations, with older persons making up a more significant proportion of the population than younger age groups. This change in the population presents several issues and concerns. According to Health Centers for Disease Control and Prevention (CDC), older people frequently experience age-related conditions that increase the need for long-term care and healthcare services. Financially speaking, they could have trouble with pension plans, retirement income, and stability, mainly if they have not saved enough for their golden years. Social and psychological problems like loneliness, mental health challenges, and the requirement for community institutions that provide support are essential. As a result of the National Institute on Aging (NIA), organizations and governments are creating laws and initiatives targeted at helping the aged, such as improved social security payments, healthcare services, and age-friendly infrastructure.

Traditionally, the term "elderly" has been defined as a person 65 years of age or older on a chronological basis. People 65 to 74 are called "early elderly," and those 75 years or older are called "late elderly." However, it is unclear what proof this definition is predicated on. There are practical, social, and historical reasons behind the designation of someone as "elderly" if their chronological age is 65. This standard gained popularity in the late 19th and early 20th centuries, especially with social security programs like the German pension system that Chancellor Otto von Bismarck instituted in 1889. Since life expectancy was shorter back then, 65 was a fair age to consider old age. This age is still considered viable despite longer life expectancies because of its strong ties to retirement and pension systems. Health and functional factors also provide credence to this classification since people usually start experiencing age-related health problems and a decline in their functional status starting in their mid-60s, which calls for more support and healthcare. Regarding finances, 65 is a reliable benchmark for retirement benefits and preparation. Social expectations also come into play because turning 65 typically denotes the end of active work and the beginning of retirement. However, given the variation in aging across individuals and the fact that many people stay active and healthy well into their 70s and beyond thanks to advancements in healthcare, there is a continuous discussion regarding whether 65 is still a helpful cutoff point for designating "elderly." This conversation emphasizes the need for more complex definitions beyond a rigid chronological age to consider a person's functional condition and overall health (Orimo et al., 2006).

# DIGITAL INCLUSION: MEANING AND CONCEPTUALIZATION

The term "digital inclusion" describes initiatives and plans to guarantee that all people and communities have access to and can use digital technologies and the Internet. It is essential to close the digital gap so everyone can take advantage of the opportunities and services that digital tools and internet platforms offer. As digital technology expands, digital inclusion is recognized as vital to social and economic advancement and empowerment of individuals and communities. The phrase "digital inclusion" has numerous possible meanings; it refers to complete, meaningful, and widespread engagement in digital activities, whether social, political, economic, or otherwise. Using digital technology to improve people's lives and means of subsistence is considered in this context. Because the digital world is influencing every part of life, from jobs and education to healthcare and social interaction, digital inclusion is essential. Marginalized populations might have difficulty obtaining opportunities and services without them (Mohan et al., 2024). This idea encompasses an array of key the following components:

A. **Access to Technology**: Ensuring everyone has the necessary devices (like smartphones, computers, tablets) and internet connectivity to participate fully in the digital world.
B. **Digital literacy**: imparting the abilities and information required to use digital platforms and tools efficiently. This covers operating software, using computers, accessing the internet, and comprehending online privacy and safety.
C. **Affordability**: Bringing internet and digital technology within reach of everyone, particularly those living in low-income homes.
D. **Inclusive material and Services**: Making sure that platforms, services, and material available online are appropriate and accessible to a range of demographics, such as older people, individuals with low literacy rates, and those with disabilities.
E. **Supportive Policies and Infrastructure**: promoting and putting into practice laws that encourage digital inclusion, such as those about broadband infrastructure, low-income housing subsidies, and educational initiatives.
F. **Social Inclusion**: Providing people with information on online privacy and safety will shield them from online risks and give them the confidence to use digital technology.

# DIGITAL INCLUSION: BOON OR BANE

Digital inclusion can be considered an advantage and a drawback, depending on how it is implemented and communicated. On the positive side, it improves access to financial services, healthcare, and education, particularly for underprivileged areas. By connecting marginalized groups to the global economy, digital tools can stimulate socioeconomic growth, promote financial inclusion, and bridge divides. Growing dependence on digital platforms may worsen inequality by increasing disparities in digital literacy, cyber threats, and unequal access to technology, leaving disadvantaged groups behind (COVID-19: Boon and Bane for Digital Payments and Financial Inclusion, 2020; Yaa Boakye-Adjei, 2020).

Digital inclusion presents both significant benefits and challenges. Studies have shown that equitable access to digital technologies can bridge gaps in education, healthcare, and economic opportunities, particularly for marginalized communities. For example, digital financial inclusion has empowered people in rural and low-income areas, fostering economic growth by enabling access to banking services and online markets (Pérez-Escolar & Canet, 2022). As technological change increases at an accelerating rate, the digital divide will only become more expensive. Those who can take advantage of the cost savings, economic opportunities, and many other benefits of the digital world will see greater returns. Those who lack access and already experience economic disadvantage will fall further behind. Many aims of public policy, such as expanding financial inclusion, improving health outcomes, and protecting human rights, are also closely tied to digital access (Kloza, 2023). Let us explore the possible advantages (boon) and difficulties (bane) of digital inclusion:

## Boon (Advantages)

A. **Economic Empowerment**: Digital inclusion, particularly for those in marginalized communities, enables people to access online job markets, digital banking, and other resources that promote economic growth and financial independence. Bhattacharjee (2024) states, *"Through digital platforms, businesses have gained unprecedented opportunities to reach wider audiences, target specific demographics, and stimulate growth through cost-effective strategies. For instance, companies like Flipkart have expanded their reach into rural areas previously overlooked by traditional marketing channels"* (p. 2).

B. **Educational Access**: It bridges the educational gap between urban and rural locations by giving students access to various online learning resources, facilitating lifelong learning. For instance, a study by (Bianchi et al., 2022) revealed that through satellite and internet technology, China's comprehensive education reform program linked rural pupils with highly educated urban professors. Thanks to this program, unavailable in their local schools, millions of students in remote areas can take advantage of resources and recorded lectures. As time passed, these pupils' academic performance increased along with their salaries, demonstrating a closing of the educational and income disparity between urban and rural areas.

C. **Healthcare Accessibility**: According to the American Academy of Family Physicians (AAFP), telemedicine involves *"the practice of medicine using technology to deliver care at a distance"* and is distinct from telehealth, which encompasses a broader range of remote healthcare services. Digital inclusion makes telemedicine and health information more accessible, especially in isolated places with a shortage of medical facilities. Through virtual training and consultations, initiatives like Project ECHO assist healthcare providers in rural areas in managing chronic illnesses more effectively. These developments have demonstrated that telemedicine lowers ER visits while increasing patient visits and improving medication adherence, especially for long-term illnesses like diabetes and heart disease (Miller, 2024).

D. **Social connectivity**: It makes it easier for people to maintain relationships with friends, family, and the community, which helps to lessen feelings of loneliness, particularly for elderly or isolated persons. Social media and video conferencing are two examples of technological technologies that have been demonstrated to increase connectivity for lonely people by providing them with a sense of emotional support and community. These therapies have shown very successful in lowering feelings of isolation experienced by older persons, which are sometimes exacerbated by limited mobility or health problems. To increase their efficacy even more, these solutions can be utilized with healthcare programs encouraging social facilitation and involvement (Lahlou & Daaleman, 2021).

E. **Access to Services**: It makes it possible to obtain necessary services that can raise one's standard of living, like online banking, social services, and government benefits. For example, Bostic et al. (2020) found that financial technology (fintech) and mobile banking have revolutionized financial services by enabling consumers to complete transactions without a bank branch, even in rural places. This change improves financial inclusion and economic mobility, especially for underbanked communities.

## Bane (Challenges)

A.  **Digital Divide**: Parsons and Hick (2008) say, *"The term digital divide was initially used by the National Telecommunications and Information Administration in the United States in its second Falling through the Net report entitled Falling Through The Net II: New Data on the Digital Divide."* Today, the digital divide is defined as the gap between people accessing digital technology and the tools to use it effectively and those without. This divide is often based on various factors, including socioeconomic status, geographic location, age, and education level. The penetration and distribution of digital tools, like many other goods and services, fail to reach the most vulnerable and disadvantaged groups. According to Persaud (2001; as cited in Parsons & Hick), The information wealthy and the information haves, as well as the poor, who are classified as the information poor and the information have-nots, have been created by this digital divide, which has also expanded the gaps in opportunities and advantages between social groups. Although digital inclusion aims to close the gap, it may unintentionally expand the separation and push certain people farther behind if it is not handled relatively.

B.  **Risks to Privacy and Security**: Privacy is at the core of human rights and is essential to individual dignity, autonomy, civil liberties, and freedom. A person's capacity to manage their own life, including the type of work they do, the people they choose to associate with, where they live, their political and religious views, and the information they reveal about themselves, is one aspect that defines their liberty (Lyon, 2001, as cited in Hiranandani, 2011). People with more access to digital technology may be more vulnerable to misinformation, cyber-attacks, and privacy violations. This is especially true for people who lack basic computer literacy. We live in an age where all information always exists in all places. For instance, Hiranandani (2001) cites Poster (1990), who remarks that Credit companies, retail stores, banks, utility companies, hospitals, health insurance companies, police agencies, state motor vehicle agencies, municipalities, and other organizations maintain detailed databases of people's daily activities. These databases are becoming increasingly commercialized, with legislation to prevent significant invasions of privacy being surpassed by the buying and selling customer and client information. Information transmission and replication efficiency have significantly risen with digital encoding for language, sounds, and images.

    **Economic Displacement**: Digitalization and automation can potentially increase employment and cause job displacement, especially in industries that depend on manual labor. This would exacerbate economic inequality.

Automation and artificial intelligence are displacing routine, physical labor more and more as technology develops, causing a significant loss of jobs in industries, including manufacturing, retail, and administrative work. Workers whose knowledge does not correlate with emerging technology may risk unemployment or underemployment due to this shift, which generates a noticeable skill gap. Comprehensive reskilling and upskilling programs that give the workers the skills they need to succeed in the changing labor market are desperately needed to address this issue. Access to technology inequality takes several essential forms. Economic barriers are vital because they exacerbate already-existing socioeconomic inequities by keeping low-income people and communities out of the digital age due to the high prices of technology and internet connections. **Over-dependence on Technology**: Excessive reliance on digital technology can result in addiction, a decline in in-person contacts, and the loss of conventional knowledge and skills, among other social and mental health problems. Furthermore, there are significant privacy and security risks when people rely too much on digital networks. People can become subject to data breaches and privacy invasions without the correct information or protections. Additionally, the growth in online activity exposes people to cyberattacks, which can harm one's finances and emotional well-being. The increased use of digital tools can also result in social isolation since fewer in-person encounters can erode community ties and hurt mental and emotional health. Furthermore, relying too much on chatbots and automated systems for customer support might annoy customers and lower the standard of individualized support. When digital services become increasingly ingrained in daily life, these groups are left behind increasingly in the absence of inexpensive solutions. Similarly, poor digital infrastructure in underserved or rural areas widens the gap between the inhabitants of these two locations, restricting access and fostering inequality.

C. **Environmental Impact**: Digital inclusion's environmental effects raise several important issues. The increasing issue of electronic garbage, or *"e-waste,"* which frequently contains dangerous elements like lead and mercury and poses significant threats to human health and the environment, is exacerbated by the rapid turnover of electronic equipment. Higher energy consumption and carbon emissions are also caused by the growing need for data centers and the widespread use of electronic gadgets, especially when those energy sources are non-renewable. Furthermore, mining minerals and metals required to create these gadgets can lead to pollution, habitat loss, and environmental deterioration. These environmental issues are made worse by the carbon footprint resulting from the construction and upkeep of digital infrastructure and the logistics of device distribution.

## DIGITAL INCLUSION AMONG THE ELDERLY

The experience and perception of aging have been profoundly impacted by two main processes: demographic change and digital transformation, sometimes known as mediatization (Hjavard, 2013). Today's governments in rich and developing countries have made the digital transformation of public and private services—like healthcare and social services—a primary focus. The hope that digitalization will increase the availability and accessibility of essential services, hence encouraging equitable access for all residents, is a major driving force behind the trend towards digitalization.

Digital media and technologies have become indispensable in many industries and integral to the workplace. Similarly, people depend increasingly on digital media, such as social media and the internet, in their daily lives to interact and plan their schedules. This change has produced a digital world where mastering these technologies is essential to being informed and connected. Though there may be advantages, researchers (Rasi-Heikkinen, 2022; Seifert et al., 2018) and policymakers (Digi arkeen-neuvottelukunta, 2019; World Health Organization, 2016) have acknowledged that the process of mediatization can also have exclusionary effects, especially for older adults, even though it promotes digital inclusion. Many older people could find it difficult or impossible to use the digital media, services, and technologies that are becoming increasingly common in society. Even those who utilize these tools may not do so in ways that optimize their daily lives, well-being, or involvement in a digitally connected society.

This problem is particularly evident in times of crisis, such as the COVID-19 epidemic, when using digital devices sparingly or not at all might have serious repercussions. Digitally excluded older individuals are more likely to experience social isolation because they may struggle to keep up social ties or obtain essential services. Due to this digital exclusion, those already marginalized by technology may have increased emotions of loneliness and obsolescence. The pandemic has brought to light how urgent it is to close these digital gaps to stop social inequality from growing and guarantee that every citizen can fully engage in an increasingly digital society.

Although digital transformation can significantly improve service accessibility and promote inclusivity, certain obstacles must be overcome. Targeted initiatives are required to boost digital literacy, offer accessible technology, and establish welcoming environments that promote the adoption and efficient use of digital tools to guarantee that older individuals are not left behind in this digital age. Without such initiatives, older populations' risk of social and digital marginalization would increase, with wider societal ramifications. The problem of digital inclusion among the elderly is significant since technology is becoming an essential part of everyday life. Older individuals must have access to and be proficient with digital tools for their general social, economic, and well-being.

## DIGITAL ACCESS AMONG THE ELDERLY: RURAL VS. URBAN

It is crucial to remember that the digital inclusion is complex and exhibits varying trends of change according on the factors taken into account. For example, certain digital gaps are closing during the past few decades, while others still exist. For instance, between 2000 and 2021, the percentage of Americans without internet access dropped sharply from 48% to 7% (Perrin & Atske, 2021). According to recent research, the majority of people own a smartphone or are technologically literate (Barrantes & Vargas, 2017). Although everyone now has better access to the internet and technology, low-income people, those living in rural areas, and members of minority groups have fewer digital devices for online access and mostly use smartphones (Vogels, 2021a). Understanding within-group heterogeneity is essential-People who are poor and have a lower socioeconomic status. According to reports, those with poorer health are more likely to be excluded from using technology (Gell et al., 2015; Silver, 2014). Additionally, older persons in suburban and rural areas expressed unfavorable opinions about technology use, which significantly restricted their use due to a lack of understanding about how they work or challenges learning how to use them. (Marston et al., 2019; O'Brien et al., 2014). The socioeconomic determinants of health paradigm (World Health Organization [WHO], 2010) effectively captures the observed digital divide by age and residence area, which holds that the root of health disparities comes from *"the conditions in which people are born, grow, work, live, and age, and the wider set of forces and systems shaping the conditions of daily life."* (WHO, 2020, p.1).

## CHALLENGES TO DIGITAL INCLUSION AMONG THE ELDERLY

Understanding the main factors contributing to digital exclusion among older adults is essential to address the present issue. While the systematic review conducted by b et al. (2022) discussed the seven factors contributing to digital exclusion by examining 24 countries, a research gap still exists in understanding the common factors contributing to the digital divide across different socio-economic settings.

Moreover, the results cannot be broadly applied because most current studies have concentrated on a particular area or demographic group. Because the leading causes of digital exclusion have not been thoroughly examined in previous studies, it is necessary to investigate the phenomenon while considering the various national contexts (High-income countries vs. Lower middle-income countries).

Multiple studies (Tomczyk et al., 2023; Lu et al., 2022; Seifert et al., 2021) found the lack of expertise to be the primary reason for digital exclusion. Some other studies (Neves et al., 2018; Elueze & Quan-Haase, 2018) attribute privacy and security concerns to using digital technologies to impact digital exclusion directly. Paez and Del (2019) suggest that designing user interfaces without considering the needs of older people introduces usability concerns. Nishijima et al. (2017); Delello and McWhorter (2017) found that ICT devices like mobile phones, tablets, and computers and internet availability impact digital exclusion rates.

Regardless of the growing adoption of Information and Communication Technologies (ICT), digital inclusion among the elderly remains a crucial issue (Mubarak & Suomi, 2022). The pie chart shown in Figure 1 depicts the global internet users based on different age groups.

*Figure 1. Distribution of internet users worldwide as of February 2024 by age group*

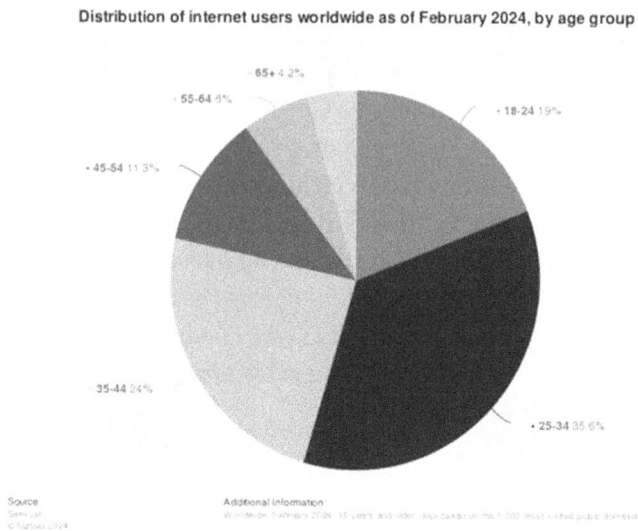

Distribution of internet users worldwide as of February 2024, by age group

*(Semrush, 2024)*

Approximately 10% fewer individuals in the 45–54, 55–64, and 65+ age groups utilize the internet than people in the younger age groups. This variation highlights the pressing need for programs that aid senior citizens in becoming digitally included.

# STRATEGIES FOR DIGITAL INCLUSION AMONG THE ELDERLY

Most UNECE countries have national digitization agendas that prioritize providing people of all ages access to technology, internet infrastructure, and lifelong learning. These proposals demonstrate how digital technology may be widely adopted to advance business, finance, healthcare, and governance. However, fewer solutions specifically address older people's needs when embracing digital technology and the advantages of being more digitally literate and engaged. Following are some strategies for digital inclusion among the elderly.

A. **Improving access**: Akinola (2021) suggests that ensuring that elderly individuals have access to devices like smartphones, tablets, or computers is the first step. This also includes access to reliable internet. The cost of devices and internet services can be a barrier. Affordable options and subsidies can help bridge this gap.

B. **Digital Literacy and support**: Training and resources tailored to the elderly can help them learn how to use digital tools. Programs should focus on basic skills like internet browsing, email use, and using apps. Regular workshops, helplines, or community support systems can help elderly individuals continue to build their digital skills (Kuoppamäki et al., 2022).

C. **Accessible Design**: Devices and software should be designed with the elderly in mind, featuring larger text, simple navigation, and voice-activated commands. Tools like screen readers, hearing aids compatible with devices, and adaptive keyboards can make technology more accessible (Mohan et al., 2024).

D. **Social Inclusion**: Digital tools can help reduce social isolation by enabling older adults to stay in touch with family and friends through social media, video calls, and messaging apps. Encouraging participation in online communities or interest groups can provide social engagement and a sense of belonging (Kuoppamäki et al., 2022).

E. **Addressing Ageism**: Combatting stereotypes that suggest older adults are less capable of using technology is also vital. Ageism creates barriers to participation, but efforts to educate the public and create inclusive digital environments can foster greater engagement (World Economic Forum, 2022). UNECE Policy Brief on Ageing No. 26 (2021) indicates that acquiring digital skills, actively using the Internet, and benefiting from digitalization can be hampered by negative stereotypes, prejudice, and self-inflicted ageism, discouraging older people from interacting with digital technologies. Governments and civil society organizations in the UNECE region attempt to dispel ageist stereotypes and alter the perception of older tech users to address this obstacle to digital inclusion. To ensure that the goods and services created are pertinent, it is crucial to encourage older generations to embrace technology in their daily lives, hone their digital skills, and make developers and service providers aware of the variety of needs and preferences among older people.

F. **Policy and Advocacy**: Government initiatives are crucial in promoting digital inclusion, especially for underserved populations like seniors. Policies that provide free or subsidized internet access and funding for digital literacy programs can help bridge the digital divide. These efforts ensure older adults have the tools and skills to engage with technology. Additionally, partnerships between governments, non-profits, and private sector companies can further expand the reach of digital inclusion programs. By working together, these entities can pool resources, share expertise, and create sustainable initiatives that benefit communities and promote equitable access to technology.

## ECONOMIC PARTICIPATION AMONG THE ELDERLY

An essential factor in increasing older people's economic involvement is digital inclusion. Giving older people the means and know-how to interact with digital technology allows them to take advantage of new job opportunities, stay financially independent, and make various economic contributions. The issue of older adults' economic participation in the digital economy is becoming more pressing as access to digital media becomes more necessary for daily living and socioeconomic engagement. Nonetheless, older people frequently encounter obstacles, including restricted use of digital devices, reduced digital literacy, and health-related difficulties like cognitive decline or visual impairment. Existing disparities across nations exacerbate these problems, mainly as poverty increasingly takes on digital aspects like restricted access to data and digital services.

In addition to addressing these technological obstacles, governments aiming to promote digital inclusion for the elderly must consider more significant financial limits. Low-income nations, for instance, could have to make difficult decisions between paying for internet infrastructure and taking care of pressing budgetary needs. Improving internet access, developing equitable technology, and providing digital literacy initiatives are all necessary to address these issues. In an increasingly digital economy, the public and commercial sectors must work together to ensure that older people are not left behind. Ensuring fair access also requires tackling problems like ageism and offering health support to those with disabilities. To close the digital divide, policymakers should prioritize intergenerational learning and technical solutions that address the unique needs of the elderly (World Economic Forum).

The following is how digital inclusion impacts economic participation for the elderly.

A. **Increased Workforce Engagement**: Owing to digital tools, seniors can continue to work after traditional retirement, enabling them to impact society positively. This can entail beginning a small internet business, consulting, freelancing, or working part-time. Gore (2021) observes that many retirees use their knowledge and expertise to launch side projects, offer advice, work as independent contractors, or take part-time jobs. Seniors can work part-time jobs while enjoying retirement, such as becoming coaches and consultants or launching home-based enterprises.

B. **Skill Development**: With online courses and tools available, older persons can more easily upgrade or gain new skills, increasing their employability in the digital economy. Seniors can locate employment possibilities that fit their experience and preferences using professional networks such as LinkedIn and online job portals (National Council on Ageing, 2023).

C. **Business Ownership**: Thanks to digital platforms, elderly individuals can establish and oversee home-based businesses. Using digital tools, they could expand their customer base, manage operations, and provide products and services online. (The Ageing, n.d)

D. **Financial Management**: With the help of digital inclusion, senior citizens can better manage their finances by using digital payment methods, investing platforms, and online banking. As a result, there is less need for in-person bank visits, increasing financial independence. Seniors can make educated decisions about their assets and income by using online platforms to access financial planning tools, watch webinars on retirement planning, and consult with financial specialists. (The Ageing, n.d).

E. **Reducing Poverty and Inequality**: By giving older people access to government services and income-generating opportunities, digital inclusion can help lower poverty and inequality. This is especially crucial for older persons who might not have as much access to typical economic prospects. Using digital tools facilitates the application process for government benefits, pensions, and social services, enabling the senior population to obtain the necessary support (Leveraging et al. for Social Inclusion | Division for Inclusive Social Development (DISD), 2021).

F. **Incentivizing Participation**: Governments might implement laws, such as tax exemptions for employers who recruit senior employees or subsidies for senior business owners, to encourage the digital inclusion of older persons in the workforce (UNECE Policy Brief on Ageing No. 26, 2021).

## POST-COVID-19 DIGITAL INCLUSION AMONG THE ELDERLY

The severe digital exclusion of older individuals has been further demonstrated by the hygienic catastrophe brought on by COVID-19. In addition, the problem has forced older folks to embrace modern technologies to make their chores easier and provide them with a powerful tool to combat the social isolation and loneliness of being confined. Because of this, everyone who has not been a part of the digital era primarily defined by their limited or nonexistent proficiency with technology needs to possess digital literacy (Martínez-Alcalá et al., 2021). The current situation has also revealed that emerging technologies and digitalization are great allies against the pandemic, offering many opportunities, such as better services, greater productivity, and ease of communication (Faraj et al., 2021). In addition to the COVID-19 pandemic, there have been other threats that have primarily affected the elderly. These threats stem from living inequality regarding access, use, and appropriation of ICT and telecommunication services; in other words, these individuals are at the forefront of a more visible digital divide (Moore et al., 2020). Since the start and aftermath of the COVID-19 pandemic, when access to the Internet and digital tools proved crucial, digital inclusion has gained significant attention from policymakers worldwide. It is now recognized as a fundamental aspect of social inclusion. Our reliance on digital technologies has grown due to stay-at-home directives, telecommuting, e-learning, and e-shopping, which makes digital inclusion more crucial than ever. The pandemic has expedited technological advancements that were already underway, like the increased use of digital platforms, cloud computing, big data, and algorithms. Without digital technologies, it would be difficult, if not impossible, to lessen the COVID-19 pandemic's effects on the economy and society. Simultaneously, it is generally acknowledged that the COVID-19 epidemic has increased digital disadvantage and exclusion globally (Promoting Social Integration through Social Inclusion - 2021 Report I Division for Inclusive Social Development (DISD), 2021).

*Figure 2. An adaptation of the Dynamics in Technology Use by Seniors (DITUS) framework*

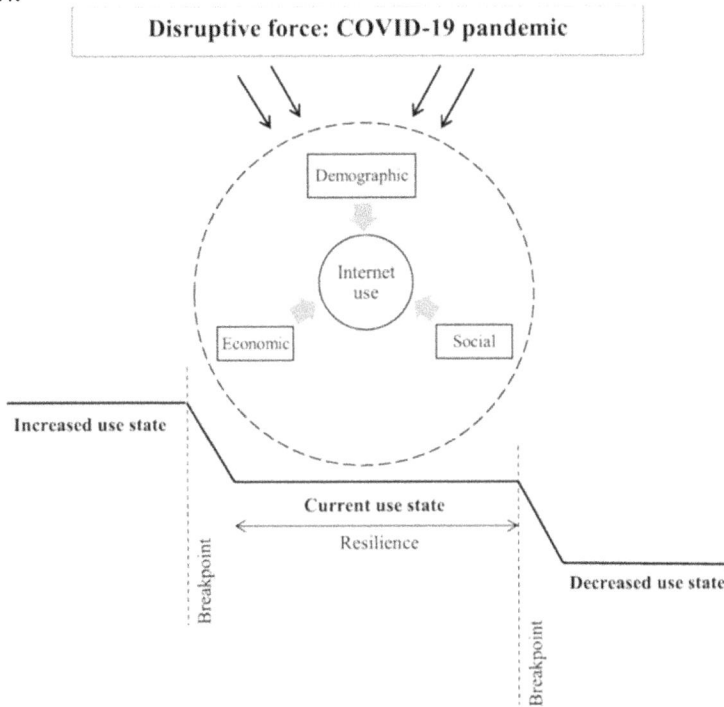

The DITUS framework was developed to explain technology use by independent-living seniors over time. The framework posits interrelated factors linked to technology use and disruptive forces that can induce changes to other use levels

The COVID-19 pandemic significantly accelerated the need for digital inclusion among the elderly, highlighting the importance of ensuring that older adults can access and use digital technologies. Post-COVID-19, the focus on digital inclusion for the elderly has only intensified, with several key trends and initiatives emerging to address this need.

The following are some of the key initiatives.

**Telehealth**: According to the Centers for Medicare & Medicaid Services (CMS), telehealth is *"The use of telecommunications technology to provide care, advice, and services to patients remotely"*. Telehealth is the delivery of healthcare services by healthcare professionals through information and communication technologies (ICT), where distance separates the participants (Doraiswamy et al., 2021). Telehealth has become an essential tool for the general population, healthcare providers, and patients with COVID-19. It enables patients to maintain real-time contact with healthcare providers for advice on their health problems, especially when people are in quarantine. Remote medical treatment using telemedicine services can promote patients' access to professional medical advice without waiting an extended period. As a result of the pandemic, telehealth services have gained popularity, and senior citizens who wish to get remote medical treatment must be digitally proficient. Even after the pandemic, telemedicine is still a vital service that enables senior citizens to manage chronic illnesses, see doctors, and get medical advice without leaving their homes.

**Online Shopping and Services**: O'Toole (2021) notes that adopting e-commerce is an important strategic priority for retailers, especially considering that COVID-19 has undoubtedly contributed to the enormous popularity of online purchasing over the previous 14 months. Many older individuals used online shopping for groceries, prescription drugs, and other necessities during the pandemic because physical distancing measures were in place. This pattern has persisted, highlighting the necessity of the digital ability to use e-commerce platforms.

**Virtual Communication**: Zoom, Skype, and WhatsApp become indispensable for senior citizens to stay in touch with friends and family during lockdowns. These resources are still essential for fostering relationships and lessening social isolation after the pandemic. Virtual communities and online support groups have grown in popularity throughout the pandemic, giving older people places to communicate socially, exchange stories, and find company even when they cannot interact (McDonnel, 2021).

**Government and Public functions**: Manfred (2021) notes that following the epidemic, several government functions have been shifted online, such as applying for aid, obtaining benefits, and receiving vaccinations. Ensuring senior citizens can use these digital platforms to receive these services is essential. The pandemic highlighted the need for older people to have better digital literacy. Programs for digital literacy geared toward senior citizens have been more prevalent since COVID-19; community centers, libraries, and nonprofit organizations typically offer these.

**Well-being and Health**: Due to the pandemic's emphasis on the value of mental health, digital tools tailored to the needs of the aged have been developed. These consist of post-pandemic virtual support groups, apps for meditation, and internet therapy services. For instance, platforms like Grouport and Sesh offer virtual group therapy that creates a sense of community and reduces the stigma of seeking mental health support (Sloan, 2021). Many senior citizens have embraced online fitness courses and wellness applications to stay active during the pandemic. These digital products are still in demand because they offer easily accessible means of preserving physical well-being.

**Overcoming the Digital Divide**: The pandemic revealed weaknesses in the digital infrastructure, especially in neglected or rural areas. Following the epidemic, a more significant push has been made to extend broadband availability and offer reasonably priced internet services so senior citizens remain connected (Nash, n.d). It is still essential to have access to reasonably priced and user-friendly gadgets. Following the pandemic, there have been ongoing efforts to provide older adults with tablets, cellphones, and other gadgets, frequently along with instructions on how to use them properly.

**Economic Involvement**: Many senior employees had to adjust to working remotely due to the pandemic. Some people have decided to stay economically active after the pandemic by continuing to work remotely or taking advantage of online learning options. Zhu et al. (2021) note that because of the pandemic's boom in online firms, several older individuals have begun digital entrepreneurship by creatively applying their talents and knowledge. They engaged in various entrepreneurial ventures using digital platforms, such as online sales of handcrafted goods and consulting.

**Privacy and Security Issues**: The demand for cyber security awareness has increased as more senior citizens use digital platforms. The post-pandemic initiatives have centered on teaching senior citizens to preserve their personal information, avoid scammers, and stay safe online. Targeted efforts have been established by organizations such as the National Cyber Security Alliance and the Cyber Security and Infrastructure Security Agency (CISA) to provide seniors with information on how to protect themselves against typical cyber risks such as identity theft, phishing, and fraudulent websites (National Council on Ageing, 2023).

## EMERGING TRENDS: ARTIFICIAL INTELLIGENCE AND ELDERLY HEALTHCARE

Artificial intelligence (AI) has been defined as any technology that simulates or surpasses human intelligence to perform a given task (European Parliament: Publications Office, 2022). There are several prospects to improve senior inclusion and assist aging populations as a result of the combination of automation and artificial intelligence (AI). The way that age interacts with other aspects of access, such as gender, income, race, and language, has a significant impact on how well a person can use, profit from, and contribute to the digital world. By 2030, there will be more than 1.4 billion persons aged 60 and beyond, according to present trends.

Given that the population spans several protected statuses and minority identities, guidelines and policies that involve and involve older individuals in AI development and implementation can promote wider inclusion (Thompson, 2024).

In the context of healthcare, artificial intelligence (AI) refers to algorithm-based computational methods that handle and evaluate enormous datasets in order to draw conclusions and forecast outcomes. AI has a wide range of possible uses in the treatment of the elderly, from wearable technology that can forecast the likelihood of a fall to clinical decision support systems that can assist in identifying delirium from clinical records (Shiwani et al., 2023).

In order to determine how AI could benefit society without compromising the autonomy, privacy, and social safety of older adults, future research should make sure that AI experts, health and social care providers, and policy makers collaborate to develop AI technologies. or the mental well-being of elderly individuals.

## SOCIAL INTEGRATION THROUGH DIGITAL INCLUSION

(Borg & Smith, 2018; Walton et al., 2013, as cited in Nguyen, 2020) Digital technology has become essential to society and societal transformation over the past ten years. Social interactions, corporate behavior, and people's daily lives all influence and are influenced by digital technologies. They can be found in all facets of society, including communication, entertainment, employment, healthcare, and education. Like electricity and water, internet connection is now considered a fundamental utility in many countries. The concept of digital inclusion has gained significant traction among policymakers worldwide. Millions of people worldwide were forced to use the internet to stay at home, work, attend school, and live remotely due to the rapidly spreading respiratory virus COVID-19. This brought attention to the importance of digital inclusion as a fundamental element of social inclusion. Due to this social isolation need, there has been a resurgence of conversations around the long-standing but now glaringly apparent digital disparities and inequalities (Samms, 2020; Woolley et al., 2020, as cited in Reisdorf & Rhinesmith, 2020).

Social integration through digital integration is increasingly important in today's interconnected world. Digital tools and platforms offer new opportunities for people of all ages, backgrounds, and abilities to connect, communicate, and participate in society. For certain groups, such as the elderly, people with disabilities, or those living in remote areas, digital integration can be a powerful means of overcoming social isolation and fostering a sense of community. Here is how digital integration can promote social integration:

*Table 1. The impact of digital integration on social integration: key areas of influence*

| 1. Enhanced Communication and Connection |
|---|
| **A. Social Media Platforms**: Digital tools like Facebook, Instagram, and Twitter allow individuals to stay in touch with friends, family, and broader social networks. For people who may be physically isolated, these platforms provide a vital connection to the outside world. Using social media can help older adults to maintain social connections. Cotton et al. (2022) opines that the relationships between social media use and older adults' well-being are poorly understood. Research that uses longitudinal designs and incorporates nuanced measures of social media use is needed. |
| **B. Access to Online Communities**: Online forums and groups cater to virtually every interest, from hobbies to professional networks. These communities offer a space for individuals to connect with others who share their passions, fostering a sense of belonging and shared identity. Digital platforms host numerous support groups for various life challenges, such as chronic illness, mental health issues, or caregiving. These groups provide emotional support, practical advice, and a sense of solidarity. |
| **C. Inclusive Participation in Society**: Digital platforms enable greater participation in civic activities, such as signing petitions, participating in online debates, and engaging with local government initiatives. This can empower marginalized groups to have a voice in societal decisions that affect them. Digital platforms allow for the sharing of cultural practices, traditions, and languages, helping preserve and promote cultural diversity. People from different backgrounds can engage with each other's cultures, fostering mutual understanding and respect. |
| **2. Educational Opportunities** |
| **A. Lifelong Learning**: Online courses and educational resources allow individuals of all ages to continue learning and developing skills. This is particularly important for those who may not have access to traditional educational institutions due to geographic or financial barriers. |
| **B. Digital Literacy**: As digital skills become increasingly important, online tutorials and programs can help bridge the gap for those less familiar with technology, ensuring they are not left behind in a rapidly digitizing world. |
| **3. Work and Economic Integration** |
| **A. Remote Work**: Digital tools enable people to work from anywhere, breaking down barriers to employment for those with mobility issues, caregiving responsibilities, or those living in remote areas. This can lead to greater economic participation and integration into the workforce. |
| **B. Digital Entrepreneurship**: The internet provides a platform for individuals to start their businesses, whether through e-commerce, content creation, or freelance services. This opens economic opportunities for those facing barriers in traditional job markets. |
| **4. Health and Well-being** |
| **A. Telehealth**: Digital health services allow individuals to access medical advice, mental health support, and wellness resources from the comfort of their homes. This is particularly beneficial for those with limited mobility or those living in areas with scarce healthcare resources. |
| **B. Health Communities**: Online platforms host communities for people managing similar health conditions, offering a space to share experiences, advice, and support. |
| **5. Breaking Down Geographical Barriers** |
| **A. Global Networks**: A. Global Networks: Digital integration allows individuals to connect with others across the globe, fostering international friendships, collaborations, and cultural exchanges. This global connectivity can lead to greater empathy and understanding between different cultures and communities. |
| **B. Access to Services**: Digital platforms provide access to essential services that might be geographically out of reach, such as online banking, government services, and telemedicine. |
| **6. Overcoming Social Stigma** |

continued on following page

*Table 1. Continued*

| |
|---|
| **A. Anonymity and Support**: Online platforms often provide anonymity that allows individuals to seek support and express themselves without fear of judgment. This is especially important for those dealing with social stigma or discrimination. |
| **B. Public Awareness Campaigns**: Social media and other digital platforms can be powerful tools for raising awareness about social issues, challenging stereotypes, and promoting social justice. |
| **7. Crisis Response and Mutual Aid** |
| **A. Community Coordination**: During crises, such as natural disasters or pandemics, digital platforms can coordinate community responses, share resources, and provide real-time information. This helps foster a sense of solidarity and collective action. |
| **B. Mutual Aid Networks**: Digital platforms have created mutual aid groups where community members can offer and request support, such as food, transportation, or financial assistance. |

# IMPACT OF DIGITAL INCLUSION ON SOCIAL ISOLATION AND WELL-BEING FOR ELDERLY

It is estimated that 28.5% of older adults globally suffer from loneliness, making social isolation and loneliness serious issues for this demographic, even if these conditions are not ubiquitous features of old age and shouldn't be portrayed as such (Chawla et al., 2021). Social isolation implies the absence of human contact or meaningful social relations that adversely impacts the quality of life of older adults, significantly deteriorating their emotional and physical health (Sen et al., 2022). Those who feel social isolation and loneliness are more likely to suffer negative consequences, including: disturbed sleep, dementia, frailty, cardiovascular events, obesity, diminished immune system functioning, poor mental health, and cognitive functioning, increased risk of Alzheimer's disease and mortality. (Choi et al., 2015; Courtin & Knapp, 2017). Many times, technology has been promoted as a tool to help vulnerable populations reduce social isolation and loneliness. Through social media sites and video conferencing apps that go beyond geographical distance, technology can help older persons who are lonely and socially isolated (Chen & Schulz, 2016). Additionally, people can have a sense of belonging and community through online groups (Lawless et al., 2022). Technology can also give people access to events and activities like online courses, which can offer fulfilling and pleasurable experiences, and healthcare services, which offer tools for maintaining wellbeing. All things considered, by offering chances for assistance, interaction, and social connection, technology treatments can lessen social isolation and loneliness among senior citizens.

## CONCLUSION

In furtherance of leading better lives, elderly individuals with increased access to digital resources may also participate more fully in the economy. Overcoming the digital divide enables older people to continue working, manage their finances, and launch their own companies—all of which are advantageous for both their financial stability and the state of the economy overall. The COVID-19 epidemic acted as a spur to the elderly's digital inclusion by drawing attention to the opportunities and difficulties they confront in a society that is quickly digitizing. After the epidemic, the emphasis has changed from immediate fixes to long-term, sustainable solutions that guarantee senior citizens' full participation in the digital society.

We can assist the elderly in thriving in the digital age by addressing access, literacy, security, and support issues. Through the provision of tools and platforms that facilitate communication, interaction, and involvement across disparate communities, digital integration acts as a potent catalyst for social integration. People may break through social, economic, and physical boundaries by using these digital technologies, which will create a more inclusive and connected society. To fully realize the promise of social integration in the digital age, it is imperative to guarantee that everyone has access to digital resources and the necessary skills to use them efficiently.

# REFERENCES

Aging and health India. (n.d.). Retrieved from Www.who.int. https://www.who.int/india/health-topics/ageing

Akinola, S. (2021, October 1). *How can we ensure digital inclusion for older adults?* World Economic Forum. https://www.weforum.org/agenda/2021/10/how-can-we-ensure-digital-inclusion-for-older-adults/

Anglen, J. (2024). AI for Elderly Care [Review of AI for Elderly Care]. Rapid Innovation. https://www.rapidinnovation.io/post/ai-for-elderly-care

Bianchi, N., Lu, Y., & Song, H. (2022). The effect of computer-assisted learning on students' long-term development. *Journal of Development Economics*, 158, 102919. DOI: 10.1016/j.jdeveco.2022.102919

Bouabida, K., Lebouché, B., & Pomey, M.-P. (2022). Telehealth and COVID-19 Pandemic: An Overview of the Telehealth Use, Advantages, Challenges, and Opportunities during COVID-19 Pandemic. *Health Care*, 10(11), 2293. DOI: 10.3390/healthcare10112293 PMID: 36421617

Chawla, K., Kunonga, T. P., Stow, D., Barker, R., Craig, D., & Hanratty, B. (2021). Prevalence of loneliness amongst older people in high-income countries: A systematic review and meta-analysis. *PLoS One*, 16(7), e0255088. DOI: 10.1371/journal.pone.0255088 PMID: 34310643

Chen, Y.-R. R., & Schulz, P. J. (2016). The Effect of Information Communication Technology Interventions on Reducing Social Isolation in the Elderly: A Systematic Review. *Journal of Medical Internet Research*, 18(1), e18. DOI: 10.2196/jmir.4596 PMID: 26822073

Choi, H., Irwin, M. R., & Cho, H. J. (2015). Impact of social isolation on behavioral health in elderly: Systematic review. *World Journal of Psychiatry*, 5(4), 432–438. DOI: 10.5498/wjp.v5.i4.432 PMID: 26740935

Coombs, C. (1920). Notes, Short Comments, and Answers to Correspondents. *Lancet*, 196(5056), 226–228. DOI: 10.1016/S0140-6736(01)18292-9

Cosco, T., Fortuna, K., Wister, A., Riadi, I., Wagner, K., & Sixsmith, A. (2021). COVID-19, Social Isolation, and Mental Health Among Older Adults: A Digital Catch-22. *Journal of Medical Internet Research*, 23(5), e21864. https://www.jmir.org/2021/5/e21864/PDF. DOI: 10.2196/21864 PMID: 33891557

Cotten, S. R., Schuster, A. M., & Seifert, A. (2021). Social media use and well-being among older adults. *Current Opinion in Psychology*, 45, 101293. Advance online publication. DOI: 10.1016/j.copsyc.2021.12.005 PMID: 35065352

Courtin, E., & Knapp, M. (2017). Social isolation, loneliness and health in old age: A scoping review. *Health & Social Care in the Community*, 25(3), 799–812. DOI: 10.1111/hsc.12311 PMID: 26712585

Delello, J. A., & McWhorter, R. R. (2017). Reducing the Digital Divide: Connecting Older Adults to iPad Technology. *Journal of applied gerontology: the official journal of the Southern Gerontological Society, 36*(1), 3–28. DOI: 10.1177/0733464815589985

Doraiswamy, S., Jithesh, A., Mamtani, R., Abraham, A., & Cheema, S. (2021). Telehealth Use in Geriatrics Care during the COVID-19 Pandemic—A Scoping Review and Evidence Synthesis. *International Journal of Environmental Research and Public Health*, 18(4), 1755. DOI: 10.3390/ijerph18041755 PMID: 33670270

Elderly Learning in the Digital Age: Towards Empowerment November 2023 Commonwealth of Learning CC BY-SA 4.0. (n.d.). Retrieved September 10, 2024, from https://oasis.col.org/server/api/core/bitstreams/7858c65d-04b1-423b-9a9a -2f318e71749b/content

ElgueraPaez, L., & Zapata Del Río, C. (2019). Elderly Users and Their Main Challenges Usability with Mobile Applications: A Systematic Review. Design, User Experience, and Usability. *Design Philosophy and Theory*, 423–438. DOI: 10.1007/978-3-030-23570-3_31

Elueze, I., & Quan-Haase, A. (2018). Privacy Attitudes and Concerns in the Digital Lives of Older Adults: Westin's Privacy Attitude Typology Revisited. *The American Behavioral Scientist*, 62(10), 1372–1391. DOI: 10.1177/0002764218787026

Fallon, C. K., & Karlawish, J. (2019). Is the WHO Definition of Health Aging Well? Frameworks for "Health" After Three Score and Ten. *American Journal of Public Health*, 109(8), 1104–1106. DOI: 10.2105/AJPH.2019.305177 PMID: 31268759

Fang, Y. X., Gill, S. S., Kunasekaran, P., Rosnon, M. R., Talib, A. T., & Abd Aziz, A. (2022). Digital divide: An inquiry on the native communities of Sabah. *Societies (Basel, Switzerland)*, 12(6), 148. DOI: 10.3390/soc12060148

Gell, N. M., Rosenberg, D. E., Demiris, G., LaCroix, A. Z., & Patel, K. V. (2015). Patterns of Technology Use Among Older Adults With and Without Disabilities. *The Gerontologist*, 55(3), 412–421. DOI: 10.1093/geront/gnt166 PMID: 24379019

Haimi, M., & Gesser-Edelsburg, A. (2022). Application and implementation of tele-health services designed for the elderly population during the COVID-19 pandemic: A systematic review. *Health Informatics Journal*, 28(1), 146045822210755. DOI: 10.1177/14604582221075561 PMID: 35175881

Hiranandani, V. (2011). Privacy and security in the digital age: Contemporary challenges and future directions. *International Journal of Human Rights*, 15(7), 1091–1106. DOI: 10.1080/13642987.2010.493360

Holgersson, J., Söderström, E., & Rose, J. (2019). *Digital inclusion of elderly citizens for a sustainable society*. In *27th European Conference on Information Systems (ECIS)*, Stockholm & Uppsala, Sweden, June 8-14, 2019. Association for Information Systems.

Kloza, B. (2023, January 3). *What Is Digital Inclusion? The Global Effort to Bring Everyone Online*. Connecting the Unconnected. https://ctu.ieee.org/what-is-digital-inclusion-the-global-effort-to-bring-everyone-online/

Kuoppamäki, S., Hänninen, R., &Taipale, S. (2022). *Enhancing Older Adults' Digital Inclusion Through Social Support: A Qualitative Interview Study*. Springer EBooks, 211–230. DOI: 10.1007/978-3-030-94122-2_11

Lahlou, R. M., & Daaleman, T. P. (2021). Addressing Loneliness and Social Isolation in Older Adults. *American Family Physician*, 104(1), 85–87. https://pubmed.ncbi .nlm.nih.gov/34264606 PMID: 34264606

Lawless, M. T., Hunter, S. C., Pinero de Plaza, M. A., Archibald, M. M., & Kitson, A. L. (2022). "You Are By No Means Alone": A Netnographic Study of Self-Care Support in an Online Community for Older Adults. *Qualitative Health Research*, 104973232211249(13), 1935–1951. Advance online publication. DOI: 10.1177/10497323221124979 PMID: 36062369

Lee, S. (2023). Internet Use and Well-Being of Older Adults Before and During the COVID-19 Pandemic: Findings from European Social Survey. *Journal of Gerontological Social Work*, 67(1), 96–113. DOI: 10.1080/01634372.2023.2217682 PMID: 37246398

Leveraging digital technologies for social inclusion | Division for Inclusive Social Development (DISD). (2021, February 18). Un.org. https://social.desa.un.org/ publications/leveraging-digital-technologies-for-social-inclusion

Loh, P., Estrella-Luna, N., & Shor, K. (2023). Pandemic Response and Mutual Aid as Climate Resilience: Learning From Community Responses in the Boston Area. *Journal of Climate Resilience & Climate Justice*, 1, 8–19. DOI: 10.1162/crcj_a_00006

Lu, X., Yao, Y., & Jin, Y. (2022). Digital exclusion and functional dependence in older people: Findings from five longitudinal cohort studies. *EClinicalMedicine*, 54, 101708. DOI: 10.1016/j.eclinm.2022.101708 PMID: 36353265

Lythreatis, S., El-Kassar, A.-N., & Singh, S. K. (2022). The digital divide: A review and future research agenda. *Technological Forecasting and Social Change*, 175(6), 121359. DOI: 10.1016/j.techfore.2021.121359

Manfred, E. (2021, July 21). *More Seniors Achieve Digital Equity*. Seniorplanet. https://seniorplanet.org/news/2021/07/21/seniors-achieve-digital-equity/

Marston, H. R., Genoe, R., Freeman, S., Kulczycki, C., & Musselwhite, C. (2019). Older Adults' Perceptions of ICT: Main Findings from the Technology In Later Life (TILL) Study. 27

McDonnell, S. (2021, February 22). *Meet and Make Friends Online*. Seniorplanet. https://seniorplanet.org/meet-and-make-friends-online/

Michel, J. P., & Sadana, R. (2017). "Healthy aging" concepts and measures. *Journal of the American Medical Directors Association*, 18(6), 460–464. DOI: 10.1016/j.jamda.2017.03.008 PMID: 28479271

Mohan, R., Saleem, F., Voderhobli, K., & Sheikh-Akbari, A. (2024). Ensuring Sustainable Digital Inclusion among the Elderly: A Comprehensive Analysis. *Sustainability (Basel)*, 16(17), 7485. DOI: 10.3390/su16177485

Mubarak, F., & Suomi, R. (2022). Elderly Forgotten? Digital Exclusion in the Information Age and the Rising Grey Digital Divide. *Inquiry*, 59(1), 004695802210962. DOI: 10.1177/00469580221096272 PMID: 35471138

Nash, S. (2020, June 4). *The pandemic has accelerated the need to close the digital divide for older adults. Stanford Center on Longevity*. https://longevity.stanford.edu/the-pandemic-has-accelerated-the-need-to-close-the-digital-divide-for-older-adults

National Council on Aging. (2015). *National Council on Aging (NCOA)*. NCOA. https://www.ncoa.org/

Neves, B. B., Waycott, J., & Malta, S. (2018). Old and afraid of new communication technologies? Reconceptualising and contesting the "age-based digital divide.". *Journal of Sociology (Melbourne, Vic.)*, 54(2), 236–248. DOI: 10.1177/1440783318766119

Nguyen, A. (2020). *Digital Inclusion*. Handbook of Social Inclusion, 1–15. DOI: 10.1007/978-3-030-48277-0_14-1

Nishijima, M., Ivanauskas, T. M., & Sarti, F. M. (2017). Evolution and determinants of digital divide in Brazil (2005–2013). *Telecommunications Policy*, 41(1), 12–24. DOI: 10.1016/j.telpol.2016.10.004

Noone, C., McSharry, J., Smalle, M., Burns, A., Dwan, K., Devane, D., & Morrissey, E. C. (2020). Video calls for reducing social isolation and loneliness in older people: A rapid review. *Cochrane Database of Systematic Reviews*, 5(5). Advance online publication. DOI: 10.1002/14651858.CD013632 PMID: 32441330

NYU Tandon School of Engineering. (2021, February 24). *Impact of online communities*. ScienceDaily. https://www.sciencedaily.com/releases/2021/02/210224120312.htm

O'Toole, M. (2021, August 23). *Leveraging eCommerce Adoption by Seniors Post-Pandemic*. Clarkston Consulting. https://clarkstonconsulting.com/insights/ecommerce-adoption-by-seniors/

Orimo, H., Ito, H., Suzuki, T., Araki, A., Hosoi, T., & Sawabe, M. (2006). Reviewing the definition of "elderly". *Geriatrics & Gerontology International*, 6(3), 149–158. DOI: 10.1111/j.1447-0594.2006.00341.x PMID: 16521795

Parson, C., & Hick, S. (2008). *Moving from the Digital Divide to Digital Inclusion*. Currents: New Scholarship in the Human Services.7. https://www.semanticscholar.org/paper/Moving-from-the-Digital-Divide-to-Digital-Inclusion-Parsons-Hick/332768fe9553feabfa7032b9415f98f66d4c39d3

Pérez-Escolar, M., & Canet, F. (2022). Research on vulnerable people and digital inclusion: Toward a consolidated taxonomical framework. *Universal Access in the Information Society*, 22(22), 1059–1072. Advance online publication. DOI: 10.1007/s10209-022-00867-x PMID: 35125988

Perrault, S. (2021). *Towards Inclusive Design of Mobile Privacy and Security for Older Adults* (Doctoral dissertation, Singapore University of Technology and Design).

Promoting social integration through social inclusion - 2021 Report | Division for Inclusive Social Development (DISD). (2021). Un.org. https://social.desa.un.org/publications/promoting-social-integration-through-social-inclusion-2021-report

Rasi-Heikkinen, P., & Doh, M.Päivi Rasi-Heikkinen. (2023). Older Adults and Digital Inclusion. *Educational Gerontology*, 49(5), 345–347. DOI: 10.1080/03601277.2023.2205743

Reisdorf, B., & Rhinesmith, C. (2020). Digital Inclusion as a Core Component of Social Inclusion. *Social Inclusion (Lisboa)*, 8(2), 132–137. https://www.researchgate.net/publication/341383220_Digital_Inclusion_as_a_Core_Component_of_Social_Inclusion/citation/download. DOI: 10.17645/si.v8i2.3184

Seifert, A., Cotten, S. R., & Xie, B. (2020). A Double Burden of Exclusion? Digital and Social Exclusion of Older Adults in Times of COVID-19. *The Journals of Gerontology. Series B, Psychological Sciences and Social Sciences*, 76(3), e99–e103. Advance online publication. DOI: 10.1093/geronb/gbaa098 PMID: 32672332

Semrush. (2024). *Distribution of internet users worldwide as of February 2024, by age group* [Review of Distribution of internet users worldwide as of February 2024, by age group]. In Statista. https://www.statista.com/statistics/272365/age-distribution-of-internet-users-worldwide/

Sen, K., Prybutok, G., & Prybutok, V. (2022). The use of digital technology for social wellbeing reduces social isolation in older adults: A systematic review. *SSM - Population Health*, 17(101020), 101020. DOI: 10.1016/j.ssmph.2021.101020 PMID: 35024424

Sen, K., Prybutok, G., & Prybutok, V. (2022). Using digital technology for social wellbeing reduces social isolation in older adults: A systematic review. *SSM - Population Health*, 17(101020), 101020. DOI: 10.1016/j.ssmph.2021.101020 PMID: 35024424

Sharit, J., & Czaja, S. J. (2017). Technology and work: Implications for older workers and organizations. *Innovation in Aging*, 1(suppl_1), 1026–1026. DOI: 10.1093/geroni/igx004.3735

Shiwani, T., Relton, S., Evans, R., Kale, A., Heaven, A., Clegg, A., Abuzour, A., Alderman, J., Anand, A., Bhanu, C., Bunn, J., Collins, J., Cutillo, L., Hall, M., Keevil, V., Mitchell, L., Ogliari, G., Penfold, R., van Oppen, J., & Todd, O. (2023). New Horizons in artificial intelligence in the healthcare of older people. *Age and Ageing*, 52(12), afad219. Advance online publication. DOI: 10.1093/ageing/afad219 PMID: 38124256

Silver, M. P. (2014). Socio-economic status over the lifecourse and internet use in older adulthood. *Ageing and Society*, 34(6), 1019–1034. DOI: 10.1017/S0144686X12001420

Sixsmith, A., Horst, B. R., Simeonov, D., & Mihailidis, A. (2022). Older people's use of digital technology during the COVID-19 pandemic. *Bulletin of Science, Technology & Society*, 42(1-2), 19–24. DOI: 10.1177/02704676221094731 PMID: 38603230

Stefanacci, G. R. (n.d.). Overview of Healthy Ageing [Review of Overview of Healthy Ageing]. *MSD Manual.* https://www.mdpi.com/2071-1050/16/17/7485

The National Council on Aging. (2023, July 06). Www.ncoa.org. https://www.ncoa.org/article/how-older-adults-can-improve-their-personal-cyber-security/

Thomson, C. (2024, May 29). Generational AI: Digital inclusion for aging populations. Atlantic Council. https://www.atlanticcouncil.org/in-depth-research-reports/report/generational-ai-digital-inclusion-for-aging-populations/

Tomczyk, Ł., Mascia, M. L., Gierszewski, D., & Walker, C. (2023). Barriers to digital inclusion among older people: A intergenerational reflection on the need to develop digital competences for the group with the highest level of digital exclusion. Innoeduca. *International Journal of Technology and Educational Innovation*, 9(1), 5–26. DOI: 10.24310/innoeduca.2023.v9i1.16433

UNECE. (2021). Ageing in the digital era policy policy brief challenging context. https://unece.org/sites/default/files/2021-07/PB26-ECE-WG.1-38_0.pdf

Vávrová, S., Recmanová, A., Kowaliková, I., Gojová, A., &Vaňharová, A. (2019). Using ICT in social work focused on e-exclusion groups. *European Proceedings of Social and Behavioral Sciences.* DOI: 10.15405/epsbs.2019.11.35

Yaa Boakye-Adjei, N. (2020). *FSI Briefs Covid-19: Boon and bane for digital payments and financial inclusion.* https://www.bis.org/fsi/fsibriefs9.pdf

Yu, C. (2024, April 12). *Will AI be a Boon to an Aging Society.* Repec.org. https://econpapers.repec.org/paper/osfthesis/a8suh.htm

Zhu, Y., Collins, A., Xu, Z., Sardana, D., & Cavusgil, S. T. (2021). Achieving aging well through senior entrepreneurship: A three-country empirical study. *Small Business Economics*, 59(2), 665–689. DOI: 10.1007/s11187-021-00564-8

# Chapter 4
# Ring Out "Ageing Miserably"; Ring In "Growing Gracefully"

**Lakshmi R. Nair**
*Christ University, India*

## ABSTRACT

*The Chapter is the fruit of research undertaken by the author who shows light to the last phases of human life. The chapter provides the cultural backdrop on growing up. The title: Ring out "Ageing Miserably;" Ring in "Growing Gracefully" suggests the author's skeptical reading of the common meanings of "ageing". At the same time the author with critical arguments revises the meaning of ageing. The researcher reaches a remedy to the problem. The research is centered on Economics of Ageing. "Heaven on Earth" a Proposed Indian Model in every Taluk numbering 6057 units located at the most healthy, hygienic, environmentally fit chosen part of the Taluk. Each center with10 acres of land instituted legally through constitutional litigation. No other financial commitment is on the part of the state. The Indian Model means for grownup citizens aged above 60 joining institution as per rules. There will be an economic design for the running of the project.*

## INTRODUCTION

The world through innovative research offers emerging trends and policy solutions. The world provides comparative analyses across among countries and regions. Contributions blend theoretical insights with empirical data, case studies, and practical recommendations. A great transformation has been diffusing the global demographic rising. Populations across the world are growing at a fast rate. This

DOI: 10.4018/979-8-3693-7753-6.ch004

shift raises challenges and opportunities. They require a specialized understanding and careful analysis. This chapter delves into the economic implications of ageing. By bringing together insights from economics, social policy, health sciences, and technology, the researcher presents a holistic view of the economics of ageing. The ageing populations exert impact on economic growth and productivity. The sustainability challenges the world faces are pension systems. Technological innovations enhance the life of older adults. Healthcare costs and delivery systems in the economic well-being of the elderly are exorbitant. Policies foster intergenerational equity and support the economic participation of older adults.

The Chapter is the fruit of research undertaken by the author who shows some light to the nation builders in some areas of human life. The paper provides the cultural backdrop on the senile retrieving pearls from mind. She uses scanner on the senescent, on the elderly in life. This has provided certain valuable cultural imperatives, from here to eternity.

The title: *Ring out "Ageing Miserably;" Ring in "Growing Gracefully"* suggests the author's skeptical reading of the common meanings of the former part of the first ageing phrase. At the same time the author with critical arguments revises and vindicates the meaning of ageing with the latter part of the self-explanatory ageing phrase. "Ageing miserably" generates skeptical senses, which have been refurbished with the complementary plethora of positive senses. The author rewrites ageing having derogatory meanings and rewrites with positive sense. The author argues that human being grows, grows through different stages from prenatal, infancy and toddler hood, early childhood, middle childhood, adolescence, early adulthood, middle adulthood, and late adulthood. None of the stages can dissociate itself from growing. The merit of this growth continuum is being ill-conceived. The writer pleads for a review on the final stage of human life continuum and recommends that man shall utilize this stage positively to human advantage. The author prescribes a design format that comprises the economics of growing during the last stage of our life. "Nations with larger older populations depend on a smaller group of people to pay for higher health costs, pension benefits, and other publicly funded programs. In 2020, there were 727 million people aged 65 or older. This number is expected to more than double by 2050."

## GROWING AND AGEING

Most people are led astray to get misled by "ageing" as something unwelcome. A lot of misunderstanding is generated by ageing as word. Growing is the phenomenon of living beings. As human beings grow, they pass through stages; they undergo newer experiences. People misconstrue the full grown human stage of life, the last stage. Every stage from childhood, youth, middle age and final stage is full of problems. People attribute a lot of issues to each stage. People say the last stage is more problematic calling it as ageing. However, they do not know what the old stage means. Here the author approaches the changes in human life as normal changes, inevitable happening. The author prescribes the functions during the stage and calls the stage as critical. Here the author has a few different observations. The author deems the age as the age that demands peaceful life. The writer exhorts that people who reach this shall lead a graceful life. The writer believes that whether food, shelter, illness, and similar other problems they may be left with for rational solutions and free living practices. These visible suggestions and approaches will help individuals and the nations with fantastic outcome. Numerous grown up people face a variety of issues, including cataracts, hearing impairment, vision problems, back pain, diabetes, neck pain, and osteoarthritis. Others may suffer from pulmonary diseases, dementia, and depression.

In the current ageing world there is a need for focus of Economic Inclusion approaches and new opportunities in partnership for Economic Inclusion need to be evolved, where old people are beneficiary. In social pension programs, opportunities may be explored in cash-plus to leverage older people's productivity, better health outcomes, and social engagement.

Technology can address economic challenges posed by an ageing population in many ways. Technology can have a supporting role for older workers. Technology can help people work longer. Technology can help caregivers be more effective and reduce the cost. Technology will maintain healthy and productive lives. Digital technologies may help the elders to maintain health. They help them purchase goods online, pay taxes, and complete financial transactions safely from home. Technology may provide better preventive care monitoring, and early interventions. Artificial intelligence will make the old smart. Voice-activated devices can also be of great use.

## "AGEING" VERSUS "GROWING": "AGEING MISERABLY" versus "GROWING GRACEFULLY"

### Ageing with Skeptical Sense

Ageing begins as one is born. It continues till its death. During certain periods more cells are formed. During other periods, birth of cells will be affected by age. The researcher gives a diagram to explain the views.

*Figure 1. Ageing with skeptical sense*

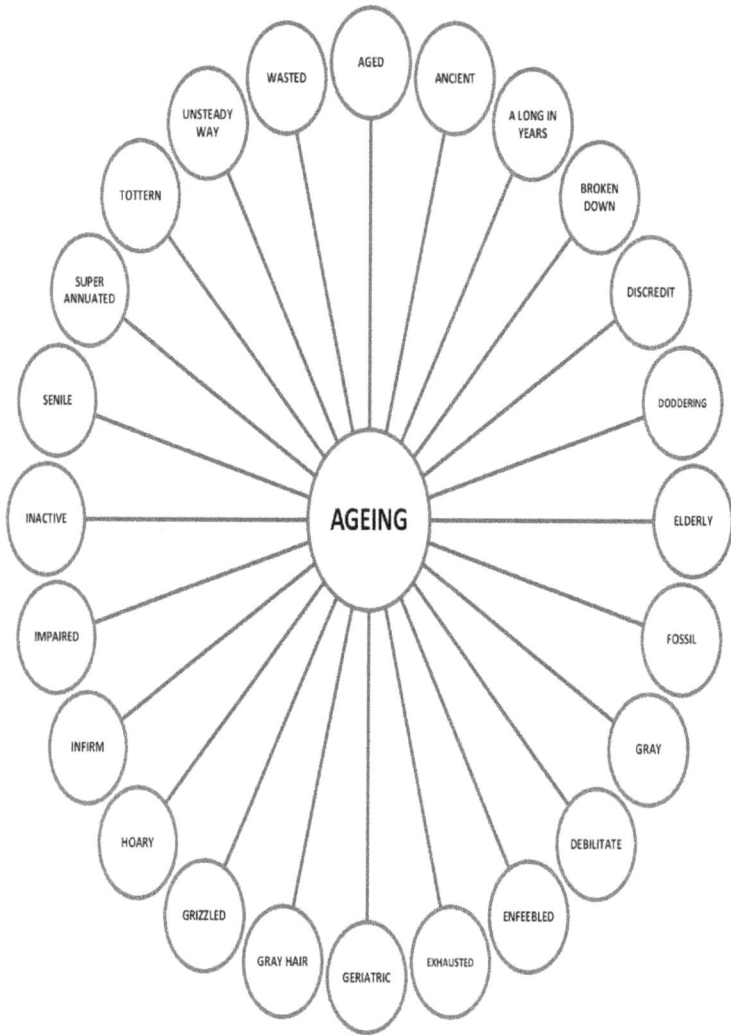

## Growing with Grace

Ageing is positive as it is inevitable. Therefore many words are synonyms with positive meaning cultural lapses let people use negative sensed words properly.

*Figure 2. Ageing with grace*

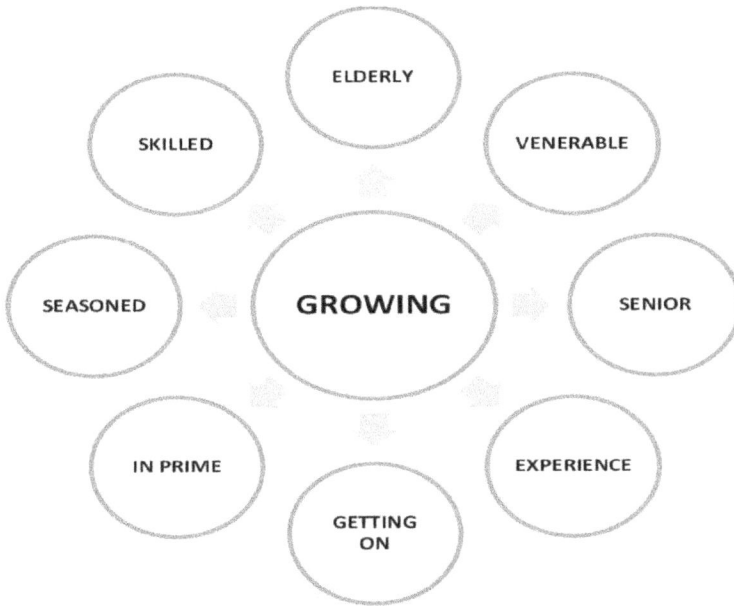

What's in a word "Growing?" It is the word people love to use. It cannot be the word "ageing." The researcher wants to launch the work on the permutations and combinations generated in the passage of time by applications of hermeneutics to know "grow" in its basic sense. It is a part of speech in basic grammar, As the word submits itself to active human mind for deeper and wider study, a proliferation of senses are generated.

The researcher confronts with a word grow, a verb, grabbles with it, and fails to solve the puzzle. The researcher initially feels a spark. The research partly wants to explain the spark forming word. The word initially born as a spark slowly expands.

## Growing: The Biology of Senescence

Every complex living thing derives its energy from the sun. It can evolve and keep its distinctiveness for a limited period. After that, the process of decline surpasses that of growth, leading to ageing. Ageing is the gradual decline in the body's essential functions for living and reproducing. The traits of getting older, as opposed to age-related illnesses like cancer and heart disease, impact every member of a species.

A number of evolutionary scientists (Medawar 1952; Kirkwood 1977) argue that ageing is not a natural part of an animal's genetic makeup. They view ageing as the normal outcome following an animal has met the needs of natural selection. Once the offspring have matured, the animal is no longer needed and can pass away. In fact, in various species, from moths to salmon, this sequence of events is common. Once the eggs are fertilized and laid, the adults perish. Nonetheless, recent research suggests that there are genetic elements involved in ageing, and that the average lifespan of a species can be influenced by changing genes or diet.

## Longevity

The notion of life span is an inherent trait of a particular species, denoting the utmost duration of years a member of said species can generally endure. Historically, human life expectancy was relatively short - in colonial America, a 65-year-old person was rare, and in 1900, 50% of American women died by age 58. However, over the past century, human longevity has increased dramatically, with 50% of American women living to age 81 by 1980. This shift reflects the growing prevalence of senescence and age-related diseases that were less common in the past. In 1900, people were more likely to succumb to infectious diseases and parasites rather than the heart attacks, cancers, and other chronic conditions that now afflict many older adults. Similarly, the outward signs of ageing, from graying hair to diminished senses, were less widespread. As Shakespeare poetically observed, those who did reach advanced age often did so *"sans teeth, sans eyes, sans taste, sans everything."*

## Geropsychology

Geropsychology may be a field inside brain research. It is committed to the ponder of developing up and the arrangement of clinical administrations for more seasoned grown-ups. Geropsychologists extend information of the typical developing handle and plan and test mental intercessions. As wellbeing care professionals, clinicians offer assistance more seasoned people & their families. They offer assistance to overcome issues, improve well-being and accomplish most extreme potential amid afterward life.

## The Growing Need for Psychological Services for Older Adults

More mental health professionals are providing nature care to older adults. As large cohorts of middle-aged people age into old age, demand will increase because this generation is more receptive to mental health services than the current one. Nearly two thirds of older adults with mental disorders, according to research, do not receive the necessary services. Certain racial and ethnic groups, as well as those living in poverty, are among the underprivileged and rural populations where this issue is most severe. According to research, most older adults would prefer to receive treatment if they experienced depression. When given the option, older adults with depression frequently choose psychological services over antidepressant medication. When receiving mental health services from licensed mental health professionals, older adults say they feel at ease.

## LITERATURE REVIEW

Psychologists are at the forefront of research on questions related to health and growing. Why do some older adults become suicidal while the majority successfully adjust to the stresses of late life? Why do some older adults experience memory loss while the majority maintain mental acuity? Studies on the ageing brain shed light on the factors that protect against and increase the risk of mental health problems throughout life. Because psychologists are skilled in psychological and neuropsychological assessment, families and healthcare providers frequently turn to them when dealing with the often complex mental and physical health issues that older adults face.

Psychologists assist senior citizens in coping with the myriad of life stressors that come with getting older, including health decline, bereavement, and moving to a new place. Psychologists treat anxiety disorders in older adults with psychotherapy and supportive counselling; the frequency of these disorders is similar to that of depression in older adults. Psychologists assist seniors in managing a variety of long-term medical conditions, such as arthritis, heart disease, and stroke, which frequently come with ageing. Preventing excessive disability and hospitalization via treatment adherence and behavioural interventions—such as exercise, biofeedback, diet, and stress management methods—is a primary objective of this kind of management. Psychologists can assist older adults in identifying situations that lead to drinking, increasing their motivation to quit, and learning new coping mechanisms for high-risk drinking situations. Some elderly people require assistance cutting back on or quitting prescription anxiety medications because they are addicted to them. Furthermore, there will probably be a rise in the prevalence of alcohol and illegal drug use as the baby boomer generation ages. The highest rates of suicide in the US are among older adults, especially the "White" men. Depression is the main risk factor for suicide. Psychologists are trained in diagnosing depression and determining a person's risk of suicide. Primary health care providers frequently fail to identify individuals who are suicidally inclined. According to reports, three-quarters of older adults who commit suicide saw a doctor within the previous month and two-fifths within the previous week. Primary care physicians frequently fail to recognize the connection that may exist between physical symptoms and mental health issues.

## Ageing Population in Industrialized Nations

H.S. Borji, a global economic and financial analyst, speaks about the effects of the ageing population in industrialized nations. He notes with concern the decrease in number in the working-age population as it ends up with shortage of qualified workers. In the elderly population a few individuals have to deal with increased expenses for healthcare retirement benefits and government programs. In 2022 the United Nations reported that there were 771 million people who were 65 years old or older. The number is predicted to increase to 994 million by 2030. By 2025 the number of older people will reach 1.6 billion. This means there will be fewer people of working-age who are part of the economy. This causes a lack of skilled workers which makes it harder for businesses to hire for needed positions. Several nations rely on immigration to ensure they have enough workers for their industries. Countries such as Australia Canada and the U.K are examples. Bring in more talented immigrants and help them join the workforce.

## ECONOMIC CHANGES

Economies differ in demands on the proportion of older adults. They will be differing in a larger working age population. Markets that are increasingly dominated by products and services related to the elderly may pose a threat to economies. It's unclear if immigration will cover the gaps in industries left by ageing populations in advanced economies or if the larger economies would need to adapt to shifting demographics. With 28.2% of its population 65 years of age or older, Japan has the largest percentage of senior adults. Ageing populations generate a number of economic effects. They comprise declining labour force, increased healthcare costs, increased dependency ratio, declining innovation and declining GDP growth. The ageing of the population affects economic growth.

## China's Economic Growth and Population Growing

China has a number of studies on these topics. Studies have been created using data from 30 Chinese provinces. Economic growth is significantly impacted by population ageing. The industrial structure generates economic growth and mediates the ageing of the population. Economic growth and the basic labour production factor are largely dependent on the population. Numerous variables, including changes in fertility intentions brought about by industrialization, increasing urbanization, and the family planning policy, have influenced China's demographic structure. China has made a number of actions to examine how population ageing affects economic expansion.

## Umpteen Economic Challenges for the Care of the Old in Nigeria

Nigeria faces great economic challenges in helping care for older people; the country does not have national policy for welfare of old people. Nigeria's healthcare system is not funded properly and it places no importance to the care of the senile. Social insurance and pension systems in Nigeria mostly cover formal employment, which is a challenge because a larger proportion of the workforce is in the informal sector. The breakdown of family structure and reduced family size are changing the home living conditions for older people. Economic migration to urban areas is expected to have an impact on elder care. Some strategies to enhance long-term care for Nigerian seniors include: awareness has been generated for making developing acceptable, affordable, and accessible with long-term care in the community and institutional settings. The country improves budgetary allocation to better the health needs of older people .The country has revised the training curriculum of all cadres of health staff to include geriatrics and utilizes primary healthcare facilities.

Nigeria and the conditions of the old may be a challenge for students of a country with several economic challenges, depreciating currency, and a need for diversification: In 2024, Nigeria's headline inflation is expected to peak at 31.7%. This is largely due to the depreciation of the naira and increased gasoline prices. The naira has devalued twice in 2023 and 2024, leading to higher prices for imported goods like foodstuffs. Nigeria's economy is heavily dependent on oil, which only contributes about 9% to the GDP. The country has significant natural and human resources that could be used to diversify its economy.

## Economically Inactive Old People of Poland

According to the findings of the Labour Force Survey (LFS), conducted in 2022, 7.8 million people between the ages of 60 and 89 were economically inactive, making up 84.3% of the population. The number of economically inactive people aged 60 to 89 increased by 0.2% compared to the previous year, while their proportion of the total population of the same age decreased by 0.1 percentage points. Women made up 62.2% of those aged 60 to 89 who were economically inactive, and urban dwellers made up 64.3%. 75.1% of men and 91.0% of women aged 60 to 89 were economically inactive. Because men and women have different retirement ages (men retire at age 65, while women retire at age 60), men tend to remain employed for longer periods of time, which accounts for the larger percentage of economically inactive women than men. There were nearly 1.5 million economically active seniors between the ages of 60 and 89 in 2022, a 1.2% increase from the year before. Men made up 67.1% of this population. The majority of economically active individuals in this age group lived in urban areas (65.8%), according to the analysis that accounts for place of residence. People between the ages of 60 and 89 made up 8.5% of the total population that was economically active. For those between the ages of 60 and 89, the economic activity ratio was 15.7% (it was 15.6% in 2021). The ratio was 9.0% for women and 24.9% for men. There was no discernible difference in the place of residence. Economically active individuals aged 60-89 made up 16.0% of the population in urban areas, compared to 15.2% in rural ones. The vast majority of seniors who are economically active—98.6%—are employed. There were 1.4 million employed people aged 60 to 89 and over in 2022, and their activity ratio was 15.5% (24.5% for men and 8.9% for women). The percentage of people between the ages of 60 and 89 who were employed was 15.8% in urban areas and 15.0% in rural ones. By the end of 2022, there were 544.4 thousand working adults aged 60 and over who were eligible for retirement benefits, a 1.9% increase from 2021. Within a year, the proportion of employed individuals aged 60 and over who are eligible for retirement benefits remained constant at 3.6% of all employed individuals in the national economy. The analysis of households with only individuals 60 years of age and older provides a better illustration of the situation of the elderly. The average disposable income per capita for the seniors residing in these households was PLN 2623. It can be said that the income increased nominally by 11.4% when compared to the amount recorded the year before. The average monthly expenses for households with all members aged 60 and over came to PLN 1896, which was a nominal increase of 13.4% over the previous year. The monthly surplus between the average income per capita and the expenses in these households was PLN 726.1. The monthly expenses incurred by elderly households accounted for 81.1% of the average income (1.7 percentage points higher than in 2021), and the surplus was PLN 497.

## Scanty Economic Support for the Elderly in Russia

Russia does not offer much economic support for the elderly. Social services and state aid are often expensive. Home services are not provided to the old people. Many old people live in poverty. They are discriminated against. Russia does not offer resources for the elderly who are disabled or suffering from dementia and other ailments. But Russia offers social policies and legislation to support older adults. Retirement system allows adults to retire at relatively young ages. It may also allow them to continue their professional career or re-establish a career.

## UK and Elderly Care

The care of the elderly in the UK has a significant economic impact. In 2019, the economic cost of informal care was £54.2 billion, which was three times the amount spent on formal long-term care. By 2039, the cost of informal care is projected to increase by 87%. In 2016, the adult social care sector in the UK employed around 1.8 million people, which was 6% of the total employment in the UK. The average earnings in this sector were estimated to be £17,300. The Office for National Statistics (ONS) estimates that 18% of people aged 50–65 who left work since the start of the pandemic reported being on a waiting list for NHS medical treatment. Some theories suggest that long waiting lists for treatment are causing people's health to deteriorate.

## India: Elders Need Organized Assistance

Older people make up only 8.9% of the total population. This amounts to 100 million elderly people, of whom over 12 million are 80 years of age or older. Many elderly people require organized assistance for long-term care; families bear the majority of this burden. Therefore, in order to increase the coverage of current long-term care, the Government of India thinks that it should implement stronger laws, policies, and programs.

## USA and Social Security

Elderly care conditions in the United States are complex and have been shaped by the search for economic security. Social Security power in US is important for economic security for older Americans. Income differences are found to be due to disparities in wages, business income, investments, pensions, and retirement accounts. Older adults with lower income are more likely to be people of color and live alone. They are also more dependent on Social Security and SSI benefits.

The author exhorts: Ring out the Current concepts of Economics of Ageing and Ring in the Economics of current global concepts of growing gracefully. The author has good faith in the efforts of the UN and its general Council along these lines. The author conceives a new world of "*grown up*" humans. While the world without doing something not scientific, working with economics, keeping humans of a matured stage as invalid, incompetent and inefficient, always working upon them as the weak, the sympathy demanding liabilities for their kith and kin, the author has a little different view to offer on the subject.

The chapter deals with how Senior citizens impact economic growth. It handles the sustainability challenges facing worldwide pension schemes, issues related to technological innovations, and how they better improve the life of the elderly. It assesses the healthcare costs and delivery system in the economic wellbeing of the elderly. The author taking consideration of these issues tries to present original and innovative research. Policy solutions are attempted at theoretical comparatistics tried among nations and regions.

The author at the outset examines the term ageing with suspicion and offers an innovative definition. Ageing is a derogatory term associating itself with the weak, the unhealthy and the incapable. An aged or ageing human being is a liability to the family, relatives, society, and the world. Instead, the author offers an interpretation offering a positive approach to all problems of senior citizens. Ageing with a derogatory sense is not the appropriate term. It is growing. Growing is a positive process. From childhood human beings grow to youth, middle age, and old age. But erroneously people give a wrong scenario of the situation.

The objectives of the paper are multidimensional. The paper aims at purging the minds of the people polluted with erroneous ageing ideas. The paper pins hopes on the grownups taking care of themselves. The grownups shall not feel themselves alienated, dejected, and depressed. They shall not think that they are the left over. They shall not feel that they are like prisons. They shall feel always that they have someone to work with, to work for, and take care of. They shall feel the breeze of love and affections. The young members of the family, they should know they are not alienating but they are striving for their own survival. The grownups should build up a world of themselves. They can continue maintaining relationship with members of the kith and kin.

## AGEING

Ageing is a natural change that occurs in various molecules and cells as time passes. This causes decline in both physical and mental abilities. It increases risk of illness. It leads to death. All these changes are due to the passage of time. The diversity seen in later life is not merely coincidental. Besides, it is related to life transitions. Common health issues among older adults include chronic obstructive pulmonary disease, diabetes, depression, dementia, back and neck pain, cataracts, refractive errors, hearing loss, and osteoarthritis. Individuals experience many health variations. Geriatric syndromes: The emergence of multiple complex health states that are collectively referred to as geriatric syndromes is another characteristic of older age. They include frailty, delirium, falls, urine incontinence, and pressure ulcers, and are frequently the result of several underlying factors.

## Both Positive and Negative

Research shows that the part of life lived healthy has remained fairly steady, suggesting that additional years are often accompanied unhealthy. If individuals can enjoy these extra years in good health and within a supportive environment, their capacity to engage in meaningful activities will be similar to that of younger individuals.

## Genetic Variations

There are genetic variations in the health of older adults. The majority of them are caused by people's social and physical surroundings, which include their homes, neighbourhoods, and communities, as well as their individual traits, like their socioeconomic class, sex, or race.

A balanced diet, regular exercise, and abstaining from tobacco use are just a few of the healthy habits that can help lower the risk of non-communicable diseases, enhance mental and physical abilities, and postpone the need for care.

The lives of older people are being affected both directly and indirectly by factors such as globalization, migration, urbanization, technological advancements (such as those in transportation and communication), and shifting gender norms. A public health response needs to assess these present and future trends and adjust policies as necessary.

## Ethnographic Studies

In ethnographies, older people have always been present, but few have dared to investigate how old age and ageing create their own cultures (and what those cultures have to do with being old) or how older people influence the cultures of younger generations.

## Ageing and Connection

Ageing provokes connection to wider narratives of cultural and national identity, to one's own past selves, and not just to other generations. According to Jordan Lewis, this connection can be found in cultural representations of "successful ageing," such as those that foster eldership in Aleut communities, thus bridging generations.

## Ageing and Disjunction

The idea itself implies movement and change, which are prompted by ageing. Growing older causes disjunction. This notion has been de-naturalized by anthropologists such as Katharine Ewing and Michael Jackson, who demonstrate that the homogenous individual self is a Western construct that is not shared by all people. Ewing (1990) and Jackson (1998) mapped the plurality of seemingly unitary selves individuals experience and enact even within a single conversation. Ageing can cause a disjunction between the mind and body in societies where youth is idolized and older age is pathologized against the backdrop of Cartesian dualism. Writing about ageing allows the writer to see the process from a perspective that feels outside of it; similar to Archimedes' lever and platform, writing about ageing conjures up the idea of an impossibly difficult physical escape from the Earth's rotation. Perhaps it accomplishes that in a subtle, symbolic way by giving rise to an idea that might endure longer than the specific body.

Emily Wentzell points out 'Growing older' causes disjunction. He frames an elderly, almost 80-year-old woman to illustrate this. She asks, "*Who is this old woman?*" when she sees her reflection because she is not aware of her age. We no longer recognize ourselves as we age. Over time, the simple act of living gradually modifies our physical characteristics, social roles in society, and appearance. Culturally prescribed life milestones like marriage, childrearing, retirement, and school graduation may also accompany these changes.

According to Jordan Lewis' notes, growing older causes a variety of profoundly beneficial changes in one's physical, mental, spiritual, and emotional aspects of life. He grew up in an Aluet Alaskan culture that valued respect for his elders. He wants to be an Elder in his own right. Being an elder in this world was a mark of honour and respect, as people looked to you for your "*knowledge and experiences.*" He departs from this conventional paradigm, suggesting that people strive to fend off the effects of ageing. In this case, social status is gained by engaging in the market economy through employment and taxation. For some people, retirement can mean leaving the working world and joining a more "*dependent*" community. This shift is frequently opposed.

Jordan Lewis uses translation as change to another form. According to Merriam-Webster Dictionary (2005), one definition of translation is the alteration or conversion to a different form or appearance. It is up to each individual to translate their own experiences. They attempt to find solace in their experiences by defining them, giving them significance, and searching through them. In the United States, the general public has certain views and beliefs about ageing. We tend to emphasize youth and beauty, avoiding ageing, and believing that we will eventually grow old. In the adult stage, people recognize the changes that occur in their bodies, minds, spirits, and emotions and try to make sense of them. They also search for people who have gone through similar things to accompany them on their journey through ageing.

## Mind and Body: Disjunction

Emily Wentzell talked about how growing older causes a disjunction between the mind and body and how our bodies don't sense our actual ages. Elderly people are respected and sought after for their wisdom and experiences. Being an elder is an honour, and people look forward to it. Four themes surfaced, all of which emphasized critical facets of what my research on eldership called successful ageing. In Bristol Bay, eldership is defined by these factors: (a) mental health; (b) involvement in the community; (c) spirituality; and (d) physical well-being. In this study, it's critical to distinguish between eldership and successful ageing. The foundation of this study was the term *"successful ageing,"* which I used to define in an Alaska Native way in order to better understand what this meant to the Elders of Bethel Bay. As I collaborated with the Elders and examined the interview data, it became evident that instead of defining successful ageing for themselves, they were characterizing traits of other Elders in their communities who they thought exemplified successful ageing.

## Growing Continuum till Death

Growing starts the moment we are born, and until the day we die, we are constantly navigating the changes, developments, and maturation of our body and mind. Emily Wentzell starts her notes by talking about how ageing itself challenges stability and stasis and causes movement.

## Fear of Ageing

Everyone should consider their attitudes toward ageing, as well as how they relate to and engage with senior citizens in their communities and families. What else have we learned about ageing from others? A comprehensive strategy is needed. How can we weigh your experiences against other people's and the public's fear of ageing?

## Social Integration in Old Age

The concept "social integration" is often used interchangeably with social support, social networks, social contacts, and social inclusion as opposed to social segregation and isolation. One definition of social integration refers to the degree to which an individual is involved in social exchanges with others, whether it is the family, social networks, or in their communities (Hooyman & Kiyak, 2008) and feels belonging and part of it. Anant (1966, p. 21) defined xzsense of belonging as a *"sense of personal involvement in a social system so that persons feel themselves to be an indispensable and integral part of the system."*

## Ageism and Social Integration

In the field of gerontology, the social integration of older people in their neighborhoods has been insufficiently addressed and almost no attention has been paid to social integration as a dependent variable (Gracia & Herrero, 2004).

Many studies take up the subject of social integration of older people in society. Some consider the labour market, the family, and social networks (de Jong Gierveld & Hagestad, 2006; Dykstra & Hagestad, 2007). Social integration is also allied with ageist stereotypes, which can encourage marginalization of older people (Butler, 1969; Basford & Thorpe, 2004; Comer, Britain, & Bond, 2007) and can hinder their social integration in society. The Prejudice Hypothesis (Allport, 1958) asserts that stereotypes and negative attitudes of one social group toward another group, based on age, gender, or race, can cause social segregation (Quillian,1995). Ageism is a systematic process of stereotyping older people just because of their older age (Butler, 1969). Ageism can be manifested in discrimination on the one hand and abuse and violence toward older people on the other (Cathalifaud, Thumala, Urquiza, & Ojeda, 2008; de Jong Gierveld & Hagestad, 2006; Palmore, 2001, 2005). Ageism is prevalent among various age groups (Bodner & Lazar, 2008; Loretto, Duncan, & White, 2000), even in traditional societies, like China, where respect for older people used to be a very important social value (Cuddy, Norton, &s Fiske, 2005; Fan, 2007). Negative images of ageing and ageism can contribute to older adults' social exclusion. Ageism is also expected to flourish in environments where cross-age interactions are limited, whereas increased social integration can reduce age stereotypes and prejudices (Uhlenberg, 2000).

## Causes of Ageing

The ubiquitous senescent phenotype is a defining feature of every species, prompting inquiry into its underlying cause, which can be explored across various levels of analysis, with a specific focus on the cellular level of organization. Despite numerous theories proposed, a definitive explanation for the mechanism of ageing remains elusive due to the lack of consensus among researchers.

## Oxidative Damage

According to a popular view, ageing is caused by changes in our metabolism. This idea states that ageing is a natural by-product of metabolism and doesn't require mutations. Reactive oxygen species (ROS) are produced when the mitochondria fail to adequately degrade 2–3% of the oxygen atoms that are taken in by them. The superoxide ion, the hydroxyl radical, and hydrogen peroxide are some of these ROS. Proteins, nucleic acids, and cell membranes can all be oxidized and harmed by ROS. The discovery that Drosophila that overexpress enzymes that break down reactive oxygen species (ROS)—catalase, which breaks down peroxide, and superoxide dismutase—live 30–40% longer than controls lends support to this notion (Orr and Sohal 1994; Parkes et al. 1998).

## General Wear-and-Tear and Genetic Instability

"Wear-and-tear" theories of ageing are among the oldest hypotheses proposed to account for the general scenescent phenotype (Weismann 1891; Szilard 1959). Little traumas to the body accumulate with age. Our genes encode enzymes with decreasing efficiency as the number of point mutations rises. Moreover, if a mutation occurred in a part of the protein synthetic apparatus, the cell would make a large percentage of faulty proteins (Orgel 1963). The rate of mutations should rise dramatically if the enzymes that synthesize DNA underwent mutations; Murray and Holliday (1981) have reported defective DNA polymerases in senescent cells. Likewise, DNA repair may be important in preventing senescence, and species whose members' cells have more efficient DNA repair enzymes live longer (Hart and Setlow 1974). Moreover, genetic defects in DNA repair enzymes, they can produce premature ageing syndromes in humans (Yu et al. 1996; Sun et al. 1998).

## Mitochondrial Genome Damage

The mutation rate in mitochondria is 10–20 times faster than the nuclear DNA mutation rate (Johnson et al. 1999). It is believed that mutations in the mitochondria may (1) cause errors in the synthesis of energy, (2) cause defective electron transport to produce ROS, and/or (3) cause apoptosis. Age-dependent declines in mitochondrial function are seen in many animals, including humans (Boffoli et al. 1994). A recent report (Michikawa et al. 1999) shows that there are "hot spots" for age-related mutations in the mitochondrial genome, and that mitochondria with these mutations have a higher replication frequency than wild-type mitochondria. As a result, the mutants can surpass the wild-type mitochondria, ultimately taking over the cell and its descendants. Additionally, these mutations might not only increase the production of Reactive Oxygen Species (ROS) but also render the mitochondrial DNA more vulnerable to damage caused by ROS.

## Genetic Ageing Programs

Numerous genes have been demonstrated to influence the process of ageing. Hutchinson-Gilford progeria syndrome, a condition in humans characterized by rapid ageing and premature death (often due to heart failure before the age of 12), is attributed to a dominant mutant gene. Symptoms of this syndrome include thin skin with age spots, decreased bone density, hair loss, and arteriosclerosis. In mice, a comparable syndrome arises from mutations in the klotho gene (Kuro-o et al. 1997). Despite extensive research, the specific functions of these gene products remain unknown.

## Economics of Ageing

The research is centred on Economics of Ageing. Quite justifiably the first part of research provides a comprehensive, interdisciplinary examination of the word "Ageing". What is ageing? What does it mean? What is growing? What does it mean? What is the difference between these two similar words? The questions are all problematic. Both of them raise great concerns.

# ECONOMICS OF AGEING VERSUS ECONOMICS OF GROWING

## Age-Structure and Economic Growth Factors

The relationship between economic growth and population age-structure is moderated by the state of health within a society. The adverse effect on the economy due to the ageing population is evident in the increased number of individuals exiting the workforce, resulting in decreased productivity, and the lack of a clearly defined correlation between the health and disability of older individuals and its impact on the economy. This study investigates how the health of the working-age population, as indicated by the number of Years Lived with Disability (YLDs) by age, affects the link between an ageing workforce and the growth of real per capita GDP in 180 countries from 1990 to 2017. Numerous analysts anticipate that an ageing population will negatively impact economic growth. However, it remains unclear whether maintaining good health among older workers can mitigate this effect. If older employees are healthy, ageing does not necessarily lead to economic downturns. Simulations indicate that substantial economic benefits could arise from investments in health.

## Ageing Population and Workforce Variation

Countries worldwide are experiencing an ageing population. This shift in the age distribution is leading to an older workforce. Between the years 2010 and 2019, the worldwide average age of the workforce—this encompasses people of working age who are either working or looking for jobs—increased from 37.6 years to 38.9 years. The largest rises were noted in Southern Europe (3.3 years), Eastern Asia (2.6 years), South Eastern Asia (2.0 years), and South America (2.0 years). In 2019, the areas with the oldest workforces included Southern Europe (median age of 43.9 years), Western Europe (43.2 years), and Eastern Asia (42.1 years) (International Labour Organization, 2020).

## Older Adults Health and Economic Outcomes

Role of health and disability among the older working-age population, one might expect that a healthy older population will be able to remain active and productive for longer, potentially moderating some of the otherwise detrimental economic effects associated with an ageing labour force (Van den Berg et al., 2010). Determining the impact of older adults' health on economic outcomes is difficult because of methodological challenges. This is largely due to the interdependence between individuals' work at older ages and their health, along with other personal characteristics. Research based on individual-level data is unable to reveal how shifts in the older population's size influence the macro economy.

## Increase in the Number and Percentage of Population

People around the globe are enjoying longer lifespans. Nowadays, the majority can anticipate living into their sixties and beyond. An increase in both the number and percentage of older individuals within their populations is noted. By 2030, 16% of individuals globally will be 60 years old or older. During this period, the population segment aged 60 and above is projected to rise from 1 billion in 1.4 billion from 2020. By 2050, the number of people aged 60 and older is expected to double, reaching 2.1 billion. Additionally, the population of those aged 80 and above is anticipated to triple from 2020 to 2050, reaching 426 million.

The trend of population ageing, characterized by an increase in the proportion of older individuals within a country's population, initially began in high-income nations. For instance, in Japan, 30% of the population is already over the age of 60.

The most significant demographic shifts are now occurring in low- and middle-income countries. By 2050, projections indicate that two-thirds of the global population aged 60 and over will live in these developing nations.

## THE "WHO" AND THE "AGE-FRIENDLY" INSTITUTIONS – THE SPARK

The research undertaken here is from a Spark out of the resolution taken by World Health Organization's to take initiative on moves to better the conditions of the human beings and the world. The Spark relates to the excitement the researcher undertakes seeing WHO's initiatives. The researcher is sceptical about the context and the contention generated by the negative phrase "ageing miserably." It is here the research finds itself as innovative and original. This enables cities inspire change by showing what can be done and how it can be done, connect cities and communities worldwide to facilitate the exchange of information, knowledge and experience and support cities and communities to find appropriate innovative and evidence-based solutions.

### WHO Response

The United Nations (UN) General Assembly has designated the years 2021 to 2030 as the UN Decade of Healthy Ageing, entrusting the World Health Organization (WHO) with its implementation. This global initiative unites governments, civil society, international organizations, professionals, academic institutions, media, and the private sector in a coordinated, collaborative, and impactful 10-year effort to promote longer, healthier lives. The Decade is founded on the WHO Global Strategy and Action Plan, as well as the United Nations Madrid International Plan of Action on Ageing. It aims to advance the objectives of the United Nations Agenda 2030 for Sustainable Development and the Sustainable Development Goals. The UN Decade of Healthy Ageing (2021–2030) aims to address health disparities and enhance the well-being of older individuals, their families, and communities through collaborative efforts in four key areas: transforming perceptions and attitudes towards ageing and ageism; creating communities that support the capabilities of older adults; offering person-centered integrated care and primary health services tailored to the needs of older individuals; and ensuring access to quality long-term care for those who require it.

## Ageing and Health

The pace of population growing/ageing is much faster than in the past. In 2050, 80% of older people will be living in low- and middle-income countries. In 2020, the global population of adults aged 60 and over surpassed the number of children under 5 years old. Over the 35-year period from 2015 to 2050, the percentage of the world's population aged 60 and above is projected to nearly double, rising from 12% to 22%.

Gerontologists embody both the roles of poets and pathologists. They view ageing as a natural aspect of life, an essential phase of human development, and frequently depict it as a positive journey. The English poet Robert Browning: "*Grow old along with me! The best is yet to be, the last of life, for which the first was made.*"

Poets serve as the interpreters of the social sciences, while pathologists are typically medical professionals or biologists. From their perspective, ageing is viewed as a detrimental process that leads to greater biological entropy, reduced reserves, an increased likelihood of illness, and ultimately, death. Their esteemed lineage is reflected in Shakespeare's words: "*Last scene of all, that ends this strange eventful history... sans teeth, sans eyes, sans taste, sans everything.*" Researchers in this field of gerontology are trained in a variety of areas, including physiology, social science, psychology, public health, and policy.

A gerontologist is a professional who studies the effects of ageing on people and promotes their well-being. Gerontologists work in many settings, including hospitals, nursing homes, community centres, and research institutes. They study the physical, mental, and social changes that occur as people age, and how these changes affect their interactions with their environment.

## From Here to Eternity

Ageing gracefully is a term used to make us feel better about the taboo that we are all getting older. It is often used as a euphemism for "looking old, but still holding on" or "showing signs of ageing, but still moving forward with life." The term is negative. But it is only interpretation. Ageing gracefully need not refer specifically to age or appearance. It mentions the attitude people have as they go through the various stages of life. Many say 'I'm so old I've got one foot in the grave'. People know from the very beginning, we grow through, to our end. As we grow old our bodies change, our faces change and our abilities change. Graceful is movement. Grace gives beauty, elegance or charm. It is the effortless beauty or charm of movement. We can grow gracefully; exercise on a regular basis, eat lots of fruit and vegetables. We can drink a lot of water; get enough sleep but not too much sleep. We will control your blood pressure.

Ageing gracefully relates to appearance. We use eye cream, face cream, neck cream and similar other things.

The researcher wishes: *"Grace on the humans who live longer."* The researcher produces an Indian model which delineates the grown up's life during the last phase of their life. The researcher vindicates that *"Those who live longer are blessed as they enjoy life longer"* and exhorts: *"The Grownups are free in their own land: the welfare home"*


## "HEAVEN ON EARTH": A PROPOSED INDIAN MODEL

**Creating age-friendly cities and communities/ Grace on them who live longer Indian Model of the Grownup's Life**

The author proposes a model each a "Heaven on Earth", City for senior citizens in every Taluk in India. There are 6057 units and they vary in their local name ranging from Taluka, Mandel, Tehsil, Subdivision and Circle. This Centre shall be located at the most healthy, hygienic, environmentally fit chosen part of the Taluk. Every center will have minimum 10 acres of land. The center will be instituted legally through constitutional litigation. All the states will have legal, economic, and general administrative control over the center. The economic accounting will be linked to the National Income of the state. Every center is located at the statutory land allotted as per the law of the land per Taluk all over India. No other financial commitment is on the part of the state or the country.

## Institution Design Framework for Grownup Citizens: Indian Model

The design is meant for a national institution each established all over in Taluks all over the state to facilitate cozy life for the grown up citizens. The state provides ten acres of land for each Taluk institution. It is meant for grownup citizens aged above 60 admitted to the institution as per rules. There is no restriction given to admission based on gender, color, race, religion, caste, community. There will be an economic system and procedure for the running of the institution. The Centre will have administrative control of the personnel selected from among the grownups like retirees from administrative take over administration (e.g.: Retired district collectors or of similar ranks), Health Officers, Police officers, Revenue Officers, Agricultural officers). The administration will be accountable to the state. Admitted person will be the member of the Centre subject to the discipline of the Centre. Freedom is the hallmark of life here. The main hallmark of the institution is freedom of thought, action, housing, and work for the institution.

Housing facilities in flats will be provided. Food and other requirements are the right of the inmates. They may feel free to travel with the permission of the Centre. They can continue with their expertise offering services to the inmates of the center. They can offer service outside and earn money for the center. Finance will be generated from the following resources. The inmates can choose any work of his/her choice and proficiency. The inmate can spend or earn, do or rest, or play with the knowledge of the personnel.

The economics of the center will rely on the income generated from manifold channels. The concept like Individual' property/pension, Income will cease to have individual's tag. All will be Centre's capital. Money through donations will go to common capital. Money will not flow out of the center. On admission the office will allot the flat. Canteen will provide food. Freedom of worship is the law of the center. It will be a *"Well living Life Centre."* Once it flourishes, it will give a Boost to National Economy.

The researcher asks the *"WH"* questions of *"Who?"*, *"What?"*, *"Why?"*, *"How?"*, *"When?"* and *"Where?"*

Who? The old shall be given the respect they deserve.
What? The grown up shall be given freedom to live and love the world.
Why?

a. The grown up condition is treated as a period of agony, suffering, poverty, diseases culminated in death, the researcher substantiates it is wrong.
b. The grown up is described as a period when the old people are outcast generally from society, community, public, etc. not always true.
c. Illness is the hall mark of the grown up, prove it is wrong.
d. It is wrong to say that most of the houses would like to terminate the grown up. All wish the fruit of freedom shall be provided in the Heaven on Earth.
e. We shall not any way all the get the Freedom of the grown up brutally curtailed.

How? First start the centres and go and step in with hope and love.
When? Now it is high time the world could have started these kinds of cities
Where? Heaven on Earth to get established all over the world

*Figure 3. Heaven on Earth (blue print)*

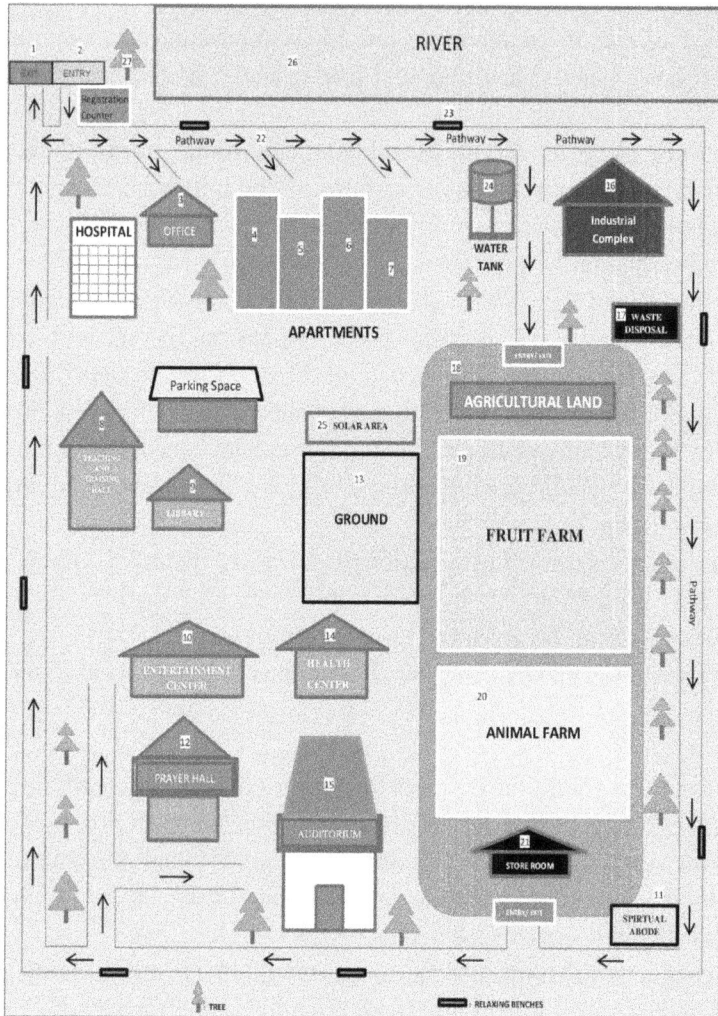

## "HEAVEN ON EARTH": FREEDOM FOR ALL

### Holacracy and Equality: All Jobs are of Equal Importance

1. Entry: The area is restricted to dwellers and visitors. The entry to the city is bifold,: One welcomes new admissions to the fold of inmates. The other welcomes visitors, relatives of the inmates and other wellwishers.

2. Exit: only with the permission, inmates can move out. The exit may be used by guests and relatives.
3. Office: office Administation is governed by a selection panel chosen by the inmates.
4. Apartment (1 BHK): Apartment (1) has a number of flats (with BHK 1). These are alloted to each who is fond of living alone.
5. Apartment (2 BHK): 2BHK flats for the grownup to occupy, where occupants are living couples or those who are happy to live together.
6. Apartment (1 BHK): Apartment (1) has a number of flats (with BHK 1). These are alloted to each who is fond of living alone.
7. Apartment (2 BHK): 2BHK flats for the grownup to occupy, where occupants are living couples or those who are happy to live together.
8. Teaching/ training: there are big rooms. If students from outside approach, they will be given teaching help.
9. Library: inmates are able to promote reading habit. They can sit, read and discuss.
10. Entertainment centre: Any entertainment as per the individual interest of the inmates.
11. Spiritual abode: For spiritual needs like prayers and songs the inmates can gather together.
12. Prayer hall: The elderly Interest in continuing their prayers will be given facilities in different prayer halls.
13. Ground: To go and Play
14. Health centre: Health Care will be provided by experienced medical personnel.
15. Auditorium: For meetings and gatherings, for organizing yoga and exercise, the auditorium can be used.
16. Industrial complex: At the inmates initiative small industrial complex may be started.
17. Waste disposal: The waste generated in the city will be disposed using modern technology.
18. Agricultural land: Using self initiatives, inmates may use this land for cultivation.
19. Fruit farm: For production of fruits for healthy those who want fruits.
20. Animal farm: For milk and food, animal farms may be used.
21. Store room: Excess materials from farm and vegitable garden.
22. Pathway: the inmates can at any time use there pathway, on the sides of which oxygen producing plants are grown.
23. Resting benches: On the side of the pathways.
24. Water Tank: Pure water storage, Tank for drinking water.
25. Solar energy: Energy for the abode will be produced. Solar panels will be spread.
26. River beside the city, the choice falls on the location as resolved by the initiators of the project.

27. Trees with in the city are planted in plenty.

The two hall marks of the 21st century are 'population ageing' and 'urbaniza-tion'. Cities and communities play a key role in enabling people to live longer and healthier. An age-friendly city or community is health promoting. It is designed for diversity, inclusion, and cohesion, including across all ages and capacities.

A Grown up-friendly city or community has accessible and safe road and transport infrastructure. The people there stay active. They keep connected. They contribute to their community's economic, social, and cultural life. A grownup-friendly city can foster solidarity among generations. It facilitates social relationships between residents of all ages. Grown up-friendly city has mechanisms to reach out to older people at risk of social isolation.

If research shows light to the nation builders in finding areas of human life to which their attention shall be immediately drawn leading to the development of the nation, this research is one. If this chapter turns into a vivifier to physical, mental, and psychological strength, the chapter as the fruit of research, this work will be a gesture of pride.

## FUTURE RESEARCH DIRECTIONS

The model proposed here is one appropriate to the conditions and ambience in India. Abiding by the general concept of the model applicable to India each country in the world scattered in different parts of the world divided by various specific reasons may develop a model each suited to the concerned country and may apply the model. This will help the grown up humans live with pleasure longer than they hope to live.

The findings of the research solve not only the results of the specific issue of the grown up people but many more issues concerning the survival of humanity on the face of the earth. The researcher stakes claims that the success of this research is unique. The study here opens up prospective research for unique future for mankind to live a life with better prosperity and peace. The researcher suggests application of holacracy, a not much applied management concept to get practised in "heaven on earth". Here there is only one caste, one community, one creed, one race, one gender; all belong to one category in every activity. Freedom flourishes here where there is no hierarchy. Freedom wins the heart of everybody where- a doctor, an engineer, an administrative officer, a carpenter, a mason, a paddy worker, all are considered equal in this city of grace.

## CONCLUSION

The researcher is contented as the study has been successful to solve the problems of the grown-ups. The study proposes a permanent solution as it is submitted to the world for perusal and implementation. The researcher feels that the conclusion will lead to a valuable suggestion to the discussions in the U.N general Assembly. At a time when even the 193 nations in the U.N. are undecided on the issue initiated by the researcher, with all humility the researcher would like to say that the proposed Indian model, which has never been implemented, and which yearns for implementation, can be a beacon light for the rest of the countries in the world. The researcher suggests the phrase "graceful growing for the grownup" to live in the ambiance of fresh cold breeze blowing on the water side with soothing, peace-getting experience.

*"Grow old along with me! The best is yet to be."- Robert Browning*

*Growing Gracefully is the proposed Indian Viable Model.*

# REFERENCES

Ageing. (2013, Oct 2) In *Social for Cultural Anthropology*. Aging | Society for Cultural Anthropology (culanth.org)

Ageing and Health. (2022, Oct 1). In *World Health Organization*. https://www.who.int/news-room/fact-sheets/detail/ageing-and-health

Aging: The Biology of Senescence. (n.d). In *National Library of Medicine*. Aging: The Biology of Senescence - Developmental Biology - NCBI Bookshelf (nih.gov)

Bata. (n.d.). In *Wikipedia*.https://en.wikipedia.org/wiki/Bata_Corporation

Bodner, E., & Lazar, A. (2008). Ageism among Israeli students: Structure and demographic influences. *International Psychogeriatrics*, 20(5), 1046–1058. DOI: 10.1017/S1041610208007151 PMID: 18405396

Boffoli, D., Scacco, S. C., Vergari, R., Solarino, G., Santacroce, G., & Papa, S. (1994). Decline with age of the respiratory chain activity in human skeletal muscle. *Biochimica et Biophysica Acta*, 1226(1), 73–82. DOI: 10.1016/0925-4439(94)90061-2 PMID: 8155742

Clarfield, M. (2011). Grow old along with me! The best is yet to be. *Canadian Medical Association Journal*, 183(10), E693–E694. DOI: 10.1503/cmaj.101431

Cuddy, A. J. C., Norton, M. I., & Fiske, S. T. (2005). This old stereotype: The pervasiveness and persistence of the elderly stereotype. *The Journal of Social Issues*, 61(2), 267–285. DOI: 10.1111/j.1540-4560.2005.00405.x

Cylus, J., & Al Tayara, L. (2021) Health, an ageing labour force, and the economy: does health moderate the relationship between population age-structure and economic growth? *Social Science and Medicine*, 287. ISSN 0277-9536. Health, an ageing labour force, and the economy: Does health moderate the relationship between population age-structure and economic growth? - ScienceDirect

de Jong Gierveld, J., & Hagestad, G. O. (2006). Perspectives on the Integration of Older Men and Women. *Research on Aging*, 28(6), 627–637. DOI: 10.1177/0164027506291871

Dykstra, P. A., & Hagestad, G. O. (2007). Roads less taken: Developing a nuanced view of older adults without children. [Google Scholar]. *Journal of Family Issues*, 28(10), 1275–1310. DOI: 10.1177/0192513X07303822

Fan, K. (2007). Zonal asymmetry of the Antarctic Oscillation. Geophysical Research Letters 34: . issn: 0094-8276.DOI: 10.1029/2006GL028045

Global Economic Issues of an Aging Population (2024,Oct 30). *In Investiopedia*. https://www.investopedia.com/articles/investing/011216/4-global-economic-issues -aging-population.asp

Gracia, E., & Herrero, J. (2004). Determinants of social integration in the community: An exploratory analysis of personal, interpersonal and situational variables. *Journal of Community & Applied Social Psychology*, 14(1), 1–15. DOI: 10.1002/casp.746

Hart, R., Setlow, R. B., & Woodhead, A. D. (1977). Evidence that pyrimidine dimers in DNA can give rise to tumors. *Proceedings of the National Academy of Sciences of the United States of America*, 74(12), 5574–5578. DOI: 10.1073/pnas.74.12.5574 PMID: 271984

Hu, B., Cartagena-Farias, J., Brimblecombe, N., Jadoolal, S., & Wittenberg, R. (2024). Projected costs of informal care for older people in England. *The European Journal of Health Economics*, 25(6), 1057–1070. DOI: 10.1007/s10198-023-01643-1 PMID: 38085432

Integration, S. (n.d.). In *Wikipedia*https://en.wikipedia.org/wiki/Social_integration #:~:text=Social%20integration%20is%20the%20process,society%20that%20is%20 receiving%20them

International Monetary Fund (IMF). (2023). "From Setbacks to Comebacks: Reforms to Build Resilience and Prosperity." *Chapter 2 in International Monetary Fund, Middle East and Central Asia Regional Economic Outlook: Building Resilence and Fostering Sustainable Growth, October 2023*, Washington, D.C.

Loretto, W., Duncan, C., & White, P. (2000). Ageism and employment: Controversies, ambiguities and younger people's perceptions. *Ageing and Society*, 20(3), 279–302. DOI: 10.1017/S0144686X00007741

Murray, V., & Holliday, R. (1981). Increased error frequency of DNA polymerases from senescent human fibroblasts. *Journal of Molecular Biology*, 146(1), 55–76. DOI: 10.1016/0022-2836(81)90366-1 PMID: 7265228

Rights of Older People. (2021, August 24). In www.hrw.org. https://www.hrw.org/ news/2021/08/24/russia-insufficient-home-services-older-people

Staying the Course on Reforms: Progress Amidst Challenges (2024, october 17) In *World Bank Group*. https://www.worldbank.org/en/news/press-release/2024/10/ 17/nigeria-staying-the-course-on-reforms-progress-amidst-challenges#:~:text=%E2 %80%9CGDP%20is%20projected%20to%20grow,naira%20and%20increased%20 gasoline%20prices

Uhlenberg, P. (2000). Why Study Age Integration? *The Gerontologist*, 40, 276–281. DOI: 10.1093/geront/40.3.276 PMID: 10853513

UNESCAP. (2016) Long-Term for Older Persons in India. SDD-SPPS Project Working Papers Series: Long-Term Care for older persons in Asia and the Pacific. https://www.unescap.org/sites/default/files/SDD%20Working%20Paper%20Ageing %20Long%20Term%20Care%20India%20v1-2.pdf

Vitman, A., Iecovich, E., & Alfasi, N. (2014, April). Ageism and Social Integration of Older Adults in Their Neighborhoods in Israel. [Ageism and Social Integration of Older Adults in Their Neighborhoods in Israel | The Gerontologist | Oxford Academic ] [oup.com]. *The Gerontologist*, 54(2), 177–189. DOI: 10.1093/geront/ gnt008 PMID: 23463803

Weismann, A. (1891). The duration of life. In Poulton, E. B., Schonland, S., & Shipley, A. E. (Eds.), *Essays on Heredity and Kindred Subjects* (2nd ed., pp. 163–256). Oxford University Press.

What is Russia like for older people? (n.d.). In *The Bearr Trust*.https://bearr.org/ regional-news/what-is-russia-like-for-older-people/#:~:text=for%20older%20 workers.-,Society%20valued%20older%20people.,vulnerable%20sectors%20of%20 the%20population

# Chapter 5
# Technology Improves the Quality of Life for Elderly People

**S. Srinivasan**
https://orcid.org/0009-0002-0179-9849

*Department of Humanities and Social Sciences, Graphic Era University, Dehradun, India*

**N. Rajavel**
https://orcid.org/0000-0001-7270-7708

*Department of Social Work, Bharathidasan University, Khajamalai Campus, Trichy, India*

## ABSTRACT

*The study focused on how technology improves the lives of elderly people. The study emphasizes life satisfaction, quality of life, social support, subjective well-being, life satisfaction among older adults, and social networks. Technology can improve the lives of elderly people. How the Theories of Specialization in Old Age can enhance the quality of life. The research study was conducted in Trichy District, Tamil Nadu, India. The research design used cross-sectional analysis. The study selected 75 rural and 75 urban samples, totaling 150 samples collected in the research. The researcher used multi-stage sampling. The findings of the study are aimed at understanding the impact of quality of life on older adults. To identify the subjective well-being and how technology usage helps older adults cope with situations.*

DOI: 10.4018/979-8-3693-7753-6.ch005

## INTRODUCTION

WHO Reports that Quality of Life (QoL) it includes the physical and mental health, emotional well being and social function. Older adult 65 years various three dimension was used QoL and needs for health behavior for the study. As per the WHO report in 2050 the number older people will be very low living middle income countries and it is reflect the population ageing is much faster than in the past. In 2020 the older adults aged 60 years and children younger than those 5 years. The report emphasis the 2015 to 2050 the proportion of population over 60 years it is nearly double the rate 12% to 22%. To examine the research study based on the clinical aspects to physical activity has on quality life for older adults. The study focused on causes change in QoL. Psychological aspects of satisfaction better geriatric outcome for the health status and health related QoL. The study deep understanding cause change in QoL has significant implication and implementation for the promotion of physical activity in the older adults (Rajeski & Mihalko, 2001).

Examine the study activities of daily living (ADL) it is associated with various dimensions. Depression focused on two dimensions and this study mainly emphasis on the memory problems. Social functioning and physical activity can implement the health care it can utilize the emotional well-being (Baernholdt et al., 2012). Explore the study reflects the importance of QoL the study 38 facets of in different 22 countries for older adults their demographic gender, age, and health of the older adults. The outcome of the study 57.8% were women, 70.1% men were healthy. This study focused on the various importance of QoL in the facet were having their energy, happiness details, well functioning the body part, and their free from pain (Molzahn et al., 2010). Good health and well-being are most important for older adults, and there is a need to address rehabilitation and resettlement support for health promotion within the system's environment (Srinivasan & Ilango, 2021).

## Impact of Technology for Older Adults

The technology support for the effects of tele monitoring system devise to useful for the QoL for older adults (Lippi et al., 2023).Technology improve more useful for older adults because the during the COVID-19 situation more supported for the technology advancement easily access the video call, with use of smart-phone digital devise play a vital role in the time more useful for the elderly people easily communicate their children and easily access the medicine and doctor appointment and suggestion received through digital way (Murciano-Hueso et al., 2022). The finding of the study there are nine groups of technologies can improve the QoL for older adults. Technology can support and impact the gender, education and age, area of residence to technologically examine. The highest rated technology to enhance the QoL for older adults. The technology can improve the QoL and new knowledge to identify their needs to expect for the future current utilized for the older adults (Halicka & Surel, 2020).

The clearly explore the study smart living it is essential for older adults their living conditions health, safety and housing. Technological can satisfy the older people their needs. The future study use for the humanoid Rudy Robot for the older adults in the smart living. How the technology can provide the revolution for the older adult's life the new technology television, internet, smart phone system (Halicka & Surel, 2022). Technology to address the needs for older adults to minimizing the negative impact of the environment and future generations. The aim of the study to provide technological improve the enhance the QoL for the adults compromising the well-being for the future aspects generation like ecological, social and ethical perspectives. Gerontological to improve the QoL and older adults while remain the sustainable (Halicka, 2024).

## Purpose of the Chapter

The purpose of the chapter, Technology to Improve Quality of Life for Older Adults, is to discuss various technologies that can enhance the lives of older adults by focusing on health and social aspects for independent living. It can address the physical conditions, cognitive, and emotional support for the older adults' challenges and barriers faced by individuals. The technology can support reducing isolation and independent living conditions to improve the overall well-being of older adults. The older adults face challenges in adopting new technology, such as digital literacy and accessibility for user-friendliness. The study addresses how the government and non-governmental organizations can support older adults by providing hands-on training for technological innovation to access the technology. The study significantly provides an understanding of technology access for older adults. The technology improves the quality of life for older adults.

## TECHNOLOGY CAN IMPROVE THE QUALITY OF LIFE FOR ADULTS

Technology can play a significant role in improving the quality of life for older adults in different aspects. There are some important factors to consider.

The study clearly explains that older adults experience a decline in their daily living conditions, and their health deteriorates. Technology plays a vital role in improving the quality of life. The technology tools support older people in accessing goods and services, as well as the infrastructure, which is important to understand for this study (Desai et al., 2022). The study emphasizes gerontechnology to enhance the quality of life for older adults in various aspects, including innovation, demand, socio-ethics, usability, and functionality. The study variables used are age and gender to influence the assessment of older adults. It explores how robots can support gerontechnologies. The study conducted in 2018 involved nearly 643 different older adults from voivodships in Poland (Halicka, 2019).

**Device Gadgets**: The health devices support older adults' fitness by enabling them to frequently track and monitor various aspects, such as heart rate, oxygen levels, sleep patterns, and physical activities. These devices provide real-time data for health assessments.

**Telemedicine**: The healthcare profession can support and reduce the need for regular hospital visits by enabling patients to utilize healthcare services in their own homes.

**Patient Monitoring System**: The device can track their diabetic levels and heart-related diseases, identify their hypertension, and support the doctor in intervening in their situations.

## AI TECHNOLOGIES SUPPORT FOR OLDER ADULTS

Mobility aids support older adults, such as wheelchairs, walkers, and electric vehicles, to help them maintain their independence. There are various devices, such as hearing aids and smart glasses, to improve sensory abilities and enhance communication effectively. Smart home technologies are becoming more viable in Western countries. Voice-activated assistants like Alexa and Google Home are more helpful for turning on lights and reminding users to take medicine, allowing control of the overall household without physical support.

Social connectivity is more useful through media such as video calls like Zoom, Skype, Google Meet, and WhatsApp calls. These platforms are particularly beneficial for older adults, as they support communication with family and friends, making it easier to speak and connect. This helps reduce feelings of loneliness and isolation. Virtual reality can support immersive environments for older adults, allowing them to easily interact with their peer groups and engage actively. They can even travel without leaving home, enabling them to stay connected (Baker et al., 2019).

## Assistive Technology Support for Mental Health

It can support memory apps that are useful for focusing and solving problems, which can help delay cognitive decline and promote brain health. They are more useful for online therapy and provide counseling services to support older adults in coping with depression, anxiety, and stress, which are more prevalent among older adults (Guay et al., 2017).

## AI Support for Older People's Safety and Security

Assistive technology can advance the safety of older adults. It can be used for home-based detection, alerting for emergencies, and automatically notifying caregivers to provide medical services. GPS trackers are more useful for tracking older adults who suffer from memory loss problems like dementia and other complications. They can be very helpful in preventing them from wandering before facing danger (Qassem, 2015).

## Assist for Robotic Support

Robotic support for caregivers of older adults can handle day-to-day activities, allowing older adults to maintain their independence for a longer period. The robot can support social connections and provide therapeutic support, such as "*Paro*." It can offer companionship to older adults, helping them feel less alone. It is useful for assisting older people (Chen et al., 2022).

## The Use of Digital Platforms for Entertainment and Learning

Online courses, such as e-learning opportunities for older people, are more useful for learning new skills, hobbies, and even languages. They help keep individuals mentally active, which seems to alleviate their worries. They can use and enjoy music, movies, series, and other digital platforms that are more useful for entertaining older adults during their leisure time (López-Sintas et al., 2017).

## Transport and Mobility Support

There are self-driving cars available due to advancements in technology. They are safer and more reliable for transportation, allowing individuals who can no longer drive to participate in social events, healthcare appointments, and errands. There is technology that is useful for transport. There are plenty of apps that can support this, such as Ola, Uber, BlaBlaCar, Savaari, Rapido, and Red Taxi. Numerous apps are available to assist with transport and mobility for older adults.

## Using Technology for Personal Care for Older Adults

Technology can be more useful in addressing the care and support needs of older adults. It can provide more support for reminders about medication, predict health risk conditions, and help manage their diets for regular activities. Real-time data can support and protect them. The smart medication device is useful for older adults to ensure their dosage levels are correct at the right time, reducing the need for medication errors (Chang et al., 2019).

## Technology can Support Financial Management

Financial management for older adults is made easier through technology, which allows them to access and process transactions without leaving their homes. They can manage all their payments using online banking tools, making it easier for older adults to pay bills such as electricity, phone, water, and housing. Everything can be done through online methods, reducing their physical trips (Kolaki, 2017).

## Geriatrics

"*Geriatrics*" is a combination of two Greek words namely "*Geron*" meaning old man and "*iatrikos*" meaning medical treatment. The term "*Geriatrics*" was coined by American Physician. Ignatz Nascher in the year 1909. It deals with that area of medical practice, which is concerned with the physiological and disease problems of the aged.

## The Process of Ageing: Biological, Social and Psychological

Biological ageing status quite early in the life period, the body loses the functional capacity at the rate of 0.8% per year after age of 30. The cumulative impact at later states is considerable. These are internal and external viable changes. Slowly the body clock winds down and ultimately stops. The mid-phase of body growth is a period when there is an essential balance between the phase of growth and decay. Biological aging occurs in a manner akin to a biological clock.I t regulates the aging lifespan. The study mainly focuses on various factors, such as biological theories like genetic damage and error theories related to cellular aging (Srinivasan & Rajavel, 2025).

So ageing involves two continuous processes that processes that proceed simultaneously in the life-time of an individual and those process an contradictory to each other. On one hand, there is the process of breaking down or shrinkage that includes their hair for gray and loss of the teeth in their body.

Psychological, ageing refer to person's adaptive capacities i.e., how well he/her adapts to changing environmental conditions with the average of his group: how well she or he can cope up in their society and the person can herself or himself to think the behavioral patterns. Psychologically speaking, ageing is associated with progressive declines in aerobic power, muscle strength, thermoregulation, and reaction speed to acuity of special senses in most environments. Socially, ageing refers to the roles or obligation for the social habits for the older people with respects of the society. Whether behaves in a manner suitable in the eyes of the society to his age (Venkateswarlu, 2008).

In late adulthood, people come to the realization that they can no longer occupy the center stage of their world. They are called upon, and increasingly call upon themselves, to reduce middle adulthood's heavy responsibilities and to live in a change relationship with society and themselves. Moving out of centre stage can be a traumatic affair since people receive less recognition and have less power and authority. Their generation is no longer the dominant one. As part of the "grandparent" generation within the family, individuals still can be helpful to their growth of spring and serve as source of wisdom, guidance and support. However, a major shift has taken place (Olson, 2022). As Levinson points out, it is time for a person's offspring, as they approach and enter middle adulthood, to assimilate the major responsibility and authority in the family. If authority is not relinquished, again the offspring may become tyrannical rulers despotic, unwise, unloved, and unloving-and their adult off-spring may become puerile adults unable to love their parents or themselves (Azar, 2003).

# THEORIES OF SPECIALIZATION OLD AGE

## Disengagement Theory

The disengagement theory was the result of a five-year investigation of a sample of 275 elderly people aged between 50 and 90 years. The study noted that disengagement was generally initiated by the individuals themselves or by the social system. Retirement, for example, is an event that release older people from specific social roels and enables them to become disengaged to some extent. Loss of a spouse serves as another example. In time, when disengagement is complete, the balance that existed between the person and society in the middle years has shifted to greater physchological distance. It is relationship and social interaction was decrease (Ragini & Salwan,)

The study argue that many of the societal conditions that have forced the elderly into restricted environments are likely to change in the future (e.g. people are retiring earlier, improved health care will enable more older people to remain more physically active; higher social security benefits may increase the economic security of the retired and enable them to engage in more active lifestyles.

## Activity Theory

Activity theory it is successful ageing suggests to retired for the individual prefer to remain productive and active. In contrast to the theory of disengagement, this view of point suggests that the aged prefer to resist preoccupation with the self and psychological distance from society. The theory emphasizes that older adults find it difficult to provide substitutes for pastimes that align with their beliefs and interests, as their abilities to perform roles relinquished beyond middle age diminish.

## Role Theory

The role theory is interlinked with older adults and their social position. Their social roles define the status of the occupants and are oriented towards their pattern of expectations regarding rights and obligations. Each person has their own status, and some have multiple statuses associated with their roles. The system can protect and is likely to change in further aspects. This can be psychologically devastating, as there is no substitute for the activities they have found. Thus, the greater the number of role resources with which individuals enter old age, the better off they will be in adjusting to the demoralizing effects of role exits (Richardson & Barusch, 2005).

## Continuity Theory

The theory provides a comprehensive understanding of people's habits, preferences, and lifestyles as they age. Older adults can adapt to the situation and consistently adjust their previous behavior to cope with aging.

## Socio-Emotional Theory

The socio-emotional well-being of individuals as they age is the focus of the theory. Older adults tend to understand the importance of relationships and social networks in providing emotional fulfillment in their lives.

## Optimization with Compensation Theory

The theory suggests that older people optimize their skills to achieve their desired goals. It can focus on older adults' physical abilities, and it can compensate through strategic planning. This can significantly help them adjust their expectations.

## Age Stratification Theory

Structural effects on individuals are based on their age. The theory plays an important role in social norms and their expectations, influencing the lifespan and affecting older adults' lives.

## Gerontranscendence Theory

This theory clearly mentions individual age and their previous materialistic rational perspectives towards the cosmic, which inspire their lives and lead to increased life satisfaction.

All the theories provide valuable insights into the complexities that aging people experience as older adults. The theories can develop policies and programs to improve the quality of life for older people.

There are four roles that change older adults. It is the first role that focuses on the attention given to the loss of life and the loss of gainful employment, which affects both partners. It is usually necessary to adapt to the changes and domestic situations (Russel, 2024). The second related loss to the elderly is the loss of income. The elderly may not be able to afford some kinds of activities. Thus, not having a sufficient income and having to make sacrifice not previously made may affect overall life satisfaction. Third, retirement coincides with declining health for many people, although many are automatically retired while they are still in good health. Either way, the elderly discover that as they age, their physical conditions deteriorate and they may have to give up some activities and moderate others. Finally, changes in the family often require role realignment. As children leave the home, the role behavior and expectations of the parents change. By the retirement years, help and assistance patterns have shifted, sometimes with assistance following from child to parent instead of the reverse. Severe illness or death of a spouse also calls for significant adjustment in the partner's role.

The reduction in role activity as worker and as parent, combined with declining health and usually reduced income. Constitute the realistic framework within which older people enacts their many roles in later life. Many person-old, young, people of influence and the man in the street must be aware of the role losses and the necessary role realignments which are an integral part of later life. There must be a clear recognition for the old age it can some period of new role and opportunities. Public and private organizations can aid in reaching broad goals of spending the new leisure time of later life constructively, and achieving positive and well-integrated roles within the family, the community and in a broad spectrum of groups and organizations.

## Subjective Well-Being and Ageing

Subjective well-being is a 'real' and universal concept. A simple linguistic review shows that an enquiry into subjective well-being is a part of a friendly greeting in many languages. Traditionally, quality of life measures tend to be 'objective' measures of income, education, availability of social and health services and the like people's feeling were considered 'subjective' and therefore irrelevant or unreliable. Certainly, there is now enough evidence of a growing incidence of low levels of well-being among the aged in Aisa, particularly in India for which enough data is currently available, people tend to develop most in areas where they reliably meet success. By middle age, most have identified preferences and competencies that predictably lead to satisfying results and have incorporated them into their identities. It is not difficult to maintain motivation toward inner continuity in the presence of proven patterns for producing a sense of inner well-being. It is social involvement and it is religious activities is essential for the well-being of the aged connecting with family members, friends, neighbors, work colleagues and community groups brings happiness to all (Waite & Das, 2010).

The affective component of SWB center's around the broad definition given above for happiness; positive over negative affect pleasant versus unpleasant affect. The "cognitive" component is identified by each individual life satisfaction it can chosen and include a measure of personal control and it can conscious cognitive judgment for the one's life and judgment up to the person that shapes SWB. Specifically, because many individuals are living longer lives and becoming increasingly aware of their well-being, age has become a major contributor to the level of SWB. In spite of increase in the likelihood of chronic illness, health declines, loss of spouses and social supports, research suggests that older people do not report being unhappier than their younger peers (Jones, 2001).

The connotation of harmony for the satisfaction of desires, goals, subjective well-being, and psychological aspects of well-being has surfaced in the conceptualization of well-being throughout the history of psychology (Srinivasan & Rajavel, 2015). It is connotative as harmonious satisfaction of one's desires and goals Subjective well-being and psychological well-being have surfaced as the two most popular conceptualizations of well-being in the history of psychology (Mehrotra et al., 2013).

## Life Satisfaction and Ageing

The life satisfaction of ageing it is successful adaption it like morale or life satisfaction or well-being perfect they happy to satisfied in their life. Neugarten, Havighurst and Topin 1961 have operationally defined life satisfaction as 1. Zest vs Apathy which relates to interest of the response and their degree of involvement 2. Resolution and fortitude which refers to the acceptance of responsibility for own life as opposed to feelings of resignation and passively accepting things 3. To congruence to achieve their life goals. 4. Positive mind and self concept 5. Happy mood and it reflects spontaneous, happy, optimistic attitude of one who enjoys life. Social production function theory assumes that people produce their own well-being by trying to optimize achievement of universal needs within constrains they are facing. In accordance with economic and psychological theory, human beings are seen as active agents who choose cost-effective ways to produce well-being (Barrett & Murk, 2006).

Cost does refer to all sort of scarce resources that one can give up, such as money, time and one more aspect is life satisfaction and is becoming little clearer that what is considered of high importance for one's sense of subjective well-being at one developmental stage may be less it relevant to another stage. Elwell and Maltbie-Crannell (1981s) found income to be having a strong, direct effect on life satisfaction for older men, but weaker and indirect effects for older women. As people age they have to deal with biological, psychological and social challenges. Further reaching old age successfully and unscathed will be influenced by the various experiences, activity, environmental stresses, social contacts and social support etc. in the last twenty years research on elderly has been given attention because of the reason increase the number elderly in worldwide and due to socio-economic and technological development, prevalence of well being among the older people has risen phenomenally, which has caused to dwell into this period for years together. The study for elderly people become essential to preserve to cure improve the life enhances their older people who are dwelling in their community.

# RELEVANT REVIEW LITERATURE

The study emphasized the need of training in adaption skills such as orientation activities of daily activities coping with relocation and memory, problem solving, self-care, coping with anxiety and depression, facing bereavement and loss and confronting death (Wanasphitaksakul, 2009). They have done study Jerome et al., (2006) on physical activity participation by presence and type of functional deficits in older people. This study sought to identified categories of functional deficits associated with activity level and evaluated the potential for older women to increase their physical activity level. The study method community dwelling women age 70-79 years from the health for ageing. Meeting physical activity recommendations was defined as 150 minutes per week to moderate the physical activity, and inactivity was defined as no weekly moderate intensity physical activity. Hierarchical categories of functional deficits were based on self-reported difficulty in four functional domains (ie., mobility/exercise tolerance, upper extremity, higher functioning and self-care) and self-reports ranged from no difficulty to difficulty in all four domains. The finding of the study the prevalence of inactivity and meeting activity recommendations were 14.4% and 12.7% respectively. The older adults could include the treatment or management and functional deficits chronic conditions and poor strength.

Explore the research study daily living functions for the elderly requiring home visits a study at a comprehensive assessment clinic for the elderly. The study community based cross sectional study lifestyle activity to depress the mood among the older people the study conducted in Japan the sample size was 656 men and women the age group between 65< older who lived in rural area in Japan, neither institutionalized nor hospitalized and who did not have symptoms of dementia. The study found that less interaction with neighbors, relations and friends they have highly associated with depressed mood for men (Arai et al., 2007).

It is important to engage in several types of activities relating to society, leisure and children/grand children to be in less depressed mood. Even if they were socially inactive, if they had frequent contact with family and children grandchildren or going out for pleasure they were less likely to be depressed. Distinguishing gender differences in lifestyle activity patterns and the association of activities with depressed mood will help to guide the development of depression intervention program (Curran et al., 2020).

Review outcome of the study to productive engagement of the physical and mental health older lives. The study representative physical and mental health for the older adults above the 60 years. They have presented secondary analysis of data from American Changing Live Study (N=1,644). Self rated health functional impairment and depressive mood were regressed on measures of engagement during the previous 12 months using generalized estimating equations, while control the socio economic conditions and health measures of the previous wave (O'Loughlin et al., 2017).

## TECHNOLOGY CAN IMPROVE THE QUALITY OF LIFE

The usage of technology is very important for maintaining a high quality of life, especially for older adults. The technology was accessible and affordable to use advanced technology for individual needs. The technology plays a crucial role in supporting the quality of life for older adults in various aspects such as health, safety, security, social engagement, and independence. The use of technology in their lives enhances the quality of their overall well-being. The study provides comprehensive results for quality of life; it includes older adults with diabetes and hypoglycemia for safety and their interpersonal support. QoL improved for the older adults' hypoglycemic safety, with nearly 86% and 85% of the respondents. The interpersonal support for nearly 37% of them is consistent with the level of independence and confidence. The satisfaction with device accuracy ($p < 0.05$) and usability ($p < 0.01$) is higher among older age groups ($p < 0.01$) and more frequent receivers. The quality of life measured for the RT-CGM is a common benefit of the satisfaction derived from device usage. The study finally provides the RT-CGM data to provide the reason that the device might enhance the QoL for older adults (Polonsky & Hessler, 2013).

The study mainly focused on three variables: socio-demographic aspects, health status, and various technology usage. The technology considered in this study includes ICT such as smartphones, computers, laptops, and tablets. The result of the study shows that nearly 3.06% of them are using smartphones, 6.65% of them own a computer, and 10.91% of them have a tablet. However, they are using these devices as "never" (Fotteler et al., 2023). The study addresses the advancement of technology, which has the main purpose of promoting independence for older adults. The older adults are less likely to adopt new technology themselves. The study conducts independently with those who are older living in rural communities and living complexes, including one of the oldest old and rural older individuals. The study covered five factors regarding older adults using technology: their frustration and usability concerns, transportation, help assistance, self-monitoring, and gaming. These factors pertain to how older adults utilize technology (Heinz et al., 2013).

### Quality of Life

The quality of life for older people enhances their well-being and satisfaction with life experiences and age. The concept of the study encompasses the physical, mental, and socio-emotional aspects of older adults. It includes several factors:

health, financial stability, emotional well-being, and social connections that support the quality of life for older adults in their environments. Today, life expectancy has increased due to improved medical technologies, which can delay death. The longevity of individuals is related to aging and the presence of diseases and disabilities. Quality of life for older adults improves with prolonged life and their individual resources, as well as a sound environment for support. It is very important to understand the psychological, social, and spiritual aspects of older adults in the context of aging care for their lives. The longer life of older individuals in the community can support the improvement of older adults' quality of life. It can investigate the aspects pertaining to the quality of life for older adults.

The study conducted 580 aged respondents 305 men and 275 women in five district of Tamil Nadu. The findings of the study women old-group and the rural elders are disadvantaged interms of economic, physical, psychological and social indication, indicating that they are having comparatively poor quality of life than their counterparts (Sundarmathy & Kannan, 2019).

The study examines the quality of life of elderly people living in rural areas. The study used multiple regression to analyze the quality of life, including chronic diseases, age, hospitalization, education, and gender. It focused on chronic-related diseases, hospitalization details, income status, and marital conditions. The results can assess the quality of life (Li & Wang, 2022).

The research study addresses the quality of life in Japanese rural areas. The study emphasizes three important aspects of quality of life: health perception, life satisfaction, and self-confidence. The study can provide insights into older adults' life satisfaction and their confidence at ages over 55 and those under 55. It examines older adults' quality of life satisfaction, women's self-confidence, and the psychotic scores related to overall satisfaction. The study covered three aspects of quality of life: psychosocial factors, health interventions, and health education care and support for older people to improve their life conditions (Kitamura et al., 2002).

The study covered various dimensions of older adults' quality of life to assess factors such as physical functioning, gender, illness, age, and habits, including tobacco use. Older adults check their health, which is significant for their social quality. Their emotional functioning is associated with their gender, illness, and medical check-ups from the last year (Gallegos et al., 2009).The condition of the incarcerated older population has also not been neglected, yet there is not much research on criminology and correctional aspects of this study (Srinivasan, 2015). The study mainly focused on the QoL health, mental health and Valuation of Life (VoL) the objective of the study longitudinal and physical. The result of the study health changes and (VoL) was little significance when QoL and mental health mediators came into the picture.

The study disability and psychosocial aspects of old age. The cross sectional analysis 999 people aged 65 years for older adults. The study variables included health problems, limitation of the study self-perceptions of health, optimism, quality of life. The result of the study the aged people 80+ years the prevalence of the health and disability, it is good for health and QoL. The oldest age group those in better health were more optimistic, but more problems meant lower for the self perception of the health and QoL, The major discussion of the study does not fully confirm the disability paradox high disability and high optimism and self for the QoLThe quality of life for elderly people is somewhat satisfactory, but some marginalized community older adults are affected by TB, respiratory diseases, and health complications at a high level (Srinivasan et al., 2023). The author emphasized the health levels of elderly people in SAARC countries, highlighting their demographic, social, and economic conditions in relation to health needs and living arrangements. While these are fairly extensive in other countries, they are woefully inadequate in India (Srinivasan et al., 2015).

## Subjective Well-Being

Subjective well-being and its relationship to physical activities have not been systematically investigated. The study identified using qualitative interviews with a purpose sample 23 community dwelling chines older adults the age group between 55-75 years and 12 women, 16 were physically active and 7 physically inactive. To use the cross case analysis 7 dimensions of SWB emerged: Physical, psychological, developmental, marital, spiritual, sociopolitical, and social. Although elements of SWB may be shared across cultures, specific distinctions were identified. Active respondents reported for the unique contributions of physical activity physical and psychological developmental elements SWB. The outcome of the study focused on the physical activity for the quality of live in Chinese older adults (Ku et al., 2007).

The major discussion of the study focuses on subjective well-being for elderly people residing in urban areas of Japan. The cross-sectional analysis aims to identify items that address ethnicity, age, gender, literacy, and living conditions related to the mental health of older adults. The Activities of Daily Living (ADL) and their past medical history impact the quality of life, which can affect the pension benefits and public assistance available to older Korean residents in Japan above the age of 65 living in the community (Moon & Mikami, 2007). The qualitative and quantitative study adjusts for gender, family ties, and educational particulars to assess the health and well-being of older adults aged between 68 and 73 years old (Ryan & Willits, 2007).

# Life Satisfaction

The study provides comprehensive insights for older life satisfaction to identify some major antecedents of life satisfaction. Regardless of age for all adults for the major life satisfaction. Life satisfaction can especially social structure, education, family, relation occupations and marital status) and including for the for family and friends and neighborhoods for the meaningful social and leisure activities (Enkvist et al., 2012).

The study investigated for the life satisfaction for predictors for coping style in the gifted men at age 62. The results indicated a high degree of consistency in affective feelings and constructs pertaining to the self. The life investigation and career choice in Terman women at age 62, Measures of satisfaction were more complex for women, as there were various patterns of child bearing and work histories for the group. Marriage was generally positive and the findings for having children vary with the particular combination of work and career paths of the women. Three types of satisfaction were studied; general life satisfaction work pattern and joy in living. Early rating of self confidence and attachments to their own parents were particularly important contributors to their sense of life satisfaction 30 years after the measurement were made (Blurton, 1992).

The study discussed from the 40 year men form Tamilnadu found the men who lived with their spouse have life satisfaction than those who had lost their wises (Chokkanathan et al., 2014). Explore the study found that older people with their spouses, living showed better social adjustment than those whose spouse were not living (Liebig & Ramamurti 2018).

In India, some have also studies different aspects of life satisfaction among the older adults. The study reported Younger activities and attitude inventory and life satisfaction index were used as tools. Health seems to be an important condition for successful ageing especially after 55 years age. In addition, after engagement in leisure and recreational activities seems to be associated with successful ageing. Those who are not well adjusted after 65 years seem to have rather poor health. Further reduced sense of economic security is not exclusively associated poor adjustment. Ageing per seems to affect sense of economic security ever among those who are well adjusted reality orientation engagement seems to aid successful ageing (Sharma, 2008). Similar study on aged women found that marital status and incase for the area residence affect life satisfaction significantly (Devi et al., 2022). In the study according Shubham and Joshi (2021) social interaction was found to be major source of life satisfaction for elderly people.

According to author find the study hopelessness, alienation for life satisfaction for the aged people 109 male and females. The study further divided into married and widowed older people.

Three variables focused on in the study are helplessness, alienation, and life satisfaction concerning older adults' psychological aspects of the test. The results of the study indicate that the married group has lower hopelessness and higher life satisfaction compared to widows and widowers (Chadha et al., 1992).

Although this study focused on mounting interest and attention, this literature is limited in several important ways. In the Indian circumstances, studies on elderly have given attention only to very few aspects pertaining to elderly problems and their mental health and not on the well-being. Indian studies based on the activity and QoL was not evident for the review to conduct by the researcher and many of the Indian studied on older people are not based on grounded theory and also not interventional. The review also indicated that studies on unique characteristics of the older people residing in the Indian cultural setting were sporadic and not aimed at theory building. There the present study focused on describe the enhance the QoL through activity as core concept for older adults.

## Smart Living for Older Adults Using Technology

Smart living for older adults using various technologies such Smartphone's, smart security technologies, digital services it is more use for the older adults. It can use for self monitoring for the health and through automation. The study emphasized the technology can improve the feature cost and smart technology which it can potential for barriers to use. Opinion of the older adults illiterate people not comfortable those who highly qualified easily able to assess the smart technology. The study support for the older adults understanding the smart system developing and deploying the smart technologies in older adults (Harris et al., 2022). The author clearly mention the smart technology can increase the ability for older adults in their home to access and monitor the health and safety conditions to protect the and prevent the fall, accidents and injuries. Smart technologies were more useful to identify for the support living place (Chabot et al., 2019).

The technology can enhance the life, safety, care for the older adults. Technologies can usage for older adults easily access but some time unable to access the technological issues. This study technology can improve the smart home it is compare the between people with direct experience technology and without experience (Ghorayeb et al., 2021).

Smart living environment it is based on the technological to moderate the effective support for older adults. Technology can support for daily activity living more viable (Tannou et al., 2023). The technology adverse support for the health system and impact quality of life to increase the social costs. Smart Living environment to involve the notion of measurement to use the several sensors. It can capture the home or person health status for a long time. Technology can more use for home support for older adults (Tannou et al., 2022).

## Objective of the Study

- To access the socio-economic conditions
- To know the QoL of older adults
- To inquire about the extent of activities among older adults
- To find out the subjective well-being of older adults
- To inquire about life satisfaction in elderly people
- To find out suitable measures for new technology support to effectively utilize older adults in improving their quality of life

## Scope of the Study

The research study mainly concentrates the older adult's well-being, life satisfaction, and quality of life. The study emphasis on demographic aspects of socio economic status, and gender wise, religious aspects, physical and psychological way to find out the results. How the technology support for the older adults and effective utilization. The various theory involved for age replacement for older is an active. The main variable quality of life, subjective well-being and life satisfaction how support for the daily activities in their life.

## RESULTS

*Table 1. Socio demographic details*

| Demographic | Socio Demographic Details | Number of Older Adults | Percentage |
|---|---|---|---|
| Age | 60 to 67 | 87 | 58 |
| | 68 to 77 | 58 | 38.7 |
| | > 77 | 5 | 3.3 |
| Gender | Male | 81 | 54 |
| | Female | 69 | 46 |

continued on following page

*Table 1. Continued*

| Demographic | Socio Demographic Details | Number of Older Adults | Percentage |
|---|---|---|---|
| Marital Status | Married | 116 | 77.3 |
| | Unmarried | 5 | 3.3 |
| | Widow | 28 | 18.4 |
| | Divorce | 1 | 1 |
| Education | Primary | 57 | 38 |
| | Secondary | 47 | 31.3 |
| | UG | 22 | 14.7 |
| | Illiterate | 24 | 16 |
| Religion | Hindu | 90 | 60 |
| | Christian | 49 | 32.7 |
| | Muslim | 11 | 7.3 |
| Area | Rural | 75 | 50 |
| | Urban | 75 | 50 |
| Family Type | Nuclear | 77 | 51.3 |
| | Joint | 57 | 38 |
| | Extended Family | 16 | 10.7 |

Table 1 focused upon the socio demographics profile of the older adults it is based on the various distribution overviews of the categories. The majority of the respondents 58 of the age group between 60 to 67 and 38.7% of the are 68 to 77 age group the majority of the age group 60 to 67 age group number it is increasing the trend. The gender distribution 54% of the older adult's male and 46% of them are female. It is nearly equal ration for the both genders among the older adults. Marital status of the respondents 77.3% of them are married and 18.4% of them widowed and remaining 3.3% of them unmarried or divorced 1%. The educational status of the respondent's primary education 38% of the older adults and remaining low level education the illiterate are 16% of them. The majority of the older adults are Hindu 60% of them. Equal chances are living rural and urban areas in older adults. 51.3% of them are nuclear families and 38% of them join families. The data clearly indicate that social demographic of older adults it is majority of are married, educated at least primary level. The data shown predominance or nuclear family.

*Table 2. Economic statuses of the respondents*

| Economic | Economic Characteristics | No of Respondents | % |
|---|---|---|---|
| Job | Private | 40 | 26.7 |
| | Retired Govt., Job | 41 | 29.8 |
| | No Job | 16 | 10.7 |
| | Agriculture | 27 | 18 |
| | No work | 26 | 14.8 |
| Current Job | Employed | 70 | 46.7 |
| | Unemployed | 80 | 53.3 |
| Housing | Rented | 26 | 17 |
| | Owned | 144 | 83 |
| Financial Problem | Financial Problem | 79 | 52.7 |
| | No Financial issues | 71 | 47.3 |

Table 2 economic characteristics of the older adults it is based on the employment status housing and financial challenges. The employment status for the respondents 26.7% of them private job and retired from the government jobs are 29.8% and 18% are involved in agriculture and 10% of them not have job. It is notable for the 14.8% of them not working at all it is possibly to indicate the dependence of other sources of income and their family support.46.7% of them are employed and unemployed are majority nearly 53.3% of them of respondents for the economic situation for the older adults it is retired for their not actively working. 83% of the respondents owned house it is indicates that stable housing situation for the most. 52.7% of the older adults face financial burden it is economic situation among the substantial problem for older adults. 47.3% of the respondents able to stand in their own financial support. The table clearly evident that the economic situation for the older adults for a number of reasonable still employed and engaged their agriculture. The older adult's ongoing challenges faced in financial aspects living cost and health expenditure or insufficient for the retirement money and old age pension scheme.

*Figure 1. Family income of the respondents*

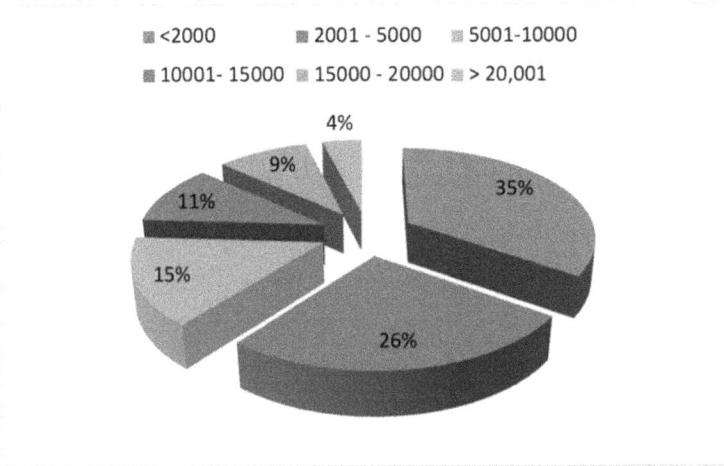

Figure 1 clearly indicate that the family income of the older adults it significant variation of the economic standing for the majority falling into lower income. The majority 52% of the respondents are getting monthly income Rs.2000 it is not sufficient to run their family and many of the unable to get pensions. 39% of the respondents are getting monthly income Rs. 2001 to 5000 it is slightly higher than the lowest group, but it is still representing the low income of their family it is a large section of the older adults struggle for their financial. 23% of the respondents are getting family income Rs. 5001 to 10,000 which could indicate a moderate income level. This cans more financial stability to compare to lower brackets. 16% of the respondents get monthly family income Rs.10001 to 15000 it is relatively comfort-able income though it is still not a high level for the joint family. Rs. 20,001 more than getting 5% of the respondents it is very smaller portion for the older adults, but it is relatively high income. The individual may can save and support for the financial system. The figure clearly mention that older adults face finical problem and especially those who are live in lower income groups the unable to run their family without assistance and minimal support for the pension meet their needs.

*Table 3. Various dimensions of QoL*

| Variables | Dimensions of QoL | No of Respondents | % |
|---|---|---|---|
| General | Low | 78 | 52 |
| | Moderate | 63 | 42 |
| | High | 9 | 6 |

continued on following page

*Table 3. Continued*

| Variables | Dimensions of QoL | No of Respondents | % |
|---|---|---|---|
| Physical Domain | Low | 44 | 29.3 |
| | Moderate | 72 | 51.3 |
| | High | 29 | 19.4 |
| Psychological Dimension | Low | 45 | 30 |
| | Moderate | 76 | 52.3 |
| | High | 29 | 17.7 |
| Social Relationship | Low | 39 | 26 |
| | Moderate | 58 | 55.7 |
| | High | 53 | 18.3 |
| Environment | Low | 39 | 26.3 |
| | Moderate | 74 | 49 |
| | High | 37 | 24.7 |
| Overall QoL | Low | 39 | 26.3 |
| | Moderate | 76 | 50.7 |
| | High | 35 | 23 |

The table provides insights among older adults Quality of Life for various dimension like general aspects, physical, psychological, social an environmental for the older adults. General aspect of QoL Low QoL 52% of the older adults it indicates that half of the older adults face struggles in the overall well being. Physical domain 51.3% of the respondents have it is manageable physical conditions without any sever impacts but 29.3% of the respondents are physical health challenges such as illness or chronic conditions affect a significant portion. Psychological aspects 52.3% of them moderate it indicate that older adults have stable but not optimal for their mental well-being. 30% of the respondents are low psychological QoL it is point to mental health concerns and stress or emotional feelings. Social relationships among majority of the older adults 55.7% moderate low level social interaction. The majority 49% of the respondent's environment satisfaction to suggest average access to services and comfort. 26.3% of the respondent's environment is very low and it is possible for due to poor living conditions and unsafe environments or lack of resources. QoL 50.7% of the respondents experience various aspects of life their fairly well but with room for improvement. The majority of older adults QoL in various dimensions it is significant portion with low QoL in the general psychological aspects. The older adult's well-being adequate it is considered number older adults face physical, mental and social challenges. The overall environment well-being to indicate the pathway for improves enhance the QoL and segment of the population.

*Table 4. Various dimensions of subjective well-being*

| Variables | Dimensions of SWB | No of Respondents | % |
|---|---|---|---|
| General well-being | Low | 92 | 61 |
| | Moderate | 42 | 28 |
| | High | 16 | 11 |
| Expectation achievement | Low | 88 | 59 |
| | Moderate | 32 | 21 |
| | High | 30 | 20 |
| Confidence in Coping | Low | 79 | 52.7 |
| | Moderate | 65 | 43 |
| | High | 6 | 4.3 |
| Transcendence | Low | 83 | 56 |
| | Moderate | 40 | 26 |
| | High | 27 | 18 |
| Family Group Support | Low | 91 | 61 |
| | Moderate | 42 | 28 |
| | High | 17 | 11 |
| Social Support | Low | 104 | 69 |
| | Moderate | 36 | 24 |
| | High | 10 | 7 |
| Primary Group Concern | Low | 61 | 41 |
| | Moderate | 57 | 38 |
| | High | 32 | 21 |
| Inadequate mental mastery | Low | 38 | 25 |
| | Moderate | 94 | 62 |
| | High | 18 | 13 |
| Perceived ill-health | Low | 40 | 27 |
| | Moderate | 87 | 58 |
| | High | 23 | 15 |
| Deficiencies in Social Contacts | Low | 38 | 26 |
| | Moderate | 87 | 57 |
| | High | 25 | 17 |
| General well-being (-) | Low | 47 | 31 |
| | Moderate | 85 | 57 |
| | High | 18 | 12 |

continued on following page

*Table 4. Continued*

| Variables | Dimensions of SWB | No of Respondents | % |
|---|---|---|---|
| Overall Subjective Well-being | Low | 40 | 26 |
| | Moderate | 74 | 50 |
| | High | 36 | 24 |

Table 4 provides various dimensions of subjective well-being among older adults to reveals the both strengths and challenges among the different areas living. General well being 61% of the respondents are low general well-being it is indicate the significant portion for the older adults their overall life satisfaction low. It is reflect older adults face life it highly pathetic conditions. Expectation achievement 59% of the respondent's low life achieving expectation it is reflect the unfulfilled desires. The coping confidence also very low 52.7% of the respondents cope with life challenges and feeling vulnerability and stress faced. Transcendence the low level 56% of the respondents has limited sense of connection to higher values of spiritual well-being. Family group support 61% of the respondents is low family support to highlight the social isolation in the family ties very weak. 69% of the respondents are low social support it is indicate that social isolation for community member very low. 41% of the respondents are having primary group concern it weaker bonds and less reliance on close social circles. Mental mastery inadequate the 62% of the respondents moderate the inadequacy to implying the manage their mental health with occasional difficulties. Perceived Ill-Health the majority 58% of the respondents feel moderate ill-health it is suggest to improve and moderate the physical conditions but not severe. 57% of the respondents are moderate for their deficiencies it is indicate the social contact it feel isolated at the times. Negative general well-being for the older adult's majority 57% of the respondents is moderate to suggest the balanced view of both positive and negative aspects of the study. Overall subjective well-being majority 50% of the respondent's moderate it is reflect that an average sense of subjective being it is improved.

The data can provide the various challenges faced among older adults in general well being like social, family, and coping with their life. It is large portion of the population to experiences for low level well-being, poor social networks, feelings, isolation and vulnerability. It is also signs of resilience of strength among the smaller groups. It can improve their social support and family involvement and improve the coping strategies it can enhance the quality of life for the older adults.

*Figure 2. Physical conditions of the respondents*

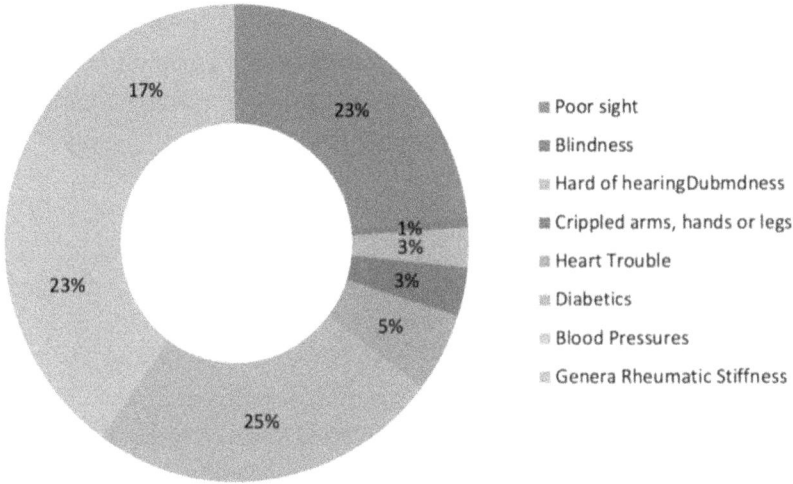

This data likely reflects the prevalence of various physical impairments and health conditions within a specific group. Here's an interpretation of each issue: Older individuals affected by their occupations face health problems such as high blood pressure, poor eyesight, and body pain, which are attributed to old age and age-related factors (Srinivasan & Ilango, 2013).

Poor Sight (35%): A significant portion of the group experiences poor vision, making it one of the most common conditions. This suggests a widespread need for corrective lenses or eye care.

Blindness (1%): Only a small percentage are completely blind, indicating that while visual impairment is prevalent, complete blindness is rare in this group.

Hard of Hearing/Dumbness (4%): A small percentage of the group faces hearing impairments or difficulties with speech (dumbness). While less common than vision problems, hearing loss still affects a notable minority.

Crippled Arms, Hands, or Legs (5%): A small percentage have mobility issues or physical impairments in their limbs, which could limit their ability to perform daily tasks or impact their quality of life.

Heart Trouble (8%): A moderate portion of the population reports heart trouble, which could include conditions like heart disease or other cardiovascular problems.

Diabetes (37%): Diabetes is one of the most prevalent conditions, affecting over a third of the population. This highlights a significant concern related to lifestyle, diet, or genetic predisposition.

Blood Pressure (34%): High blood pressure is also a widespread issue, affecting a large segment of the group. This could be linked to stress, poor diet, or other health factors.

General Rheumatic Stiffness (26%): A quarter of the group suffers from stiffness in the joints or muscles, possibly related to arthritis or age-related issues, making it a common problem affecting mobility and comfort.

## Summary

Diabetes (37%), poor sight (35%), and high blood pressure (34%) are the most common health conditions, suggesting that lifestyle-related health issues (e.g., diet, stress) are prominent in this group.

Rheumatic stiffness (26%) is also a common problem, potentially indicating widespread joint or muscular pain, likely related to aging or physical stress.

Heart trouble (8%) is less frequent but still a concern, while blindness (1%), hearing impairment (4%), and mobility issues (5%) are relatively rare compared to the other conditions.

Overall, the data points to prevalent chronic conditions like diabetes, blood pressure issues, and poor vision, alongside mobility and joint concerns that could impact quality of life.

*Figure 3. Problem face often*

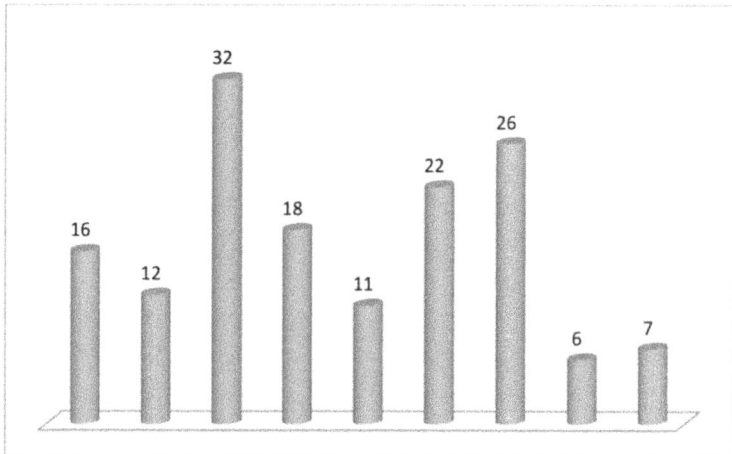

This data reflects the frequency of various physical and health-related problems experienced by a group of individuals. Here's a breakdown and interpretation of each issue:

- Breath Problem (16%): A moderate number of individuals experience breathing difficulties, which could be related to respiratory issues such as asthma, allergies, or anxiety.
- Heartburn (12%): A smaller portion of the group suffers from heartburn, likely caused by acid reflux or digestive problems.
- Feeling Tired (32%): A significant portion of individuals frequently feel tired, making it one of the more common issues, possibly related to stress, lack of sleep, or underlying health problems.
- Constipation (18%): This suggests that digestive issues are somewhat prevalent, affecting nearly a fifth of the population.
- Urinary Problem (11%): A relatively small percentage report urinary problems, which could be due to infections, dehydration, or other health concerns.
- Headache (22%): Over one-fifth of the group experiences headaches, a fairly common problem that could be linked to stress, dehydration, vision problems, or other causes.
- Body Pain (26%): A quarter of the population deals with body pain, indicating that physical discomfort is a relatively common issue, possibly due to posture, lifestyle, or chronic conditions.
- Aching Issues (6%): A smaller subset of individuals reports general aches, which might be a less frequent but still notable problem.
- Nervous Problem (7%): A minor portion experiences nervous issues, possibly related to anxiety, stress, or neurological conditions.
- Feeling tired (32%) and body pain (26%) are the most commonly reported problems, suggesting a high level of fatigue and physical discomfort in this group.
- Headaches (22%) and constipation (18%) are also significant issues, while breathing problems (16%) and heartburn (12%) are moderately common.
- Nervous problems (7%) and aching issues (6%) are the least reported concerns, indicating they affect only a small portion of the population.

Overall, the data highlights that fatigue, pain, and digestive issues are the most common health complaints in this group, possibly pointing to lifestyle factors or stress affecting well-being.

*Figure 4. Problems trouble often*

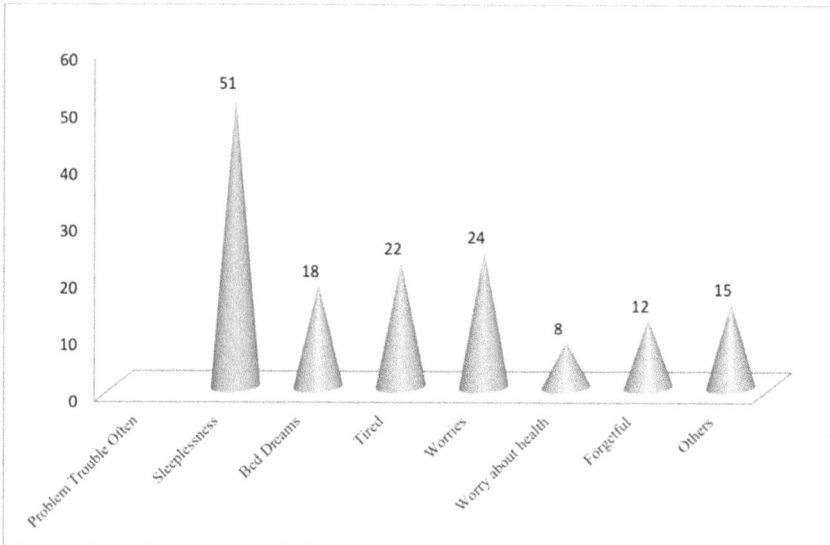

This data appears to represent the frequency of various problems or troubles experienced by a group, with percentages likely corresponding to how often individuals report each issue. Here's an interpretation of each problem: Older adults often face poor mental health issues and physical health problems, which are exacerbated by the harsh conditions of confinement (Srinivasan & Ilango, 2021).

Sleeplessness (51%): More than half of the individuals experience sleeplessness, making it the most common issue. This could point to stress, anxiety, or other health factors affecting sleep quality.

Bad Dreams (18%): A smaller portion of the group struggles with bad dreams, which may contribute to sleep disturbances but is less frequent compared to sleeplessness.

Tired (22%): About a fifth of the group often feels tired, possibly due to insufficient rest, physical strain, or mental exhaustion.

Worries (24%): A quarter of the population experiences general worry, which could be linked to stressors related to personal, professional, or social life.

Worry About Health (8%): A relatively small percentage are specifically concerned about their health, suggesting that for most individuals, health is not a major source of anxiety, or that they may be coping well with health concerns.

Forgetful (12%): A minority report forgetfulness, indicating that memory issues are not as prevalent, though still significant enough to be noted.

Others (15%): This category could include various other troubles not specifically listed, affecting a notable portion of the group but not as common as sleeplessness or worries.

In summary, sleeplessness is the most frequent trouble faced by this group, followed by worry and tiredness. Concerns about health and forgetfulness are less common but still affect certain individuals. These issues may suggest underlying stress or lifestyle factors affecting well-being.

*Figure 5. Technology used*

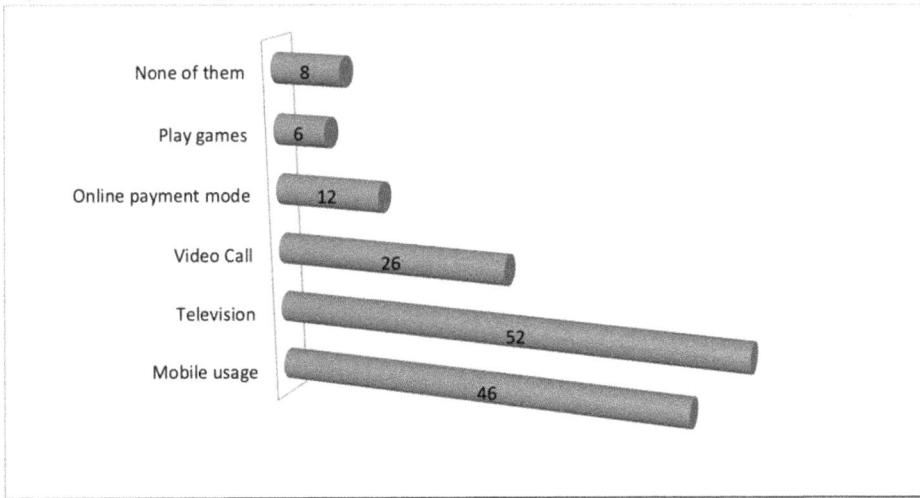

This data seems to represent the usage distribution of different technologies, possibly within a specific group of individuals or a demographic. Here's an interpretation of each technology's usage:

- Mobile Usage (46%): A significant portion of the population uses mobile phones, possibly for communication, accessing information, or entertainment.
- Television (52%): This shows that television is the most widely used technology among the group, suggesting that traditional media still plays a crucial role in their daily lives.
- Video Call (26%): Around a quarter of the group engages in video calls, which indicates a moderate usage of communication technologies that offer face-to-face interaction, possibly used for both personal and professional purposes.

- Online Payment Mode (12%): A smaller percentage of individuals use online payment methods, showing that this group may be slower in adopting digital financial services or could have limited access to such technologies.
- Play Games (6%): Gaming is the least popular activity, indicating that entertainment through gaming is not a primary use of technology for this group.
- None of them (8%): A small fraction of individuals do not use any of the listed technologies, highlighting that some may have limited access to or interest in modern technological platforms.

In summary, the data indicates that television and mobile phones are the most widely used technologies, while activities like online payments and gaming are less common in this population.

## DISCUSSION

Ageing has been always accompanied with risks of ill-health, disability, insecurity, social isolation, dependency, inactive, poverty and poor of QoL. Older improve improve the QoL to great extent. Family income for the older adults between Rs. 2000 to 3000 19% of the respondents educational qualification were up to SSLC. Since the older people were not educated high and doing agriculture, they were in poor economic status and also could not find better job because of their quality of life was moderate. Majority of the older people were Hindu 60% of the respondents and as our country is filled with majority of Hindu religious people it is obvious to have this number.

Majority of the older adult's family head is the husband or the male respondents. In India patriarchal family system is still in existence from ancient days and through. Women are education they cannot exercise the power due to several factors in the family. Nearly half of the respondents 47% are still in workforce. In many ways, the elderly are victims of ageism.

Majority of the older adults have economic problem and most of the previous studies discussed on elderly revealed the same. Most of the older people are spiritual and they believe that ageing is incomplete if they do not depend on supreme power and their problems are solved by praying and offering pooja. In this study income and monthly expenditure of the respondents are significantly correlated with their life QoL, SWB and life satisfaction.

The quality of life for older adults is important for healthy aging. The quality of life for older adults is associated with an increasing number of higher expectations in their lives within society. The quality of life is a useful concept (Netuveli & Blane, 2008). Assistive technology supports older people in terms of care, such as monitoring, health monitoring, detectors, and electronic sensors used to identify needs. It is more useful for older adults in their lifestyle. Digital technology supports older people; it is not usually the only one using it (Miskelly, 2001; Dascalu et al., 2018).

The usage of ICT for older adults is not important for their day-to-day life, and there is low usage of the technology. The research study highlights that there are many technologies supporting interventions. However, people feel that using them is time-consuming and increases costs, which leads to a lack of acceptance of technology (Chen & Chan, 2011). There are many studies discussing the improvement of older adults' acceptance of using ICT (Ijsselsteijn et al., 2007; Gaßner & Conrad, 2010; Sánchez-Rico et al., 2017; Bong et al., 2019). Technology is useful, but older adults face barriers in using and handling information technology. The study highlights the importance of new technology for older adults who are suffering (Fischer et al., 2014).

The study addresses the technology that advances the quality of life of older adults in the telecare program in Taiwan. It emphasizes older adults who use telecare and receive better social welfare. This technology is accepted for improving quality of life (Chou et al., 2013). The major discussion of the study on quality of life indicates that it is negative rather than a long-term good quality of life, which is possible. The improvement of older adults' quality of life can be included as a goal of their lives (Netuveli & Blane, 2008).

## Technology's Benefits for Older People

The use of technology enriches their lives by facilitating better interpersonal relationships. The study clearly examined the technology for social, physical, and psychological aspects of health for older adults. The study was conducted with 591 older people regarding the health and retired older adults, with a mean value of 68.18 and an SD value of 10.75; 55.5% of them were female. The technology-based behaviors of older adults include using email, social networks, online video calls, online chatting, and instant messaging through smartphones. The technology is usable for older adults and contributes to their positive attitude toward technology. Older adults use better health-related resources for chronic illnesses and fevers, subjective well-being, and depressive symptoms. The use of technology for physical and psychological support reduces their loneliness. Technology offers more benefits for people's close relationships regarding physical health and mental well-being. Through technology, successful relationships are fostered for older people (Chopik, 2016).

The findings of the study clearly mention that older adults' usage of technology maximizes the tools available to support their everyday independent life. The study focused on older adults and their attitudes toward the usage of technology in a variety of contexts, i.e., their daily life, home environments, workplaces, and health.

The study addresses the supplement to past research (Mitzner et al., 2010). The outcome of the study shows that older adults support social encouragement, but the stereotype of computers presents complexity and inappropriateness. The computer literacy training was significantly used by nearly 38 to 81% of older adults, and internet usage increased from 21 to 62% (Bakaev et al., 2008).

## Technology Advancement

## Technology Advancement

There are some aspects that affect the quality of life for adults, including healthcare, social engagement, financial security, and advanced technologies, which are not sufficiently considered. The technologies provide practical implementation for the quality of life of older adults (Damant et al., 2017).

## Lack of Technological Integration

The quality of life for older adults focuses on care and support for health, family care, and community support. It is a crucial part of AI technology use, such as telemedicine, smart home devices, and health monitors. Technology advancement plays a vital role in all fields of elderly care; however, it may still have limitations. The older adults are unable to use health apps and digital tools and need help from others; they may depend on others to learn the technology (Charness & Boot, 2009).

## A Lack of Technical Skill Among Older Adults

The advanced technology enhances the lives of older adults. It is advanced utilization in European countries, but those literate are able to understand. For illiterate and rural older adults, it is very difficult to utilize the technologies. The cost-wise, older adults suffer when using advanced technology, particularly rural and low-income older adults who face barriers.

## Progress in technology Has Not Reached Its Full Potential

There are many new advanced technologies to improve older adults' lives, especially AI-powered care systems, telehealth, mobile apps, and robotic care support. The elderly care support involves human and social elements to increase caregiver services that support physical needs (Muramatsu et al., 2024).

## CONCLUSION

The conclusion of the study the impact of quality of life for older adults in technological aspects and subjective well being and general well being for the older adults. The study cans overall well-being to address the various to improve the older adult's life physical, cognitive and social challenges. The impact of technology can continue to evolve for the path in healthier way in independent and socially connected for lives for the ageing population. It is ultimately to improve the quality of life. The technologies provide major aspects of the improve the elderly individual and enhance their quality of life. The future research can improve the individual person for solutions, usability and cost-effectiveness to address the ethical concerns. It is investigate the feature implications for the further research study. The research can develop more effective technologies that not only meet the physical need cognitive need for the older adults it can enhance their social life and mental health independently.

## Suggestions for Future Studies

The future studies it country lack behind in the some of the aging problems it is social problems, widowhood, utilization of older people in national development and economic development it is the most important aspects of special needs for the aged in their society and family structure, intergenerational gap, problems due to migration and development of technology. It is a essential for the researcher aim to develop and evolving the technological aspects and sociological theories to enhance the aging population in the country. The study can conduct comparative analysis to in rural and urban aspects and physiological aspects and social aspects between the two groups. The study can psychological aspects depression, anxiety, stress, feeling, emotions self esteem can take the activity of daily living for the further research study. Study based on the social work interventions must be forced and theory formation with regard to Indian culture. The study cans emphasis in feature aspects older adults' life satisfaction, QoL, social support, Social Network, subjective well-being in feature researchers.

# REFERENCES

Arai, A., Ishida, K., Tomimori, M., Katsumata, Y., Grove, J. S., & Tamashiro, H. (2007). Association between lifestyle activity and depressed mood among home-dwelling older people: A community-based study in Japan. *Aging & Mental Health*, 11(5), 547–555. DOI: 10.1080/13607860601086553 PMID: 17882593

Azar, S. T. (2003). Adult development and parenthood: A social-cognitive perspective. *Handbook of adult development*, 391-415. DOI: 10.1007/978-1-4615-0617-1_20

Baernholdt, M., Hinton, I., Yan, G., Rose, K., & Mattos, M. (2012). Factors associated with quality of life in older adults in the United States. *Quality of Life Research: An International Journal of Quality of Life Aspects of Treatment, Care and Rehabilitation*, 21(3), 527–534. DOI: 10.1007/s11136-011-9954-z PMID: 21706127

Bakaev, M., Ponomarev, V., & Prokhorova, L. (2008, July). E-learning and elder people: Barriers and benefits. In *2008 IEEE Region 8 International Conference on Computational Technologies in Electrical and Electronics Engineering* (pp. 110-113). Doi: DOI: 10.1109/SIBIRCON.2008.4602586

Baker, S., Kelly, R. M., Waycott, J., Carrasco, R., Hoang, T., Batchelor, F., Ozanne, E., Dow, B., Warburton, J., & Vetere, F. (2019). Interrogating social virtual reality as a communication medium for older adults. *Proceedings of the ACM on human-computer interaction, 3*(CSCW), 1-24. DOI: 10.1145/3359251

Barrett, A. J., & Murk, P. J. (2006). Life Satisfaction Index for the Third Age (LSITA): A measurement of successful aging. https://core.ac.uk/download/pdf/46955647.pdf

Blurton, E. U. (1992). *Gender and history: An analysis of the patterns of change in levels of aspirations, satisfaction, achievement and personal adjustment in gifted and nongifted men and women*. University of California, Riverside. https://www.proquest.com/openview/ecb04cc4b6d8e0b32de7855c53b18512/1?pq-origsite=gscholar&cbl=18750&diss=y

Bong, W. K., Bergland, A., & Chen, W. (2019). Technology acceptance and quality of life among older people using a TUI application. *International Journal of Environmental Research and Public Health*, 16(23), 4706. DOI: 10.3390/ijerph16234706 PMID: 31779170

Chabot, M., Delaware, L., McCarley, S., Little, C., Nye, A., & Anderson, E. (2019). Living in place: The impact of smart technology. *Current Geriatrics Reports*, 8(3), 232–238. DOI: 10.1007/s13670-019-00296-4

Chadha, N. K., Aggarwal, V., & Mangla, A. P. (1992). Hopelessness, alienation and life satisfaction among aged. *Indian Journal of Gerontology*, 6(3), 82–92.

Chang, D., Gu, Z., Li, F., & Jiang, R. (2019). A user-centric smart product-service system development approach: A case study on medication management for the elderly. *Advanced Engineering Informatics*, 42, 100979. DOI: 10.1016/j.aei.2019.100979

Charness, N., & Boot, W. R. (2009). Aging and information technology use: Potential and barriers. *Current Directions in Psychological Science*, 18(5), 253–258. DOI: 10.1111/j.1467-8721.2009.01647.x

Chen, K., & Chan, A. H. (2011). A review of technology acceptance by older adults. *Gerontechnology (Valkenswaard)*, 10(1). Advance online publication. DOI: 10.4017/gt.2011.10.01.006.00

Chen, S. C., Davis, B. H., Kuo, C. Y., Maclagan, M., Chien, C. O., & Lin, M. F. (2022). Can the Paro be my Buddy? Meaningful experiences from the perspectives of older adults. *Geriatric Nursing*, 43, 130–137. DOI: 10.1016/j.gerinurse.2021.11.011 PMID: 34883391

Chokkanathan, S., Natarajan, A., & Mohanty, J. (2014). Elder abuse and barriers to help seeking in Chennai, India: A qualitative study. *Journal of Elder Abuse & Neglect*, 26(1), 60–79. DOI: 10.1080/08946566.2013.782786 PMID: 24313798

Chou, C. C., Chang, C. P., Lee, T. T., Chou, H. F., & Mills, M. E. (2013). Technology acceptance and quality of life of the elderly in a telecare program. *CIN: Computers, Informatics. Computers, Informatics, Nursing*, 31(7), 335–342. DOI: 10.1097/NXN.0b013e318295e5ce PMID: 23728446

Curran, E., Rosato, M., Ferry, F., & Leavey, G. (2020). Prevalence and factors associated with anxiety and depression in older adults: Gender differences in psychosocial indicators. *Journal of Affective Disorders*, 267, 114–122. DOI: 10.1016/j.jad.2020.02.018 PMID: 32063562

Damant, J., Knapp, M., Freddolino, P., & Lombard, D. (2017). Effects of digital engagement on the quality of life of older people. *Health & Social Care in the Community*, 25(6), 1679–1703. DOI: 10.1111/hsc.12335 PMID: 26919220

Dascălu, M., Rodideal, A., & Popa, L. (2018). In Romania, Elderly People Who Most Need ICT Are Those Who Are Less Probable to Use It. *Social Work Review/ Revista de Asistenta Sociala, 17*(2).

Desai, S., McGrath, C., McNeil, H., Sveistrup, H., McMurray, J., & Astell, A. (2022). Experiential value of technologies: A qualitative study with older adults. *International Journal of Environmental Research and Public Health*, 19(4), 2235. DOI: 10.3390/ijerph19042235 PMID: 35206435

Devi, B. N., Megala, M., & Saravanakumar, P. (2022). Social and health concerns of elderly women in rural area in Tirupur District, Tamil Nadu. *Journal of Family Medicine and Primary Care, 11*(8), 4447-4451. doi:DOI: 0.4103/jfmpc.jfmpc_42_22

Elwell, F., & Maltbie-Crannell, A. D. (1981). The impact of role loss upon coping resources and life satisfaction of the elderly. *Journal of Gerontology*, 36(2), 223–232. DOI: 10.1093/geronj/36.2.223 PMID: 7204904

Enkvist, Å., Ekström, H., & Elmståhl, S. (2012). What factors affect life satisfaction (LS) among the oldest-old? *Archives of Gerontology and Geriatrics*, 54(1), 140–145. DOI: 10.1016/j.archger.2011.03.013 PMID: 21555158

Fischer, S. H., David, D., Crotty, B. H., Dierks, M., & Safran, C. (2014). Acceptance and use of health information technology by community-dwelling elders. *International Journal of Medical Informatics*, 83(9), 624–635. DOI: 10.1016/j.ijmedinf.2014.06.005 PMID: 24996581

Fotteler, M. L., Kocar, T. D., Dallmeier, D., Kohn, B., Mayer, S., Waibel, A. K., Swoboda, W., & Denkinger, M. (2023). Use and benefit of information, communication, and assistive technology among community-dwelling older adults–a cross-sectional study. *BMC Public Health*, 23(1), 2004. DOI: 10.1186/s12889-023-16926-8 PMID: 37833689

Gallegos-Carrillo, K., Mudgal, J., Sánchez-García, S., Wagner, F. A., Gallo, J. J., Salmerón, J., & García-Peña, C. (2009). Social networks and health-related quality of life: a population based study among older adults. *Salud publica de Mexico, 51*(1), 06-13. https://www.scielosp.org/pdf/spm/v51n1/04.pdf

Gaßner, K., & Conrad, M. (2010). ICT enabled independent living for elderly. *A status-quo analysis on products and the research landscape in the field of Ambient Assisted Living (AAL) in EU-27*. https://ifap.ru/library/book467.pdf

Ghorayeb, A., Comber, R., & Gooberman-Hill, R. (2021). Older adults' perspectives of smart home technology: Are we developing the technology that older people want? *International Journal of Human-Computer Studies*, 147, 102571. DOI: 10.1016/j.ijhcs.2020.102571

Guay, C., Auger, C., Demers, L., Mortenson, W. B., Miller, W. C., Gélinas-Bronsard, D., & Ahmed, S. (2017). Components and outcomes of internet-based interventions for caregivers of older adults: Systematic review. *Journal of Medical Internet Research*, 19(9), e313. DOI: 10.2196/jmir.7896 PMID: 28928109

Halicka, K. (2019). Gerontechnology—The assessment of one selected technology improving the quality of life of older adults. *Engineering Management in Production and Services*, 11(2), 43–51. DOI: 10.2478/emj-2019-0010

Halicka, K. (2024). Assessment of chosen technologies improving seniors' quality of life in the context of sustainable development. *Technological and Economic Development of Economy*, 30(1), 107–128. DOI: 10.3846/tede.2024.20614

Halicka, K., & Surel, D. (2020). Evaluation and selection of technologies improving the quality of life of older people. https://www.um.edu.mt/library/oar/handle/123456789/57531

Halicka, K., & Surel, D. (2022). Smart living technologies in the context of improving the quality of life for older people: The case of the humanoid Rudy Robot. *Human Technology*, 18(2), 191–208. DOI: 10.14254/1795-6889.2022.18-2.5

Harris, M. T., Blocker, K. A., & Rogers, W. A. (2022). Older adults and smart technology: Facilitators and barriers to use. *Frontiers of Computer Science*, 4, 835927. DOI: 10.3389/fcomp.2022.835927

Heinz, M., Martin, P., Margrett, J. A., Yearns, M., Franke, W., Yang, H. I., Wong, J., & Chang, C. K. (2013). Perceptions of technology among older adults. *Journal of Gerontological Nursing*, 39(1), 42–51. DOI: 10.3928/00989134-20121204-04 PMID: 23244061

Ijsselsteijn, W., Nap, H. H., de Kort, Y., & Poels, K. (2007). Digital game design for elderly users. In *Proceedings of the 2007 conference on Future Play* (pp. 17-22). DOI: 10.1145/1328202.1328206

Jerome, G. J., Glass, T. A., Mielke, M., Xue, Q. L., Andersen, R. E., & Fried, L. P. (2006). Physical activity participation by presence and type of functional deficits in older women: The Women's Health and Aging Studies. *The Journals of Gerontology. Series A, Biological Sciences and Medical Sciences*, 61(11), 1171–1176. DOI: 10.1093/gerona/61.11.1171 PMID: 17167158

Jones, T. G. (2001). *Cognitive and psychosocial predictors of subjective well-being in older adults*. Wayne State University. https://www.proquest.com/openview/415f4968bdfd8aaf6888fde9a5f030fe/1?pq-origsite=gscholar&cbl=18750&diss=y

Karaoglu, G., Hargittai, E., Hunsaker, A., & Nguyen, M. H. (2021). Changing technologies, changing lives: Older adults' perspectives on the benefits of using new technologie. *International Journal of Communication*, 15, 3887–3907. DOI: 10.5167/uzh-207350

Kitamura, T., Kawakami, N., Sakamoto, S., Tanigawa, T., Ono, Y., & Fujihara, S. (2002). Quality of life and its correlates in a community population in a Japanese rural area. *Psychiatry and Clinical Neurosciences*, 56(4), 431–441. DOI: 10.1046/j.1440-1819.2002.01033.x PMID: 12109962

Kolaki, M. (2017). Mobile payment use and mobile payment transactions by older adults: A qualitative study. https://www.diva-portal.org/smash/record.jsf?pid=diva2%3A1127590&dswid=2831

Ku, P. W., McKenna, J., & Fox, K. R. (2007). Dimensions of subjective well-being and effects of physical activity in Chinese older adults. *Journal of Aging and Physical Activity*, 15(4), 382–397. DOI: 10.1123/japa.15.4.382 PMID: 18048943

Li, J., & Wang, Q. (2022). Religiosity and health among Chinese older adults: A meta-analytic review. *Ageing and Society*, 42(2), 271–305. DOI: 10.1017/S0144686X20000835

Liebig, P., & Ramamurti, P. V. (2018). Living arrangements and social support for older adults in India. In *Handbook of Asian aging* (pp. 237–260). Routledge., https://www.taylorfrancis.com/chapters/edit/10.4324/9781315224503-10/living-arrangements-social-support-older-adults-india-phoebe-liebig-ramamurti DOI: 10.4324/9781315224503-10

Lippi, L., Turco, A., Folli, A., D'Abrosca, F., Curci, C., Mezian, K., Sire, A. D., & Invernizzi, M. (2023). Technological advances and digital solutions to improve quality of life in older adults with chronic obstructive pulmonary disease: A systematic review. *Aging Clinical and Experimental Research*, 35(5), 953–968. DOI: 10.1007/s40520-023-02381-3 PMID: 36952118

López-Sintas, J., Rojas-DeFrancisco, L., & García-Álvarez, E. (2017). Home-based digital leisure: Doing the same leisure activities, but digital. *Cogent Social Sciences*, 3(1), 1309741. DOI: 10.1080/23311886.2017.1309741

Miskelly, F. G. (2001). Assistive technology in elderly care. *Age and Ageing*, 30(6), 455–458. DOI: 10.1093/ageing/30.6.455 PMID: 11742772

Mitzner, T. L., Boron, J. B., Fausset, C. B., Adams, A. E., Charness, N., Czaja, S. J., Dijkstra, K., Fisk, A. D., Rogers, W. A., & Sharit, J. (2010). Older adults talk technology: Technology usage and attitudes. *Computers in Human Behavior*, 26(6), 1710–1721. DOI: 10.1016/j.chb.2010.06.020 PMID: 20967133

Molzahn, A., Skevington, S. M., Kalfoss, M., & Makaroff, K. S. (2010). The importance of facets of quality of life to older adults: An international investigation. *Quality of Life Research: An International Journal of Quality of Life Aspects of Treatment, Care and Rehabilitation*, 19(2), 293–298. DOI: 10.1007/s11136-009-9579-7 PMID: 20063124

Moon, J. S., & Mikami, H. (2007). Difference in subjective well-being between ethnic Korean and Japanese elderly residents in an urban community in Japan. *Geriatrics & Gerontology International*, 7(4), 371–379. DOI: 10.1111/j.1447-0594.2007.00427.x

Muramatsu, N., Žefran, M., Stiehl, E., & Cornwell, T. (2024). AI-based technology in home-based care in aging societies: challenges and opportunities. *Handbook of Artificial Intelligence at Work*, 166-190. DOI: 10.4337/9781800889972.00017

Murciano-Hueso, A., Martín-García, A. V., & Cardoso, A. P. (2022). Technology and quality of life of older people in times of COVID: A qualitative study on their changed digital profile. *International Journal of Environmental Research and Public Health*, 19(16), 10459. DOI: 10.3390/ijerph191610459 PMID: 36012093

Netuveli, G., & Blane, D. (2008). Quality of life in older ages. *British Medical Bulletin*, 85(1), 113–126. DOI: 10.1093/bmb/ldn003 PMID: 18281376

O'Loughlin, K., Loh, V., & Kendig, H. (2017). Carer characteristics and health, wellbeing and employment outcomes of older Australian baby boomers. *Journal of cross-cultural gerontology, 32*, 339-356. doi: , R. P. (2022). *The Grandparent Vocation: Wisdom, Legacies, and Spiritual Growth*. Rowman & Littlefield. https://www.google.co.in/books/edition/The_Grandparent_Vocation/xdKUEAAAQBAJ?hl=en&gbpv=1&dq=As+part+of+the+%E2%80%9Cgrandparent%E2%80%9D+generation+within+the+family,+individuals+still+can+be+helpful+to+their+growth+of+spring+and+serve+as+source+of+wisdom,+guidance+and+support.+However,+a+major+shift+has+taken+place.+&pg=PR9&printsec=frontcoverDOI: 10.1007/s10823-017-9321-Olson

Polonsky, W. H., & Hessler, D. (2013). What are the quality of life-related benefits and losses associated with real-time continuous glucose monitoring? A survey of current users. *Diabetes Technology & Therapeutics*, 15(4), 295–301. DOI: 10.1089/dia.2012.0298 PMID: 23427866

Qassem, T. (2015). Emerging technologies for dementia patient monitoring. *Advanced Technological Solutions for E-Health and Dementia Patient Monitoring*, 62-104. DOI: 10.4018/978-1-4666-7481-3.ch004

Rejeski, W. J., & Mihalko, S. L. (2001). Physical activity and quality of life in older adults. *The Journals of Gerontology. Series A, Biological Sciences and Medical Sciences*, 56(suppl_2), 23–35. DOI: 10.1093/gerona/56.suppl_2.23 PMID: 11730235

Richardson, V. E., & Barusch, A. S. (2005). *Gerontological practice for the twenty-first century: A social work perspective*. Columbia University Press., https://www.google.co.in/books/edition/Gerontological_Practice_for_the_Twenty_f/OsWQ2U0HoBkC?hl=en&gbpv=1&dq=Thus+the+greater+the+number+of+role+resources+with+which+individual+enter+old+age+the+better+off+they+will+be+adjusting+to+the+demoralizing+effects+of+role+exits+(Blau,+1973).&pg=PR7&printsec=frontcover

Russell, C. (2024). *The aging experience*. Taylor & Francis., DOI: 10.4324/9781032683720

Ryan, A. K., & Willits, F. K. (2007). Family ties, physical health, and psychological well-being. *Journal of Aging and Health*, 19(6), 907–920. DOI: 10.1177/0898264307308340 PMID: 18165288

Sánchez-Rico, A., Garel, P., Notarangelo, I., Quintana, M., Hernández, G., Asteriadis, S., Popa, M., Vretos, N., Solachidis, V., Burgos, M., & Girault, A. (2017). ICT services for life improvement for the elderly. In *Harnessing the Power of Technology to Improve Lives* (pp. 600–605). IOS Press.

Sharma, K. (2008) a quarterly journal devoted to research on ageing Vol. 22, No. 2,. *Book Reviews*, 256, 262.

Shubham, S., & Joshi, A. K. (2021). *Challenges and opportunities in social care of elderly in urban India*. Ageing. DOI: 10.1007/978-981-16-5827-3_19

Srinivasan, S., Ilango (2013). Work Problems Faced by Aged Construction Workers in Thanjavur District, Tamil Nadu. SLAP Journal of Social Science ISSN-0975 9999

Srinivasan, S. (2015). Situation of Older People: A Comparative Study of Countries in the SAARC Region. Perpustakaan Negara Malaysia Cataloging-in Publication Data, The 2nd International Social Work Conference 2015 – Celebrating Diversity in One World, Proceeding: ISBN 978-967-394-244-2.

Srinivasan, S. (2015). The Elderly Inmates in the Indian Prisons – A Psychosocial Perspective, Perpustakaan Negara Malaysia Cataloging-in Publication Data, the 2nd International Social Work Conference 2015 – Celebrating Diversity in One World, Proceeding: ISBN 978-967-394-244-2.

Srinivasan, S. Ilango (2021). Health Problem Faced by Elderly Inmates in Central Prisons in India, A Quarterly International Multilateral Thamizh Journal, Modern Thamizh Research, Arts and Humanities, Vol 28, No 7, ISSN: 2121-984X, Raja Publication, UGC Care Listed (Group – I).

Srinivasan, S. Ilango (2021). Mental Health Problems faced by Aged Inmates due to Overcrowding of Central Prison in Tamil Nadu, A Quarterly International Multilateral Thamizh Journal, Modern Thamizh Research, Arts and Humanities, Vol 28, No 7, ISSN: 2121-984X, Raja Publication, UGC Care Listed (Group – I).

Srinivasan, S. (2023). Situation of Elderly Person with TB: A Comparative Study of Countries in the SAARC Region. International Journal for Multidisciplinary Research (IJFMR), E-ISSN: 2582-2160, IJFMR23057862, Volume 5, Issue 5, September-October 2023.10.28.SJIF Impact Factor(2023) is 8.224 & ISI:1.188, Journal DOI:DOI: 10.36713/epra2013

Srinivasan, S., & Rajavel, N. (2025). A Study of the Psychological Well-Being of Tamil Nadu Prison Inmates With Special Reference of AI. In *AI Technologies and Advancements for Psychological Well-Being and Healthcare* (pp. 219–254). IGI Global., DOI: 10.4018/979-8-3693-9158-7.ch009

Srinivasan, S., & Rajavel, N. (2025). Artificial Intelligence Approach to Psychological Wellbeing Among the Ageing Population. In *AI Technologies and Advancements for Psychological Well-Being and Healthcare* (pp. 187–218). IGI Global., DOI: 10.4018/979-8-3693-9158-7.ch008

Sudarmathy, S., & Kannan, M. (2019). Quality of Life of Senior Citizens Residing at the Home for Aged.

Tannou, T., Lihoreau, T., Couture, M., Giroux, S., Wang, R. H., Spalla, G., Zarshenas, S., Roy, M. G., Aboujaoude, A., Yaddaden, A., Morin, L., & Bier, N. (2023). Is research on 'smart living environments' based on unobtrusive technologies for older adults going in circles? Evidence from an umbrella review. *Ageing Research Reviews*, 84, 101830. DOI: 10.1016/j.arr.2022.101830 PMID: 36565962

Tannou, T., Lihoreau, T., Gagnon-Roy, M., Grondin, M., & Bier, N. (2022). Effectiveness of smart living environments to support older adults to age in place in their community: An umbrella review protocol. *BMJ Open*, 12(1), e054235. DOI: 10.1136/bmjopen-2021-054235 PMID: 35078843

Venkateswarlu, V. (2008). *Problems of Rural Aged: A Sociological Perspective.* Gyan Publishing House.

Waite, L., & Das, A. (2010). Families, social life, and well-being at older ages. *Demography*, 47(Suppl 1), S87–S109. DOI: 10.1353/dem.2010.0009 PMID: 21302422

Wanasphitaksakul, S. (2009). Factors influencing concern about death and dying, coping with death and dying, and satisfaction with life among elderly Thai and Chinese. https://repository.au.edu/server/api/core/bitstreams/05971af4-54de-4866-bcb1-d9e5d80505a7/content

## ADDITIONAL READING

https://www.who.int/news-room/fact-sheets/detail/ageing-and-health

https://www.google.co.in/books/edition/Problems_of_Rural_Aged/AI7nTBZaoUAC?hl=en&gbpv=1&dq=Socially,+ageing+refers+to+the+roles+or+obligation+for+the+social+habits+for+the+older+people

# Chapter 6
# Designing for Longevity:
## Economic Perspectives on Age–Friendly Housing and Urban Development

**Tiago Manuel Horta Reis da Silva**
https://orcid.org/0000-0001-5220-1718
*King's College London, UK*

## ABSTRACT

*This article explores the intersection of age-friendly housing and urban planning within the broader context of the economics of aging. As populations worldwide continue to age, there is a growing need to adapt housing and urban environments to meet the specific needs of older adults. This chapter examines the economic implications of age-friendly housing initiatives and the role of urban planning in creating sustainable, inclusive environments for the elderly. By analysing current trends, policies, and economic models, the chapter aims to provide a comprehensive understanding of how age-friendly urban planning can contribute to the well-being of older adults while also benefiting society at large. The discussion includes case studies from various global contexts, highlighting best practices and innovative solutions. The chapter concludes by offering policy recommendations and identifying areas for future research.*

## INTRODUCTION

As global populations age, the demand for age-friendly environments has become increasingly urgent, particularly in the realms of housing and urban planning (Reis da Silva, 2023a; Reis da Silva, 2023b). This demographic shift is not merely

DOI: 10.4018/979-8-3693-7753-6.ch006

a concern for social policy but also an economic imperative, as the design and accessibility of urban environments significantly influence the quality of life and well-being of older adults (Reis da Silva, 2023c; Reis da Silva, 2024a). The World Health Organization (WHO) has emphasized the importance of creating age-friendly built environments, which encompass housing, transportation, and public spaces, to foster active aging and optimize the living conditions for older adults (Chau & Jamei, 2021; Fitzpatrick et al., 2023). The integration of age-friendly principles into urban planning is essential for addressing the unique challenges posed by an aging population, including social isolation, accessibility, and health disparities (Hou, 2021). The economic implications of an aging population are profound. As the number of older adults increases, so does the need for supportive housing models that provide care while allowing for independence. Research indicates that supportive housing with care can significantly enhance the well-being of older adults, reducing the burden on healthcare systems by enabling individuals to age in place (Hou, 2021; Reis da Silva, 2023a). In Ireland, for example, policies have been directed towards public provision of care for older adults, primarily through nursing homes, which may not fully address the diverse needs of this demographic (Hou, 2021). Thus, urban planners and policymakers must consider innovative housing solutions that facilitate aging in place, thereby promoting both individual well-being and economic sustainability (Horta Reis da Silva, 2022a; Horta Reis da Silva, 2022c; Horta Reis da Silva, 2022d; Reis da Silva, 2023a).

Neighborhood quality plays a crucial role in the health and well-being of older adults. Studies have shown that access to affordable and usable housing developments, which provide opportunities for social engagement and proximity to essential services, is vital for successful aging (Wright et al., 2022). The design of neighborhoods should prioritize accessibility, safety, and social connectivity to mitigate the risks of isolation and promote active participation in community life (Wright et al., 2022; Reis da Silva, 2024b). Furthermore, the economic benefits of investing in age-friendly neighborhoods are substantial, as they can lead to reduced healthcare costs and improved quality of life for older residents (Scheckler, 2020). Housing affordability is another critical factor influencing the ability of older adults to age in place. The relationship between housing costs and community-based aging is complex; inadequate housing can impede healthy aging, while affordable housing options can empower older adults to maintain their independence (Scheckler, 2020; Reis da Silva, 2023a). The economic burden of housing costs often leads to difficult choices for older adults, forcing them to prioritize between healthcare and housing stability (Yu et al., 2021). Therefore, it is imperative that urban planning incorporates strategies to enhance housing affordability and accessibility, ensuring that older adults can live comfortably within their communities. The importance of community-based support services cannot be overstated in the context of aging populations. Access to community support services is integral to the aging process, particularly for older adults living in social housing (Binette, 2023). Research has highlighted the need for integrated service delivery models that co-locate health and social services within housing developments, thereby facilitating easier access for older tenants (Binette, 2023). This approach not only enhances the quality of life for older adults but also reduces the strain on healthcare systems by promoting preventive care and early intervention (Dalistan et al., 2022).

Moreover, the role of technology in supporting aging in place is increasingly recognized. The integration of smart technologies within housing can enhance the independence of older adults by providing tools for monitoring health and safety (Fields, 2023). However, disparities in technology access must be addressed to ensure that all older adults can benefit from these advancements (Berlinger, 2022). Policymakers should prioritize initiatives that promote digital literacy and access to technology, particularly for low-income and marginalized populations (Berlinger, 2022). The intersectionality of aging, housing, and health is further complicated by social determinants such as race, socioeconomic status, and geographic location. Research indicates that older adults from minority backgrounds often face significant barriers to accessing affordable and appropriate housing (Berlinger, 2022). These disparities can exacerbate health inequities and limit opportunities for social engagement, highlighting the need for targeted interventions that address the unique challenges faced by diverse populations (Ige, 2019).

# THE DEMOGRAPHIC OF AGING

## Global Aging Trends and Projections

The global demographic landscape is currently undergoing a significant transformation characterized by an unprecedented increase in the proportion of older adults. According to projections by the United Nations, the number of individuals aged 60 and above is expected to more than double by 2050, reaching approximately 2.1 billion (Nojomi, 2023). This demographic shift is particularly pronounced in developed countries but is increasingly becoming a reality in developing regions as well. The aging population is primarily driven by increased life expectancy and declining birth rates, which together result in a higher dependency ratio and a greater demand for age-specific services and infrastructure (Nojomi, 2023). This demographic transition necessitates a comprehensive understanding of the implications for various sectors, particularly housing and urban development. The economic impact of an aging population is profound, affecting labor markets, public finances, and overall economic growth. As the proportion of older adults rises, there is a corresponding increase in the demand for healthcare, pensions, and social services, which places significant strain on public resources (Nojomi, 2023). Moreover, the shift in demographic structure necessitates adjustments in housing and urban planning to accommodate the unique needs of older adults. This has implications for the construction industry, real estate markets, and urban development policies, as communities must adapt to ensure that they are equipped to support an aging population (Hartt et al., 2022). The need for age-friendly environments is not merely a social concern; it is an economic imperative that requires immediate attention from policymakers and urban planners.

In terms of housing and urban development, the aging population presents specific challenges that traditional models of urban planning often fail to address. Many existing urban environments are not designed with the needs of older adults in mind, leading to issues of accessibility, safety, and social isolation (Rodrigues et al., 2021). This demographic shift requires a rethinking of urban environments, with a focus on creating inclusive, accessible, and sustainable communities. Age-friendly housing and urban planning are essential components of this approach, offering solutions that enhance the quality of life for older adults while also benefiting the broader community (Klann et al., 2019). For instance, walkable neighborhoods with high-quality pedestrian infrastructure can significantly improve the mobility and independence of older adults, thereby promoting active aging (Lenstra, 2017; Horta Reis da Silva, 2022b; Reis da Silva, 2024a).

The concept of age-friendly communities encompasses various elements, including physical infrastructure, social services, and community engagement. Research indicates that neighborhoods designed with older adults in mind can lead to improved health outcomes and greater social participation (Li et al., 2014; Reis da Silva, 2024b). For example, the presence of well-maintained sidewalks, accessible public transportation, and community centers can facilitate social interactions and reduce feelings of isolation among older adults (Reis da Silva, 2024b). Additionally, the integration of green spaces and recreational facilities can promote physical activity, which is crucial for maintaining health and well-being in later life (Brüchert et al., 2022). Therefore, urban planners must prioritize the development of age-friendly environments that cater to the diverse needs of older adults.

The integration of age-friendly housing and urban planning is essential for fostering environments that support healthy aging, echoing the principles of holistic care emphasized in various nursing domains. The concept of age-friendly environments aligns with the insights provided in recent healthcare literature. Age-friendly housing and urban planning prioritize the emotional and physical well-being of older adults, ensuring that urban spaces are designed to meet their specific needs, thereby promoting inclusivity and accessibility.

Older adults have complex intricacies (Reis da Silva, 2024c; Reis da Silva, 2024d; Reis da Silva, 2024e). It is important to ensure adequate hydration and nutrition, chronic conditions that requires careful consideration of the physiological changes that accompany aging, urban planners must similarly account for the unique needs of older adults in the design of housing and community infrastructure (Reis da Silva, 2024f; Reis da Silva, 2024g; Reis da Silva, 2024h). This includes considerations for accessibility, safety, and the facilitation of social connections, which are critical for preventing issues such as loneliness and falls—key topics also explored in the context of community nursing and older adult care (Reis da Silva, 2024a; Reis da Silva, 2024b). Thus, the interdisciplinary nature of age-friendly planning underscores the importance of collaborative approaches that integrate insights from healthcare, urban design, and social policy to create environments that support the holistic well-being of aging populations (Reis da Silva, 2024i).

## Emotional Intelligence in Older Adults

Emotional intelligence (EI) in nursing for older adults is crucial not only for patient care but also for broader socio-economic outcomes, particularly in the context of age-friendly housing and urban planning (da Silva, 2022; Reis da Silva, 2024j). Nurses with high EI contribute to improved health outcomes, reducing healthcare costs associated with chronic diseases and long-term care. This aligns with the economic goals of sustainable healthcare systems, as healthier older adults require fewer medical interventions, easing the financial burden on public services (da Silva, 2022; Reis da Silva, 2024j).

Moreover, EI-informed nursing enhances the effectiveness of age-friendly housing and urban planning. These initiatives aim to create environments that support the physical and emotional well-being of older adults. Nurses play a pivotal role in assessing and advocating for housing designs that accommodate the emotional and social needs of the elderly, such as reducing isolation and promoting community engagement. This advocacy is critical in influencing urban planning policies that prioritize affordable, accessible, and emotionally supportive living spaces for older populations. Thus, the integration of EI in gerontological nursing not only improves individual care but also supports economic and urban development strategies aimed at enhancing the quality of life for aging populations (da Silva, 2022; Reis da Silva, 2024j).

## Sustainable Development Goals and Age-Friendly Housing

The Sustainable Development Goals (SDGs), particularly Goal 11 (Sustainable Cities and Communities) and Goal 3 (Good Health and Well-being), are directly linked to the economic and social imperatives of age-friendly housing and urban planning (Reis da Silva and Rodrigues, 2023). These goals emphasize creating inclusive, safe, and sustainable urban environments that cater to all age groups, including older adults. Integrating these principles into urban planning not only addresses the needs of an aging population but also promotes economic sustainability.

Age-friendly housing that meets the SDG criteria can reduce healthcare costs by providing environments that support healthy aging, thereby lowering the incidence of chronic illnesses and falls among older adults. Economically, this reduces the burden on healthcare systems and fosters a more resilient economy by enabling older adults to live independently for longer periods. Moreover, age-friendly urban planning that prioritizes accessibility and social inclusion contributes to the well-being and productivity of older adults, allowing them to continue contributing to the economy, whether through formal employment, volunteer work, or caregiving roles. Thus, aligning urban planning with the SDGs creates a virtuous cycle of economic and social benefits, enhancing the quality of life for older populations.

## Economic Impact of an Aging Population

The implications of an aging population extend beyond housing and urban development; they also encompass broader societal changes. As the demographic landscape shifts, there is a growing recognition of the importance of social infrastructure in supporting older adults. Social infrastructure refers to the networks and services that facilitate social connections and community engagement, which are vital for combating loneliness and isolation among older adults (Jiang et al., 2023; Reis da Silva, 2024b). Studies have shown that strong social networks can enhance the mental and emotional well-being of older adults, thereby contributing to their overall quality of life (Merom et al., 2015; Reis da Silva, 2024g). Therefore, fostering social connections through community programs and initiatives is essential for creating age-friendly environments.

## Implications for Housing and Urban Development

Moreover, the intersection of technology and aging presents both challenges and opportunities. The rapid advancement of technology has the potential to improve the lives of older adults by enhancing their access to information, services, and social connections (Keskinen et al., 2020). However, disparities in technology access and digital literacy must be addressed to ensure that all older adults can benefit from these advancements (Jessiman et al., 2023). Policymakers should prioritize initiatives that promote digital literacy and access to technology, particularly for low-income and marginalized populations (Adlakha et al., 2021; Cowley et al., 2023). By leveraging technology, communities can create innovative solutions that support the needs of older adults and enhance their quality of life.

# CONCEPTUAL FRAMEWORK OF AGE-FRIENDLY HOUSING

## Definition and Key Features of Age-Friendly Housing

Age-friendly housing is a concept that encompasses residential environments specifically designed or adapted to meet the diverse needs of older adults, enabling them to live independently and safely as they age (Reis da Silva, 2023a). This housing model is closely linked to the broader goal of "aging in place," which emphasizes the importance of allowing older adults to remain in their homes and communities as they grow older (Reis da Silva, 2023a). Key features of age-friendly housing include barrier-free design, easy access to healthcare and social services, and proximity to public transportation and community amenities (Peek et al., 2017). These features not only enhance the quality of life for older adults but also contribute to their overall well-being by promoting independence and reducing the risk of social isolation (Eriksson et al., 2016).

## Principles of Universal Design and Accessibility

The principles of universal design are central to the development of age-friendly housing. Universal design refers to the creation of environments that are inherently accessible to people of all ages and abilities, eliminating the need for adaptation or specialized design (Zuiderveen et al., 2016). Key elements of universal design in housing include step-free entrances, wide doorways and hallways, lever handles on doors and faucets, and non-slip flooring. These features benefit not only older adults but also enhance the overall safety and usability of the home for all residents, thereby fostering an inclusive environment (Melchiorre et al., 2022; Reis da Silva, 2023c; Reis da Silva, 2024a). By integrating universal design principles, housing can accommodate the changing needs of residents over time, ensuring that homes remain functional and accessible as individuals age (Tanlamai et al., 2022).

Technology plays an increasingly vital role in the development of age-friendly housing. Smart home technologies, such as automated lighting, temperature control, and security systems, can significantly enhance the safety and comfort of older adults (Soósová, 2016). These technologies allow for greater control over the living environment, enabling seniors to manage their homes more effectively and independently. Additionally, telehealth services and remote monitoring technologies facilitate access to healthcare and support services from the comfort of home, reducing the need for frequent hospital visits and enhancing the overall quality of life for older adults (Abril-Jiménez et al., 2019; Reis da Silva and Mitchell, 2024). The integration of these technologies into age-friendly housing not only improves the living experience for seniors but also alleviates the burden on healthcare systems by promoting preventive care and timely interventions (Lahti et al., 2021).

## The Role of Technology in Age-Friendly Housing

In examining the role of technology in age-friendly housing, it is essential to consider the barriers that older adults may face in adopting these innovations. Research indicates that while many seniors express a desire to use technology to enhance their independence, factors such as lack of familiarity, perceived complexity, and concerns about privacy can hinder their engagement with new technologies (Mareš et al., 2016). Therefore, it is crucial to provide education and support to older adults, ensuring they feel confident in utilizing technology to improve their living conditions (Zhang et al., 2021). Furthermore, the design of technological solutions should prioritize usability, ensuring that they are intuitive and accessible to seniors with varying levels of technological proficiency (Cunha-Diniz et al., 2023).

The concept of age-friendly housing also extends to the broader community context, emphasizing the importance of social infrastructure in supporting older adults. Access to community resources, such as healthcare facilities, recreational areas, and social services, is critical for promoting active aging and enhancing the quality of life for seniors (Cunha-Diniz et al., 2023). Communities that prioritize age-friendly principles in their planning and development can create environments that foster social connections, reduce isolation, and promote overall well-being among older residents (Billis et al., 2013; Reis da Silva, 2024b). For instance, neighborhoods designed with walkable streets, accessible public transportation, and community centers can significantly improve the mobility and social engagement of older adults, thereby enhancing their quality of life (Koirala et al., 2022). Moreover, the integration of age-friendly housing within a supportive community framework can lead to significant economic benefits. By enabling older adults to age in place, communities can reduce the demand for costly institutional care and healthcare services, ultimately leading to lower public expenditures (Haufe & Peek, 2019; Reis da Silva, 2023a). Additionally, age-friendly housing can stimulate local economies by attracting older residents who contribute to the community through their participation in local activities and services (Wolinsky et al., 2020). Therefore, investing in age-friendly housing not only addresses the needs of older adults but also supports the economic vitality of communities as a whole.

# ECONOMIC IMPLICATIONS OF AGE-FRIENDLY HOUSING

## Cost-Benefit Analysis of Age-Friendly Initiatives

Investing in age-friendly housing initiatives presents significant economic benefits for both older adults and society as a whole. A comprehensive cost-benefit analysis reveals that the initial costs associated with developing age-friendly housing are outweighed by the long-term savings in healthcare and social care expenditures (Reis da Silva, 2023c; Reis da Silva, 2024a). For instance, accessible housing designs can significantly reduce the incidence of falls and injuries among older adults, which in turn leads to lower healthcare costs associated with emergency services and rehabilitation (Steels, 2015). Moreover, age-friendly housing can delay or prevent the need for more expensive institutional care, such as nursing homes, thereby further reducing public spending on elder care (Yamada, 2023). This economic rationale underscores the importance of prioritizing age-friendly housing initiatives as a means to enhance the quality of life for older adults while simultaneously alleviating financial pressures on healthcare systems.

## Economic Models for Sustainable Aging Communities

Various economic models have been proposed to support the development of sustainable aging communities, emphasizing the necessity of public-private partnerships, community-based initiatives, and innovative financing mechanisms. For example, social impact bonds and community land trusts have emerged as effective funding strategies for age-friendly housing projects, leveraging private investment to achieve public benefits (Buffel & Phillipson, 2018). These models not only facilitate the financing of age-friendly initiatives but also encourage collaboration among stakeholders, including government agencies, non-profit organizations, and private developers. Additionally, the concept of "age-friendly cities" has gained traction globally, with numerous municipalities adopting policies and practices that promote the well-being of older adults while simultaneously stimulating economic growth (Torku et al., 2020). Such initiatives can lead to the creation of jobs in construction, healthcare, and social services, thereby contributing to local economies.

# CASE STUDIES: ECONOMIC IMPACT OF AGE-FRIENDLY HOUSING IN DIFFERENT CONTEXT

Several case studies illustrate the economic impact of age-friendly housing initiatives in diverse contexts. In Japan, for instance, the government has implemented a comprehensive strategy to address the needs of its rapidly aging population, which includes the development of age-friendly housing and urban environments (Yamada, 2023). This strategy has resulted in significant economic benefits, including increased employment in the construction and healthcare sectors, as well as improved quality of life for older adults. Similarly, in the United States, the AARP (formerly the American Association of Retired Persons) has promoted age-friendly communities through its "Livable Communities" initiative, which has been shown to enhance economic resilience and social cohesion in participating neighborhoods (Ying et al., 2021). These examples highlight the potential for age-friendly housing initiatives to drive economic growth while addressing the needs of an aging population. The economic implications of age-friendly housing extend beyond immediate financial savings; they also encompass broader societal benefits. By enabling older adults to age in place, communities can foster social inclusion and reduce the risk of isolation, which is often associated with negative health outcomes (Scott, 2021). Research indicates that age-friendly environments can enhance the mental and emotional well-being of older adults, leading to lower healthcare costs associated with mental health issues (Warner & Zhang, 2023). Furthermore, the integration of age-friendly housing within a supportive community framework can lead to increased civic engagement and participation among older residents, further enriching community life and fostering intergenerational connections (Ng et al., 2022).

## Urban Planning and Age-Friendly Communities

### The Role of Urban Planning in Supporting Aging Populations

Urban planning plays a critical role in supporting aging populations by creating environments conducive to healthy aging. Age-friendly urban planning involves the integration of housing, transportation, public spaces, and services to create communities that are accessible, inclusive, and supportive of older adults. Key elements of age-friendly urban planning include walkable neighborhoods, accessible public transportation, safe and inviting public spaces, and proximity to healthcare and social services (Torku et al., 2020). These features not only enhance the quality of life for older adults but also promote their independence and social engagement, which are essential for maintaining physical and mental well-being as they age (Che, 2024).

## Integrating Age-Friendly Concepts into Urban Development Plans

Integrating age-friendly concepts into urban development plans requires a multi-disciplinary approach that involves collaboration between urban planners, architects, policymakers, and community stakeholders. This process entails identifying the specific needs and preferences of older adults and developing design and policy solutions that address these needs. For instance, urban planners may collaborate with healthcare providers to ensure that new developments are located near medical facilities, or with transportation authorities to improve access to public transit for older adults (Buffel & Phillipson, 2018). Such collaborative efforts can lead to the creation of environments that not only accommodate older adults but also foster intergenerational interactions and community cohesion.

## Best Practices and Lessons from Global Examples

Global examples of age-friendly urban planning provide valuable lessons for other cities and regions. The World Health Organization's "Global Network for Age-Friendly Cities and Communities" includes cities that have successfully implemented age-friendly policies and practices. Cities such as New York, Copenhagen, and Melbourne have adopted a range of strategies to enhance the liveability of their environments for older adults. Common features of these cities include comprehensive public transportation systems, pedestrian-friendly streets, accessible public spaces, and community engagement programs that involve older adults in the planning process (Fatmah et al., 2019). These examples highlight the importance of tailoring urban planning initiatives to the specific contexts and needs of local populations.

## Policy Considerations and Recommendations

### National and Local Policies for Age-Friendly Housing and Urban Planning

National and local policies play a crucial role in the development of age-friendly housing and urban planning. Supportive policies should focus on removing barriers to accessibility, incentivizing the development of age-friendly housing, and ensuring that older adults have access to essential services and amenities. Additionally, policies should promote the participation of older adults in the decision-making process, ensuring that their voices are heard, and their needs are met (Guillemot & Warner, 2023). This participatory approach not only empowers older adults but also leads to more effective and relevant urban planning outcomes.

## Challenges and Barriers to Implementation

Despite the clear benefits of age-friendly housing and urban planning, several challenges and barriers to implementation persist. High costs associated with retrofitting existing housing and infrastructure, resistance to change from developers and policymakers, and a lack of awareness or understanding of the needs of older adults can hinder progress (Faber et al., 2020). Overcoming these barriers requires a concerted effort from all stakeholders, including government agencies, private sector actors, and civil society organizations. For instance, public-private partnerships can leverage resources and expertise to develop sustainable age-friendly communities (Boer et al., 2020).

## Strategic Recommendations for Policymakers

To promote the development of age-friendly housing and urban planning, policymakers should consider several strategic recommendations. First, incentivizing the development of age-friendly housing through tax credits, grants, or low-interest loans can encourage developers to incorporate age-friendly features into their projects (Зиганшина et al., 2020). Second, enhancing public awareness through education and outreach campaigns can increase understanding of the importance of age-friendly environments and garner community support for such initiatives (Ivan et al., 2020). Third, fostering community engagement by involving older adults in the planning and development process ensures that their needs and preferences are reflected in the final outcomes (Aboderin et al., 2017).

## Future Directions in Age-Friendly Housing and Urban Planning

### Emerging Trends and Innovations

As the field of age-friendly housing and urban planning continues to evolve, several emerging trends and innovations are noteworthy. One significant trend is the adoption of green building practices, which prioritize sustainability and environmental responsibility in the construction and renovation of housing. These practices not only reduce the ecological footprint of buildings but also enhance the health and well-being of older adults by improving indoor air quality and reducing energy costs Simpson et al. (2022). Additionally, the integration of technology in housing and urban design is becoming increasingly prevalent. Smart home technologies, such as automated lighting and security systems, are being incorporated into age-friendly housing to enhance safety and convenience for older residents (Mohamad et al., 2019). Furthermore, the development of intergenerational living arrangements is gaining traction, promoting social interaction and support between different age groups, which can combat loneliness and foster community cohesion (Kim et al., 2021).

## The Role of Stakeholders in Promoting Age-Friendly Environments

The successful development of age-friendly environments relies heavily on the active involvement of a diverse range of stakeholders. This includes older adults, policymakers, urban planners, architects, healthcare providers, and community organizations. Collaboration among these stakeholders is essential to ensure that age-friendly initiatives are effective, sustainable, and responsive to the needs of older adults (Kimpel, 2024). Engaging older adults in the planning process not only empowers them but also ensures that their preferences and experiences inform the design of age-friendly spaces (Black & Jester, 2020). For instance, participatory design approaches can lead to more relevant and impactful outcomes, as they incorporate the voices of those who will ultimately inhabit these spaces (Lee & Edmonston, 2019).

## Areas for Further Research

Despite significant progress in the field of age-friendly housing and urban planning, there remain many areas that require further research. One critical area is the economic impact of age-friendly initiatives. Understanding the cost-effectiveness of these projects, particularly in terms of healthcare savings and improved quality of life for older adults, is essential for justifying investments in age-friendly housing (Park et al., 2023). Additionally, research should explore the effectiveness of different policy approaches in promoting age-friendly environments. This includes examining how various regulatory frameworks and funding mechanisms can support the development of age-friendly housing and urban spaces (Yamada, 2023). Furthermore, the long-term outcomes of age-friendly communities need to be assessed, particularly in relation to their sustainability and resilience in the face of demographic changes (Chang et al., 2022). Future research should also delve into the intersection of age-friendly housing with other areas of urban development, such as environmental sustainability and social equity. As cities grapple with the dual challenges of aging populations and climate change, it is crucial to explore how age-friendly initiatives can be aligned with broader sustainability goals (Applebaum et al., 2021). This includes investigating how eco-friendly housing designs can be integrated into age-friendly communities, thereby promoting both environmental stewardship and the well-being of older residents (Black & Jester, 2020). Additionally, examining the social equity implications of age-friendly housing is vital, as it ensures that all older adults, regardless of socioeconomic status, have access to safe and supportive living environments (K & Sia, 2022).

## CONCLUSION

The aging population presents both challenges and opportunities for housing and urban planning. Age-friendly housing and urban planning are essential components of a comprehensive approach to aging, offering solutions that enhance the quality of life for older adults while also benefiting society as a whole. By adopting age-friendly policies and practices, communities can create environments that are inclusive, accessible, and supportive of healthy aging. The economic and social benefits of these initiatives are clear, making age-friendly housing and urban planning a critical area of focus for policymakers, urban planners, and community leaders. The development of age-friendly housing and urban planning requires a collaborative and multi-disciplinary approach, supported by evidence-based policies and innovative solutions. As the global population continues to age, the need for age-friendly environments will only become more pressing, making it essential to prioritize the creation of sustainable, inclusive communities for older adults.

The relationship between age-friendly housing, urban planning, and the economics of aging is multifaceted and requires a comprehensive approach. Policymakers and urban planners must collaborate to create environments that support the needs of older adults, fostering independence, social engagement, and overall well-being. By prioritizing age-friendly principles in housing and urban development, communities can not only enhance the quality of life for older residents but also achieve significant economic benefits through reduced healthcare costs and increased social cohesion. The global aging trend presents a complex set of challenges and opportunities that require a multifaceted approach. The demographic shift towards an older population necessitates significant changes in housing, urban planning, and social infrastructure to accommodate the unique needs of older adults. By prioritizing age-friendly principles in urban development, communities can enhance the quality of life for older residents while also achieving economic benefits through reduced healthcare costs and increased social cohesion. The integration of technology and social infrastructure further underscores the importance of creating inclusive environments that support the well-being of older adults. As we move forward, it is imperative that policymakers, urban planners, and community leaders work collaboratively to develop sustainable solutions that address the needs of an aging population.

The conceptual framework of age-friendly housing encompasses a multifaceted approach that integrates universal design principles, technological innovations, and community support systems. By prioritizing the needs of older adults in housing development, communities can create environments that promote independence, enhance quality of life, and foster social connections. The role of technology in this framework is crucial, as it provides tools and solutions that empower older adults to manage their homes and health effectively. Ultimately, the development of age-friendly housing is not only a response to demographic changes but also an opportunity to create inclusive, vibrant communities that support the well-being of all residents. The economic implications of age-friendly housing initiatives are multifaceted and far-reaching. By investing in age-friendly housing, communities can achieve significant long-term savings in healthcare and social care costs while simultaneously enhancing the quality of life for older adults. The development of sustainable aging communities through innovative financing models and public-private partnerships can stimulate local economies and create jobs in various sectors. Furthermore, age-friendly housing contributes to social inclusion and community cohesion, ultimately benefiting society as a whole. As the global population continues to age, prioritizing age-friendly housing initiatives will be essential for fostering healthy, vibrant communities that support the well-being of all residents.

Urban planning is essential for creating age-friendly communities that support the needs of older adults. By integrating age-friendly concepts into urban development plans, cities can enhance the quality of life for older residents while promoting social inclusion and community cohesion. The role of national and local policies in facilitating this process cannot be overstated, as supportive policies are crucial for removing barriers and ensuring that older adults have access to the services and amenities they need. Despite the challenges that exist, strategic recommendations for policymakers can pave the way for the development of sustainable, age-friendly urban environments that benefit all residents. The future directions in age-friendly housing and urban planning are shaped by emerging trends, stakeholder collaboration, and the need for further research. By embracing innovations such as green building practices, smart technologies, and intergenerational living arrangements, communities can create inclusive and sustainable environments for older adults. The active involvement of diverse stakeholders is essential to ensure that age-friendly initiatives are responsive to the needs of older residents. Furthermore, ongoing research into the economic impacts, policy effectiveness, and intersections with sustainability and equity will be crucial for advancing the field of age-friendly housing and urban planning.

# REFERENCES

Зиганшина, Л., Yudina, E., Talipova, L., Sharafutdinova, G., & Khairullin, R. (2020). Smart and age-friendly cities in russia: An exploratory study of attitudes, perceptions, quality of life and health information needs. *International Journal of Environmental Research and Public Health*, 17(24), 9212. DOI: 10.3390/ijerph17249212 PMID: 33317150

Aboderin, I., Rosenberg, M., & Owii, H. (2017). Toward "age-friendly slums"? health challenges of older slum dwellers in Nairobi and the applicability of the age-friendly city approach. *International Journal of Environmental Research and Public Health*, 14(10), 1259. DOI: 10.3390/ijerph14101259 PMID: 29053576

Abril-Jiménez, P., Lacal, J., Pérez, S., Páramo, M., Colomer, J., & Arredondo, M. (2019). Aging-friendly cities for assessing older adults' decline: IOT-based system for continuous monitoring of frailty risks using smart city infrastructure. *Aging Clinical and Experimental Research*, 32(4), 663–671. DOI: 10.1007/s40520-019-01238-y PMID: 31228029

Adlakha, D., Chandra, M., Krishna, M., Smith, L., & Tully, M. (2021). Designing age-friendly communities: Exploring qualitative perspectives on urban green spaces and aging in two Indian megacities. *International Journal of Environmental Research and Public Health*, 18(4), 1491. DOI: 10.3390/ijerph18041491 PMID: 33557432

Applebaum, J., Horecka, K., Loney, L., & Graham, T. (2021). Pet-friendly for whom? an analysis of pet fees in Texas rental housing. *Frontiers in Veterinary Science*, 8, 767149. Advance online publication. DOI: 10.3389/fvets.2021.767149 PMID: 34820439

Berlinger, N. (2022). Housing, aging, and health: New findings and frameworks from housing-focused research in the context of covid-19. *Innovation in Aging*, 6(Supplement_1), 337–337. DOI: 10.1093/geroni/igac059.1329

Billis, A., Konstantinidis, E., Zilidou, V., Wadhwa, K., Ladas, A., & Bamidis, P. (2013). Biomedical engineering and elderly support. *International Journal of Reliable and Quality E-Healthcare*, 2(2), 21–37. DOI: 10.4018/ijrqeh.2013040102

Binette, J. (2023). Where we live, where we age: home is at the heart of older adults' well-being - fact sheet.. DOI: 10.26419/res.00479.006

Black, K., & Jester, D. (2020). Examining older adults' perspectives on the built environment and correlates of healthy aging in an American age-friendly community. *International Journal of Environmental Research and Public Health*, 17(19), 7056. DOI: 10.3390/ijerph17197056 PMID: 32992480

Boer, B., Bozdemir, B., Jansen, J., Hermans, M., Hamers, J., & Verbeek, H. (2020). The homestead: Developing a conceptual framework through co-creation for innovating long-term dementia care environments. *International Journal of Environmental Research and Public Health*, 18(1), 57. DOI: 10.3390/ijerph18010057 PMID: 33374761

Brüchert, T., Quentin, P., & Bolte, G. (2022). The relationship between perceived built environment and cycling or e-biking for transport among older adults–a cross-sectional study. *PLoS One*, 17(5), e0267314. DOI: 10.1371/journal.pone.0267314 PMID: 35503760

Buffel, T., & Phillipson, C. (2018). A manifesto for the age-friendly movement: Developing a new urban agenda. *Journal of Aging & Social Policy*, 30(2), 173–192. DOI: 10.1080/08959420.2018.1430414 PMID: 29364777

Buffel, T., & Phillipson, C. (2018). A manifesto for the age-friendly movement: Developing a new urban agenda. *Journal of Aging & Social Policy*, 30(2), 173–192. DOI: 10.1080/08959420.2018.1430414 PMID: 29364777

Chang, C., Lim, X., Supramaniam, P., Chew, C., Ding, L., & Rajan, P. (2022). Perceived gap of age-friendliness among community-dwelling older adults: Findings from Malaysia, a middle-income country. *International Journal of Environmental Research and Public Health*, 19(12), 7171. DOI: 10.3390/ijerph19127171 PMID: 35742420

Chau, H., & Jamei, E. (2021). Age-friendly built environment. *Encyclopedia*, 1(3), 781–791. DOI: 10.3390/encyclopedia1030060

Che, S., Lei, W. I., Hung, T., & Leong, S. M. (2024). Attitudes to aging mediates the relationship between perception of age-friendly city and life satisfaction among middle-aged and older people in Macao: A cross-sectional study. *BMC Geriatrics*, 24(1), 362. Advance online publication. DOI: 10.1186/s12877-024-04961-y PMID: 38654157

Cowley, S. A., Tzouvara, V., & Horta Reis da Silva, T. (2023). Public Health: healthy aging and well-being. In Redfern's Nursing Older People. Fifth edition. Editors: Ross, Harris, Fitzpatrick and Abley. Elsevier.

Cunha-Diniz, F., Taveira-Gomes, T., Santos, A., Teixeira, J., & Magalhães, T. (2023). Are there any differences in road traffic injury outcomes between older and younger adults? setting the grounds for posttraumatic senior personal injury assessment guidelines. *Journal of Clinical Medicine*, 12(6), 2353. DOI: 10.3390/jcm12062353 PMID: 36983355 da Silva, T. H. R. (2022). Emotional awareness and emotional intelligence. *British Journal of Community Nursing*, 27(12), 573–574. DOI: 10.12968/bjcn.2022.27.12.573 PMID: 36519463

Dalistan, R., George, S., Lane, R., Block, H., & Laver, K. (2022). Middle aged and older adult's perspectives of their own home environment: a qualitative meta-synthesis. DOI: 10.21203/rs.3.rs-2067454/v1

Eriksson, J., Hildingh, C., Buer, N., & Thulesius, H. (2016). Seniors' self-preservation by maintaining established self and defying deterioration – a grounded theory. *International Journal of Qualitative Studies on Health and Well-being*, 11(1), 30265. DOI: 10.3402/qhw.v11.30265 PMID: 27172511

Faber, M., Tavy, Z., & Pas, S. (2020). Engaging older people in age-friendly cities through participatory video design. *International Journal of Environmental Research and Public Health*, 17(23), 8977. DOI: 10.3390/ijerph17238977 PMID: 33276604

Fatmah, F., Dewi, V., & Priotomo, Y. (2019). Developing age-friendly city readiness: A case study from Depok city, Indonesia. *SAGE Open Medicine*, 7, 205031211985251. DOI: 10.1177/2050312119852510 PMID: 31205701

Fields, B., Skrove, Z., Tredinnick, R., Sprecher, B., Lee, J., Shields, R., Ponto, K., & Shin, J. (2023). The usability and acceptability of the augmented reality home assessment tool (arhat). *Innovation in Aging*, 7(Supplement_1), 1142–1143. DOI: 10.1093/geroni/igad104.3668

Fitzpatrick, J. M., Bianchi, L. A., Hayes, N., Da Silva, T., & Harris, R. (2023). Professional development and career planning for nurses working in care homes for older people: A scoping review. *International Journal of Older People Nursing*, 18(1), e12519. DOI: 10.1111/opn.12519 PMID: 36441621

Guillemot, J., & Warner, M. (2023). Age-friendly cities in Latin America: A human ecological framework. *Geriatrics (Basel, Switzerland)*, 8(3), 46. DOI: 10.3390/geriatrics8030046 PMID: 37218826

Hartt, M., DeVerteuil, G., & Potts, R. (2022). Age-unfriendly by design. *Journal of the American Planning Association*, 89(1), 31–44. DOI: 10.1080/01944363.2022.2035247

Haufe, M., Peek, S., & Luijkx, K. G. (2019). Matching gerontechnologies to independent-living seniors' individual needs: Development of the GTM tool. *BMC Health Services Research*, 19(1), 26. Advance online publication. DOI: 10.1186/s12913-018-3848-5 PMID: 30634971

Horta Reis Da Silva, T. (2022a). Muskuloskeletal minor injuries: assessment and treatment. In Curr, S., & Fordham-Clarke, C. (Eds.), *Clinical Skills at Glance* (1st ed., pp. 128–129). Wiley. [55]

Horta Reis Da Silva, T. (2022b). Falls - prevention, assessment and management. In Curr, S., & Fordham-Clarke, C. (Eds.), *Clinical Skills at Glance* (pp. 130–131). Wiley. [56]

Horta Reis Da Silva, T. (2022c). Moving and Handling. In Curr, S., & Fordham-Clarke, C. (Eds.), *Clinical Skills at Glance* (pp. 20–21). Wiley.

Horta Reis Da Silva, T. (2022d). Moving and Handling: turning in bed, transfer and hoisting. In Curr, S., & Fordham-Clarke, C. (Eds.), *Clinical Skills at Glance* (pp. 22–23). Wiley.

Hou, S. I. (2021). Physical activity and social relationships on social engagement among community-dwelling older adults. *Innovation in Aging*, 5(Suppl 1), 28. DOI: 10.1093/geroni/igab046.099

Ige, J. (2019). Environmental health and housing: Issues for public health. *Housing Studies*, 34(3), 561–562. DOI: 10.1080/02673037.2019.1558597

Ivan, L., Beu, D., & Hoof, J. (2020). Smart and age-friendly cities in Romania: An overview of public policy and practice. *International Journal of Environmental Research and Public Health*, 17(14), 5202. DOI: 10.3390/ijerph17145202 PMID: 32708488

Jessiman, T., Rowe, R., & Jago, R. (2023). A qualitative study of active travel amongst commuters and older adults living in market towns. *BMC Public Health*, 23(1), 840. Advance online publication. DOI: 10.1186/s12889-023-15573-3 PMID: 37165327

Jiang, X., Lu, W., Luo, H., Yang, J., Chen, M., Wang, J., Wu, M., Chen, X., Tang, Y., Hu, Y., & Zhang, L. (2023). Spirituality and attitudes toward death among older adults in rural and urban China: A cross-sectional study. *Journal of Religion and Health*, 62(5), 3070–3094. DOI: 10.1007/s10943-023-01794-8 PMID: 37012553

K, A. and Sia, S. (2022). Theory of planned behavior in predicting the construction of eco-friendly houses. Management of Environmental Quality an International Journal, 33(4), 938-954. DOI: 10.1108/MEQ-10-2021-0249

Keskinen, K., Rantakokko, M., Suomi, K., Rantanen, T., & Portegijs, E. (2020). Environmental features associated with older adults' physical activity in different types of urban neighborhoods. *Journal of Aging and Physical Activity*, 28(4), 540–548. DOI: 10.1123/japa.2019-0251 PMID: 31860829

Kim, K., Buckley, T., Burnette, D., Kim, S., & Cho, S. (2021). Measurement indicators of age-friendly communities: Findings from the AARP age-friendly community survey. *The Gerontologist*, 62(1), e17–e27. DOI: 10.1093/geront/gnab055 PMID: 33909074

Kimpel, C., Dietrich, M. S., Lauderdale, J., Schlundt, D. G., & Maxwell, C. A. (2024). Using the age-friendly environment framework to assess advance care planning factors among older adults with limited income: A cross-sectional, descriptive survey study. *The Gerontologist*, 64(7), gnae059. Advance online publication. DOI: 10.1093/geront/gnae059 PMID: 38813768

Klann, A., Vu, L., Ewing, M., Fenton, M., & Pojednic, R. (2019). Translating urban walkability initiatives for older adults in rural and under-resourced communities. *International Journal of Environmental Research and Public Health*, 16(17), 3041. DOI: 10.3390/ijerph16173041 PMID: 31443359

Koirala, P., Shrestha, S., & Koirala, M. (2022). Functional status of senior citizens of a metropolitan city in Morang. *Kathmandu University Medical Journal*, 20(4), 493–498. DOI: 10.3126/kumj.v20i4.54276 PMID: 37795731

Lahti, A., Mikkola, T., Salonen, M., Wasenius, N., Sarvimäki, A., Eriksson, J., & Bonsdorff, M. (2021). Mental, physical and social functioning in independently living senior house residents and community-dwelling older adults. *International Journal of Environmental Research and Public Health*, 18(23), 12299. DOI: 10.3390/ijerph182312299 PMID: 34886019

Lee, S. and Edmonston, B. (2019). Living alone among older adults in Canada and the U.S.. Healthcare, 7(2), 68. DOI: 10.3390/healthcare7020068

Lenstra, N. (2017). The community-based information infrastructure of older adult digital learning. *Nordicom Review*, 38(s1), 65–77. DOI: 10.1515/nor-2017-0401

Li, L., Liu, J., Zhang, Z., & Xu, H. (2014). Late-life depression in rural China: Do village infrastructure and availability of community resources matter? *International Journal of Geriatric Psychiatry*, 30(7), 729–736. DOI: 10.1002/gps.4217 PMID: 25333218

Mareš, J., Cígler, H., & Vachková, E. (2016). Czech version of opqol-35 questionnaire: The evaluation of the psychometric properties. *Health and Quality of Life Outcomes*, 14(1), 93. Advance online publication. DOI: 10.1186/s12955-016-0494-7 PMID: 27317441

Melchiorre, M., D'Amen, B., Lamura, G., & Socci, M. (2022). Health emergencies, falls, and use of communication technologies by older people with functional and social frailty: Aging in place in deprived areas of Italy. *International Journal of Environmental Research and Public Health*, 19(22), 14775. DOI: 10.3390/ijerph192214775 PMID: 36429499

Merom, D., Gebel, K., Fahey, P., Astell-Burt, T., Voukelatos, A., Rissel, C., & Sherrington, C. (2015). Neighborhood walkability, fear and risk of falling and response to walking promotion: The easy steps to health 12-month randomized controlled trial. *Preventive Medicine Reports*, 2, 704–710. DOI: 10.1016/j.pmedr.2015.08.011 PMID: 26844140

Mohamad, Z., Nee, A., Yang, F., Rehman, M., & Yin, Y. (2019). *Achieving community happiness through affordable eco-friendly smart houses*. Kne Social Sciences., DOI: 10.18502/kss.v3i21.5021

Ng, S., Lim, X., Hsu, H., & Chou, C. (2022). Age-friendliness of city, loneliness and depression moderated by internet use during the covid-19 pandemic. *Health Promotion International*, 38(3), daac040. Advance online publication. DOI: 10.1093/heapro/daac040 PMID: 35437585

Nojomi, M., Goharinezhad, S., Saraei, R., Goharinejad, S., Ramezani, G., & Aalaa, M. (2023). Exploring the attitudes of general medical students toward older adult's care in a lower middle-income country: Implications for medical education. *BMC Medical Education*, 23(1), 649. Advance online publication. DOI: 10.1186/s12909-023-04626-1 PMID: 37684593

Park, S., Kim, Y., Kwon, O., & Lee, J. (2023). Influence of consumer innovativeness and cosmetic selection attributes on purchase intention of eco-friendly cosmetics. *The Journal of Cosmetic Medicine*, 7(1), 29–37. DOI: 10.25056/JCM.2023.7.1.29

Peek, S., Luijkx, K., Vrijhoef, H., Nieboer, M., Aarts, S., Voort, C., & Wouters, E. (2017). Origins and consequences of technology acquirement by independent-living seniors: Towards an integrative model. *BMC Geriatrics*, 17(1), 189. Advance online publication. DOI: 10.1186/s12877-017-0582-5 PMID: 28830444

Reis da Silva. Tiago Horta (2024d). Death and Its Significance in Nursing Practice. Palliat Med Care Int J. 2024; 4(3): 555640. DOI: https://juniperpublishers.com/pmcij/pdf/PMCIJ.MS.ID.555640.pdf

Reis da Silva, T. (2024c). The Evolution of Nursing for Older Adult: A Historical Perspective. Associative J Health Sci. 3(3). *AJHS*, 000561, 2024. DOI: 10.31031/AJHS.2024.03.000561

Reis da Silva, T. (2024g). Can supplementing vitamin B12 improve mental health outcomes?: A literature review. *British Journal of Community Nursing*, 29(3), 137–146. DOI: 10.12968/bjcn.2024.29.3.137 PMID: 38421889

Reis da Silva, T. H. (2023a). Moving and Handling in the Community. *British Journal of Community Nursing*, 28(8), 369. DOI: 10.12968/bjcn.2023.28.8.369 PMID: 37527217

Reis da Silva, T. H. (2023b). Aging in place: Aging at home and in the community. *British Journal of Community Nursing*, 28(5), 213–214. DOI: 10.12968/bjcn.2023.28.5.213 PMID: 37130715

Reis da Silva, T. H. (2023c). Falls assessment and prevention in the nursing home and community. *British Journal of Community Nursing*, 28(2), 68–72. DOI: 10.12968/bjcn.2023.28.2.68 PMID: 36735363

Reis da Silva, T. H. (2024a). Falls prevention in older people and the role of nursing. *British Journal of Community Nursing*, 29(7), 335–339. DOI: 10.12968/bjcn.2024.0005 PMID: 38963269

Reis da Silva, T. H. (2024b). Loneliness in older adults. *British Journal of Community Nursing*, 29(2), 60–66. DOI: 10.12968/bjcn.2024.29.2.60 PMID: 38300245

Reis da Silva, T. H (2024e). Oncology and Cancer Medicine: Understanding the complexities in Older Patients. Biomed J Sci & Tech Res 55(3)-2024. DOI: DOI: 10.26717/BJSTR.2024.55.008720

Reis da Silva, T. H. (2024f). Understanding body fluid balance, dehydration and intravenous fluid therapy. *Emergency Nurse*. Advance online publication. DOI: 10.7748/en.2024.e2201 PMID: 38978385

Reis da Silva, T. H. (2024h). Chronic kidney disease in older adults: Nursing implications for community nurses. *Journal of Kidney Care*, 9(4), 174–179. DOI: 10.12968/jokc.2024.9.4.174

Reis da Silva, T. H. (2024i). Pharmacokinetics in older people: An overview of prescribing practice. *Journal of Prescribing Practice*, 6(8), 2–9. DOI: 10.12968/jprp.2024.6.9.374

Reis da Silva, T. H., & Mitchell, A. (2024a). Integrating Digital Transformation in Nursing Education: Best Practices and Challenges in Curriculum Development. In Lytras, M., Serban, A. C., Alkhaldi, A., Malik, S., & Aldosemani, T. (Eds.), *Digital Transformation in Higher Education, Part B Cases, Examples and Good Practices*. Emerald Publishing Limited.

Reis da Silva, T. H., & Rodrigues, E. C. P. (2023). Body Image Related Discrimination. In Leal Filho, W., Azul, A. M., Brandli, L., Lange Salvia, A., Özuyar, P. G., & Wall, T. (Eds.), *Reduced Inequalities. Encyclopedia of the UN Sustainable Development Goals*. Springer., DOI: 10.1007/978-3-319-71060-0_61-1

Reis da Silva Tiago. (2024j) The Value of Emotional Intelligence in Midwifery: Enhancing Care and Outcomes for Mothers and Infants through Sustainable Development Goals and Leadership. Journal of Womens Healthcare & Midwifery Research. SRC/JWHMR-133. Link: https://www.onlinescientificresearch.com/articles/the-value-of-emotional-intelligence-in-midwifery-enhancing-care-and-outcomes-for-mothers-and-infants-through-sustainable-developme.pdf

Rodrigues, N., Han, C., Su, Y., Klainin-Yobas, P., & Wu, V. (2021). Psychological impacts and online interventions of social isolation amongst older adults during covid-19 pandemic: A scoping review. *Journal of Advanced Nursing*, 78(3), 609–644. DOI: 10.1111/jan.15063 PMID: 34625997

Scheckler, S. (2020). Housing, affordability, and community-based aging. *Innovation in Aging*, 4(Supplement_1), 690–691. DOI: 10.1093/geroni/igaa057.2415

Scott, M. (2021). Planning for age-friendly cities. *Planning Theory & Practice*, 22(3), 457–492. DOI: 10.1080/14649357.2021.1930423

Simpson, M., Oetzel, J., Wilson, Y., Nock, S., Johnston, K., & Reddy, R. (2022). Codesigning a culture-centered age-friendly community for Māori Kaumātua: Cultural principles and practices. *The Journals of Gerontology. Series B, Psychological Sciences and Social Sciences*, 77(12), 2265–2275. DOI: 10.1093/geronb/gbac092 PMID: 35796864

Soósová, M. (2016). Determinants of quality of life in the elderly. *Central European Journal of Nursing and Midwifery*, 7(3), 484–493. DOI: 10.15452/CE-JNM.2016.07.0019

Steels, S. (2015). Key characteristics of age-friendly cities and communities: A review. *Cities (London, England)*, 47, 45–52. DOI: 10.1016/j.cities.2015.02.004

Tanlamai, U., Jaikengkit, A., Jarutach, T., Rajkulchai, S., & Ritbumroong, T. (2022). Use of daily posture and activity tracking to assess sedentary behavior, toss-and-turns, and sleep duration of independently living Thai seniors. *Health Informatics Journal*, 28(1), 146045822110702. DOI: 10.1177/14604582211070214 PMID: 35220815

Torku, A., Chan, A., & Yung, E. (2020). Age-friendly cities and communities: A review and future directions. *Aging and Society*, 41(10), 2242–2279. DOI: 10.1017/S0144686X20000239

Torku, A., Chan, A., & Yung, E. (2020). Implementation of age-friendly initiatives in smart cities: Probing the barriers through a systematic review. *Built Environment Project and Asset Management*, 11(3), 412–426. DOI: 10.1108/BEPAM-01-2020-0008

Warner, M., & Zhang, X. (2023). Representative bureaucracy, age-friendly planning, and the role of gender, public engagement, and professional management. *Administration & Society*, 55(9), 1738–1757. DOI: 10.1177/00953997231183000

Wolinsky, F., Jones, M., & Dotson, M. (2020). Does visual speed of processing training improve health-related quality of life in assisted and independent living communities?: A randomized controlled trial. *Innovation in Aging*, 4(4), igaa029. Advance online publication. DOI: 10.1093/geroni/igaa029 PMID: 32964141

Wright, R., Gamaldo, A., & Lee, A. (2022). Neighborhood quality as it relates to health and well-being in older African Americans. *Innovation in Aging*, 6(Supplement_1), 113–114. DOI: 10.1093/geroni/igac059.452

Yamada, K., Murotani, K., Mano, M., Lim, Y., & Yoshimatsu, J. (2023). Age-friendly approach is necessary to prevent depopulation: Resident architectural designers and constructors' evaluation of the age-friendliness of Japanese municipalities. *International Journal of Environmental Research and Public Health*, 20(17), 6626. DOI: 10.3390/ijerph20176626 PMID: 37681766

Yamada, K., Murotani, K., Mano, M., Lim, Y., & Yoshimatsu, J. (2023). Age-friendly approach is necessary to prevent depopulation: Resident architectural designers and constructors' evaluation of the age-friendliness of Japanese municipalities. *International Journal of Environmental Research and Public Health*, 20(17), 6626. DOI: 10.3390/ijerph20176626 PMID: 37681766

Ying, L., Lai, M., & Hwa, L. (2021). Modelling age-friendly environment for social connectedness: A cross-sectional study. *F1000 Research*, 10, 955. DOI: 10.12688/f1000research.73032.1 PMID: 35035892

Yu, J., Ma, G., & Wang, S. (2021). Do age-friendly rural communities affect quality of life? a comparison of perceptions from middle-aged and older adults in China. *International Journal of Environmental Research and Public Health*, 18(14), 7283. DOI: 10.3390/ijerph18147283 PMID: 34299736

Zhang, Y., Wang, J., Zu, Y., & Hu, Q. (2021). Attitudes of Chinese college students toward aging and living independently in the context of China's modernization: A qualitative study. *Frontiers in Psychology*, 12, 609736. Advance online publication. DOI: 10.3389/fpsyg.2021.609736 PMID: 34135797

Zuiderveen, A., Ivey, C., Dordan, S., & Leiras, C. (2016). Encouraging occupation: A systematic review of the use of life review and reminiscence therapy for the treatment of depressive symptoms in older adults. *Occupational Therapy in Mental Health*, 32(3), 281–298. DOI: 10.1080/0164212X.2016.1145090

# Chapter 7
# The Effects of Türkiye's Ageing Problem on the Elderly

**Bilal Göde**
https://orcid.org/0000-0001-8377-5909
*Pamukkale University, Turkey*

## ABSTRACT

*Old age is one of the life stages that every living being will encounter if they live a normal life course. Thanks to the opportunities provided by developing technology and economic development, the average life expectancy is gradually increasing and the number of people who manage to reach the old age stage is increasing day by day. In old age, people's employment opportunities decrease and this may cause economic bottlenecks for the elderly. It is becoming more and more likely that elderly people who try to survive in old age by relying solely on public resources will experience economic difficulties. The relationship between the elderly population and GDP per capita and health expenditures is tested with Johansen cointegration test and toda yamamoto causality test. A cointegration relationship was found between the variables. According to the model results, a causality relationship was found between the elderly population and GDP per capita and health expenditures.*

## INTRODUCTION

Aging is a stage of life that every living being will experience. In this phase, many differences emerge compared to other phases experienced before. In particular, factors such as deterioration in health and decreased productivity have economically challenging effects on the elderly. Many different definitions have been made by

DOI: 10.4018/979-8-3693-7753-6.ch007

looking at the concept of aging from different perspectives. Aging has been handled with many different approaches such as biological, chronological, psychological and economic aging. Despite the disadvantaged situation of the elderly, it is necessary to prevent their economic well-being from falling to a challenging level. In addition to individuals making preparations for their own future, the state needs to develop policies especially against economic aging.

Economic ageing refers to the economic effects of changes in the demographic structure of a society or country. Generally, population ageing is associated with declining fertility rates and longer life expectancy. The decline in the working-age population causes economic challenges, such as the burden on pension systems and health systems. As an older population reduces the number of people working in the economy, there will be a reduction in the labor force. A declining labor force will also put pressure on all pension- related financial systems. More retirees will also increase health expenditures of the aging population. The aging of the population poses a major threat to the sustainability of public finances due to the decrease in public revenue and increase in public expenditures (Aydın, 2024). Rather than excluding the elderly population, it would be beneficial to ensure that they remain within the system as much as possible to reduce their burden on public finances and to ensure that their past experiences guide the new generation (Ayabakan, 2022). Attempts to mitigate the negative effects of population aging are essential, especially for the survival of pension systems.

The human life cycle is basically composed of the stages of birth, aging and death. Analyzing this cycle for societies helps to predict the structural changes of the population. Births and deaths are very important for the survival of a socio-economically balanced society. The increase in the elderly population in a society will endanger the economic and social balance and emphasize the necessity of death for the increase and sustainability of social welfare (Gölçek & Göde, 2023).

This study will focus on the concept of economic aging and examine its effects on the elderly in Türkiye. The economic consequences of the aging population, social security systems, economic policy recommendations and the relationship between economy and aging in general will be discussed. The relationship between the elderly population, health expenditures and GDP per capita will be investigated by cointegration and causality tests. Model results will be interpreted and policy recommendations will be presented. The aim of the study is to provide readers with an overview of the economic effects of population aging and to evaluate Türkiye's situation in this regard by comparing it with international examples.

# AGING AND TYPES OF AGING

Although aging and old age are basically considered as a biological process, they are too broad to be limited to these concepts. The reason why aging, which has many aspects, has such a wide range is that the human being is a complex being in itself (Yaman & Acar, 2015).

Poverty is a problem that individuals may face in all periods of their lives. Poverty can have different effects in every period of life. Poverty in old age is a major problem. It is more difficult for individuals to escape poverty in old age. The risk of poverty increases for the elderly who have lost their working power significantly compared to their youth. For this reason, the effects of poverty in old age can be more severe (Karadeniz & Öztepe, 2013).

Population aging is accompanied by a wide range of social and economic changes. Declines in birth rates, changes in marriage, cohabitation and divorce patterns, rising levels of education and economic prosperity, as well as migration are also influential in the process of social aging (UN, 2020).

*Table 1. Societies by proportion of elderly population*

| 1-Young societies | Populations with less than 4% of the population aged 65 and over |
|---|---|
| 2-Mature Societies | Societies with a population aged 65 and over between 4-7% of the total population |
| 3-Elder Societies | Societies where the proportion of the population aged 65 and over to the entire population is between 7-10% (such as Canada, Australia, Japan, Türkiye) |
| 4 - Very Old Societies | Societies where the ratio of the elderly population to the total population is above 10%. In these societies fertility rates are very low or the young population has emigrated. Developed European countries are usually in this group (e.g. Norway, Sweden) |

Source: Bölüktaş (2019)

It is possible to analyze societies in 4 groups based on the ratio of the elderly to the total population. Table 1 presents these 4 groups and their definitions. Türkiye is among the elderly societies with its current proportion of elderly and Türkiye's elderly population continues to increase rapidly.

There are definitions of old age according to many different criteria, not only the age dimension. Considering these definitions, biological, social, psychological and chronological aging classifications come to the fore (Yerli, 2017):

- *Chronological Ageing*: Chronological age, also referred to as calendar age or birth age, is the age of an individual counted starting from birth. It is obtained by subtracting the date of birth from the date of the current period. Those with a higher calendar age are considered older than those with a lower calendar age (Aslan & Hocaoğlu, 2017). According to the chronological approach, someone who is 70 years old is older than someone who is 50 years old. According to the World Health Organization (WHO), 65 is the age of old age, while the United Nations' age limit is 60 (Türkiye Eleventh Development Plan, 2018). Considering a complex concept such as old age only in chronological terms is incomplete in terms of understanding the importance of old age.

- *Biological Aging*: Biological aging is the anatomical and physiological changes that an individual experiences over time (Öksüzokyar et al., 2016). Biological aging may vary from individual to individual. The conditions in which the individual lives, work life, social life are among the factors that can affect the course of biological aging. The changes that occur due to physical and chemical reactions occurring in cells are the technical explanation of biological aging. In addition to these reactions, external factors can accelerate or slow down this process. The decrease in the durability and regeneration rate of tissues brings about biological aging. The aging process is realized when the rate of wear and tear exceeds the rate of regeneration (Bulut and Özçakar, 2011).

- *Psychological Aging*: This type of aging is the changes in the mental, behavioral and social position of individuals during the aging process. Especially adapting to the changes in their social status is one of the biggest problems (Bölüktaş 2019). The difficulties experienced in the process of adapting to the new social status are considered within the scope of psychological aging.

- *Economic Aging*: Changes in the lifestyle and welfare level of individuals caused by the loss of income that individuals suffer after ending their active working life constitute the subject of economic aging. With aging, individuals are able to work less or cannot work (MEB, 2011). Accordingly, the capacity to generate income also decreases. When the wealth accumulation of individuals is not taken into account, public resources and individuals' own work are the sources of income. As work opportunities and capacity decline with aging, the main source of income is generally public resources.

Aging is a process that cannot be stopped or reversed within the existing possibilities. The only possible policy is to make this process as bearable and comfortable as possible for individuals. For this reason, facilitating the lives of aging individuals is one of the important policies of states. Reducing the risks of poverty by improving the financial situation of individuals is one of the tasks undertaken by social states.

# OLD AGE PROFILE OF TÜRKİYE

Countries' rising levels of indebtedness confront the twin goals of spending on the elderly and reducing budget deficits. Many countries feel compelled to reconsider the composition of their pension and health expenditures, which account for almost 40% of total expenditures. By 2050, the world's elderly population is expected to equalize with the young population, with more than 2 billion elderly people (Harper, 2014). This situation makes old age a common problem for the whole world.

*Table 2. Türkiye's population structure and future projections*

|  | (65+) | 15-64 | 0-14 | Total | 0-14/65+ | 15-64/65+ | 65+/Total |
|---|---|---|---|---|---|---|---|
| 1950 | 791627 | 11696980 | 8531915 | 21020522 | 10,78 | 14,78 | 0,038 |
| 1980 | 2120321 | 25215983 | 18071786 | 45408090 | 8,52 | 11,89 | 0,047 |
| 1990 | 2653705 | 33298281 | 20061892 | 56013878 | 7,56 | 12,55 | 0,047 |
| 2000 | 3800740 | 41854609 | 19768657 | 65424006 | 5,20 | 11,01 | 0,058 |
| 2010 | 5275938 | 49076202 | 18993247 | 73345387 | 3,60 | 9,30 | 0,072 |
| 2020 | 7714241 | 58771559 | 19602989 | 86088789 | 2,54 | 7,62 | 0,090 |
| 2023 | 8725568 | 59482915 | 19059642 | 87268125 | 2,18 | 6,82 | 0,100 |
| 2024 | 8992923 | 59715661 | 18762174 | 87470758 | 2,09 | 6,64 | 0,103 |
| 2025 | 9265463 | 59982227 | 18434022 | 87681712 | 1,99 | 6,47 | 0,106 |
| 2030 | 11250397 | 61140363 | 16631081 | 89021841 | 1,48 | 5,43 | 0,126 |
| 2050 | 20188826 | 57436139 | 13614302 | 91239267 | 0,67 | 2,84 | 0,221 |
| 2070 | 26405225 | 47648673 | 10231503 | 84285401 | 0,39 | 1,80 | 0,313 |
| 2090 | 26355496 | 37158644 | 8300219 | 71814359 | 0,31 | 1,41 | 0,367 |
| 2100 | 24387386 | 33470784 | 7166749 | 65024919 | 0,29 | 1,37 | 0,375 |

Source: UN World Population Prospects (2024)

The increase in the proportion of the elderly population in the total population causes a deteriorating effect on socioeconomic balances. The increase in the elderly population has the effect of reducing the proportional difference between the population with productive capacity and the dependent population. This situation affects the intergenerational income distribution and changes the expectations for the retirement period (Karadeniz & Öztepe, 2013). It is also taken into account as an important decision input for policy makers.

In industrializing societies, the problem of old age arises spontaneously. With the increasing participation of people in the labor force, the size of families is gradually shrinking. With the resulting increase in welfare, the average human life span is gradually increasing. The decrease in births and the increase in the average

age also bring about the aging of the society. Developments in the field of medicine also support this process (Yaman & Acar, 2015).

Table 2 shows the population of Türkiye in three categories: elderly population (65+), 15-64 (able to work) and young population (0-14). Considering the population structure according to this classification is necessary in order to know the size of the group that can be called needy (elderly + young). In 1950, the ratio of the working population to the elderly population was 14.77, while this ratio was 11.01 in 2000 and decreased to 6.81 in 2023. Accordingly, for every elderly person, the number of people who can work in the society has decreased from 14.77 to 6.81. The ratio of the elderly population to the total population has increased from only 3.8% in 1950 to 10% in 2023. This ratio means that 100 out of every 1000 people in society are elderly.

According to the projections made by the UN, population changes in these three categories have been estimated. In 2050, the ratio of the elderly population to the total population will be 22%, while in 2100 this ratio will rise to 37.5%. In this case, 375 out of every 1000 people in the society will be elderly. If these rates are realized, Türkiye will join the ranks of very old societies by 2030.

## FERTILITY IN TÜRKIYE

In industrial societies, it is becoming more difficult to have children with labor force participation and the size of families is shrinking. With the resulting prosperity, life expectancy increases. This situation becomes a vicious circle. The functioning of the system reveals the problem as a natural process. The increase in the level of education leads to a worse situation by reducing birth rates.

*Table 3. Fertility levels in Türkiye and selected countries*

|  | 1962 | 1982 | 2002 | 2022 | 2042 | 2062 |  | 1962 | 1982 | 2002 | 2022 | 2042 | 2062 |
|---|---|---|---|---|---|---|---|---|---|---|---|---|---|
| Australia | 3,39 | 1,93 | 1,76 | 1,60 | 1,65 | 1,67 | Mexico | 6,77 | 4,44 | 2,62 | 1,80 | 1,70 | 1,67 |
| Austria | 2,80 | 1,66 | 1,37 | 1,47 | 1,55 | 1,59 | Netherlands | 3,17 | 1,50 | 1,73 | 1,64 | 1,66 | 1,67 |
| Belgium | 2,60 | 1,62 | 1,64 | 1,59 | 1,65 | 1,67 | New Zealand | 4,13 | 1,94 | 1,87 | 1,76 | 1,69 | 1,68 |
| Canada | 3,73 | 1,70 | 1,49 | 1,47 | 1,53 | 1,55 | Norway | 2,87 | 1,71 | 1,76 | 1,51 | 1,59 | 1,62 |
| Chile | 4,60 | 2,65 | 1,92 | 1,54 | 1,55 | 1,58 | Poland | 2,74 | 2,32 | 1,25 | 1,46 | 1,54 | 1,57 |
| Colombia | 6,65 | 3,62 | 2,43 | 1,69 | 1,64 | 1,63 | Portugal | 3,27 | 2,07 | 1,46 | 1,37 | 1,45 | 1,51 |
| Costa Rica | 6,51 | 3,53 | 2,18 | 1,52 | 1,53 | 1,56 | Slovak Republic | 2,84 | 2,29 | 1,19 | 1,57 | 1,62 | 1,64 |
| Czechia | 2,11 | 1,99 | 1,18 | 1,70 | 1,72 | 1,72 | Slovenia | 2,29 | 1,92 | 1,21 | 1,63 | 1,68 | 1,69 |

continued on following page

*Table 3. Continued*

|  | 1962 | 1982 | 2002 | 2022 | 2042 | 2062 |  | 1962 | 1982 | 2002 | 2022 | 2042 | 2062 |
|---|---|---|---|---|---|---|---|---|---|---|---|---|---|
| Denmark | 2,54 | 1,42 | 1,73 | 1,72 | 1,72 | 1,73 | Spain | 2,78 | 1,93 | 1,24 | 1,29 | 1,41 | 1,48 |
| Estonia | 1,95 | 2,08 | 1,36 | 1,68 | 1,67 | 1,68 | Sweden | 2,22 | 1,61 | 1,65 | 1,67 | 1,68 | 1,69 |
| Finland | 2,66 | 1,72 | 1,71 | 1,40 | 1,50 | 1,56 | Switzerland | 2,56 | 1,54 | 1,37 | 1,50 | 1,57 | 1,60 |
| France | 2,77 | 1,92 | 1,86 | 1,79 | 1,78 | 1,76 | Türkiye | 6,22 | 4,14 | 2,32 | 1,88 | 1,76 | 1,72 |
| Germany | 2,50 | 1,49 | 1,33 | 1,53 | 1,57 | 1,59 | United Kingdom | 2,89 | 1,77 | 1,62 | 1,57 | 1,63 | 1,66 |
| Greece | 2,30 | 2,10 | 1,32 | 1,37 | 1,45 | 1,50 | United States | 3,34 | 1,82 | 2,00 | 1,66 | 1,69 | 1,70 |
| Hungary | 1,80 | 1,78 | 1,30 | 1,58 | 1,62 | 1,64 | Saudi Arabia | 7,44 | 6,95 | 3,71 | 2,39 | 1,96 | 1,82 |
| Iceland | 3,97 | 2,28 | 1,94 | 1,73 | 1,68 | 1,65 | South Africa | 6,04 | 4,62 | 2,31 | 2,34 | 2,00 | 1,84 |
| Ireland | 3,91 | 2,95 | 1,95 | 1,76 | 1,72 | 1,71 | Argentina | 3,09 | 3,19 | 2,48 | 1,88 | 1,77 | 1,72 |
| Israel | 3,76 | 3,15 | 2,88 | 2,95 | 2,54 | 2,21 | Brazil | 5,97 | 3,82 | 2,08 | 1,63 | 1,60 | 1,62 |
| Italy | 2,46 | 1,56 | 1,27 | 1,29 | 1,41 | 1,47 | China | 6,07 | 3,00 | 1,55 | 1,18 | 1,35 | 1,43 |
| Japan | 1,99 | 1,70 | 1,33 | 1,31 | 1,44 | 1,50 | India | 5,90 | 4,57 | 3,20 | 2,01 | 1,83 | 1,75 |
| Korea | 5,64 | 2,46 | 1,19 | 0,87 | 1,11 | 1,27 | Indonesia | 5,53 | 4,20 | 2,45 | 2,15 | 1,92 | 1,81 |
| Latvia | 1,92 | 1,99 | 1,26 | 1,59 | 1,61 | 1,63 | EU27 | 2,59 | 1,93 | 1,44 | 1,53 | 1,59 | 1,62 |
| Lithuania | 2,49 | 1,97 | 1,24 | 1,62 | 1,67 | 1,70 | **OECD** | **3,30** | **2,15** | **1,65** | **1,59** | **1,62** | **1,63** |
| Luxembourg | 2,26 | 1,49 | 1,62 | 1,39 | 1,50 | 1,55 |  |  |  |  |  |  |  |

Source: United Nations, Department of Economic and Social Affairs (2022)

As of 2023, there are approximately 8.7 million elderly people in Türkiye. Considering that the fertility rate is declining and the average human life expectancy is gradually increasing, it is estimated that the weight of the elderly in society will gradually increase. From 6.22 in 1962, the fertility rate declined to 4.22 in 1982 and to 1.88 in 2022. According to UN estimates, it is expected to decline to 1.76 in 2042 and to 1.72 in 2062. Such a rapid decline in the fertility rate is a major problem for Türkiye's demographic structure. In 1962, the OECD average was 3.3, while Türkiye's average was almost twice the OECD average, but rapidly converged to the OECD average in 2002 and 2022. Throughout this period, average speeds in most OECD countries have been parallel or very close to the OECD average. Therefore, for many countries, this situation can be considered normal. For Türkiye, however, this rapid decline may have a challenging impact on policy development. In 25 countries in the table, average fertility is equal to or above the OECD average, while in 20 countries it is below the average.

*Figure 1. Median age level in Türkiye*

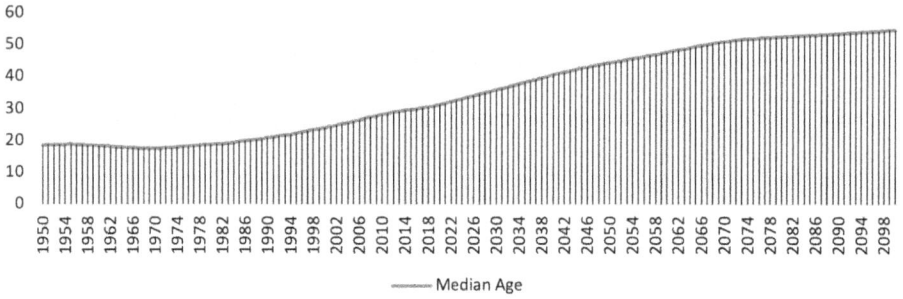

Median Age

*(UN, World Population Prospects, 2024)*

By the end of the 21st century, demographic structures will be characterized by declining birth rates, an aging society and a numerically stable nature. Figure 1 shows the median age graph of Türkiye starting from 1950. While the median age was below 20 until the 1970s, it rose above 30 by 2024. While it was possible to easily talk about a young society structure until 1990, the median age started to increase rapidly after this period. According to the projections made by the UN, the median age is expected to be 54 in 2100. Such a rapid increase in the median age is an important indicator that Turkish society is aging very rapidly. The increase in the weight of the upper segments of the population pyramid is one of the most important factors that increase the median age. This is due to the fact that while the elderly population is gradually increasing, the increase in the young population does not follow the same course.

*Figure 2. Life expectancy at birth in Türkiye*

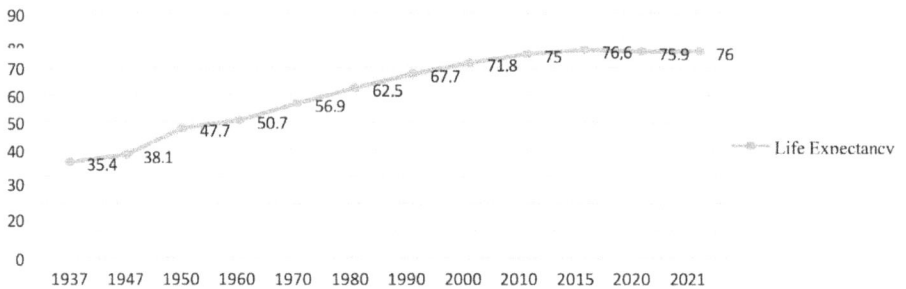

Life Expectancy

*(UN WPP, 2022; HMD, 2023; Zijdeman et al., 2015; Riley, 2005)*

The figure shows the average life expectancy in Türkiye between 1937 and 2021. While in 1937 the average life expectancy was 35.4 years, this number increased to 76 in 2021. According to this data, considering the age limit of 65 years, after the 1990s, almost all of the society had the expectation that they could reach old age. This is one of the most important signs of social aging. Life expectancy is continuously increasing thanks to the increase in economic prosperity and advances in the medical field. Considering the progress of the current economic system and technological developments, it will be possible to conclude that the average life expectancy will increase further.

## OLD AGE AND PENSION SYSTEM IN TÜRKİYE

Premiums are one of the most important sources of income for a social security system to survive. As the number of employees increases, the premiums collected will increase, while a decrease in the number of employees will lead to a decrease in premiums. The fact that the elderly leave the working life with retirement, terminate their premium payments and receive a pension has a challenging effect on the system. In this respect, the fact that the elderly who are able to work remain in the labor force means that they will continue to generate premiums and support the system.

*Figure 3. Income sources of older people (2020)*

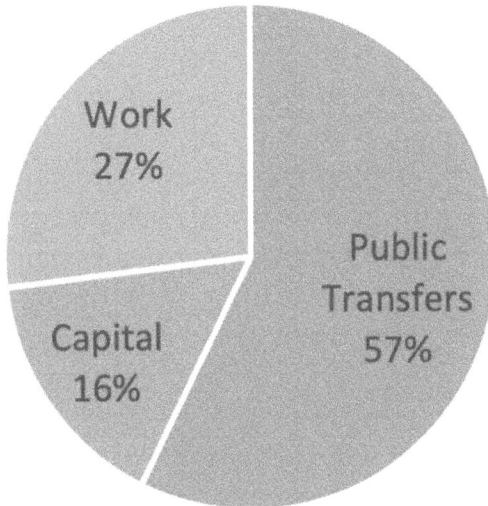

Work
27%

Capital
16%

Public
Transfers
57%

*(OECD Income Distribution Database, 2023)*

Figure 3 shows the sources of income of pensioners in Türkiye. Public transfers are the largest source of income with 57%. The state ranks first in terms of income sources of retirees. The second largest source of income is income from work. 27% share of income from work means that individuals continue to work despite retirement. The 16% contribution from capital shows that retirees derive the least income from their own assets and private pension systems, and thus the number of wealthy retirees is quite low. When the sources of income of retirees in Türkiye are taken into account, the sources received from the state rank first. As the elderly population increases in the coming years, the number of retirees will also increase and the burden on the social security system will gradually increase. Incentives for retirees to diversify their income sources should be implemented. It should be made clear to the society that it will become increasingly difficult to live solely on state-sourced income and that they should take their own precautions for the future. Retired people should be given the opportunity to work after retirement by enabling them to age more properly. It is essential to create an active aging and thus a more economically and socially active elderly population by preventing the elderly from being cut off from society with retirement.

*Table 4. Transfers to social security institutions (Thousand TL)*

| Years | Total Transfer | Total Transfer/Total Budget |
|-------|----------------|----------------------------|
| 2011 | 16.660.893 | 0,12 |
| 2012 | 21.809.382 | 0,13 |
| 2013 | 20.545.353 | 0,11 |
| 2014 | 21.485.116 | 0,10 |
| 2015 | 12.248.203 | 0,05 |
| 2016 | 20.601.684 | 0,08 |
| 2017 | 25.713.555 | 0,08 |
| 2018 | 16.800.805 | 0,04 |
| 2019 | 110.036.558 | 0,23 |
| 2020 | 153.572.409 | 0,27 |
| 2021 | 122.940.128 | 0,18 |
| 2022 | 215.251.560 | 0,20 |
| 2023 | 391.696.349 | 0,17 |
| Total | 1.149.361.995 | |

Source: Social Security Institutions Budget Statistics (2024)

Table 4 shows the transfers made to the social security institution by the administrations included in the Central Government Budget. Transfers made over the years have been on a continuous and increasing trend. Between 2011 and 2023, a total transfer of approximately TL 1.15 trillion was realized from the central government to the social security institution. The inability of the social security institution to meet its expenses with its own revenues is not sustainable in the long run. It is of great importance to prevent these chronic deficits and to transform the social security institution into a self-sufficient structure. In proportional terms, transfers fell to 5% of the total budget in 2015 but reached a record high of 27% in 2019. For every 100 liras that entered the SSI budget, 27 liras came from transfers. The sustainability of a system in which deficits are persistent and which is necessarily sustained by transfers is a matter of debate.

*Figure 4. The normal retirement age in OECD countries*

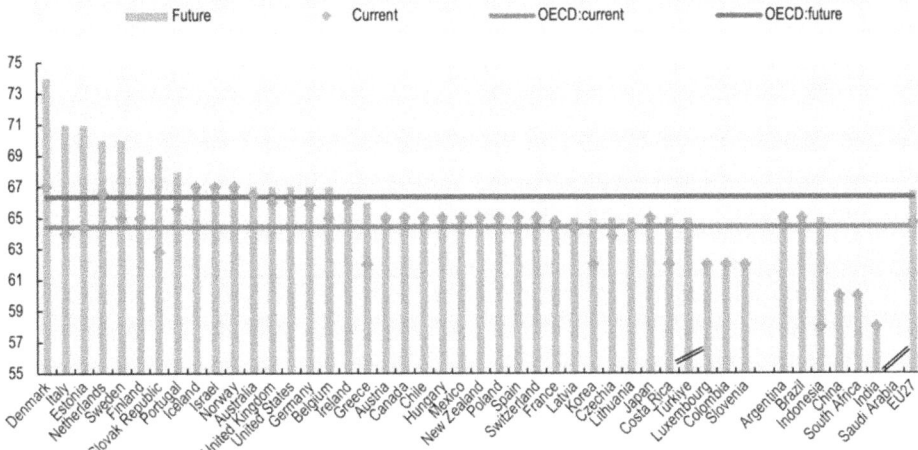

(*OECD Pensions at a Glance, 2023*)

The figure shows the retirement ages of OECD member countries. Looking at the horizontal lines, the lower line shows the current OECD retirement age level, while the upper line shows the expected OECD retirement age level in the future. Many countries have retirement ages below the current OECD average. According to the current outlook, many countries will have to raise their retirement ages in the upcoming period. Türkiye is an exceptional case, with a current retirement age of 52. The retirement age, which has increased after the recent regulations, is expected and required to increase further in the future.

The aging of the population also affects the consumption-saving decisions of the society. While consumption tendency is high in societies with a large young population, consumption tendency gradually decreases and saving tendency increases in societies with a large elderly population. This situation is also effective in shaping the production decisions of the supply side. In addition, the consumption decisions of the elderly population are different from those of the young population. While societies with a predominantly young population adapt to innovations faster, the elderly population cannot adapt to innovations quickly. This, in turn, affects demand and closely affects the export-import composition (Hunjira et al., 2022).

In societies with relatively lower consumption and higher savings, a decline in production and hence employment would be an expected outcome. A decline in employment may also lead to a decline in the revenues of social security systems. The possibility of a decrease in the revenues of the social security system, whose expenditures have to increase with the aging population, may put the system into a serious bottleneck.

The effects of aging are also seen in the context of fiscal policies. The demands of the elderly population for public services (social welfare and health) are increasing in line with their needs. In addition to these, there are also increases in service demands such as security (Sanz and Velázquez, 2007).

In addition, it creates changes in the areas where public expenditures will be directed. In a society with a predominantly young population, education expenditures will take precedence, while in a society with a predominantly elderly population, social security and elderly care expenditures will take priority. In societies with more retirees, the share of social security also increases. The state's shifting of resources to these areas may also restrict the resources to be allocated to investments and negatively affect sustainable development (Wang et al., 2024). States need to take demographic factors into account when formulating employment, fiscal, tax, health, investment and migration policies.

## EMPIRICAL LITERATURE SUMMARY

Previous studies in the literature are instructive in determining the data to be used in the model and the type of model. By examining the previous studies, it will be possible to identify the missing parts in the literature and to carry out studies in these areas.

*Table 5. Selected studies on the relationship between health expenditures, elderly population, and income*

| Author | Study | Conclusion |
|--------|-------|------------|
| Newhouse (1977) | Medical-Care Expenditure: A Cross- National Survey | In this study, the relationship between income and health expenditures is investigated using panel data set. It is concluded that as income increases, health expenditures also increase. |
| Culyer (1989) | Cost containment in Europe | Using panel data set, the study concludes that income is the determinant of health expenditures in Europe. |
| Zweifel et al. (1999) | Ageing Of Population and Health Care Expenditure: A Red Herring? | The study concludes that not only the income level but also the aging structure of Sweden has an impact on health expenditures. |
| Gerdtham et al. (2000) | On stationarity and cointegration of international health expenditure and GDP | The study concluded that the GDP and health expenditures of 21 OECD countries are cointegrated. |
| Taban & Kar (2003) | The impacts of the disaggregated public expenditure on economic growth | In this study, the relationship between health expenditures and economic growth in Türkiye was investigated through cointegration analysis. They concluded that there is a negative relationship between health expenditures and economic growth. |
| Clemente et al. (2004) | On the international stability of health care expenditure functions: are government and private functions similar? | The study concluded that there is a long-run cointegration relationship between health expenditures and GDP in a sample of OECD countries. |
| Erdil &Yetkiner (2004) | A Panel Data Approach for Income-Health Causality | The study concluded that there is a long-run cointegration relationship between health expenditures and GDP in a sample of OECD countries. In the study, a causality relationship operating from economic growth to health expenditures in low- and middle-income countries |
| Wang & Rettenmaier (2007) | A Note On Cointegration Of Health Expenditures And Income | The study investigates the stationarity and cointegration of health expenditures and gross state product (GSP) using a panel data set of 50 US states. The study concludes that the two series form a cointegrated relationship. |

continued on following page

*Table 5. Continued*

| Author | Study | Conclusion |
|---|---|---|
| Payne et al. (2007) | Counting Backward to Health Care's Future: Using Time-to-Death Modeling to Identify Changes in End-of-Life Morbidity and the Impact of Aging on Health Care Expenditures | The study concluded that health expenditures increase more than the increase in income.<br>According to the results of the study, there will be an increase in health expenditures due to the increase in old age. |
| Narayan & Narayan (2008) | The Role Of Permanent And Transitory Shocks In Explaining International Health Expenditures | In this study, the relationship between health expenditures and per capita income in the USA, the UK, Japan, Canada, and Switzerland is investigated. In the UK, Japan and Switzerland, temporary shocks are more important in explaining per capita health expenditures, while in the USA and Canada, permanent shocks are dominant in changes in per capita health expenditures. |
| Arisoy et al. (2010) | Social Expenditures and Economic Growth Relationship: Turkish Economy A Study for the 1960 - 2005 Period Dynamic Analysis | The results of the study emphasize the positive impact of both social expenditures and their subcomponents such as education, health and social protection expenditures on economic growth. |
| Cetin & Ecevit (2010) | The Impact of Health Expenditures on Economic Growth: A Panel Regression Analysis on OECD Countries | In this study, the relationship between health expenditures and economic growth in 15 OECD countries was tested by panel data analysis.<br>According to the empirical model results, there is no statistically significant relationship between health expenditures and economic growth. |
| Moscone & Tosetti (2010) | Health Expenditure And Income In The United States | This study investigates income and health expenditures in the United States using a panel data set. According to the study, there is a long- run cointegration relationship between personal income and health expenditures. According to the study, it is concluded that health care is not a luxury but a necessity. |
| de Meijer et al. (2013) | The effect of population aging on health expenditure growth: a critical review | In the study, population aging increases acute care costs and increases health expenditures in the long run. |

continued on following page

*Table 5. Continued*

| Author | Study | Conclusion |
|---|---|---|
| de la Maisonneuvei et al. (2013) | Public Spending on Health and Long-term Care | On average, total health and long-term care expenditures in OECD countries are projected to increase by 3.3 and 7.7 percent of GDP between 2010 and 2060 under cost constraint and cost pressure scenarios, respectively. In the same period for BRICS, it is projected to increase by |
| Tamakoshi & Hamori (2015) | Health-care expenditure, GDP and share of the elderly in Japan: a panel cointegration analysis | In the study, using panel data set, it is concluded that the increasing elderly population in Japan increases health expenditures. |
| Kurt (2015) | Government Health Expenditures and Economic Growth: A Feder-Ram Approach for the Case of Türkiye | According to the results of the study, the direct effect of government health expenditures on economic growth in Türkiye is positive and significant, while the indirect effect is negative and significant. |
| Pascual-Saez et al. (2017) | Public health expenditure, GDP and the elderly population: a comparative study | The study concluded that there is a cointegration relationship between health expenditure per capita, GDP per capita and population over 65 in Spanish autonomous communities. It is concluded that the increase in health expenditures due to the aging population may have challenging effects on health systems. |
| Nyamweya (2017) | Healthcare Expenditure And Economic Growth: The Kenyan Case (1970 - 2016) | The study finds that health expenditures are positively and significantly associated with economic growth measured by real GDP. |
| Piabuo et al. (2017) | Health expenditure and economic growth - a review of the literature and an analysis between the economic community for central African states (CEMAC) and selected African countries | The study finds that there is a positive and significant relationship between health expenditures and economic growth in CEMAC countries and 5 other African countries. The relationship is long-run and significant. While there is an increase of 0.38% in five African countries, there is an increase of 0.30% in CEMAC countries. |

continued on following page

*Table 5. Continued*

| Author | Study | Conclusion |
|--------|-------|------------|
| Karasac & Sağın (2018) | The Effect Of Health Expenditures On Economic Growth In Oecd Economies | According to the findings of the study, there is a linear relationship between health expenditures and Gross Domestic Product in OECD countries. In these economies, increases in health expenditures also increase national income. In addition, according to the VECM Model, there is a bidirectional causality relationship between the variables. |
| Alwago (2023) | The nexus between health expenditure, life expectancy, and economic growth: ARDL model analysis for Kenya | The study concluded that health expenditures have a positive effect on GDP and life expectancy has a positive effect on GDP in Kenya in the long run. According to the causality test results, there is a unidirectional causality from health expenditures to economic growth. |

## METHOD AND DATA SET

In this study, Johansen Cointegration Test and Toda-Yamamoto (1995) causality model are used to examine the relationship between GDP per capita, health expenditures and elderly population. While the Johansen Cointegration Test is used to investigate whether there is one or more relationships between series with unit roots, the Toda-Yamamoto test is a method designed to determine the existence of a causal relationship between variables and the direction of the relationship if it exists. One of the biggest advantages of the Toda- Yamamoto method is that it does not require the existence of a cointegration relationship between the variables used in the model.

First, a series of preliminary analyses are required to determine the structural characteristics of the data set to be used and to identify an appropriate model. These analyses include various statistical tests such as unit root test, heteroscedasticity and LM autocorrelation test. The unit root test is used to determine whether the time series data are stationary or not, while the LM test is used to test whether the errors of the model are autocorrelated or not and the varying variance test is used to test whether the variance of the errors in the model is constant or not. These tests are important for determining the structural properties of the data set and thus ensuring the accuracy of the model.

*Table 6. Variables used in the study and their explanations*

| Variables | Abbreviations | Description | Data Source | Period |
|---|---|---|---|---|
| GDP Per Capita | GDP | Türkiye's GDP per Capita | World Bank | 1975-2022 |
| Elderly Population | Elder | Türkiye's Population Over 65+ | United Nations | 1975-2022 |
| Health Spending (%GDP) | Health | Türkiye's Health Spending (%GDP) | Ourworld In Data | 1975-2022 |

The aim of the analysis is to investigate how GDP per capita, health expenditures and elderly population are related to each other using the data set in the table. There are 3 variables in the model and the data set between 1975-2022 is used. Logarithms of the data are used in the model to minimize computational and model setting errors.

*Table 7. Unit root test results*

| Series Name | Model | | ADF | |
|---|---|---|---|---|
| | | | Statistics | Probe. |
| GDP (GDP Per Capita) | Level | None | 1.211 | 0.9401 |
| | | Constant | -0.403 | 0.9000 |
| | | Constant Trend | -1.732121 | 0.7210 |
| | First Difference | None | -5.732135 | 0.0000*** |
| | | Constant | -6.051116 | 0.0000*** |
| | | Constant Trend | -5.992618 | 0.0000*** |
| ELDER (Elderly Population) | Level | None | 2.551070 | 0.9968 |
| | | Constant | 3.626269 | 1.0000 |
| | | Constant Trend | 0.256203 | 0.9977 |
| | First Difference | None | 1.227369 | 0.9416 |
| | | Constant | 0.004371 | 0.9538 |
| | | Constant Trend | -4.678729 | 0.0031*** |
| HEALTH (Health Spending-%GDP) | Level | None | 0.696804 | 0.8626 |
| | | Constant | -1.024909 | 0.7369 |
| | | Constant Trend | -1.020597 | 0.9311 |
| | First Difference | None | -5.465528 | 0.0000*** |
| | | Constant | -5.601450 | 0.0000*** |
| | | Constant Trend | -5.641811 | 0.0001*** |

Notes: *** denotes significance at 1%, ** denotes significance at 5%, * denotes significance at 1% level. In ADF unit root tests, the lag length criterion is set as Schwarz information criterion.

Table 7. shows the unit root results of the variables subject to the model. It is observed that all three variables contain unit roots at their levels and become stationary in their first differences. The fact that all series contain unit root at the same level (I1) makes it possible to conduct cointegration test. In order to perform the cointegration test, it is necessary to determine the appropriate VAR model.

*Figure 5. VAR(3) AR roots graph*

## Inverse Roots of AR Characteristic Polynomial

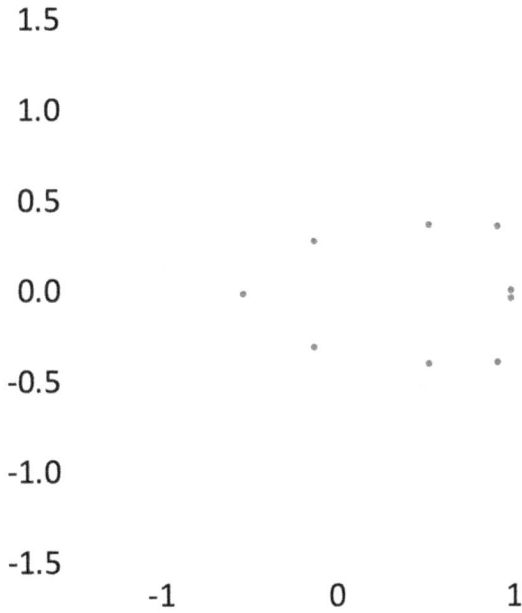

*Table 8. VAR(3) model AR roots table*

| Root | Modulus |
|---|---|
| 0.987646 - 0.021961i | 0.987890 |
| 0.987646 + 0.021961i | 0.987890 |
| 0.912673 - 0.376114i | 0.987134 |
| 0.912673 + 0.376114i | 0.987134 |
| 0.526015 - 0.382751i | 0.650531 |
| 0.526015 + 0.382751i | 0.650531 |
| -0.531020 | 0.531020 |
| -0.127085 - 0.292903i | 0.319285 |
| -0.127085 + 0.292903i | 0.319285 |

Figure 4 and Table 8 show the status of the inverse roots for the VAR(3) model. At the specified stationarity of the variables and at the appropriate lag level (3), all the inverse roots are inside the unit circle. This indicates that the unit VAR(3) model satisfies the stability condition.

*Table 9. Serial correlation LM test and White heteroskedasticity test results*

| | Chi-sq | Prob. |
|---|---|---|
| White Heteroskedasticity | 109.8670 | 0.4319 |
| | **Rao F-stat** | **Prob.** |
| Serial Correlation LM Test | 1.313055 | 0.2451 |

The fact that the probability values of the LM Test and White test are higher than 10% indicates the reliability of the model. According to these results, the model does not suffer from autocorrelation and heteroscedasticity problems, and there is no model fitting error. VAR (3) model satisfies the stability conditions.

*Table 10. Johansen cointegration test results*

| Hypothesized | | Trace | 0.1 | |
|---|---|---|---|---|
| No. of CE(s) | Eigenvalue | Statistic | Critical Value | Prob. |
| None * | 0.386615 | 46.68527 | 39.75526 | 0.0200** |
| At most 1 | 0.287510 | 25.17975 | 23.34234 | 0.0608* |
| At most 2 | 0.208067 | 10.26423 | 10.66637 | 0.1157 |

The table shows the results of the Johansen cointegration test. There are 2 cointegrations in the model at 10% level. According to the model results, there is a cointegration relationship between health expenditures, elderly population and GDP per capita.

In order to conduct the Toda Yamamoto test, a VAR model with a degree of k+dmax should be estimated. In order to estimate an accurate VAR model, the stationarity level of the series should be determined and the appropriate lag (k) should be determined by constructing the VAR model. The VAR(3) model was used to perform the Johansen cointegration test. It is seen that the VAR(3) model meets the stability conditions. Since it was determined by the unit root test that the variables subject to the model contain 1st order unit roots, the model with k+dmax (VAR(3)+1=VAR(4)) was estimated for the Toda- Yamamoto test.

*Table 11. Toda-Yamamoto causality test results*

| Null Hypothesis | $\chi^2$ Statistic | Significance Level | Decision | Decision Explanation |
|---|---|---|---|---|
| GDP↛ELDER | 6,536 | 0,1625 | GDP↛ELDER | No Causality |
| HEALTH↛ ELDER | 3.729 | 0.4438 | HEALTH↛ ELDER | No Causality |
| Joint Value | 8.247 | 0,4097 | HEALTH & GDP ↛ ELDER | No Causality |
| ELDER ↛ GDP | 6.593 | 0.1590 | ELDER ↛ GDP | No Causality |
| HEALTH ↛ GDP | 4.569 | 0.3344 | HEALTH ↛ GDP | No Causality |
| Joint Value | 17.016 | 0.0299** | ELDER & HEALTH → GDP | Causality Exists |
| ELDER ↛ HEALTH | 13.150 | 0.0106** | ELDER → HEALTH | Causality Exists |
| GDP ↛ HEALTH | 12.980 | 0.0114** | GDP → HEALTH | Causality Exists |
| Joint Value | 23.799 | 0.0025*** | ELDER & GDP→ HEALTH | Causality Exists |

Table presents the results of the analysis of the causality relationship between GDP per capita, elderly population and health expenditures. In the table, the existence of causality is interpreted according to the 10% significance level. It is determined that there is a causality relationship from GDP per capita and elderly population to health expenditures. According to these results, health expenditures are expected to increase due to the increase in GDP per capita and the increase in the elderly population.

## CONCLUSION

Old age is one of the life stages that every living being will encounter if they live a normal life course. Thanks to the opportunities provided by developing technology and economic development, the average life expectancy is gradually increasing and the number of people reaching old age is increasing day by day. Population aging is a growing problem for both Türkiye and other countries around the world. In old age, people have fewer opportunities to work, which can lead to economic bottlenecks for the elderly. Elderly people who rely solely on public resources to survive in old age are increasingly likely to experience economic difficulties. For this reason, in addition to public resource transfers, it is of great importance both to encourage them to participate in complementary pension systems and to increase the awareness of saving for old age.

During their active working life, individuals need to determine their savings and consumption habits with their old age in mind. A savings-consumption balance adjusted without taking into account the old age period may lead to the risk of poverty for the individual reaching old age. The state's policies for the elderly should not be based solely on transfers such as salaries and aid. A financial bottleneck that the state may experience may affect the elderly in the same way. In this respect, the state needs to establish an infrastructure where elderly individuals can guarantee themselves economically. Individuals should be made aware of the importance of diversifying their sources of income as much as possible. Otherwise, an economic model based solely on public resources may significantly restrict the mobility of elderly individuals. Since the determination of policies for retirees will be within the framework of the political process, the attitude to be adopted by the political will also be effective. For this reason, it would be in the interests of older individuals not to depend on a single source for their fate.

According to the Johansen cointegration test results, it is concluded that there is cointegration between the variables. A causality relationship was found from the elderly population and GDP per capita to health expenditures. As population aging increases and income increases, the share of health expenditures in GDP has increased. Under the assumption that the current conditions will continue, this process will continue in the following periods.

The most permanent solution to the aging population problem is to encourage births. This would allow the young population to start growing again and pave the way for the state to provide the resources needed by the elderly population. If fertility increases, a decline in the median age would be possible. This would also increase the number of people eligible to join the labor force. Increased premium production would also give a breathing space to the pension system. The sustainability of public finances is also closely linked to reducing the severity of the population problem. In economies where the young population is protected and encouraged, the labor force will be sufficient and will have a relaxing effect on public finance.

# REFERENCES

Alwago, W. O. (2023). The nexus between health expenditure, life expectancy, and economic growth: ARDL model analysis for Kenya. *Regional Science Policy & Practice*, 15(5), 1064–1086. DOI: 10.1111/rsp3.12588

Arısoy, İ., Ünlükaplan, İ., & Ergen, Z. (2010). The relationship between social expenditures and economic growth: A dynamic analysis intended for 1960-2005 period of the Turkish economy. *The Journal of Finance*, 158, 398–421.

Aslan, M., & Hocaoğlu, Ç. (2017). Psychiatric problems associated with aging and aging period. *Journal of Düzce University Institute of Health Sciences*, 7(1), 53–62.

Ayabakan, B. Ç. (2022). Covid-19 update on the relationship between aging, active aging and intergenerational conflict in Europe. In Journal of Social Policy Conferences (No. 83, pp. 225-247). Istanbul University.

Aydin, M. (2024). Aging Society and Tax Policy. Pamukkale University Journal of Social Sciences Institute, (63).

Bölüktaş, R. P. (2019). *Theories of aging and geriatric assessment*. Istanbul University Faculty of Open and Distance Education.

Bulut, Ü., & Özçakar, N. (2011). How we age. *The Journal of Turkish Family Physician*, 3(1), 1–5.

Çetin, M., & Ecevit, E. (2010). The Impact of Health Expenditures on Economic Growth: A Panel Regression Analysis on Oecd Countries. *Journal of Doğuş University*, 11(2), 166–182.

Clemente, J., Marcuello, C., Montañés, A., & Pueyo, F. (2004). On the international stability of health care expenditure functions: Are government and private functions similar? *Journal of Health Economics*, 23(3), 589–613. DOI: 10.1016/j.jhealeco.2003.08.007 PMID: 15120472

Culyer, A. J. (1989). Cost containment in Europe. *Health Care Financing Review*, (Suppl), 21. PMID: 10313433

De la Maisonneuve, C., & Oliveira Martins, J. (2013). Public Spending on Health and Long-term Care: A new set of projections. In *OECD Economic Policy Papers, No. 6*. OECD Publishing., DOI: 10.1787/5k44t7jwwr9x-

De Meijer, C., Wouterse, B., Polder, J., & Koopmanschap, M. (2013). The effect of population aging on health expenditure growth: A critical review. *European Journal of Ageing*, 10(4), 353–361. DOI: 10.1007/s10433-013-0280-x PMID: 28804308

Dickey, D. A., & Fuller, W. A. (1981). Likelihood Ratio Statistics for Autoregressive Time Series with a Unit Root. *Econometrica*, 49(4), 1057–1072. DOI: 10.2307/1912517

Erdil, E., & Yetkiner, I. H. (2004). A panel data approach for income-health causality.

Gerdtham, U. G., & Löthgren, M. (2000). On stationarity and cointegration of international health expenditure and GDP. *Journal of Health Economics*, 19(4), 461–475. DOI: 10.1016/S0167-6296(99)00036-3 PMID: 11010235

Gölçek, A. G., & Göde, B. (2023). The Course of Tax Revenue During the Process of Population Aging: Empirical Evidence from Turkey. *Fiscaoeconomia*, 7(Özel Sayı), 614–640. DOI: 10.25295/fsecon.1348960

Harper, S. (2014). Economic and social implications of aging societies. *Science*, 346(6209), 587–591. DOI: 10.1126/science.1254405 PMID: 25359967

Hunjra, A. I., Azam, M., Bruna, M. G., & Taskin, D. (2022). Role of financial development for sustainable economic development in low middle income countries. *Finance Research Letters*, 47, 102793. DOI: 10.1016/j.frl.2022.102793

Income Distribution Database, O. E. C. D. (2023). www.oecd.org/social/income-distribution- database.htm, (Accessed: 08.10.2024).

Johansen, S. (1995). *Likelihood-based inference in cointegrated vector autoregressive models*. OUP Oxford. DOI: 10.1093/0198774508.001.0001

Johansen, S., & Juselius, K. (1990). Maximum likelihood estimation and inference on cointegration-with appucations to the demand for money. *Oxford Bulletin of Economics and Statistics*, 52(2), 169–210. DOI: 10.1111/j.1468-0084.1990.mp52002003.x

Kar, M., & Taban, S. (2003). The impacts of the disaggregated public expenditure on economic growth. Ankara University Faculty of Political Science, 53(3), 145-169.

Karadeniz, O., & Öztepe, N. D. (2013). Elderly Poverty in Türkiye. *Labour and Society*, 3(38), 77–102.

Kurt, S. (2015). Government Health Expenditures and Economic Growth: A Feder-Ram Approach for the Case of Türkiye. *International Journal of Economics and Financial Issues*, 5(2), 441–447.

Miraç, Ö. Y., & Acar, M. (2015). *Türkiye Sosyal Hizmet Birikiminde Yaşlılık: Bibliographic Bir Değerlendirme (1950-2013)* (1st ed.). Açılımkitap Publications.

Moscone, F., & Tosetti, E. (2010). Health expenditure and income in the United States. *Health Economics*, 19(12), 1385–1403. DOI: 10.1002/hec.1552 PMID: 19842092

Narayan, P. K., & Narayan, S. (2008). The role of permanent and transitory shocks in explaining international health expenditures. *Health Economics*, 17(10), 1171–1186. DOI: 10.1002/hec.1316 PMID: 18076005

Newhouse, J. P. (1977). Medical care expenditure: A cross-national survey. *The Journal of Human Resources*, 12(1), 115–125. DOI: 10.2307/145602 PMID: 404354

Nyamweya, N. K. (2017). Healthcare expenditure and economic growth: The kenyan case (1970- 2016).

OECD Pensions at a Glance (2023), https://www.oecd.org/en/publications/pensions -at-a-glance- 2023_678055dd-en.html, (Accessed: 08.10.2024).

Öksüzokyar, M. M., Eryiğit, S. Ç., Düzen, K. Ö., Mergen, B. E., Sökmen, Ü. N., & Öğüt, S. (2016). Causes and effects of biological aging. Mehmet Akif Ersoy University Journal of Health Sciences Institute, 4(1).

Our World In Data based on Lindert (1994), OECD (1993), OECD Stat - processed by Our World in Data. "public_health_expenditure_pc_gdp" [dataset]. Our World In Data based on, Lindert (1994), OECD (1993), OECD Stat [original data], (Accessed: 12.10.2024).

Pascual-Saez, M., Cantarero-Prieto, D., & Castañeda, D. (2017). Public health expenditure, GDP and the elderly population: A comparative study. *International Journal of Social Economics*, 44(10), 1390–1400. DOI: 10.1108/IJSE-03-2016-0106

Payne, G., Laporte, A., Deber, R., & Coyte, P. C. (2007). Counting backward to health care's future: Using time-to-death modeling to identify changes in end-of-life morbidity and the impact of aging on health care expenditures. *The Milbank Quarterly*, 85(2), 213–257. DOI: 10.1111/j.1468-0009.2007.00485.x PMID: 17517114

Piabuo, S. M., & Tieguhong, J. C. (2017). Health expenditure and economic growth-a review of the literature and an analysis between the economic community for central African states (CEMAC) and selected African countries. *Health Economics Review*, 7(1), 23. DOI: 10.1186/s13561-017-0159-1 PMID: 28593509

Sağın, A., & Karasaç, F. (2018). The Effect of Health Expenditures on Economic Growth in Oecd Economies. *Kirklareli University Journal of Faculty of Economics and Administrative Sciences*, 7(1), 72–86.

Sanz, I., & Velázquez, F. J. (2007). The role of ageing in the growth of government and social welfare spending in the OECD. *European Journal of Political Economy*, 23(4), 917–931. DOI: 10.1016/j.ejpoleco.2007.01.003

Social Security Institutions Budget Statistics. (2023). https://muhasebat.hmb.gov.tr/ sosyal- guvenlik-kurumlari-butce-istatistikleri, (Accessed: 11.10.2024).

Tamakoshi, T., & Hamori, S. (2015). Health-care expenditure, GDP and share of the elderly in Japan: A panel cointegration analysis. *Applied Economics Letters*, 22(9), 725–729. DOI: 10.1080/13504851.2014.972540

Toda, H. Y., & Yamamoto, T. (1995). Statistical inference in vector autoregressions with possibly integrated processes. *Journal of Econometrics*, 66(1-2), 225–250. DOI: 10.1016/0304-4076(94)01616-8

UN. World Population Prospects (2024) - processed by Our World in Data. "Median age, medium projection - UN WPP" [dataset]. United Nations, "World Population Prospects" [original data], (Accessed: 09.10.2024).

UN. World Population Prospects (2024) - processed by Our World in Data. "Population,ages 0-14 - UN WPP" [dataset]. United Nations, "World Population Prospects" [original data], (Accessed: 09.10.2024).

UN. World Population Prospects (2024). - processed by Our World in Data. "Population, ages 0- 14, ages 15-64, ages 65+ - UN WPP" [dataset]. United Nations, "World Population Prospects" [original data], (Accessed: 09.10.2024).

United Nations Department of Economic and Social Affairs, Population Division (2020). World Population Ageing 2020 Highlights: Living arrangements of older persons (ST/ESA/SER.A/451).

Wang, L., Liang, J., & Wang, B. (2024). Population aging and sustainable economic development: An analysis based on the role of green finance. *Finance Research Letters*, 70, 106239. DOI: 10.1016/j.frl.2024.106239

Worldbank Indicators. (2024). Economic Indicators, https://databank.worldbank.org/ indicator/NY.GDP.PCAP.CD/1ff4a498/Popular-Indicators, (Accessed: 11.10.2024).

Yerli, G. (2017). Characteristics Of Ageing Period And Social Works For The Elderly. *Journal Of International Social Research*, 10(52).

Zijdeman, (2015);Riley (2005) - with minor processing by Our World in Data. "Life expectancy at birth - Various sources - period tables" [dataset]. Human Mortality Database, "Human Mortality Database"; United Nations, "World Population Prospects 2022"; United Nations, "World Population Prospects"; Zijdeman et al., "Life Expectancy at birth 2"; James C. Riley, "Estimates of Regional and Global Life Expectancy, 1800-2001", (Accessed: 09.10.2024).

Zweifel, P., Felder, S., & Meiers, M. (1999). Ageing of population and health care expenditure: A red herring? *Health Economics*, 8(6), 485–496. DOI: 10.1002/(SICI)1099-1050(199909)8:6<485::AID-HEC461>3.0.CO;2-4 PMID: 10544314

# Chapter 8
# Intergenerational Caregiving on Grandparents Health:
## A Case Study

**Priya S. Dev**
https://orcid.org/0000-0002-5626-2208
*Department of Social Work, Bharathidasan University, Trichy, India*

**J. O. Jeryda Gnanajane Eljo**
*Department of Social Work, Bharathidasan University, Trichy, India*

**S. Srinivasan**
https://orcid.org/0009-0002-0179-9849
*Department of Humanities and Social Sciences, Graphic Era University, Dehradun, India*

## ABSTRACT

*In contemporary society, parents strive to provide a better life for their children by pursuing job opportunities. There is a significant increase in parents entrusting the duty of baby care to their own parents or in-laws. Taking care of grandchildren is a herculean task for some, while for others; it brings happiness and enjoyment during their retirement life. In these circumstances, they have their own concerns regarding health, family, children, as well as the grandchildren in their care. The findings of the study reveals that, the positive, as well as negative, aspects of intergenerational caregiving have substantial importance in the area of policy making. The study conclude with a statement regarding the need of Social support policies, that can play a pivotal role in identifying the needs of grandparents during the caregiving process and the essentiality to establish intergenerational bonding between grand-*

DOI: 10.4018/979-8-3693-7753-6.ch008

*parents and young adults.*

## INTRODUCTION

As age increases, there is a chance of decrease in energy levels and associated physical and psychological problems, especially health issues due to the decline in the ability to repair and regenerate body cells. This will affect the capacity to take care of the grandchild both physically and mentally. Unfortunately, some grandparents have poor financial assistance or face pressure from their children to take care of the grandchild, forcing them to participate in the caregiving process without considering the physical and psychological problems associated with aging. This study envisages the role of grandparents in taking care of their grandchildren and how it affects their health. In an optimistic approach, the caregiving aspect would be better with appropriate financial backing from family members, providing support for regular health check-ups, comfort in spiritual aspects, and the opportunity to maintain good societal interaction.

Aging is also a time period of loneliness if it lacks a social support system or experiences the immediate loss of a loved one, or due to retirement (Dev & Eljo, 2022). It needs to be recognized, and the chance of taking care of the grandchild will help them overcome feelings of loneliness and engage in day-to-day life. The concept of care provision could have a significant impact on the lives of grandparents by reducing their stress levels, depression, anxiety, and fear of death. It automatically enriches their quality of life and mental health, while physical activeness makes them strong and independent. Today, grandparents are taking on multiple roles as they grow older (Vidovićová, 2018). Increasing age leads to an increase in dependency towards others (Guo et al., 2022). However, a new common scenario is emerging in families where adult parents have jobs (Stephen, 2023). This places the responsibility of caring for the grandchildren solely in the hands of grandparents staying at home (Brunello & Yamamura, 2023). As we are aware, people who are 60 and above face physical, psychological, and social problems, along with associated comorbidities (WHO, 2019). Due to financial instability, lack of a social network system, and ill-health, some among the grandparents are forced to work assigned by their grownup children. This will affect them positively or negatively throughout their life (Zamarro, 2020).

On the other side, grandparents play a vital role in the lives of their grandchildren (Wetzel & Hank, 2020). Considering the family as an institution, a positive interconnection between grandparents and grandchildren can enrich the understanding of values, standards, cultural beliefs, and important life lessons (Thomas et al., 2017). The generational bond between grandparents and grandchildren will have high impact in molding the personality of the grandchildren. There are studies which shows that intergenerational bonding has a great impact on children's scholastic performance (Yeh et al., 2022). There are also studies indicate an increase in depression among grandparents is due to engagement in the caregiving process without willingness (Earl & Marais, 2023). The fast-growing changes in socio political and financial aspects have a visible impact on grandchildren, who show respect and obedience towards their grandparents (Brunello & Rocco, 2019). The traditional treatment of grandparents also faces significant challenges and risk factors (Ministry of Social and Family Development, 2022).

*Figure 1. Share of seniors in developed countries who had been told by a doctor they had depression, anxiety, or another mental health condition as of 2021, by country*

Share of seniors in developed countries who had been told by a doctor they had depression, anxiety, or another mental health condition as of 2021, by country*

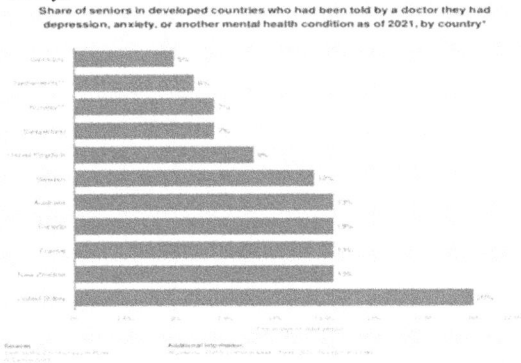

*(CIHI, 2023)*

Furthermore, issues associated with loneliness, social isolation, dependency, psychological and physical imbalances lead to grandparents being less active and socially excluded (Peters et al., 2021). Disease associated with ageing and related comorbidities also affect the Quality of Life and Mental Health of older grandparents (Leong et al., 2022).

## Intergenerational Bonding for Improving Ageing

Intergenerational bonding is an essential tool for boosting mental health by enhancing the lives of older adults through enriching experiences like grand parenting. It also promotes communication among family members (Bagnasco et al., 2020). Thus, intergenerational bonding plays a crucial role in dignifying the lives of older adults. Through this, it can enhance social intelligence and generate a sense of we-feeling and togetherness. Nevertheless, the lack of awareness about the positive outcomes of intergenerational bonding results in negligence, loss of worth, and dignity for older adults, who are often seen merely as caregivers. Without proper support and assistance, they are sometimes forced to care for children at various stages of life (Kroll, 2011).

Positive intergenerational bonding helps reduce generational gaps and strengthens values. It enriches discussions and knowledge exchange between grandparents and grandchildren. Family, as an integrated system that includes all age groups, can be termed 'truly age-integrated.' Due to the overlap of societal norms and increasing numbers of old age homes, issues such as divorce, suicide, psychological problems, addiction to alcohol and drugs, and changes in attitudes toward respecting elders have become more common. In this context, intergenerational bonding can effectively uplift family solidarity through cross-age understanding and connectedness (Reynolds et al., 2022).

## Intergenerational Exchange between Grandparents

Weak intergenerational exchanges between grandparents and grandchildren can disrupt these relationships. A digitalized society often neglects older adults by labeling them as illiterate regarding technology, contributing to increased depression and anxiety among them. Underestimating older adults and prejudging their contributions in economic and cultural contexts can marginalize them from family and societal events. Intergenerational bonding programs in various countries help grandparents adapt to a digitized society. Recent studies show that 3.08% of grandchildren reside with grandparents and have stronger intergenerational bonds compared to those who live separately (Statista, 2022).

## Intergenerational Understanding Between Young and Old

In today's modernized world, industrialization has contributed to generational segregation. The gap between generations varies according to the social structures in different communities. Transitioning from joint to nuclear family systems has widened the gap between grandparents and grandchildren (Silverstein & Bengston, 2003). "Institutional age segregation" is a key factor in this divide, leading to negative attitudes toward older adults (Niazi et al., 2020). This segregation often results in older adults being institutionalized while younger generations are placed in hostels or daycare centers for their studies. This separation promotes distance and creates psychological issues among older adults, contributing to age-associated diseases and disabilities (Bland, 2006).

When three or more generations live under the same roof, they tend to have strong inter-connectedness and a sense of we-feeling. Even when young and older adults live in the same premises, they often have separate ideologies and outlooks, leading to 'separate islands of activity.' In the new generation era, the lack of intimacy and love forces grandparents to find happiness in TV or exclude them from decision-making processes and other household activities. Their children are often busy managing household chores, balancing work and personal life, and striving for an elevated status.

On the other hand, many grandchildren are heavily engaged in school activities and extracurricular, making time with older adults seem irrelevant or less important. Such stereotypes need to be addressed by initiating intergenerational bonding programs. Increased mobile phone use among children and their parents can also create loneliness among older adults, leading to isolation and the perception that older adults are disturbances. These negative practices and the lack of respect for older adults need to be addressed, and proactive measures for intergenerational bonding should be enforced.

## BACKGROUND OF THE STUDY

Supporting older adults is a serious issue during the drastic increase in the older population due to the triumphs of modernity (United Nations, Department of Economic and Social Affairs, Population Division, 2019). Age-associated diseases, disabilities, and comorbidities significantly impact the mental health and quality of life of older adults (Scotté, et al., 2018). Intergenerational bonding also promotes socialization between grandparents and their grandchildren (Ding, 2024). This bonding has evident positive outcomes for both older grandparents and their grandchildren. Among grandchildren, intergenerational bonding reduces age-old stereotypes, helps children establish purposeful relationships, and improves their communication and socialization skills (Gualano et al., 2018). Older grandparents benefit from intergenerational bonding by reporting increased well-being, feeling relaxed, and energized (Bagnasco et al., 2020). Intergenerational bonding is also influenced by the quality of relationships between both groups (Bagnasco et al., 2020). Furthermore, intergenerational bonding is an essential tool in maintaining care, trust, and affection (Leong et al., 2022).

The increase in nuclear families and the decrease in the number of joint families following urbanization may result in a reduction in the strong connection between grandparents and grandchildren. In the current scenario, nuclear families with both parents working often rely on older in-laws or parents to care for their children (Lim et al., 2019). This situation leads to negative outcomes for both grandchildren and grandparents. Grandparents may not have enough time for their daily activities, leisure, or other entertaining activities. They are fully engaged in taking care of the grandchildren while their own children work. If older adults have age-related diseases or comorbidities, they face physical, psychological, and social issues related to intergenerational caregiving. These psychological disturbances while taking care of the grandchildren can also affect the care they provide for the children (Watson, 2023). This affects both the quality of life and mental health of older adults.

Grandparents play an important role in the caregiving process for their grandchildren, especially in joint and extended families, where support is prevalent. The study is associated with full-time caregiving for their grandchildren. It provides various roles that grandparents play in caregiving.

> *Primary Caregivers:* Due to occupational circumstances, parents cannot focus on their children's education and health aspects. They may face financial problems and migrate for work, while grandparents often provide primary caregiving for their grandchildren (Settless et al., 2009).
> *Supplementary Support*: They can be involved with their grandchildren to handle tasks such as helping with schooling activities and extracurricular activities.
> *Cultural Transmission*: The grandparents regularly provide their traditions and family history to focus on their grandchildren (Kemp, 2007).
> *Emotional Support*: Older adults provide for their grandchildren by sharing previous experiences and positive storytelling, which motivates their children emotionally. They can support and improve their well-being in a positive way, enhancing the lives of their grandchildren (Wallbaum et al., 2018).

## Grandparents Involvement in Taking Care of Their Grandchildren

Grandparents provide emotional support, social skills, and a sense of security for their grandchildren. They can also help reduce stress, offer financial support, and provide reliable assistance. They can support strengthening family bonds and increasing positive thoughts, mental health, and well-being for the grandchildren.

## Challenges for Grandparents in Caregiving for Grandchildren

Grandparents involve themselves with their grandchildren's health problems, especially physical and mental health issues. To provide parenting support to avoid conflict. They can provide support for the financial strain, even when they have limited income.

## SIGNIFICANCE AND SCOPE OF THE STUDY

Intergenerational bonding acts as a fundamental need for older grandparents in terms of improving their health and well-being (Bagnasco et al., 2020). This bonding is enriched by strong connectedness between grandparents and their grandchildren. The relationship and the sharing of experiences can reduce isolation and loneliness, and enhance cognition and conation in older adults in a positive way (Wong & Hsiesh, 2019). This can lead to fostering a high-quality relationship that reduces dependency and helps older adults face daily challenges with greater freedom (Lim et al., 2019). Thus, the quality of life and mental health of older adults will improve, making them feel valued and accepted, and fostering a positive attitude towards life.

Energetic older grandparents can be seen when they are in a positive environment interacting with their grandchildren (Canedo-Garcia et al., 2017). This fosters a renewed sense of existence for older grandparents. At different dimensions of healthy aging, strong grandparent-grandchild bonds emphasize deep personal connections and the sharing of experiences (Gualano et al., 2018). This focus not only improves the mental health and quality of life of older grandparents but also helps reduce social isolation, stereotypes, and false beliefs associated with aging, thereby promoting worth and dignity among older grandparents and paving the way for healthy aging (Bagnasco et al., 2020).

## REVIEW OF LITERATURE

A study on "Grandparents' relations to grandchildren in the transition to adulthood" by Wetzel and Hank (2020) explained that busy schedules of children lead to a crisis in taking care of older parents as well as their own children. This results in increased psychosocial problems for grandparents, who are often forced to take on the role of caregiver for their grandchildren despite their own health problems (Morais et al., 2019). Another study conducted by Mebane and Pezzutti (2020) on positive intergenerational solidarity among grandparents and grandchildren highlighted a positive view from both respondents.

The research study aims to provide comprehensive insights into the physical health of grandparents in the context of their intergenerational roles among older adults. The study emphasizes the well-being of older adults through a path analysis of grandparents' previous experiences as caregivers. Non-caregivers provided insights into grandparent caregiving aspects. The study focused on nearly 799 grandparents aged 60 and above in rural areas. The study covered three aspects: financial, emotional, and instrumental support. Grandparents provide caregiving and self-rated health (SRH) for the limitations of non-caregivers. Emotional support can mediate the relationship between caregiving and SRH in caregivers. The findings highlight health improvements and benefits for grandparents (Zhou et al., 2017).

The findings of the study could provide a better association between caregiving for grandchildren and the physical and mental health of older adults in the Chinese context. The study focused on three aspects of child policy. This can provide care for grandchildren and have a positive impact on the physical health of grandparents, reducing depression and the likelihood of related issues (Wang & Tang, 2023).

The study highlighted that the majority of older adults, nearly 30% of whom are grandparents, represent the fourth generation in their families. The majority of them are great-grandparents or both. Especially grandfathers in urban areas, who experience health-related benefits from intergenerational caregiving. Rural grandmothers also suffer from health risks due to intergenerational caregiving (Xu, 2019).

## Intergenerational Understanding and Generational Cohesion

Finding and bridging the generational gap can be effectively achieved through intergenerational bonding between grandparents and grandchildren (Xu & Wu, 2005). The demographic shift in the older population is characterized by depression, anxiety, societal stereotypes, economic instability, and a sense of dependency due to a lack of positive attitudes towards life. Lack of supportive hands and space to ventilate emotions are associated with psychological issues that cause older grandparents to withdraw from pleasurable activities. Financial instability in meeting basic needs also creates dependency, lack of confidence, ignorance, and neglect. These challenges can be addressed when older adults have opportunities to interact with younger generations. Sharing their experiences, ideologies, and informative stories with younger generations increases the self-efficacy of grandparents and improves their self-esteem (Fong-Chong, 2003).

Increased age segregation presents both opportunities and challenges. Utilizing the knowledge and experience of grandparents by respecting their worth and dignity positively contributes to healthy aging (Thang, 2011). Modernization has contributed to the rise in nuclear families, leading to decreased multi-generational households and resulting in a lack of communication, relationship bonds, psychosocial problems due to a lack of good advisors or listeners, and a shortage of individuals to spend time with children if both parents are working (Ng & James, 2013). This causes mobile addiction, dependency on alcohol and drugs, violent behavior, negative peer influences, and more. Initiating activities that promote intergenerational bonding by providing a platform for older grandparents and younger children to share ideas, ventilate emotions freely, receive advice and suggestions, can bring a positive outlook on aging and dispel existing stereotypes (Fong-Chong, 2003). This will help combat ageism and forecast better aging in the future.

Intergenerational bonding can be achieved through various platforms, such as providing awareness to school children, establishing, and maintaining strong intergenerational connections within the family, ensuring the physical and psychological health of older adults, and treating them with non-judgmental and acceptable behavior. This approach can help older adults feel proud and worthy and serve as resources for future generations (Kaplan, 2002). An empathetic attitude is necessary in intergenerational bonding. All family members should be aware of the immediate needs and desires of older adults and how much they are willing to engage in establishing meaningful relationships. A structured opportunity must be provided for both young and older adults (McCrea & Smith, 2014).

The ultimate aim of intergenerational bonding between older adults and younger generations is to establish meaningful engagement (Aw et al., 2017). This platform will provide younger generations with an in-depth understanding of aging and parameters for healthy aging. It will also foster mutual respect. Intergenerational bonding encompasses strategies to establish social connectedness and promote policies and programs to mainstream cross-generational cohesion and dialogue. Integrating these aspects of healthy aging can promote social harmony, thereby creating an age-friendly society where older adults experience positive outcomes from interactions with younger generations (Thang, 2011).

## Age Segregation and Consequences

Discrimination of older adults by younger generations still exists in the current scenario. This is one of the main reasons for age segregation, which creates negative stereotypes and increases the number of institutionalized older adults. This segregation promotes horizontal relationships (relationships maintained within the same age group) and is against vertical relationships (relationships across all age categories). This disengagement between young and older adults needs to be addressed, and policy formulation should focus on initiating strong intergenerational bonding.

The demographic transition in population aging underscores the need for assistance for older adults to meet the psychosocial and physical challenges associated with aging (Dev & Eljo, 2024). These challenges can be mitigated through proactive measures to foster intergenerational bonding and connectedness between young and old. Generational re-engagement is an effective tool to promote intergenerational bonding and emphasize its importance. Families, societies, and the environments where older adults live should be aware of the desirable outcomes that intergenerational bonding can offer and consider it an effective intervention strategy for mutual learning. This practice should be adopted both nationally and internationally, considering the projected aging population in 2050. Social workers and social bodies play a significant role in promoting intergenerational bonding among grandparents and children through developmental efforts. This should begin within families and schools, where children start to build their knowledge base.

## Trends in Intergenerational Bonding

Family is considered the origin of care, love, and support. The drastic decline in morbidity rates and the increase in aging pose challenges and opportunities for families and society. Delays in marriage and an increased desire for singlehood also contribute to changes in natality. The trends in family structures have been notably affected by demographic trends and the rise of nuclear families. There is evidence that changes in household sizes due to a lack of adjustment and a reluctance to live jointly with parents and grandparents point to a reduction in the number of family members per household. The number of family members in each household was reported to be 4.9 in 1980 and decreased to 3.5 by 2010. This indicates that grand-children are less connected to grandparents due to the smaller household size and age segregation within families.

## Strategies to Promote Intergenerational Bonding

Truly integrated individuals from different age groups can be seen in each family. The family system can effectively unite all members under one platform. Therefore, the concept of intergenerational bonding should originate within the family, fostering purposeful relationships between family members, including older grandparents. Historically, intergenerational mutual benefits have been promoted, but practical state policies and strategies for intergenerational bonding remain a question mark. Task forces have played an instrumental role in creating awareness among families and societies where older adults reside.

Celebrating 'Grandparents Day' is also a wonderful strategy that makes people aware of how precious our older adults are. This also emphasizes the need for binding families. Interconnectedness and intergenerational bonding can be achieved through a variety of programs, activities, and tasks that help to engage and entertain them sActive aging can be possible in an inclusive society where all individuals' worth and dignity are respected. An equal platform and consideration for all, rather than just an elderly-friendly environment, need to be initiated. The activities, projects, and programs that are planned to be implemented in society must be intergenerational in nature (Murayama et al., 2015).

## Intergenerational Solidarity

Like climate change, which affects everyone in society equally, the problems generated due to the absence of intergenerational solidarity also affect society as a whole. This showcases that intergenerational solidarity is an essential factor for societal advancement. Intergenerational solidarity can contribute to the allocation of resources for society's upliftment as well as the efficient utilization of resources. Integrating all people without categorizing them by age, intergenerational solidarity can help share expectations and generate and allocate new proactive measures for a healthier future. Ageist stereotyping always acts as a barrier against intergenerational solidarity. Social support networks can act as a shield to strengthen intergenerational solidarity (Cordella et al., 2021).

## Four-Dimensional Aspects of Grandparents

The study emphasizes the physical, social, psychological, and economic aspects of grandparents in raising grandchildren. The objective of the study is to highlight the psychological problems of older adults and provide care. In the aspects of social, family, physical, and economic factors, it raises the distress of grandparents and affects their grandchildren. The results of the study provide insights into the psychological problems faced by grandparents. It predicts family sources that can involve their physical health, social support, and emotional well-being (Kelley et al., 200).

## MATERIALS METHOD

### Aim of the Study

This case study focuses on intergenerational bonding and its impact on grandparents' health. It addresses the gap in understanding the positive and negative effects of intergenerational bonding between grandparents and grandchildren. The study also contributes to future research by highlighting the long-term effects of intergenerational bonding.

### Objectives

1. To understand the role of grandparents in the caregiving process for their grandchildren.
2. To evaluate the positive and negative outcome of intergenerational caregiving on grandparents' health.

3. To find out social work intervention strategies for the intergenerational bonding of grandparents and grandchildren.
4. To envisage the economic implications of intergenerational caregiving.

## Area of the Study

The study was conducted in the Convent Street area of Crawford, Tiruchirappalli. In this locality, there are grandparents who are actively involved in the caregiving process for their grandchildren and the sample size of the study was five. This study area was specifically chosen by the researcher due to the significant trend of both the parents went for job and older grandparents are responsible in taking care of the grandchildren below five years, which played a pivotal role in the selection criteria. This residential area is the mix of both financially sound and economically poor people residing and have a notable residents who have high educational qualification and good standard of living. When compared to urban areas there is a significant proportion posse's basic education and are struggling to manage their day today needs.

## Research Questions

1. How does intergenerational care giving affect the health of grandparents?
2. What were the positive and negative outcomes of intergenerational bonding?
3. What kinds of roles are performed by grandparents in the caregiving process?

## Research Design and Sampling

This study is qualitative in nature, employing the case study method and observation. To obtain a sample of 5 respondents from Convent Street, Crawford, located in Tiruchirappalli, the researcher adopted a purposive sampling method. Specific recruitment criteria were adopted by the researcher for collecting the sample to gain in-depth knowledge about the complex experiences. The recruitment criteria comprised:

1. A grandparent who is currently performing the role of raising a grandchild below the age of three and who has been performing the role of a caregiver for over a year.
2. Grandchildren whose parents are employed and are physically absent.
3. Grandchildren who are willing to participate in the study.

Participants who showed willingness to participate were given a detailed description of the study, including its purpose, scope, and effectiveness. Informed consent was collected, and a total of five respondents were selected for the study. By choosing this sample size, the gender proportion could not be balanced, as female grandparents predominantly take care of the grandchildren.

## Tools for Data Collection

Semi-structured Interview Schedule: The overall caregiving role of grandparents was assessed using a semi-structured interview schedule. The interview also inquired about the health issues they are experiencing due to caregiving. The researcher placed significant importance on the effects of caregiving on grandparents' health, with a focus on the psychosocial aspects of both positive and negative outcomes throughout the caregiving process.

## Data Collection and Analysis

The data collection process was conducted through a semi-structured interview schedule, gathering information on the dimensions of physical, social, psychological, and economic aspects that affect grandparents' health. The discussion also explored the importance of grandparents in raising grandchildren. Each interview lasted approximately 30 to 40 minutes, resulting in fifteen pages of transcribed material. Each transcript was read several times to extract conceptual information from the transcribed verbatim. The selected grandparents were providing care for children under the age of 3 and resided in the geographical location of the study area. The researcher scheduled prior appointments before conducting the data collection, and all data collection was carried out in their residential areas. The data collection began by asking sociodemographic details of the respondents, followed by open-ended questions such as: How long have you been in the caregiving process? Do you receive any support and assistance from anyone? How are you able to manage your grandchildren? What challenges have you faced during the caregiving process, and what strategies have you adopted to cope with these challenges? What psychosocial and physical issues have you encountered in the caregiving process? How do you feel about the care you are providing, and what are the positive and negative implications of your care for the grandchildren? What is the current status of your health and your grandchildren's health? Are your children supportive in fulfilling your needs, and if you are sick, do they allow you to take care of the children?

## RESULTS AND DISCUSSION

In this case study, two of the respondents are in the age group of 70 and 72, while the others are in the age categories of 60, 62, and 68. There are two male respondents and three female respondents in the study. Only two of the respondents belong to a high economic status, two have a middle economic status, and one belongs to a low economic condition. The reason for their involvement in caregiving is that their children, daughters, and sons-in-law are busy with jobs outside.

Three of the respondents feel that it is their duty to care for their grandchild because they represent the future generations of our society. One respondent said, "If the children are busy with their jobs, I will provide adequate food, ensure comfortable sleep, allocate appropriate time to play with my grandchild, and develop learning habits."

All respondents in the study population had health issues before taking care of their grandchildren. They reported having age-associated disorders such as diabetes, heart disease, cholesterol, cataracts, and arthritis. Respondents with high economic status had no health issues due to caregiving because they employed domestic help and received proper medication on time with the support of their children. However, this was different for respondents from middle and low economic backgrounds. The results show that the absence of a daughter-in-law creates more problems in managing household work and providing care for the grandchild, leading to increased physical pain, psychological disturbances, and a lack of socialization. Forty percent of the respondents experience sleep disturbances due to the irregular sleeping patterns of their grandchildren.

Respondents who own a house, have domestic help, and receive a retirement pension experience fewer physical, psychological, and social problems related to caregiving. One respondent said, "Luckily we have a pension; it's God's grace, so I can spend enough money on my grandchild." Considering the positive impact of caregiving, all respondents strongly agreed that "the foundation of caregiving is love and affection," and they are happy to take care of their grandchild. The roles performed by the grandparents include involving the child in the socialization process with neighbors and friends, providing food at the right time, engaging in teaching and learning new things, and providing childcare. One respondent expressed their current feelings about taking care of the grandchild: "Tasting the baby's innocent behavior, we want another grandchild." The researcher focused on the positive and negative impacts of caregiving among grandparents and grandchildren. This includes psychological challenges and strengths, physical health and caregiving burden, social and economic issues, availability of leisure time, unmet needs, and worries. All this information was collected from the older grandparents.

## Positive Impacts of Caregiving

All the grandparents included in the present study accepted that they felt a sense of purpose after getting the chance to care for their grandchildren. Before this, they felt lonely, sad, and depressed because their children were away for work, and their earnings were the only source of income for running the family. They were alone in the house with limited interaction. Lack of self-confidence in old age forced them to stay home and not participate in community or family-oriented programs. When given the opportunity to care for the baby, they felt satisfaction and considered it a duty to contribute to their children's well-being. Grandparents in the study spent almost every day caring for the baby from morning till evening or night. When the older adults were sick or had health issues, all children were understanding and co-operated by allowing them to relax and take medication. Spending time with their grandchildren helped them stay engaged. One male grandparent, aged 72, said, "By seeing my child's smile, I think it was a miracle and God's gift. My one and only son decided not to get married, but at the age of 36, he changed his mind, and now he has a three-year-old baby girl. We are very happy about this role of grandparenting." Another respondent, a 70-year-old grandmother, said, "Spending time with my granddaughter is one of the happiest parts of old age. Feeding her and hearing her call me 'ammachi' and imitate me makes me happy and engaged. I waited so long to see a grandchild, and now caregiving makes me more active. Each day, I think about what I need to teach the baby, which also activates my brain. Playing with her is an effective strategy to activate my body muscles. So, I am blessed to do this caregiving.

## Negative Impacts of Caregiving

The negative impacts of caregiving correlate with older grandparents' worries about their health problems and associated caregiving. There is no one else to care for the grandchildren, so they must provide grandparenting despite their physical issues. A 68-year-old grandmother said, "My daughter and son-in-law work in a hotel and receive poor pay, and they are the breadwinners for the family. They spend a huge amount on my health issues in the hospital. So, I need to help by taking care of the baby. Sometimes, due to pain, I show some anger towards my grandchild, but later I feel regret." Poor economic conditions force older grandparents into caregiving roles, and engaging with physical illness makes them stressed, resulting in aggressive behavior, anxiety, and anger towards their grandchild. Taking care of children under the age of 3 is a herculean task because they constantly explore their surroundings, often putting objects in their mouths. Therefore, grandparents must be highly vigilant to prevent falls, accidents, or ingestion of harmful materials. Paying attention to the grandchild from morning until evening or night, when their parents return home, is challenging for almost all grandparents involved in caregiving.

A 62-year-old female grandparent revealed, "I am okay with taking care of the baby, but she is so naughty and inattentive. When I feed her, she deliberately spits out the food. When her mother, my daughter-in-law, comes home, she shouts at me, saying I am not feeding the baby properly. This hurts me because I have no one to share my feelings with. My son always sides with her. I am treated like a servant, and my needs are not considered. I love my grandchild the most; I do not act intentionally. Despite my physical issues and psychological stress from my daughter-in-law, I am still ready to care for the baby and provide as much love as possible. My daughter-in-law goes to work every day without doing any household chores, so I wash the plates when the baby is sleeping. I never get a moment to relax. Almost every night, I cry and wish to be with my late husband." This data highlights the suffering of the older grandmother, who lacks support to express her emotions and needs. This situation can have a serious impact on both her psychological well-being and the care she provides to her grandchild.

## Impact of Caregiving on Grandchildren

Grandparents who are financially sound and receiving a retirement pension often show a positive attitude towards intergenerational caregiving. The support of household staff allows them to focus solely on caregiving without the pressure or tension of household chores. For instance, a 72-year-old grandfather disclosed, "Teaching my grandchild new words is entertaining for me. The first word she said was 'thatha.' She is super quick to learn and shows eagerness to understand each thing. She asks me what an object is. I can't tell how time flies when she is with me. Now, she is one and a half years old. She can recite the alphabet, count from 1 to 5, and knows all the body parts I've taught her." This demonstrates a clear, positive relationship between the grandfather and granddaughter. Positive relationships help the child learn quickly and engage actively in the learning process. This suggests that the grandfather's mental health is well, and he enjoys a good quality of life. This, in turn, positively impacts the grandchild's mind and health.

Conversely, a 60-year-old grandfather providing care for a 3-year-old granddaughter shared, "I am over-tensed about the behavior of my grandchild. He is always picking objects off the floor and eating them. I have said no several times, but he does not obey me. Due to poor eyesight, I can't see these small things on the floor; he finds them immediately and eats them. I have scolded him many times. Now, at this small age, when I start to scold him, he uses bad words. I don't know where he learns them. Listening to his parents fight might be a reason. Now, he runs in unsafe areas. I am so old I can't keep up with him. Running after him increases my blood pressure. His favorite activity is climbing. Climbing on furniture and windows makes me very stressed. There have been several instances where he has fallen and injured his head. He is addicted to mobile phones, knows how to swipe through YouTube shorts, and always wants the phone. If we don't give it to him, he will turn the house upside down and scream, throwing whatever he finds. I am not at an age to take care of small kids. Running to catch him sometimes causes me to lose my balance. By God's grace, I haven't sustained a severe injury." This case exemplifies the challenges of disobedience from grandchildren. The use of bad words, throwing things, screaming, and showing disregard for grandparents often results from mobile phone addiction. However, it's important not to blame older grandparents, as they are unable to manage all the child's naughty behavior.

In this case, the grandparent, who is a hypertension patient and takes regular medication, has resorted to giving the child a mobile phone to manage his behavior. He believes that if the child has the phone, he will sit quietly, eliminating worries. He is not concerned about the consequences of mobile phone use. Prolonged mobile phone use among children under three can lead to serious health issues, including delays in cognitive, speech, and language development. It can also impair social skills, attention, behavior, motor skills, and lead to obesity and physical inactivity in the future.

## Economic Implications of Intergenerational Caregiving

In the case of people living in low or average economic backgrounds, a substantial amount of money can be saved by entrusting the care of their children to grandparents in the absence of the parents (Fuller-Thomson & Minkler, 2001). Traditional Indian cultures also advocate grandparenting for the betterment of younger generations, which can reduce additional expenses for daycare services. If the grandparents live separately and the children are responsible for taking care of their elderly parents, they have to pay extra money for residence, utilities, and food. However, residing in the same house with grandparents can reduce this financial burden. On the other hand, after retirement or at age 60 and above, older grandparents who are willing to switch to a new job and earn an income may be unable to do so if they take on the responsibility of caregiving for their grandchildren (Glaser et al., 2018). This can also lead to financial dependency on their children. Health is a serious factor in caregiving. Health-related problems associated with caregiving can lead to increased medical costs, healthcare expenses, and higher charges for medical attention (Agrawal & Keshri, 2014). The caregiving provided by grandparents to grandchildren is mostly unpaid; however, the financial worth of this care is of substantial importance (Hayslip et al., 2019). Generational wealth transfer is another significant area where grandchildren have the chance to receive financial support for their education or future inheritance. This can be an important aid in reducing the financial stress of the parents regarding their children's future.

## Economic Implications Among Grandparents Providing Care for Grandchildren

The study provides a comprehensive review of the economic aspects of later life. It highlights the growing number of older adults or grandparents who can provide care for their grandchildren, which is increasing in Korea. The study provides various aspects of grandparents' economic influence on the care of their grandchildren. This study highlights the intergenerational exchange theory, providing the relationship between grandparents and grandchildren. It is associated with care and the economic aspects of their later life. The data clearly indicate that nearly 2,599 grandmothers are living in Korea after retirement. They can provide income to support their grandchildren under the age of ten. The study focused on 279 grandchildren and their support for education, marital needs, and household support for grandparents. The economic aspects of grandparents include receiving financial support from compensation and providing related economic support for care and other economic aspects (Kim et al., 2018).

The study discussed several key factors involving the economic aspects for grandparents, including their ability to afford the costs and benefits of supporting and raising their grandchildren. To provide heterogeneous support for grandparents in caregiving. The critical aspects of the study focus on support for the social custodial role of grandparents. It can emphasize the parents' attitudes toward grandparents raising their grandchildren. This can help with the multiple aspects of custodial care for grandparents. The direction of the research practices on custodial care for grandparents (Hayslip & Kaminski, 2005).

The existing review provides the economic aspects, which are growing inexorably for the older population. The study emphasizes the major economic aspects of social change, which are important for increasing the older adult population. The study can explore further aspects of older adults' retirement plans, which can support additional financial needs and reduce market pressures. The financial crisis is predicted to crash the housing market, with economic implications for older adults. The study is likely to improve the challenges they face and enhance the future direction of retirees (Angel & Settersten, 2013).

## Economic Aspects Grandparents

The past study highlights the parent and their adolescent problem it is especially for the economic stress and depression. The main aspects of the study to extend the family it is associate between their economic adversity and depression faced for parenting. The grandparent are highly in economic pressure for parenting pull and push facts. The grandparent are harsh of parent and fall for the depression. The study conducted in Bulgaria for the grandparent nearly 62 family adolescent and grandparent they are economic situation. The study provide comprehensive understanding for their economic burden and parent push and pull grandparents it is highly affected for the grandparents. The outcome of the study economic stress for the parents and it fall for depression due to harsh of parenting their parents. The finding of the study to address the family due to economic economic affect they can face extended for the family relation in the role of cultural aspects (Botcheva & Shirley Feldman, 2004).

## Health Risks of Intergenerational Caregiving

The study enlightens the previous review, which can reveal the pathway to caring for their grandchildren that may be detrimental to their health. They can provide caregiving for the physically demanding tasks, and even grandparents themselves experience challenges due to normal aging (Sampson, 2008).Caring for grandchildren may limit grandparents' time and opportunities to participate in leisure and recreation, leading to an imbalance. They can be involved in social engagement activities (Pruchno, 1999; Gladstone et al., 2009; Marken & Howard, 2014).

The existing review enlightens the study on health problems faced by grandparents in raising grandchildren and identifies various directions for future research. The study adopted a literature review method based on the findings of health-related studies. It began by examining the relationship associated with the concepts. The study is a longitudinal design, which varies across cross-cultural aspects and compares the knowledge of grandparents to provide caregivers with insights into their health and conditions (Grinstead et al., 2003).

According to the author's point of view, many grandparents face problems when raising grandchildren. They can encounter health-related risks within the family structure, which can affect the child's improvement. The significance of the study is to address the problems faced by grandparents due to high health risks, compared to their counterparts. The study provides insights into the physical health, mental health, and behavior of grandparents as primary caregivers for their grandchildren. The findings of the study indicate that the functioning of grandmothers can jeopardize the quality of life for their grandchildren. The study reported that they are unable to stand up to their physical conditions and face emotional aspects of community practices (Whitley et al., 2001).

The findings of the study provide insights into caregiving for grandparents, with nearly 50% of them requiring assistance with Activities of Daily Living (ADL). The study report highlighted the lower health levels of older adults and their satisfaction levels. It indicates that caregivers have low-level health conditions. Further research studies can be implemented to assess functional abilities and focus on health measures. The study needs to improve policy-level support for grandparents raising grandchildren to help reduce their stress levels (Minkler & Fuller-Thomson, 1999).

## Grandparents and Grandchildren: Transition in Relationships

The existing review provides a comprehensive understanding of the major themes, such as the grandparent's role in parent-child relations and its mutual impact on family relationships. Parent-child relation is ongoing and infrequent, with sporadic contact. The study addresses the social implications from a social work perspective, including the need to provide more awareness among family members. It highlights family issues and their long-term influence on intergenerational family relations (Weber & Waldrop, 2000).

The study highlighted the physical, social, psychological, and economic aspects of grandparents and the importance of their health in raising grandchildren. The study provides some of the reviews cited here. Thank you for providing valuable suggestions to enhance the research paper.

## Intergenerational Approach for Grandparents

The approach emphasis for their strengths and skill of age group. It can lead the social aspects of issues in the specific challenges faced by practitioners. Intergeneration approach can implement in higher education to segregate the challenges and services. The study emphasis on permanent implement for the intergenerational events or activities in school level. To meet the social, mental health aspects and improve the grandparents and raising their grandchildren. The effective research study provide the relationship for the intergeneration program. To enhance the various people involve in the intergenerational aspects and to develop intergeneration program model it can emphasis on children life cycle view in the world (Flint & Perez-Porter, 2013). The intergenerational approach can involve various aspects of ageing for the nursing home, day care center, senior care, geriatric home. It can innovate for their idea and support for the develop to improve the intergeneration activities. The academic aspects involve in the curriculum to improve the intergenerational activities to build various reference and variety social issues aspects of the study.

# FINDINGS

The positive cross-age attitude of grandparents has a wide-ranging impact on improving the skills and abilities of grandchildren (Belgrave & Keown, 2018). It reduces the intergenerational gap, increases comfort, and establishes strong connectedness (Halpin et al., 2017). This also helps dispel stereotypes associated with both grandparents and their grandchildren (Sun et al., 2019). During the caregiving process, if grandparents allow their grandchildren to interact with neighbors, relatives, and individuals in their close circle, it fosters good socialization and behavioral patterns among the children under their care (Dev & Eljo, 2023). Increasing social networks and supportive relationships later help grandchildren develop good friendships and effective social networks (Grossman & Gruenewald, 2020). Through social engagement with grandchildren, grandparents are also involved in the socialization process, which helps them alleviate stress, anxiety, and depression (Halpin et al., 2017).

Providing intergenerational caregiving frequently for children under the age of 3 can cause health deterioration and physical and psychological challenges. Children who do not obey can create high blood pressure and stress for the caregivers (Schneiders et al., 2021). Mobile addiction among children under 3 creates more serious issues, including delays in cognitive, speech, language, and motor skill development (Kardefelt-Winther, 2017). Lack of support from children and unmet basic needs also create psychological issues such as anxiety, stress, and depression (Brunissen et al., 2020). To alleviate psychological issues due to caregiving, grandparents can use strategies like sharing their problems with their children, neighbors, and close circles and seeking financial and instrumental assistance to relieve stress associated with intergenerational caregiving (Treleaven & Ngin, 2021). If grandparents do not receive adequate consideration, treatment for their medical conditions, and have no time for themselves, it can create mental health problems and reduce quality of life (Czapanskiy, 1993).

# LIMITATIONS AND FUTURE PROSPECTS

There are certain limitations to which the study is restricted from generalizing to the entire universe. The first limitation is that the sample was collected from an economically sound area. Consequently, their caregiving process receives supportive assistance due to financial stability. The second limitation is that the study was conducted using a self-prepared interview schedule and directly posed to the respondents. This introduces a chance of bias in reporting and makes it susceptible to social desirability. Finally, the sample size was limited, and thus the information is confined within that boundary.

## SOCIAL WORK INTERVENTION

Professional social workers can offer planned intergenerational projects for the welfare of both grandparents and grandchildren. They can aim to create an age-friendly community by providing opportunities for grandparents and grandchildren to share their viewpoints, ideas, and experiences freely with one another. This also helps in finding solutions for present problems and forecasting the future. This connectedness and sense of belonging create emotional attachment, and social workers can encourage them to participate in various activities that enhance their well-being, quality of life, and mental health.

Intergenerational learning is another area where social workers can promote bonding. In this learning concept, social workers can create opportunities to help both grandparents and grandchildren become aware of how they can support one another. Learning from generation to generation provides a deeper understanding of life lessons.

An age-friendly college is an essential factor in which social workers can play a significant role in fostering intergenerational bonding. In this concept, activities for enhancing intergenerational bonding need to be organized on the same premises where grandparents and grandchildren can meet on one platform. This will showcase the importance of experience sharing, intergenerational connectedness, and socialization and make them aware of their privileges.

## INNOVATION AND FUTURE OUTCOMES OF THE STUDY

This exploratory study highlights the importance of intergenerational bonding and its impact on grandparents' health. The study demonstrates a comprehensive approach to both the positive and negative impacts of caregiving on grandparents and the grandchildren they care for. It provides a holistic intergenerational caregiving framework with detailed implications beyond the traditional caregiving process. This study contributes to the intersection of health and intergenerational caregiving by highlighting how the emotional well-being of grandparents affects the development and future of children. The study also addresses the physical, psychological, and social aspects of intergenerational caregiving and the challenges faced by both grandparents and grandchildren. An innovative aspect of the study is the detailed examination of the consequences of mobile phone use among children under the age of 3 and the growing concern within the intergenerational caregiving process.

The study recommends balanced media usage to prevent developmental delays and negative outcomes associated with excessive mobile phone use. It also incorporates a novel dimension by focusing on the health and needs of older adults.

Future research should focus on policy development to ensure holistic health for both grandparents and children involved in caregiving, including stress reduction techniques, therapeutic interventions, awareness on balancing caregiving and health requirements, and health management. Additionally, educational initiatives through training programs and elder-friendly programs should be explored. The study opens avenues for future research on mitigating the negative effects of intergenerational caregiving, strategies to prevent developmental delays due to mobile phone overuse, and examining intergenerational caregiving in various sociocultural perspectives.

## CONCLUSION

The study concludes that if grandparents receive adequate consideration and facilities to fulfill their needs, it helps them attain healthy aging along with their grandchildren. Intergenerational caregiving also has a positive effect on both grandparents and grandchildren, rather than just negative impacts. The findings of the study show that intergenerational caregiving can have both positive and negative impacts on grandparents' health. It can reduce anxiety, depression, and stress, and promote peace and happiness. However, lack of family support, unmet needs, and the pressure of caregiving, coupled with adamant behavior from children, can create stress, anxiety, and worsen physical issues. This will contribute to grandchildren receiving better care and nurture from their grandparents. Therefore, researchers can emphasize that intergenerational caregiving has both strong positive and negative impacts on the health of grandparents and grandchildren.

# REFERENCES

Agrawal, G., & Keshri, K. (2014). Morbidity patterns and health care seeking behavior among older widows in India. *PLoS One*, 9(4), e94295. DOI: 10.1371/journal.pone.0094295 PMID: 24718291

Angel, J. L., & Settersten, R. A., Jr. (2013). The new realities of aging: Social and economic contexts. Perspectives on the future of the sociology of aging, 95-119. https://www.google.co.in/books/edition/Perspectives_on_the_Future_of_the_Sociol/1b7_RjfR3YwC?hl=en&gbpv=1&dq=current+realities+of+conditioned+and+economic+aspects+grandparents&pg=SA2-PA1&printsec=frontcover

Aw, S., Koh, G., Oh, Y. J., Wong, M. L., Vrijhoef, H. J., Harding, S. C., Geronimo, M. A. B., Lai, C. Y. F., & Hildon, Z. J. (2017). Explaining the continuum of social participation among older adults in Singapore: From'closed doors' to active ageing in multi-ethnic community settings. *Journal of Aging Studies*, 42, 46–55. DOI: 10.1016/j.jaging.2017.07.002 PMID: 28918821

Bagnasco, A., Hayter, M., Rossi, S., Zanini, M. P., Pellegrini, R., Aleo, G., Catania, G., & Sasso, L. (2020). Experiences of participating in intergenerational interventions in older people's care settings: A systematic review and meta-synthesis of qualitative literature. *Journal of Advanced Nursing*, 76(1), 22–33. DOI: 10.1111/jan.14214 PMID: 31566788

Belgrave, M. J., & Keown, D. J. (2018). Examining cross-age experiences in a distance-based intergenerational music project: Comfort and expectations in collaborating with opposite generation through "virtual" exchanges. *Frontiers in Medicine*, 5, 214. DOI: 10.3389/fmed.2018.00214 PMID: 30151363

Bland, R. (2006). Senior citizens, good practice and quality of life in residential care homes. https://dspace.stir.ac.uk/handle/1893/70

Botcheva, L. B., & Shirley Feldman, S. (2004). Grandparents as family stabilizers during economic hardship in Bulgaria. *International Journal of Psychology*, 39(3), 157–168. DOI: 10.1080/00207590344000321

Brunello, G., & Rocco, L. (2019). Grandparents in the blues. The effect of childcare on grandparents' depression. *Review of Economics of the Household*, 17(2), 587–613. DOI: 10.1007/s11150-018-9432-2

Brunello, G., & Yamamura, E. (2023). Reciprocity and the matrilineal advantage in European grand-parenting. *Review of Economics of the Household*, 21(2), 397–433. DOI: 10.1007/s11150-022-09630-w

Brunissen, L., Rapoport, E., Fruitman, K., & Adesman, A. (2020). Parenting challenges of grandparents raising grandchildren: Discipline, child education, technology use, and outdated health beliefs. GrandFamilies: The Contemporary Journal of Research, Practice and Policy, 6(1), 6. https://scholarworks.wmich.edu/grandfamilies/vol6/iss1/6/

Canedo-Garcia, A., Garcia-Sanchez, J. N., & Pacheco-Sanz, D. I. (2017). A systematic review of the effectiveness of intergenerational programs. *Frontiers in Psychology*, 8, 1882. DOI: 10.3389/fpsyg.2017.01882 PMID: 29163269

Cordella, M., Poiani, A., Cordella, M., & Poiani, A. (2021). The Social Dimension of Older Ages. Fulfilling Ageing: Psychosocial and Communicative Perspectives on Ageing, 461-632. DOI: 10.1007/978-3-030-60071-6_6

Czapanskiy, K. (1993). Grandparents, Parents and Grandchildren: Actualizing Interdependency in Law. Conn. L. Rev., 26, 1315. https://heinonline.org/HOL/LandingPage?handle=hein.journals/conlr26&div=50&id=&page=

Dev, P. S., & Eljo, J. G. (2024). Addressing the Ethical and Legal Complexities in Elderly Care: A Study from India. *Nusantara Journal of Behavioral and Social Science*, 3(3), 111–118. DOI: 10.47679/njbss.202456

Dev, P. S., & Eljo, J. J. G. (2022). COVID-19 impacts on elderly with disability. DOI: DOI: 10.21522/TIJPH.2013.SE.22.01.Art005

Dev, P. S., & Eljo, J. J. G. (2023). Inclusive Wash for Elderly with Disabilities. *Journal for ReAttach Therapy and Developmental Diversities*, 6(5s), 285–291. http://jrtdd.com/index.php/journal/article/view/518

Ding, K. (2024). The Impact of Grandparents and Intergenerational Living on Children's Social and Emotional Development. Journal of Education. *Humanities and Social Sciences*, 29, 403–412. DOI: 10.54097/paw2mg46

Earl, E. J., & Marais, D. (2023). The experience of intergenerational interactions and their influence on the mental health of older people living in residential care. *PLoS One*, 18(7), e0287369. DOI: 10.1371/journal.pone.0287369 PMID: 37405973

Flint, M. M., & Perez-Porter, M. (2013). Grandparent caregivers: Legal and economic issues. In *Intergenerational Approaches in Aging* (pp. 63–76). Routledge., https://www.taylorfrancis.com/chapters/edit/10.4324/9780203047293-8/grandparent-caregivers-margaret-flint-melinda-perez-porter

Fong-Chong, A. (2003). Tampines 3-in-1 Family Centre, Singapore. *Journal of Intergenerational Relationships*, 1(1), 169–171. DOI: 10.1300/J194v01n01_14

Fuller-Thomson, E., & Minkler, M. (2001). American grandparents providing extensive child care to their grandchildren: Prevalence and profile. *The Gerontologist*, 41(2), 201–209. DOI: 10.1093/geront/41.2.201 PMID: 11327486

Gladstone, J. W., Brown, R. A., & Fitzgerald, K. A. J. (2009). Grandparents raising their grandchildren: Tensions, service needs and involvement with child welfare agencies. *International Journal of Aging & Human Development*, 69(1), 55–78. DOI: 10.2190/AG.69.1.d PMID: 19803340

Glaser, K., Stuchbury, R., Price, D., Di Gessa, G., Ribe, E., & Tinker, A. (2018). Trends in the prevalence of grandparents living with grandchild (ren) in selected European countries and the United States. *European Journal of Ageing*, 15(3), 237–250. DOI: 10.1007/s10433-018-0474-3 PMID: 30310371

Grinstead, L. N., Leder, S., Jensen, S., & Bond, L. (2003). Review of research on the health of caregiving grandparents. *Journal of Advanced Nursing*, 44(3), 318–326. DOI: 10.1046/j.1365-2648.2003.02807.x PMID: 14641402

Grossman, M. R., & Gruenewald, T. L. (2020). Failure to meet generative self-expectations is linked to poorer cognitive–affective well-being. The Journals of Gerontology: Series B, 75(4), 792-801. DOI: 10.1093/geronb/gby069

Gualano, M. R., Voglino, G., Bert, F., Thomas, R., Camussi, E., & Siliquini, R. (2018). The impact of intergenerational programs on children and older adults: A review. *International Psychogeriatrics*, 30(4), 451–468. DOI: 10.1017/S104161021700182X PMID: 28988548

Guo, J., Huang, X., Dou, L., Yan, M., Shen, T., Tang, W., & Li, J. (2022). Aging and aging-related diseases: From molecular mechanisms to interventions and treatments. *Signal Transduction and Targeted Therapy*, 7(1), 391. DOI: 10.1038/s41392-022-01251-0 PMID: 36522308

Halpin, S. N., Dillard, R. L., Idler, E., Clevenger, C., Rothschild, E., Blanton, S., Wilson, J., & Flacker, J. M. (2017). The benefits of being a senior mentor: Cultivating resilience through the mentorship of health professions students. *Gerontology & Geriatrics Education*, 38(3), 283–294. DOI: 10.1080/02701960.2015.1079707 PMID: 26251869

Hayslip, B.Jr, Fruhauf, C. A., & Dolbin-MacNab, M. L. (2019). Grandparents raising grandchildren: What have we learned over the past decade? *The Gerontologist*, 59(3), e152–e163. DOI: 10.1093/geront/gnx106 PMID: 28666363

Hayslip, B.Jr, & Kaminski, P. L. (2005). Grandparents raising their grandchildren: A review of the literature and suggestions for practice. *The Gerontologist*, 45(2), 262–269. DOI: 10.1093/geront/45.2.262 PMID: 15799992

Hodgson, H. (2019). The Grandma Force: Grandmothers Changing Grandchildren, Families, and Themselves. BQB Publishing. https://www.google.co.in/books/edition/The_Grandma_Force/LC2MDwAAQBAJ?hl=en&gbpv=1&dq=Celebrating+%E2%80%98Grandparents+Day%E2%80%99+is+also+a+wonderful+strategy+that+makes+people+aware+of+how+precious+our+older+adults+are.+This+also+emphasizes+the+need+for+binding+families.+&pg=PT15&printsec=frontcover

Kaplan, M. S. (2002). International programs in schools: Considerations of form and function. *International Review of Education*, 48(5), 305–334. DOI: 10.1023/A:1021231713392

Kardefelt-Winther, D. (2017). How does the time children spend using digital technology impact their mental well-being, social relationships and physical activity?: an evidence-focused literature review. https://www.eukidsonline.de/wp-content/uploads/Children-digital-technology-wellbeing.pdf

Kelley, S. J., Whitley, D., Sipe, T. A., & Yorker, B. C. (2000). Psychological distress in grandmother kinship care providers: The role of resources, social support, and physical health. *Child Abuse & Neglect*, 24(3), 311–321. DOI: 10.1016/S0145-2134(99)00146-5 PMID: 10739075

Kemp, C. L. (2007). Grandparent—grandchild ties: Reflections on continuity and change across three generations. *Journal of Family Issues*, 28(7), 855–881. DOI: 10.1177/0192513X07299599

Kim, H. J., Lapierre, T. A., & Chapin, R. (2018). Grandparents providing care for grandchildren: Implications for economic preparation for later life in South Korea. *Ageing and Society*, 38(4), 676–699. DOI: 10.1017/S0144686X16001215

Kroll, D. H. (2011). To care or not to care: the ultimate decision for adult caregivers in a rapidly aging society. Temp. Pol. & Civ. Rts. L. Rev., 21, 403. https://heinonline.org/HOL/LandingPage?handle=hein.journals/tempcr21&div=22&id=&page=

Leong, K. S., Klainin-Yobas, P., Fong, S. D., & Wu, X. V. (2022). Older adults' perspective of intergenerational programme at senior day care centre in Singapore: A descriptive qualitative study. *Health & Social Care in the Community*, 30(1), e222–e233. DOI: 10.1111/hsc.13432 PMID: 34028921

Lim, C. C. L., Low, C. L. T., Hia, S. B., Thang, L. L., & Thian, A. L. (2019). Generativity: Establishing and nurturing the next generation. *Journal of Intergenerational Relationships*, 17(3), 368–379. DOI: 10.1080/15350770.2019.1617603

Marken, D. M., & Howard, J. B. (2014). Grandparents raising grandchildren: The influence of a late-life transition on occupational engagement. *Physical & Occupational Therapy in Geriatrics*, 32(4), 381–396. DOI: 10.3109/02703181.2014.965376

McCrea, J. M., & Smith, T. B. (2014). Types and models of intergenerational programs. In *Intergenerational programs* (pp. 81–93). Taylor & Francis., https://www.taylorfrancis.com/chapters/edit/10.4324/9781315783451-7/types-models-intergenerational-programs-james-mccrea-thomas-smith

Mebane, M. E., & Pezzuti, L. (2020). Intergenerational solidarity in triads of adult grandchild, parent, and grandparent: The positive view of elders, positive expectations towards the future and young-elders divide. *Educational Gerontology*, 46(9), 512–524. DOI: 10.1080/03601277.2020.1785672

Ministry of Social and Family Development, Republic of Singapore. 2022. Ageing Families in Singapore, 2010–2020. Insight Series Paper 01/2022.

Minkler, M., & Fuller-Thomson, E. (1999). The health of grandparents raising grandchildren: Results of a national study. *American Journal of Public Health*, 89(9), 1384–1389. DOI: 10.2105/AJPH.89.9.1384 PMID: 10474557

Morais, D. M. D. C. B., Faria, C. M. G. M., & Fernandes, L. P. N. S. (2019). Intergenerational caregiving: The role of attachment and mental representation of caregiving in filial anxiety of middle-aged children. *Journal of Intergenerational Relationships*, 17(4), 468–487. DOI: 10.1080/15350770.2019.1596187

Murayama, Y., Ohba, H., Yasunaga, M., Nonaka, K., Takeuchi, R., Nishi, M., Sakuma, N., Uchida, H., Shinkai, S., & Fujiwara, Y. (2015). The effect of intergenerational programs on the mental health of elderly adults. *Aging & Mental Health*, 19(4), 306–314. DOI: 10.1080/13607863.2014.933309 PMID: 25010219

Ng, C. T. C., & James, S. (2013). "Directive approach" for Chinese clients receiving psychotherapy: Is that really a priority? *Frontiers in Psychology*, 4, 49. DOI: 10.3389/fpsyg.2013.00049 PMID: 23408043

Niazi, A. R. K., Mubeen, M., Niazi, M. H. K., & Asnan, C. M. (2020). Generation gap is a difference i Generation Gap in Pakistan: Antecedents and Effects. *The Dialogue*, 15(4), 64–75. https://journals.qurtuba.edu.pk/ojs/index.php/thedialogue/article/view/222

Peters, R., Ee, N., Ward, S. A., Kenning, G., Radford, K., Goldwater, M., Dodge, H. H., Lewis, E., Xu, Y., Kundrna, G., Hamilton, M., Peters, J., Anstey, K. J., Lautenschlager, N. T., Fitzgerald, A., & Rockwood, K. (2021). Intergenerational programmes bringing together community dwelling non-familial older adults and children: A systematic review. *Archives of Gerontology and Geriatrics*, 94, 104356. DOI: 10.1016/j.archger.2021.104356 PMID: 33567363

Pruchno, R. (1999). Raising grandchildren: The experiences of black and white grandmothers. *The Gerontologist*, 39(2), 209–221. DOI: 10.1093/geront/39.2.209 PMID: 10224717

Reynolds, C. F.III, Jeste, D. V., Sachdev, P. S., & Blazer, D. G. (2022). Mental health care for older adults: Recent advances and new directions in clinical practice and research. *World Psychiatry; Official Journal of the World Psychiatric Association (WPA)*, 21(3), 336–363. DOI: 10.1002/wps.20996 PMID: 36073714

Sampson, D. (2008). The experience of grandparents raising grandchildren: A phenomenological study. https://digitalscholarship.unlv.edu/rtds/2429/

Schneiders, M. L., Phou, M., Tum, V., Kelley, M., Parker, M., & Turner, C. (2021). Grandparent caregiving in Cambodian skip-generation households: Roles and impact on child nutrition. *Maternal and Child Nutrition*, 17(S1), e13169. DOI: 10.1111/mcn.13169 PMID: 34241960

Scotté, F., Bossi, P., Carola, E., Cudennec, T., Dielenseger, P., Gomes, F., Knox, S., & Strasser, F. (2018). Addressing the quality of life needs of older patients with cancer: A SIOG consensus paper and practical guide. *Annals of Oncology : Official Journal of the European Society for Medical Oncology*, 29(8), 1718–1726. DOI: 10.1093/annonc/mdy228 PMID: 30010772

Settles, B. H., Zhao, J., Mancini, K. D., Rich, A., Pierre, S., & Oduor, A. (2009). Grandparents caring for their grandchildren: Emerging roles and exchanges in global perspectives. *Journal of Comparative Family Studies*, 40(5), 827–848. DOI: 10.3138/jcfs.40.5.827

Silverstein, M., Giarrusso, R., & Bengtson, V. L. (2003). Grandparents and grandchildren in family systems. Global aging and challenges to families, 75-102. https://www.google.co.in/books/edition/Global_Aging_and_Challenges_to_Families/AnMIEQAAQBAJ?hl=en&gbpv=1&dq=Transitioning+from+joint+to+nuclear+family+systems+has+widened+the+gap+between+grandparents+and+grandchildren.+&pg=PA75&printsec=frontcover

Statista, (2022). Annual number of adult social care homes in England from 2009 to 2019, Statistia.

Sun, Q., Lou, V. W., Dai, A., To, C., & Wong, S. Y. (2019). The effectiveness of the young–old link and growth intergenerational program in reducing age stereotypes. *Research on Social Work Practice*, 29(5), 519–528. DOI: 10.1177/1049731518767319

Thang, L. L. (2011). Promoting intergenerational understanding between the young and old: the case of Singapore. In UN report of the expert group meeting in Qatar (pp. 8-9). https://www.un.org/esa/socdev/family/docs/egm11/EGM_Expert_Paper _Theng_Leng_Leng.pdf

Thomas, P. A., Liu, H., & Umberson, D. (2017). Family relationships and well-being. *Innovation in Aging*, 1(3), igx025. Advance online publication. DOI: 10.1093/geroni/igx025 PMID: 29795792

Treleaven, E., & Ngin, C. (2021). When parents are not present: Decision-making dynamics for young children's health and illness in migrant-sending households in rural Cambodia. *Social Science & Medicine*, 287, 114327. DOI: 10.1016/j.socscimed.2021.114327 PMID: 34509896

Vidovićová, L. (2018). New roles for older people. *Journal of Population Ageing*, 11(1), 1–6. DOI: 10.1007/s12062-017-9217-z

Wallbaum, T., Matviienko, A., Ananthanarayan, S., Olsson, T., Heuten, W., & Boll, S. C. (2018, April). Supporting communication between grandparents and grandchildren through tangible storytelling systems. In *Proceedings of the 2018 CHI Conference on Human Factors in Computing Systems* (pp. 1-12). DOI: 10.1145/3173574.3174124

Wang, L., & Tang, Y. (2023). Impacts of intergenerational caregiving on grandparents' health: Implications for SDG-3. *Economic Analysis and Policy*, 79, 584–598. DOI: 10.1016/j.eap.2023.06.015

Watson, J. (2023). Skipped Generation Parenting: A Program to Enhance the Grandparent Caregiver Experience (Doctoral dissertation, John F. Kennedy University).

Weber, J. A., & Waldrop, D. P. (2000). Grandparents raising grandchildren: Families in transition. *Journal of Gerontological Social Work*, 33(2), 27–46. DOI: 10.1300/J083v33n02_03

Wetzel, M., & Hank, K. (2020). Grandparents' relationship to grandchildren in the transition to adulthood. *Journal of Family Issues*, 41(10), 1885–1904. DOI: 10.1177/0192513X19894355

Whitley, D. M., Kelley, S. J., & Sipe, T. A. (2001). Grandmothers raising grandchildren: Are they at increased risk of health problems? *Health & Social Work*, 26(2), 105–114. DOI: 10.1093/hsw/26.2.105 PMID: 11378995

Wong, E. L., Lau, J. Y., & Yeoh, E. K. (2018). Thinking intergenerationally: Intergenerational solidarity, health and active aging in Hong Kong: Policy. *Journal of Intergenerational Relationships*, 16(4), 478–492. DOI: 10.1080/15350770.2018.1489328

Wong, J. S., & Hsieh, N. (2019). Functional status, cognition, and social relationships in dyadic perspective. The Journals of Gerontology: Series B, 74(4), 703-714. DOI: 10.1093/geronb/gbx024

Xu, H. (2019). Physical and mental health of Chinese grandparents caring for grandchildren and great-grandparents. *Social Science & Medicine*, 229, 106–116. DOI: 10.1016/j.socscimed.2018.05.047 PMID: 29866373

Xu, L., Chi, I., & Wu, S. (2018). Grandparent–grandchild relationships in Chinese immigrant families in Los Angeles: Roles of acculturation and the middle generation. *Gerontology & Geriatric Medicine*, 4, 2333721418778196. DOI: 10.1177/2333721418778196 PMID: 30035201

Yeh, I. L., Wong, S. Y. X., Safaruan, L. S. B., Kang, Y. Q., Wong, M. S., & Wilson, I. M. (2022). Development and Implementation of an Intergenerational Bonding Program in a Co-Located Model: A Case Study in Singapore. *Social Sciences (Basel, Switzerland)*, 11(12), 557. DOI: 10.3390/socsci11120557

Zamarro, G. (2020). Family labor participation and child care decisions: The role of grannies. *SERIEs*, 11(3), 287–312. DOI: 10.1007/s13209-020-00213-5

Zhou, J., Mao, W., Lee, Y., & Chi, I. (2017). The impact of caring for grandchildren on grandparents' physical health outcomes: The role of intergenerational support. Research on Aging, 39(5), 612-634. doi:s10.1177/0164027515623332

# Conclusion

Aging, as a natural part of human life, is one of the most significant processes that individuals and societies face. However, we now know that aging is not merely a biological phenomenon; it also creates a complex interplay within economic, social, and political contexts. The chapters explored throughout this book have sought to examine the multifaceted impacts, opportunities, and challenges of aging. Now, it is time to return to the questions we posed at the beginning of the book and evaluate the points where we found answers to these questions.

At the beginning of the book, we questioned whether aging is a problem or an opportunity. As we have seen throughout the chapters, aging encompasses both aspects. The first chapter, titled ***The Economics of Aging: Global Trends and Perspectives***, addressed the global trends of aging, discussing the economic pressures and changes this phenomenon creates on societies. The impact of the aging population on social security systems, the sustainability of retirement policies, and the increase in healthcare expenditures are the main factors that cause this process to be perceived as a "*problem*." However, at the same time, the concept of the "silver economy" discussed in this chapter revealed that aging also creates economic opportunities. In this context, the chapter suggested that the knowledge, experience, and spending power of older individuals can contribute to societies' economic growth and innovation.

So, how much are these opportunities being utilized? As we have seen throughout the book, aging is often perceived as a "*burden*" in political and social systems. But it is possible to change this perception. For example, the chapter titled ***Ring Out 'Ageing Miserably'; Ring In 'Growing Gracefully'*** argued that aging should be approached with a more positive perspective. Offering a cultural and philosophical approach, it emphasized that aging can be a new beginning for individuals, not an end. This showed us that it could be a powerful call for societies to reshape their policies and perceptions towards older individuals.

Another important question was how older individuals can be integrated into the social and economic system. The chapter ***Lifelong Learning: Demographic Trends and Economic Participation in Older Adults*** discussed the critical role of education in encouraging the active participation of older individuals in society. Lifelong learning programs for older individuals not only increase economic participation but also strengthen social bonds and support individuals' self-actualization processes. So, are these programs widespread enough? As discussed in the book, many countries still fail to sufficiently encourage older individuals' access to education. However, this emerges as an important policy area that can be addressed in the future.

Similarly, the chapter titled ***Digital Inclusion and Economic Participation of the Elderly: Challenges and Strategies*** emphasized the critical role that technology can play in improving the quality of life for older individuals. However, shortcomings in technology accessibility and digital literacy prevent older individuals from benefiting sufficiently from these opportunities. This raises another question that needs to be answered: Should technology be designed only for younger generations, or should it evolve to meet the needs of older individuals? It seems that the future will be shaped by the answer to this question.

The role of technology in improving the quality of life for older individuals is not limited to digital inclusion. The chapter titled ***Technology Improves the Quality of Life for Elderly People: A Pathway to Well-Being*** discussed how gerontechnology, in particular, can increase the independence of older individuals and their access to healthcare services. It showed that innovative solutions such as telemedicine, wearable health devices, and smart home technologies can play a critical role in supporting the physical and mental well-being of older individuals while reducing health inequalities in society. The integration of these technologies not only improves individual quality of life but also alleviates pressure on healthcare systems. However, the accessibility and economic costs of these technologies remain significant issues to be resolved in the future.

The book did not only address aging from global perspectives but also examined the situation of countries with unique demographic and cultural structures, such as Türkiye. The chapter titled ***The Effects of Türkiye's Ageing Problem on the Elderly*** analyzed Türkiye's aging problem. Issues such as the weakness of social support systems, inequalities in access to healthcare services, and the weakening of intergenerational ties revealed how complex an issue aging is in the Turkish context. The policies that Türkiye has developed to address the problem of aging can be evaluated not only in a national context but also in the context of global trends. So, will countries like Türkiye see aging as a "*crisis*," or will they evaluate this process as an opportunity to transform their societies?

The aging process affects not only individuals and states but also family structures and intergenerational relationships. The chapter titled *Intergenerational Caregiving on Grandparents' Health: A Case Study* analyzed the impact of family ties and intergenerational solidarity on the well-being of older individuals. In particular, taking on roles such as childcare for grandchildren can have both positive and negative effects on the physical and mental health of older individuals. This indicates that social policies need to be rethought not only at the individual level but also at the family and societal level.

The chapter titled *Designing for Longevity: Economic Perspectives on Age-Friendly Housing and Urban Development* discussed how to design age-friendly environments to improve the quality of life for older individuals. Safe, accessible, and inclusive urban areas and housing are critical to meeting the needs of the aging population. It showed that such designs can not only improve individual living standards but also increase social cohesion and sustainability.

## QUESTION FOR THE FUTURE

The chapters of this book aimed to answer important questions by addressing different dimensions of the aging process. However, this process has also brought new questions to the forefront:

o     What kind of policies should be developed to increase the labor force participation of older individuals?

o     How can family structures and social systems be redesigned to strengthen intergenerational solidarity?

o     How can technology improve the quality of life for older individuals while reducing social inequalities?

o     What innovative financing models can be used to ensure the sustainability of healthcare and social security systems?

o     How can cultural perceptions and policies be transformed to address aging from a more positive perspective?

These questions not only constitute an area of academic discussion but also offer a roadmap for the future sustainability of societies.

## A FINAL CALL TO ACTION

Aging is a process that every individual will encounter. However, this process is not just an individual matter, but a societal responsibility. This book represents a modest effort to explore ways of seeing aging not as a problem, but as an opportunity. While the topics discussed provide a foundation for understanding the multifaceted impacts of aging, what will be built upon this foundation will only be possible through the joint efforts of not just academics, but also policymakers, civil society organizations, and individuals.

The future will be shaped by how we address aging. Will we see aging as a burden, or as an opportunity to transform our societal structures? The answers we give to these questions will determine not only our present but also our future. Therefore, understanding and managing aging is not just a necessity, but also an opportunity for a more just, inclusive, and sustainable future!

**Ali Gökhan Gölçek**
*Nigde Ömer Halisdemir University, Turkey*

# Compilation of References

Aboderin, I., Rosenberg, M., & Owii, H. (2017). Toward "age-friendly slums"? health challenges of older slum dwellers in Nairobi and the applicability of the age-friendly city approach. *International Journal of Environmental Research and Public Health*, 14(10), 1259. DOI: 10.3390/ijerph14101259 PMID: 29053576

Abril-Jiménez, P., Lacal, J., Pérez, S., Páramo, M., Colomer, J., & Arredondo, M. (2019). Aging-friendly cities for assessing older adults' decline: IOT-based system for continuous monitoring of frailty risks using smart city infrastructure. *Aging Clinical and Experimental Research*, 32(4), 663–671. DOI: 10.1007/s40520-019-01238-y PMID: 31228029

Adlakha, D., Chandra, M., Krishna, M., Smith, L., & Tully, M. (2021). Designing age-friendly communities: Exploring qualitative perspectives on urban green spaces and aging in two Indian megacities. *International Journal of Environmental Research and Public Health*, 18(4), 1491. DOI: 10.3390/ijerph18041491 PMID: 33557432

Ageing and Health. (2022, Oct 1). In *World Health Organization*. https://www.who.int/news-room/fact-sheets/detail/ageing-and-health

Ageing. (2013, Oct 2) In *Social for Cultural Anthropology*. Aging | Society for Cultural Anthropology (culanth.org)

Aging and health India. (n.d.). Retrieved from Www.who.int. https://www.who.int/india/health-topics/ageing

Aging: The Biology of Senescence. (n.d). In *National Library of Medicine*. Aging: The Biology of Senescence - Developmental Biology - NCBI Bookshelf (nih.gov)

Agrawal, G., & Keshri, K. (2014). Morbidity patterns and health care seeking behavior among older widows in India. *PLoS One*, 9(4), e94295. DOI: 10.1371/journal.pone.0094295 PMID: 24718291

Akinola, S. (2021, October 1). *How can we ensure digital inclusion for older adults?* World Economic Forum. https://www.weforum.org/agenda/2021/10/how-can-we -ensure-digital-inclusion-for-older-adults/

Alwago, W. O. (2023). The nexus between health expenditure, life expectancy, and economic growth: ARDL model analysis for Kenya. *Regional Science Policy & Practice*, 15(5), 1064–1086. DOI: 10.1111/rsp3.12588

Angel, J. L., & Settersten, R. A., Jr. (2013). The new realities of aging: Social and economic contexts. Perspectives on the future of the sociology of aging, 95-119. https://www.google.co.in/books/edition/Perspectives_on_the_Future_of_the _Sociol/1b7_RjfR3YwC?hl=en&gbpv=1&dq=current+realities+of+conditioned+ and+economic+aspects+grandparents&pg=SA2-PA1&printsec=frontcover

Anglen, J. (2024). AI for Elderly Care [Review of AI for Elderly Care]. Rapid Innovation. https://www.rapidinnovation.io/post/ai-for-elderly-care

Applebaum, J., Horecka, K., Loney, L., & Graham, T. (2021). Pet-friendly for whom? an analysis of pet fees in Texas rental housing. *Frontiers in Veterinary Science*, 8, 767149. Advance online publication. DOI: 10.3389/fvets.2021.767149 PMID: 34820439

Arai, Y., & Khan, I. A. (2023). *Silver Hues: Building Age-Ready Cities*. World Bank, EAP Regional Paper.

Arai, A., Ishida, K., Tomimori, M., Katsumata, Y., Grove, J. S., & Tamashiro, H. (2007). Association between lifestyle activity and depressed mood among home-dwelling older people: A community-based study in Japan. *Aging & Mental Health*, 11(5), 547–555. DOI: 10.1080/13607860601086553 PMID: 17882593

Arısoy, İ., Ünlükaplan, İ., & Ergen, Z. (2010). The relationship between social expenditures and economic growth: A dynamic analysis intended for 1960-2005 period of the Turkish economy. *The Journal of Finance*, 158, 398–421.

Aslan, M., & Hocaoğlu, Ç. (2017). Psychiatric problems associated with aging and aging period. *Journal of Düzce University Institute of Health Sciences*, 7(1), 53–62.

Aw, S., Koh, G., Oh, Y. J., Wong, M. L., Vrijhoef, H. J., Harding, S. C., Geronimo, M. A. B., Lai, C. Y. F., & Hildon, Z. J. (2017). Explaining the continuum of social participation among older adults in Singapore: From 'closed doors' to active ageing in multi-ethnic community settings. *Journal of Aging Studies*, 42, 46–55. DOI: 10.1016/j.jaging.2017.07.002 PMID: 28918821

Ayabakan, B. Ç. (2022). Covid-19 update on the relationship between aging, active aging and intergenerational conflict in Europe. In Journal of Social Policy Conferences (No. 83, pp. 225-247). Istanbul University.

Aydin, M. (2024). Aging Society and Tax Policy. Pamukkale University Journal of Social Sciences Institute, (63).

Azar, S. T. (2003). Adult development and parenthood: A social-cognitive perspective. *Handbook of adult development*, 391-415. DOI: 10.1007/978-1-4615-0617-1_20

Baernholdt, M., Hinton, I., Yan, G., Rose, K., & Mattos, M. (2012). Factors associated with quality of life in older adults in the United States. *Quality of Life Research: An International Journal of Quality of Life Aspects of Treatment, Care and Rehabilitation*, 21(3), 527–534. DOI: 10.1007/s11136-011-9954-z PMID: 21706127

Bagnasco, A., Hayter, M., Rossi, S., Zanini, M. P., Pellegrini, R., Aleo, G., Catania, G., & Sasso, L. (2020). Experiences of participating in intergenerational interventions in older people's care settings: A systematic review and meta-synthesis of qualitative literature. *Journal of Advanced Nursing*, 76(1), 22–33. DOI: 10.1111/jan.14214 PMID: 31566788

Bakaev, M., Ponomarev, V., & Prokhorova, L. (2008, July). E-learning and elder people: Barriers and benefits. In *2008 IEEE Region 8 International Conference on Computational Technologies in Electrical and Electronics Engineering* (pp. 110-113). Doi: DOI: 10.1109/SIBIRCON.2008.4602586

Baker, S., Kelly, R. M., Waycott, J., Carrasco, R., Hoang, T., Batchelor, F., Ozanne, E., Dow, B., Warburton, J., & Vetere, F. (2019). Interrogating social virtual reality as a communication medium for older adults. *Proceedings of the ACM on human-computer interaction, 3*(CSCW), 1-24. DOI: 10.1145/3359251

Balatti, J., & Falk, I. (2002). Socioeconomic contributions of adult learning to community: A social capital perspective. *Adult Education Quarterly*, 52(4), 281–298. DOI: 10.1177/074171302400448618

Barrett, A. J., & Murk, P. J. (2006). Life Satisfaction Index for the Third Age (LSITA): A measurement of successful aging. https://core.ac.uk/download/pdf/46955647.pdf

Barrouillet, P. (2015). Theories of cognitive development: From Piaget to today. *Developmental Review*, 38, 1–12. DOI: 10.1016/j.dr.2015.07.004

Bashkireva, A. S., Bogdanova, D. Y., Bilyk, A. Y., Shishko, A. V., Kachan, E. Y., & Arutyunov, V. A. (2018). Quality of life and physical activity among elderly and old people. *Advances in gerontology=. Uspekhi Gerontologii*, 31(5), 743–750. PMID: 30638330

Bata. (n.d.). In *Wikipedia*.https://en.wikipedia.org/wiki/Bata_Corporation

Behzadnia, B., Deci, E. L., & DeHaan, C. R. (2020). Predicting relations among life goals, physical activity, health, and well-being in elderly adults: a self-determination theory perspective on healthy aging. *Self-determination theory and healthy aging: Comparative contexts on physical and mental well-being*, 47-71.

Belgrave, M. J., & Keown, D. J. (2018). Examining cross-age experiences in a distance-based intergenerational music project: Comfort and expectations in collaborating with opposite generation through "virtual" exchanges. *Frontiers in Medicine*, 5, 214. DOI: 10.3389/fmed.2018.00214 PMID: 30151363

Berglund, G. (2007). Adapt or you're toast?–Remodelling the individual in lifelong learning. *Nordic Studies in Education*, 27(2), 120–129. DOI: 10.18261/ISSN1891-5949-2007-02-02

Berlinger, N. (2022). Housing, aging, and health: New findings and frameworks from housing-focused research in the context of covid-19. *Innovation in Aging*, 6(Supplement_1), 337–337. DOI: 10.1093/geroni/igac059.1329

Bessant, J. C., Emslie, M., & Watts, R. (2011). Accounting for Future Generations: Intergenerational Equity in Australia 1. *Australian Journal of Public Administration*, 70(2), 143–155. DOI: 10.1111/j.1467-8500.2011.00723.x

Bianchi, N., Lu, Y., & Song, H. (2022). The effect of computer-assisted learning on students' long-term development. *Journal of Development Economics*, 158, 102919. DOI: 10.1016/j.jdeveco.2022.102919

Biggs, S., Carstensen, L., & Hogan, P. (2012). Social capital, lifelong learning and social Innovation. In World Economic Forum, Global Population Ageing: Peril or Promise? (pp. 39–41). Retrieved November 16, 2013, from http://www3.weforum.org/docs/WEF_ GAC_GlobalPopulationAgeing_Report_2012.pdf

Billis, A., Konstantinidis, E., Zilidou, V., Wadhwa, K., Ladas, A., & Bamidis, P. (2013). Biomedical engineering and elderly support. *International Journal of Reliable and Quality E-Healthcare*, 2(2), 21–37. DOI: 10.4018/ijrqeh.2013040102

Binette, J. (2023). Where we live, where we age: home is at the heart of older adults' well-being - fact sheet.. DOI: 10.26419/res.00479.006

Bjorklund, B. R. (2011). *The journey of adulthood* (7th ed.). Prentice Hall.

Black, K., & Jester, D. (2020). Examining older adults' perspectives on the built environment and correlates of healthy aging in an American age-friendly community. *International Journal of Environmental Research and Public Health*, 17(19), 7056. DOI: 10.3390/ijerph17197056 PMID: 32992480

Bland, R. (2006). Senior citizens, good practice and quality of life in residential care homes. https://dspace.stir.ac.uk/handle/1893/70

Blurton, E. U. (1992). *Gender and history: An analysis of the patterns of change in levels of aspirations, satisfaction, achievement and personal adjustment in gifted and nongifted men and women.* University of California, Riverside. https://www.proquest.com/openview/ecb04cc4b6d8e0b32de7855c53b18512/1?pq-origsite=gscholar&cbl=18750&diss=y

Bodner, E., & Lazar, A. (2008). Ageism among Israeli students: Structure and demographic influences. *International Psychogeriatrics*, 20(5), 1046–1058. DOI: 10.1017/S1041610208007151 PMID: 18405396

Boer, B., Bozdemir, B., Jansen, J., Hermans, M., Hamers, J., & Verbeek, H. (2020). The homestead: Developing a conceptual framework through co-creation for innovating long-term dementia care environments. *International Journal of Environmental Research and Public Health*, 18(1), 57. DOI: 10.3390/ijerph18010057 PMID: 33374761

Boffoli, D., Scacco, S. C., Vergari, R., Solarino, G., Santacroce, G., & Papa, S. (1994). Decline with age of the respiratory chain activity in human skeletal muscle. *Biochimica et Biophysica Acta*, 1226(1), 73–82. DOI: 10.1016/0925-4439(94)90061-2 PMID: 8155742

Bölüktaş, R. P. (2019). *Theories of aging and geriatric assessment.* Istanbul University Faculty of Open and Distance Education.

Bong, W. K., Bergland, A., & Chen, W. (2019). Technology acceptance and quality of life among older people using a TUI application. *International Journal of Environmental Research and Public Health*, 16(23), 4706. DOI: 10.3390/ijerph16234706 PMID: 31779170

Boström, A. K. (2002). Informal learning in a formal context: Problematizing the concept of social capital in a contemporary Swedish context. *International Journal of Lifelong Education*, 21(6), 510–524. DOI: 10.1080/0260137022000016730

Botcheva, L. B., & Shirley Feldman, S. (2004). Grandparents as family stabilizers during economic hardship in Bulgaria. *International Journal of Psychology*, 39(3), 157–168. DOI: 10.1080/00207590344000321

Bouabida, K., Lebouché, B., & Pomey, M.-P. (2022). Telehealth and COVID-19 Pandemic: An Overview of the Telehealth Use, Advantages, Challenges, and Opportunities during COVID-19 Pandemic. *Health Care*, 10(11), 2293. DOI: 10.3390/healthcare10112293 PMID: 36421617

Brewster, P. W., Melrose, R. J., Marquine, M. J., Johnson, J. K., Napoles, A., MacKay-Brandt, A., Farias, S., Reed, B., & Mungas, D. (2014). Life experience and demographic influences on cognitive function in older adults. *Neuropsychology*, 28(6), 846–858. DOI: 10.1037/neu0000098 PMID: 24933483

Brookfield, S. (2012). The impact of lifelong learning on communities. In Aspin, D. N., Chapman, J., Evans, K., & Bagnall, R. (Eds.), *Second international handbook of lifelong learning*. Part 2 (pp. 875–886). Springer. DOI: 10.1007/978-94-007-2360-3_53

Brüchert, T., Quentin, P., & Bolte, G. (2022). The relationship between perceived built environment and cycling or e-biking for transport among older adults–a cross-sectional study. *PLoS One*, 17(5), e0267314. DOI: 10.1371/journal.pone.0267314 PMID: 35503760

Brunello, G., & Rocco, L. (2019). Grandparents in the blues. The effect of child-care on grandparents' depression. *Review of Economics of the Household*, 17(2), 587–613. DOI: 10.1007/s11150-018-9432-2

Brunello, G., & Yamamura, E. (2023). Reciprocity and the matrilineal advantage in European grand-parenting. *Review of Economics of the Household*, 21(2), 397–433. DOI: 10.1007/s11150-022-09630-w

Brunissen, L., Rapoport, E., Fruitman, K., & Adesman, A. (2020). Parenting challenges of grandparents raising grandchildren: Discipline, child education, technology use, and outdated health beliefs. GrandFamilies: The Contemporary Journal of Research, Practice and Policy, 6(1), 6. https://scholarworks.wmich.edu/grandfamilies/vol6/iss1/6/

Buffel, T., & Phillipson, C. (2018). A manifesto for the age-friendly movement: Developing a new urban agenda. *Journal of Aging & Social Policy*, 30(2), 173–192. DOI: 10.1080/08959420.2018.1430414 PMID: 29364777

Bulut, Ü., & Özçakar, N. (2011). How we age. *The Journal of Turkish Family Physician*, 3(1), 1–5.

Butler, R. N., & Gleason, H. P. (1985). *Productive aging*. Springer.

Canedo-Garcia, A., Garcia-Sanchez, J. N., & Pacheco-Sanz, D. I. (2017). A systematic review of the effectiveness of intergenerational programs. *Frontiers in Psychology*, 8, 1882. DOI: 10.3389/fpsyg.2017.01882 PMID: 29163269

Çetin, M., & Ecevit, E. (2010). The Impact of Health Expenditures on Economic Growth: A Panel Regression Analysis on Oecd Countries. *Journal of Doğuş University*, 11(2), 166–182.

Chabot, M., Delaware, L., McCarley, S., Little, C., Nye, A., & Anderson, E. (2019). Living in place: The impact of smart technology. *Current Geriatrics Reports*, 8(3), 232–238. DOI: 10.1007/s13670-019-00296-4

Chadha, N. K., Aggarwal, V., & Mangla, A. P. (1992). Hopelessness, alienation and life satisfaction among aged. *Indian Journal of Gerontology*, 6(3), 82–92.

Chang, C., Lim, X., Supramaniam, P., Chew, C., Ding, L., & Rajan, P. (2022). Perceived gap of age-friendliness among community-dwelling older adults: Findings from Malaysia, a middle-income country. *International Journal of Environmental Research and Public Health*, 19(12), 7171. DOI: 10.3390/ijerph19127171 PMID: 35742420

Chang, D., Gu, Z., Li, F., & Jiang, R. (2019). A user-centric smart product-service system development approach: A case study on medication management for the elderly. *Advanced Engineering Informatics*, 42, 100979. DOI: 10.1016/j.aei.2019.100979

Charness, N., & Boot, W. R. (2009). Aging and information technology use: Potential and barriers. *Current Directions in Psychological Science*, 18(5), 253–258. DOI: 10.1111/j.1467-8721.2009.01647.x

Chau, H., & Jamei, E. (2021). Age-friendly built environment. *Encyclopedia*, 1(3), 781–791. DOI: 10.3390/encyclopedia1030060

Chawla, K., Kunonga, T. P., Stow, D., Barker, R., Craig, D., & Hanratty, B. (2021). Prevalence of loneliness amongst older people in high-income countries: A systematic review and meta-analysis. *PLoS One*, 16(7), e0255088. DOI: 10.1371/journal.pone.0255088 PMID: 34310643

Chen, K., & Chan, A. H. (2011). A review of technology acceptance by older adults. *Gerontechnology (Valkenswaard)*, 10(1). Advance online publication. DOI: 10.4017/gt.2011.10.01.006.00

Chen, M. F., Wang, R. H., & Hung, S. L. (2015). Predicting health-promoting self-care behaviors in people with pre-diabetes by applying Bandura social learning theory. *Applied Nursing Research*, 28(4), 299–304. DOI: 10.1016/j.apnr.2015.01.001 PMID: 26608429

Chen, S. C., Davis, B. H., Kuo, C. Y., Maclagan, M., Chien, C. O., & Lin, M. F. (2022). Can the Paro be my Buddy? Meaningful experiences from the perspectives of older adults. *Geriatric Nursing*, 43, 130–137. DOI: 10.1016/j.gerinurse.2021.11.011 PMID: 34883391

Chen, Y.-R. R., & Schulz, P. J. (2016). The Effect of Information Communication Technology Interventions on Reducing Social Isolation in the Elderly: A Systematic Review. *Journal of Medical Internet Research*, 18(1), e18. DOI: 10.2196/jmir.4596 PMID: 26822073

Che, S., Lei, W. I., Hung, T., & Leong, S. M. (2024). Attitudes to aging mediates the relationship between perception of age-friendly city and life satisfaction among middle-aged and older people in Macao: A cross-sectional study. *BMC Geriatrics*, 24(1), 362. Advance online publication. DOI: 10.1186/s12877-024-04961-y PMID: 38654157

Chiţiba, C. A. (2012). Lifelong learning challenges and opportunities for traditional universities. *Procedia: Social and Behavioral Sciences*, 46, 1943–1947. DOI: 10.1016/j.sbspro.2012.05.408

Choi, H., Irwin, M. R., & Cho, H. J. (2015). Impact of social isolation on behavioral health in elderly: Systematic review. *World Journal of Psychiatry*, 5(4), 432–438. DOI: 10.5498/wjp.v5.i4.432 PMID: 26740935

Chokkanathan, S., Natarajan, A., & Mohanty, J. (2014). Elder abuse and barriers to help seeking in Chennai, India: A qualitative study. *Journal of Elder Abuse & Neglect*, 26(1), 60–79. DOI: 10.1080/08946566.2013.782786 PMID: 24313798

Chou, C. C., Chang, C. P., Lee, T. T., Chou, H. F., & Mills, M. E. (2013). Technology acceptance and quality of life of the elderly in a telecare program. *CIN: Computers, Informatics. Computers, Informatics, Nursing*, 31(7), 335–342. DOI: 10.1097/NXN.0b013e318295e5ce PMID: 23728446

Clarfield, M. (2011). Grow old along with me! The best is yet to be. *Canadian Medical Association Journal*, 183(10), E693–E694. DOI: 10.1503/cmaj.101431

Clemente, J., Marcuello, C., Montañés, A., & Pueyo, F. (2004). On the international stability of health care expenditure functions: Are government and private functions similar? *Journal of Health Economics*, 23(3), 589–613. DOI: 10.1016/j.jhealeco.2003.08.007 PMID: 15120472

Cocquyt, C., Diep, N. A., Zhu, C., De Greef, M., & Vanwing, T. (2017). Examining social inclusion and social capital among adult learners in blended and online learning environments. *European journal for Research on the Education and Learning of Adults, 8*(1), 77-101

Colarusso, C. A. (1992). *Child and adult development: A psychoanalytic introduction for clinicians.* Springer Science & Business Media. DOI: 10.1007/978-1-4757-9673-5

Coombs, C. (1920). Notes, Short Comments, and Answers to Correspondents. *Lancet*, 196(5056), 226–228. DOI: 10.1016/S0140-6736(01)18292-9

Cordella, M., Poiani, A., Cordella, M., & Poiani, A. (2021). The Social Dimension of Older Ages. Fulfilling Ageing: Psychosocial and Communicative Perspectives on Ageing, 461-632. DOI: 10.1007/978-3-030-60071-6_6

Cornelius, S. W. (1984, March). The classic pattern of intellectual aging: Test familiarity, difficulty, and performance. *Journal of Gerontology*, 39(2), 201–206. DOI: 10.1093/geronj/39.2.201 PMID: 6699376

Cosco, T., Fortuna, K., Wister, A., Riadi, I., Wagner, K., & Sixsmith, A. (2021). COVID-19, Social Isolation, and Mental Health Among Older Adults: A Digital Catch-22. *Journal of Medical Internet Research*, 23(5), e21864. https://www.jmir.org/2021/5/e21864/PDF. DOI: 10.2196/21864 PMID: 33891557

Cotten, S. R., Schuster, A. M., & Seifert, A. (2021). Social media use and well-being among older adults. *Current Opinion in Psychology*, 45, 101293. Advance online publication. DOI: 10.1016/j.copsyc.2021.12.005 PMID: 35065352

Courtin, E., & Knapp, M. (2017). Social isolation, loneliness and health in old age: A scoping review. *Health & Social Care in the Community*, 25(3), 799–812. DOI: 10.1111/hsc.12311 PMID: 26712585

Cowley, S. A., Tzouvara, V., & Horta Reis da Silva, T. (2023). Public Health: healthy aging and well-being. In Redfern's Nursing Older People. Fifth edition. Editors: Ross, Harris, Fitzpatrick and Abley. Elsevier.

Croezen, S., Haveman-Nies, A., Alvarado, V. J., Van't Veer, P., & De Groot, C. P. G. M. (2009). Characterization of different groups of elderly according to social engagement activity patterns. *JNHA-The Journal of Nutrition. Health and Aging*, 13, 776–781. PMID: 19812867

Cuddy, A. J. C., Norton, M. I., & Fiske, S. T. (2005). This old stereotype: The pervasiveness and persistence of the elderly stereotype. *The Journal of Social Issues*, 61(2), 267–285. DOI: 10.1111/j.1540-4560.2005.00405.x

Culyer, A. J. (1989). Cost containment in Europe. *Health Care Financing Review*, (Suppl), 21. PMID: 10313433

Cumming, E., & Henry, W. E. (1961). *Growing old: The process of disengagement.* Basic Books.

Cunha-Diniz, F., Taveira-Gomes, T., Santos, A., Teixeira, J., & Magalhães, T. (2023). Are there any differences in road traffic injury outcomes between older and younger adults? setting the grounds for posttraumatic senior personal injury assessment guidelines. *Journal of Clinical Medicine*, 12(6), 2353. DOI: 10.3390/jcm12062353 PMID: 36983355

Curran, E., Rosato, M., Ferry, F., & Leavey, G. (2020). Prevalence and factors associated with anxiety and depression in older adults: Gender differences in psychosocial indicators. *Journal of Affective Disorders*, 267, 114–122. DOI: 10.1016/j.jad.2020.02.018 PMID: 32063562

Cylus, J., & Al Tayara, L. (2021) Health, an ageing labour force, and the economy: does health moderate the relationship between population age-structure and economic growth? *Social Science and Medicine*, 287. ISSN 0277-9536. Health, an ageing labour force, and the economy: Does health moderate the relationship between population age-structure and economic growth? - ScienceDirect

Czaja, S. J. (1994). Employment opportunities for older adults: Engineering design and research issues. *Experimental Aging Research*, 20(4), 265–273. DOI: 10.1080/03610739408253976 PMID: 7843213

Czapanskiy, K. (1993). Grandparents, Parents and Grandchildren: Actualizing Interdependency in Law. Conn. L. Rev., 26, 1315. https://heinonline.org/HOL/LandingPage?handle=hein.journals/conlr26&div=50&id=&page=

da Silva, T. H. R. (2022). Emotional awareness and emotional intelligence. *British Journal of Community Nursing*, 27(12), 573–574. DOI: 10.12968/bjcn.2022.27.12.573 PMID: 36519463

Dalistan, R., George, S., Lane, R., Block, H., & Laver, K. (2022). Middle aged and older adult's perspectives of their own home environment: a qualitative meta-synthesis. DOI: 10.21203/rs.3.rs-2067454/v1

Damant, J., Knapp, M., Freddolino, P., & Lombard, D. (2017). Effects of digital engagement on the quality of life of older people. *Health & Social Care in the Community*, 25(6), 1679–1703. DOI: 10.1111/hsc.12335 PMID: 26919220

Dantas, R. G., Perracini, M. R., Guerra, R. O., Ferriolli, E., Dias, R. C., & Padula, R. S. (2017). What are the sociodemographic and health determinants for older adults continue to participate in work? *Archives of Gerontology and Geriatrics*, 71, 136–141. DOI: 10.1016/j.archger.2017.04.005 PMID: 28458105

Dascălu, M., Rodideal, A., & Popa, L. (2018). In Romania, Elderly People Who Most Need ICT Are Those Who Are Less Probable to Use It. *Social Work Review/ Revista de Asistenta Sociala, 17*(2).

de Jong Gierveld, J., & Hagestad, G. O. (2006). Perspectives on the Integration of Older Men and Women. *Research on Aging*, 28(6), 627–637. DOI: 10.1177/0164027506291871

De la Maisonneuve, C., & Oliveira Martins, J. (2013). Public Spending on Health and Long-term Care: A new set of projections. In *OECD Economic Policy Papers, No. 6*. OECD Publishing., DOI: 10.1787/5k44t7jwwr9x-

De Meijer, C., Wouterse, B., Polder, J., & Koopmanschap, M. (2013). The effect of population aging on health expenditure growth: A critical review. *European Journal of Ageing*, 10(4), 353–361. DOI: 10.1007/s10433-013-0280-x PMID: 28804308

Delello, J. A., & McWhorter, R. R. (2017). Reducing the Digital Divide: Connecting Older Adults to iPad Technology. *Journal of applied gerontology: the official journal of the Southern Gerontological Society, 36*(1), 3–28. DOI: 10.1177/0733464815589985

Dench, S., & Regan, J. (2000, February). Learning in later life: Motivation and impact (Research Brief No. 183). Retrieved November 16, 2013, from https://www .employment-studies.co.uk/pubs/summary.php?id=rr183

Desai, S., McGrath, C., McNeil, H., Sveistrup, H., McMurray, J., & Astell, A. (2022). Experiential value of technologies: A qualitative study with older adults. *International Journal of Environmental Research and Public Health*, 19(4), 2235. DOI: 10.3390/ijerph19042235 PMID: 35206435

Dev, P. S., & Eljo, J. J. G. (2022). COVID-19 impacts on elderly with disability. DOI: DOI: 10.21522/TIJPH.2013.SE.22.01.Art005

Development Through Life. (2022). *A Psychosocial Approach" by Barbara M* (11th ed.). Newman and Philip R. Newman.

Devi, B. N., Megala, M., & Saravanakumar, P. (2022). Social and health concerns of elderly women in rural area in Tirupur District, Tamil Nadu. *Journal of Family Medicine and Primary Care, 11*(8), 4447-4451. doi:DOI: 0.4103/jfmpc.jfmpc_42_22

Dev, P. S., & Eljo, J. G. (2024). Addressing the Ethical and Legal Complexities in Elderly Care: A Study from India. *Nusantara Journal of Behavioral and Social Science*, 3(3), 111–118. DOI: 10.47679/njbss.202456

Dev, P. S., & Eljo, J. J. G. (2023). Inclusive Wash for Elderly with Disabilities. *Journal for ReAttach Therapy and Developmental Diversities*, 6(5s), 285–291. http://jrtdd.com/index.php/journal/article/view/518

Di Nuovo, S., De Beni, R., Borella, E., Marková, H., Laczó, J., & Vyhnálek, M. (2020). Cognitive impairment in old age: Is the shift from healthy to pathological aging responsive to prevention? *European Psychologist*, 25(3), 174–185. DOI: 10.1027/1016-9040/a000391

Dickey, D. A., & Fuller, W. A. (1981). Likelihood Ratio Statistics for Autoregressive Time Series with a Unit Root. *Econometrica*, 49(4), 1057–1072. DOI: 10.2307/1912517

Diggs, J. (2008). Activity theory of aging. In Loue, S., & Sajatovie, M. (Eds.), *Encyclopedia of Aging and Public Health* (pp. 79–81). Springer. DOI: 10.1007/978-0-387-33754-8_9

Ding, K. (2024). The Impact of Grandparents and Intergenerational Living on Children's Social and Emotional Development. Journal of Education. *Humanities and Social Sciences*, 29, 403–412. DOI: 10.54097/paw2mg46

Doraiswamy, S., Jithesh, A., Mamtani, R., Abraham, A., & Cheema, S. (2021). Telehealth Use in Geriatrics Care during the COVID-19 Pandemic—A Scoping Review and Evidence Synthesis. *International Journal of Environmental Research and Public Health*, 18(4), 1755. DOI: 10.3390/ijerph18041755 PMID: 33670270

Dorsett, R., Lui, S., & Weale, M. (2010). *Economic benefits of lifelong learning*. Centre for Learning and Life Chances in Knowledge Economies and Societies.

Dykstra, P. A., & Hagestad, G. O. (2007). Roads less taken: Developing a nuanced view of older adults without children. [Google Scholar]. *Journal of Family Issues*, 28(10), 1275–1310. DOI: 10.1177/0192513X07303822

Earl, E. J., & Marais, D. (2023). The experience of intergenerational interactions and their influence on the mental health of older people living in residential care. *PLoS One*, 18(7), e0287369. DOI: 10.1371/journal.pone.0287369 PMID: 37405973

Elderly Learning in the Digital Age: Towards Empowerment November 2023 Commonwealth of Learning CC BY-SA 4.0. (n.d.). Retrieved September 10, 2024, from https://oasis.col.org/server/api/core/bitstreams/7858c65d-04b1-423b-9a9a-2f318e71749b/content

ElgueraPaez, L., & Zapata Del Río, C. (2019). Elderly Users and Their Main Challenges Usability with Mobile Applications: A Systematic Review. Design, User Experience, and Usability. *Design Philosophy and Theory*, 423–438. DOI: 10.1007/978-3-030-23570-3_31

Elueze, I., & Quan-Haase, A. (2018). Privacy Attitudes and Concerns in the Digital Lives of Older Adults: Westin's Privacy Attitude Typology Revisited. *The American Behavioral Scientist*, 62(10), 1372–1391. DOI: 10.1177/0002764218787026

Elwell, F., & Maltbie-Crannell, A. D. (1981). The impact of role loss upon coping resources and life satisfaction of the elderly. *Journal of Gerontology*, 36(2), 223–232. DOI: 10.1093/geronj/36.2.223 PMID: 7204904

Enkvist, Å., Ekström, H., & Elmståhl, S. (2012). What factors affect life satisfaction (LS) among the oldest-old? *Archives of Gerontology and Geriatrics*, 54(1), 140–145. DOI: 10.1016/j.archger.2011.03.013 PMID: 21555158

Erdil, E., & Yetkiner, I. H. (2004). A panel data approach for income-health causality.

Eriksson, J., Hildingh, C., Buer, N., & Thulesius, H. (2016). Seniors' self-preservation by maintaining established self and defying deterioration – a grounded theory. *International Journal of Qualitative Studies on Health and Well-being*, 11(1), 30265. DOI: 10.3402/qhw.v11.30265 PMID: 27172511

Esping-Andersen, G. (1999). *Social Foundation of Postindustrial Economies*. Oxford University Press. DOI: 10.1093/0198742002.001.0001

Esping-Andersen, G., & Myles, J. (2009). Sustainable and Equitable Retirement in a Life Course Perspective. In Clark, G., Munnell, A. H., & Orszag, M. (Eds.), *The Oxford Handbook of Pensions and Retirement Income* (pp. 839–858). Oxford University Press., DOI: 10.1093/oxfordhb/9780199272464.003.0042

Faber, M., Tavy, Z., & Pas, S. (2020). Engaging older people in age-friendly cities through participatory video design. *International Journal of Environmental Research and Public Health*, 17(23), 8977. DOI: 10.3390/ijerph17238977 PMID: 33276604

Fallon, C. K., & Karlawish, J. (2019). Is the WHO Definition of Health Aging Well? Frameworks for "Health" After Three Score and Ten. *American Journal of Public Health*, 109(8), 1104–1106. DOI: 10.2105/AJPH.2019.305177 PMID: 31268759

Fan, K. (2007). Zonal asymmetry of the Antarctic Oscillation. Geophysical Research Letters 34: . issn: 0094-8276.DOI: 10.1029/2006GL028045

Fang, Y. X., Gill, S. S., Kunasekaran, P., Rosnon, M. R., Talib, A. T., & Abd Aziz, A. (2022). Digital divide: An inquiry on the native communities of Sabah. *Societies (Basel, Switzerland)*, 12(6), 148. DOI: 10.3390/soc12060148

Fatmah, F., Dewi, V., & Priotomo, Y. (2019). Developing age-friendly city readiness: A case study from Depok city, Indonesia. *SAGE Open Medicine*, 7, 205031211985251. DOI: 10.1177/2050312119852510 PMID: 31205701

Field, J. (2005). *Social capital and lifelong learning*. Policy Press.

Field, J. (2009). *Well-being and happiness: Inquiry into the future of lifelong learning (Thematic paper 4)*. National Institute of Adult Continuing Education.

Fields, B., Skrove, Z., Tredinnick, R., Sprecher, B., Lee, J., Shields, R., Ponto, K., & Shin, J. (2023). The usability and acceptability of the augmented reality home assessment tool (arhat). *Innovation in Aging*, 7(Supplement_1), 1142–1143. DOI: 10.1093/geroni/igad104.3668

Fischer, S. H., David, D., Crotty, B. H., Dierks, M., & Safran, C. (2014). Acceptance and use of health information technology by community-dwelling elders. *International Journal of Medical Informatics*, 83(9), 624–635. DOI: 10.1016/j.ijmedinf.2014.06.005 PMID: 24996581

Fitzpatrick, J. M., Bianchi, L. A., Hayes, N., Da Silva, T., & Harris, R. (2023). Professional development and career planning for nurses working in care homes for older people: A scoping review. *International Journal of Older People Nursing*, 18(1), e12519. DOI: 10.1111/opn.12519 PMID: 36441621

Fledsberg, S., Svensson, M., & Johansson, N. (2023). Lifetime healthcare expenditures across socioeconomic groups in Sweden. *European Journal of Public Health*, 33(6), 994–1000. DOI: 10.1093/eurpub/ckad140 PMID: 37649353

Flint, M. M., & Perez-Porter, M. (2013). Grandparent caregivers: Legal and economic issues. In *Intergenerational Approaches in Aging* (pp. 63–76). Routledge., https://www.taylorfrancis.com/chapters/edit/10.4324/9780203047293-8/grandparent-caregivers-margaret-flint-melinda-perez-porter

Fong-Chong, A. (2003). Tampines 3-in-1 Family Centre, Singapore. *Journal of Intergenerational Relationships*, 1(1), 169–171. DOI: 10.1300/J194v01n01_14

Formosa, M. (Ed.). (2019). *The University of the third age and active aging: European and Asian-Pacific perspectives*. Springer. DOI: 10.1007/978-3-030-21515-6

Fotteler, M. L., Kocar, T. D., Dallmeier, D., Kohn, B., Mayer, S., Waibel, A. K., Swoboda, W., & Denkinger, M. (2023). Use and benefit of information, communication, and assistive technology among community-dwelling older adults–a cross-sectional study. *BMC Public Health*, 23(1), 2004. DOI: 10.1186/s12889-023-16926-8 PMID: 37833689

Fuller-Thomson, E., & Minkler, M. (2001). American grandparents providing extensive child care to their grandchildren: Prevalence and profile. *The Gerontologist*, 41(2), 201–209. DOI: 10.1093/geront/41.2.201 PMID: 11327486

Gajewski, P. D., Falkenstein, M., Thönes, S., & Wascher, E. (2020). Stroop task performance across the lifespan: High cognitive reserve in older age is associated with enhanced proactive and reactive interference control. *NeuroImage*, 207, 116430. DOI: 10.1016/j.neuroimage.2019.116430 PMID: 31805383

Gallegos-Carrillo, K., Mudgal, J., Sánchez-García, S., Wagner, F. A., Gallo, J. J., Salmerón, J., & García-Peña, C. (2009). Social networks and health-related quality of life: a population based study among older adults. *Salud publica de Mexico, 51*(1), 06-13. https://www.scielosp.org/pdf/spm/v51n1/04.pdf

Gaßner, K., & Conrad, M. (2010). ICT enabled independent living for elderly. *A status-quo analysis on products and the research landscape in the field of Ambient Assisted Living (AAL) in EU-27*. https://ifap.ru/library/book467.pdf

Gell, N. M., Rosenberg, D. E., Demiris, G., LaCroix, A. Z., & Patel, K. V. (2015). Patterns of Technology Use Among Older Adults With and Without Disabilities. *The Gerontologist*, 55(3), 412–421. DOI: 10.1093/geront/gnt166 PMID: 24379019

Gerdtham, U. G., & Löthgren, M. (2000). On stationarity and cointegration of international health expenditure and GDP. *Journal of Health Economics*, 19(4), 461–475. DOI: 10.1016/S0167-6296(99)00036-3 PMID: 11010235

Ghorayeb, A., Comber, R., & Gooberman-Hill, R. (2021). Older adults' perspectives of smart home technology: Are we developing the technology that older people want? *International Journal of Human-Computer Studies*, 147, 102571. DOI: 10.1016/j.ijhcs.2020.102571

Gladstone, J. W., Brown, R. A., & Fitzgerald, K. A. J. (2009). Grandparents raising their grandchildren: Tensions, service needs and involvement with child welfare agencies. *International Journal of Aging & Human Development*, 69(1), 55–78. DOI: 10.2190/AG.69.1.d PMID: 19803340

Glaser, K., Stuchbury, R., Price, D., Di Gessa, G., Ribe, E., & Tinker, A. (2018). Trends in the prevalence of grandparents living with grandchild (ren) in selected European countries and the United States. *European Journal of Ageing*, 15(3), 237–250. DOI: 10.1007/s10433-018-0474-3 PMID: 30310371

Global Economic Issues of an Aging Population (2024,Oct 30). *In Investiopedia*. https://www.investopedia.com/articles/investing/011216/4-global-economic-issues -aging-population.asp

Gölçek, A. G., & Göde, B. (2023). The Course of Tax Revenue During the Process of Population Aging: Empirical Evidence from Turkey. *Fiscaoeconomia*, 7(Özel Sayı), 614–640. DOI: 10.25295/fsecon.1348960

Golding, B. G. (2011). Social, local, and situated: Recent findings about the effectiveness of older men's informal learning in community contexts. *Adult Education Quarterly*, 61(2), 103–120. DOI: 10.1177/0741713610380437

Gordon, D., Levitas, R., Pantazis, C., Patsios, D., Payne, S., Townsend, P., Adelman, L., Ashworth, K., Middleton, S., Bradshaw, J., & Williams, J. (2000). *Poverty and Social Exclusion in Britain*.

Gracia, E., & Herrero, J. (2004). Determinants of social integration in the community: An exploratory analysis of personal, interpersonal and situational variables. *Journal of Community & Applied Social Psychology*, 14(1), 1–15. DOI: 10.1002/casp.746

Grinstead, L. N., Leder, S., Jensen, S., & Bond, L. (2003). Review of research on the health of caregiving grandparents. *Journal of Advanced Nursing*, 44(3), 318–326. DOI: 10.1046/j.1365-2648.2003.02807.x PMID: 14641402

Grossman, M. R., & Gruenewald, T. L. (2020). Failure to meet generative self-expectations is linked to poorer cognitive–affective well-being. The Journals of Gerontology: Series B, 75(4), 792-801. DOI: 10.1093/geronb/gby069

Gualano, M. R., Voglino, G., Bert, F., Thomas, R., Camussi, E., & Siliquini, R. (2018). The impact of intergenerational programs on children and older adults: A review. *International Psychogeriatrics*, 30(4), 451–468. DOI: 10.1017/S104161021700182X PMID: 28988548

Guarino, A., Forte, G., Giovannoli, J., & Casagrande, M. (2020). Executive functions in older people with mild cognitive impairment: A systematic review on motor and cognitive inhibition, conflict control and cognitive flexibility. *Aging & Mental Health*, 24(7), 1028–1045. DOI: 10.1080/13607863.2019.1584785 PMID: 30938193

Guay, C., Auger, C., Demers, L., Mortenson, W. B., Miller, W. C., Gélinas-Bronsard, D., & Ahmed, S. (2017). Components and outcomes of internet-based interventions for caregivers of older adults: Systematic review. *Journal of Medical Internet Research*, 19(9), e313. DOI: 10.2196/jmir.7896 PMID: 28928109

Guillemot, J., & Warner, M. (2023). Age-friendly cities in Latin America: A human ecological framework. *Geriatrics (Basel, Switzerland)*, 8(3), 46. DOI: 10.3390/geriatrics8030046 PMID: 37218826

Guo, J., Huang, X., Dou, L., Yan, M., Shen, T., Tang, W., & Li, J. (2022). Aging and aging-related diseases: From molecular mechanisms to interventions and treatments. *Signal Transduction and Targeted Therapy*, 7(1), 391. DOI: 10.1038/s41392-022-01251-0 PMID: 36522308

Guo, Y., Liu, M., Wang, J., Xia, Y., & Zhao, D. (2023). Demographic Challenge: The Rise of the Silver Economy in China. *Advances in Economics. Management and Political Sciences*, 34(1), 120–125. DOI: 10.54254/2754-1169/34/20231688

Haimi, M., & Gesser-Edelsburg, A. (2022). Application and implementation of telehealth services designed for the elderly population during the COVID-19 pandemic: A systematic review. *Health Informatics Journal*, 28(1), 146045822210755. DOI: 10.1177/14604582221075561 PMID: 35175881

Halicka, K., & Surel, D. (2020). Evaluation and selection of technologies improving the quality of life of older people. https://www.um.edu.mt/library/oar/handle/123456789/57531

Halicka, K. (2019). Gerontechnology—The assessment of one selected technology improving the quality of life of older adults. *Engineering Management in Production and Services*, 11(2), 43–51. DOI: 10.2478/emj-2019-0010

Halicka, K. (2024). Assessment of chosen technologies improving seniors' quality of life in the context of sustainable development. *Technological and Economic Development of Economy*, 30(1), 107–128. DOI: 10.3846/tede.2024.20614

Halicka, K., & Surel, D. (2021). Gerontechnology—New opportunities in the service of older adults. *Engineering Management in Production and Services*, 13(3), 114–126. DOI: 10.2478/emj-2021-0025

Halicka, K., & Surel, D. (2022). Smart living technologies in the context of improving the quality of life for older people: The case of the humanoid Rudy Robot. *Human Technology*, 18(2), 191–208. DOI: 10.14254/1795-6889.2022.18-2.5

Halpin, S. N., Dillard, R. L., Idler, E., Clevenger, C., Rothschild, E., Blanton, S., Wilson, J., & Flacker, J. M. (2017). The benefits of being a senior mentor: Cultivating resilience through the mentorship of health professions students. *Gerontology & Geriatrics Education*, 38(3), 283–294. DOI: 10.1080/02701960.2015.1079707 PMID: 26251869

Hao, L., Xu, X., Dupre, M. E., Guo, A., Zhang, X., Qiu, L., Zhao, Y., & Gu, D. (2020). Adequate access to healthcare and added life expectancy among older adults in China. *BMC Geriatrics*, 20(1), 129. DOI: 10.1186/s12877-020-01524-9 PMID: 32272883

Harper, S. (2014). Economic and social implications of aging societies. *Science*, 346(6209), 587–591. DOI: 10.1126/science.1254405 PMID: 25359967

Harris, M. T., Blocker, K. A., & Rogers, W. A. (2022). Older adults and smart technology: Facilitators and barriers to use. *Frontiers of Computer Science*, 4, 835927. DOI: 10.3389/fcomp.2022.835927

Hart, R., Setlow, R. B., & Woodhead, A. D. (1977). Evidence that pyrimidine dimers in DNA can give rise to tumors. *Proceedings of the National Academy of Sciences of the United States of America*, 74(12), 5574–5578. DOI: 10.1073/pnas.74.12.5574 PMID: 271984

Hartt, M., DeVerteuil, G., & Potts, R. (2022). Age-unfriendly by design. *Journal of the American Planning Association*, 89(1), 31–44. DOI: 10.1080/01944363.2022.2035247

Haufe, M., Peek, S., & Luijkx, K. G. (2019). Matching gerontechnologies to independent-living seniors' individual needs: Development of the GTM tool. *BMC Health Services Research*, 19(1), 26. Advance online publication. DOI: 10.1186/s12913-018-3848-5 PMID: 30634971

Havighurst, R. J. (1961). Successful aging. *The Gerontologist*, 1(1), 8–13. DOI: 10.1093/geront/1.1.8

Hayslip, B.Jr, Fruhauf, C. A., & Dolbin-MacNab, M. L. (2019). Grandparents raising grandchildren: What have we learned over the past decade? *The Gerontologist*, 59(3), e152–e163. DOI: 10.1093/geront/gnx106 PMID: 28666363

Hayslip, B.Jr, & Kaminski, P. L. (2005). Grandparents raising their grandchildren: A review of the literature and suggestions for practice. *The Gerontologist*, 45(2), 262–269. DOI: 10.1093/geront/45.2.262 PMID: 15799992

Heinz, M., Martin, P., Margrett, J. A., Yearns, M., Franke, W., Yang, H. I., Wong, J., & Chang, C. K. (2013). Perceptions of technology among older adults. *Journal of Gerontological Nursing*, 39(1), 42–51. DOI: 10.3928/00989134-20121204-04 PMID: 23244061

Hendlin, Y. H. (2014). The Threshold Problem in Intergenerational Justice. *Ethics and the Environment*, 19(2), 1–38. DOI: 10.2979/ethicsenviro.19.2.1

Hertzog, C., Kramer, A. F., Wilson, R. S., & Lindenberger, U. (2008). Enrichment effects on adult cognitive development: Can the functional capacity of older adults be preserved and enhanced? *Psychological Science in the Public Interest*, 9(1), 1–65. DOI: 10.1111/j.1539-6053.2009.01034.x PMID: 26162004

Herzog, A. R., Ofstedal, M. B., & Wheeler, L. M. (2002). Social engagement and its relationship to health. *Clinics in Geriatric Medicine*, 18(3), 595–609. DOI: 10.1016/S0749-0690(02)00025-3 PMID: 12424874

Hiranandani, V. (2011). Privacy and security in the digital age: Contemporary challenges and future directions. *International Journal of Human Rights*, 15(7), 1091–1106. DOI: 10.1080/13642987.2010.493360

Hodgson, H. (2019). The Grandma Force: Grandmothers Changing Grandchildren, Families, and Themselves. BQB Publishing. https://www.google.co.in/books/edition/The_Grandma_Force/LC2MDwAAQBAJ?hl=en&gbpv=1&dq=Celebrating+%E2%80%98Grandparents+Day%E2%80%99+is+also+a+wonderful+strategy+that+makes+people+aware+of+how+precious+our+older+adults+are.+This+also+emphasizes+the+need+for+binding+families.+&pg=PT15&printsec=frontcover

Holgersson, J., Söderström, E., & Rose, J. (2019). *Digital inclusion of elderly citizens for a sustainable society*. In *27th European Conference on Information Systems (ECIS)*, Stockholm & Uppsala, Sweden, June 8-14, 2019. Association for Information Systems.

Honey, A., Kariuki, M., Emerson, E., & Llewellyn, G. (2014). Employment status transitions among young adults, with and without disability. *The Australian Journal of Social Issues*, 49(2), 151–170. DOI: 10.1002/j.1839-4655.2014.tb00306.x

Horsley, T., Grimshaw, J., & Campbell, C. (2010). *How to create conditions for adapting physicians' skills to new needs and lifelong learning*. WHO Regional Office for Europe.

Horta Reis Da Silva, T. (2022a). Muskuloskeletal minor injuries: assessment and treatment. In Curr, S., & Fordham-Clarke, C. (Eds.), *Clinical Skills at Glance* (1st ed., pp. 128–129). Wiley. [55]

Hou, S. I. (2021). Physical activity and social relationships on social engagement among community-dwelling older adults. *Innovation in Aging*, 5(Suppl 1), 28. DOI: 10.1093/geroni/igab046.099

Hou, X., Liu, L., & Cain, J. (2022). Can higher spending on primary healthcare mitigate the impact of ageing and non-communicable diseases on health expenditure? *BMJ Global Health*, 7(12), e010513. DOI: 10.1136/bmjgh-2022-010513 PMID: 36564087

Hu, B., Cartagena-Farias, J., Brimblecombe, N., Jadoolal, S., & Wittenberg, R. (2024). Projected costs of informal care for older people in England. *The European Journal of Health Economics*, 25(6), 1057–1070. DOI: 10.1007/s10198-023-01643-1 PMID: 38085432

Hult, M., Pietilä, A. M., & Saaranen, T. (2020). Improving employment opportunities for the unemployed through health and workability promotion in Finland. *Health Promotion International*, 35(3), 518–526. DOI: 10.1093/heapro/daz048 PMID: 31132120

Hunjra, A. I., Azam, M., Bruna, M. G., & Taskin, D. (2022). Role of financial development for sustainable economic development in low middle income countries. *Finance Research Letters*, 47, 102793. DOI: 10.1016/j.frl.2022.102793

Ige, J. (2019). Environmental health and housing: Issues for public health. *Housing Studies*, 34(3), 561–562. DOI: 10.1080/02673037.2019.1558597

Ijsselsteijn, W., Nap, H. H., de Kort, Y., & Poels, K. (2007). Digital game design for elderly users. In *Proceedings of the 2007 conference on Future Play* (pp. 17-22). DOI: 10.1145/1328202.1328206

Income Distribution Database, O. E. C. D. (2023). www.oecd.org/social/income-distribution- database.htm, (Accessed: 08.10.2024).

Integration, S. (n.d.). In *Wikipedia*https://en.wikipedia.org/wiki/Social_integration#:~:text=Social%20integration%20is%20the%20process,society%20that%20is%20receiving%20them

International Monetary Fund (IMF). (2023). "From Setbacks to Comebacks: Reforms to Build Resilience and Prosperity." *Chapter 2 in International Monetary Fund, Middle East and Central Asia Regional Economic Outlook: Building Resilence and Fostering Sustainable Growth, October 2023*, Washington, D.C.

Ivan, L., Beu, D., & Hoof, J. (2020). Smart and age-friendly cities in Romania: An overview of public policy and practice. *International Journal of Environmental Research and Public Health*, 17(14), 5202. DOI: 10.3390/ijerph17145202 PMID: 32708488

Janssens, J. (2002). *Innovations in Lifelong Learning: Capitalising on ADAPT. CEDEFOP Panorama Series*. CEDEFOP, PO Box 22427, Thessaloniki, GR-55102 Greece

Jerome, G. J., Glass, T. A., Mielke, M., Xue, Q. L., Andersen, R. E., & Fried, L. P. (2006). Physical activity participation by presence and type of functional deficits in older women: The Women's Health and Aging Studies. *The Journals of Gerontology. Series A, Biological Sciences and Medical Sciences*, 61(11), 1171–1176. DOI: 10.1093/gerona/61.11.1171 PMID: 17167158

Jessiman, T., Rowe, R., & Jago, R. (2023). A qualitative study of active travel amongst commuters and older adults living in market towns. *BMC Public Health*, 23(1), 840. Advance online publication. DOI: 10.1186/s12889-023-15573-3 PMID: 37165327

Jiang, X., Lu, W., Luo, H., Yang, J., Chen, M., Wang, J., Wu, M., Chen, X., Tang, Y., Hu, Y., & Zhang, L. (2023). Spirituality and attitudes toward death among older adults in rural and urban China: A cross-sectional study. *Journal of Religion and Health*, 62(5), 3070–3094. DOI: 10.1007/s10943-023-01794-8 PMID: 37012553

Johansen, S. (1995). *Likelihood-based inference in cointegrated vector autoregressive models*. OUP Oxford. DOI: 10.1093/0198774508.001.0001

Johansen, S., & Juselius, K. (1990). Maximum likelihood estimation and inference on cointegration-with appucations to the demand for money. *Oxford Bulletin of Economics and Statistics*, 52(2), 169–210. DOI: 10.1111/j.1468-0084.1990.mp52002003.x

Jones, T. G. (2001). *Cognitive and psychosocial predictors of subjective well-being in older adults*. Wayne State University. https://www.proquest.com/openview/415f4968bdfd8aaf6888fde9a5f030fe/1?pq-origsite=gscholar&cbl=18750&diss=y

K, A. and Sia, S. (2022). Theory of planned behavior in predicting the construction of eco-friendly houses. Management of Environmental Quality an International Journal, 33(4), 938-954. DOI: 10.1108/MEQ-10-2021-0249

Kallestrup-Lamb, M., Marin, A. O. K., Menon, S., & Søgaard, J. (2024). Aging populations and expenditures on health. *The Journal of the Economics of Ageing*, 29, 100518. DOI: 10.1016/j.jeoa.2024.100518

Kaplan, M. S. (2002). International programs in schools: Considerations of form and function. *International Review of Education*, 48(5), 305–334. DOI: 10.1023/A:1021231713392

Kar, M., & Taban, S. (2003). The impacts of the disaggregated public expenditure on economic growth. Ankara University Faculty of Political Science, 53(3), 145-169.

Karadeniz, O., & Öztepe, N. D. (2013). Elderly Poverty in Türkiye. *Labour and Society*, 3(38), 77–102.

Karaoglu, G., Hargittai, E., Hunsaker, A., & Nguyen, M. H. (2021). Changing technologies, changing lives: Older adults' perspectives on the benefits of using new technologie. *International Journal of Communication*, 15, 3887–3907. DOI: 10.5167/uzh-207350

Kardefelt-Winther, D. (2017). How does the time children spend using digital technology impact their mental well-being, social relationships and physical activity?: an evidence-focused literature review. https://www.eukidsonline.de/wp-content/uploads/Children-digital-technology-wellbeing.pdf

Kelley, S. J., Whitley, D., Sipe, T. A., & Yorker, B. C. (2000). Psychological distress in grandmother kinship care providers: The role of resources, social support, and physical health. *Child Abuse & Neglect*, 24(3), 311–321. DOI: 10.1016/S0145-2134(99)00146-5 PMID: 10739075

Kemp, C. L. (2007). Grandparent—grandchild ties: Reflections on continuity and change across three generations. *Journal of Family Issues*, 28(7), 855–881. DOI: 10.1177/0192513X07299599

Keskinen, K., Rantakokko, M., Suomi, K., Rantanen, T., & Portegijs, E. (2020). Environmental features associated with older adults' physical activity in different types of urban neighborhoods. *Journal of Aging and Physical Activity*, 28(4), 540–548. DOI: 10.1123/japa.2019-0251 PMID: 31860829

Kim, H. J., Lapierre, T. A., & Chapin, R. (2018). Grandparents providing care for grandchildren: Implications for economic preparation for later life in South Korea. *Ageing and Society*, 38(4), 676–699. DOI: 10.1017/S0144686X16001215

Kim, K., Buckley, T., Burnette, D., Kim, S., & Cho, S. (2021). Measurement indicators of age-friendly communities: Findings from the AARP age-friendly community survey. *The Gerontologist*, 62(1), e17–e27. DOI: 10.1093/geront/gnab055 PMID: 33909074

Kimpel, C., Dietrich, M. S., Lauderdale, J., Schlundt, D. G., & Maxwell, C. A. (2024). Using the age-friendly environment framework to assess advance care planning factors among older adults with limited income: A cross-sectional, descriptive survey study. *The Gerontologist*, 64(7), gnae059. Advance online publication. DOI: 10.1093/geront/gnae059 PMID: 38813768

Kiri, L. (2023). Demographic transition - Global population patterns and trends: The case of Albania. *Academic Journal of Business, Administration. Law and Social Sciences*, 9(2), 29–36. DOI: 10.2478/ajbals-2023-0004

Kitamura, T., Kawakami, N., Sakamoto, S., Tanigawa, T., Ono, Y., & Fujihara, S. (2002). Quality of life and its correlates in a community population in a Japanese rural area. *Psychiatry and Clinical Neurosciences*, 56(4), 431–441. DOI: 10.1046/j.1440-1819.2002.01033.x PMID: 12109962

Klann, A., Vu, L., Ewing, M., Fenton, M., & Pojednic, R. (2019). Translating urban walkability initiatives for older adults in rural and under-resourced communities. *International Journal of Environmental Research and Public Health*, 16(17), 3041. DOI: 10.3390/ijerph16173041 PMID: 31443359

Klimczuk, A. (2016). Comparative analysis of national and regional models of the silver economy in the European Union. *International Journal of Ageing and Later Life*, 10(2), 31–59. DOI: 10.3384/ijal.1652-8670.15286

Kloza, B. (2023, January 3). *What Is Digital Inclusion? The Global Effort to Bring Everyone Online*. Connecting the Unconnected. https://ctu.ieee.org/what-is-digital-inclusion-the-global-effort-to-bring-everyone-online/

Koirala, P., Shrestha, S., & Koirala, M. (2022). Functional status of senior citizens of a metropolitan city in Morang. *Kathmandu University Medical Journal*, 20(4), 493–498. DOI: 10.3126/kumj.v20i4.54276 PMID: 37795731

Kolaki, M. (2017). Mobile payment use and mobile payment transactions by older adults: A qualitative study. https://www.diva-portal.org/smash/record.jsf?pid=diva2%3A1127590&dswid=2831

Kola, L., & Owumi, B. (2019). Causes of Poverty in Old Age, Not a Structural Failing? *Journal of Aging & Social Policy*, 31(5), 467–485. DOI: 10.1080/08959420.2019.1642692 PMID: 31328675

Kroll, D. H. (2011). To care or not to care: the ultimate decision for adult caregivers in a rapidly aging society. Temp. Pol. & Civ. Rts. L. Rev., 21, 403. https://heinonline.org/HOL/LandingPage?handle=hein.journals/tempcr21&div=22&id=&page=

Kuoppamäki, S., Hänninen, R., &Taipale, S. (2022). *Enhancing Older Adults' Digital Inclusion Through Social Support: A Qualitative Interview Study*. Springer EBooks, 211–230. DOI: 10.1007/978-3-030-94122-2_11

Ku, P. W., McKenna, J., & Fox, K. R. (2007). Dimensions of subjective well-being and effects of physical activity in Chinese older adults. *Journal of Aging and Physical Activity*, 15(4), 382–397. DOI: 10.1123/japa.15.4.382 PMID: 18048943

Kurt, S. (2015). Government Health Expenditures and Economic Growth: A Feder-Ram Approach for the Case of Türkiye. *International Journal of Economics and Financial Issues*, 5(2), 441–447.

Lahlou, R. M., & Daaleman, T. P. (2021). Addressing Loneliness and Social Isolation in Older Adults. *American Family Physician*, 104(1), 85–87. https://pubmed.ncbi.nlm.nih.gov/34264606 PMID: 34264606

Lahti, A., Mikkola, T., Salonen, M., Wasenius, N., Sarvimäki, A., Eriksson, J., & Bonsdorff, M. (2021). Mental, physical and social functioning in independently living senior house residents and community-dwelling older adults. *International Journal of Environmental Research and Public Health*, 18(23), 12299. DOI: 10.3390/ijerph182312299 PMID: 34886019

Lawless, M. T., Hunter, S. C., Pinero de Plaza, M. A., Archibald, M. M., & Kitson, A. L. (2022). "You Are By No Means Alone": A Netnographic Study of Self-Care Support in an Online Community for Older Adults. *Qualitative Health Research*, 104973232211249(13), 1935–1951. Advance online publication. DOI: 10.1177/10497323221124979 PMID: 36062369

Lee, S. and Edmonston, B. (2019). Living alone among older adults in Canada and the U.S.. Healthcare, 7(2), 68. DOI: 10.3390/healthcare7020068

Lee, S. (2023). Internet Use and Well-Being of Older Adults Before and During the COVID-19 Pandemic: Findings from European Social Survey. *Journal of Gerontological Social Work*, 67(1), 96–113. DOI: 10.1080/01634372.2023.2217682 PMID: 37246398

Lenstra, N. (2017). The community-based information infrastructure of older adult digital learning. *Nordicom Review*, 38(s1), 65–77. DOI: 10.1515/nor-2017-0401

Leong, K. S., Klainin-Yobas, P., Fong, S. D., & Wu, X. V. (2022). Older adults' perspective of intergenerational programme at senior day care centre in Singapore: A descriptive qualitative study. *Health & Social Care in the Community*, 30(1), e222–e233. DOI: 10.1111/hsc.13432 PMID: 34028921

Lerner, R. M. (Ed.), *Handbook of Child Psychology and Developmental Science.* DOI: 10.1002/9781118963418

Levasseur, , MTribble, , D. S. CDesrosiers, , J. (2009). Meaning of quality of life for older adults: importance of human functioning components. *Archives of Gerontology and Geriatrics, 49*(2), e91–e100.

Leveraging digital technologies for social inclusion | Division for Inclusive Social Development (DISD). (2021, February 18). Un.org. https://social.desa.un.org/publications/leveraging-digital-technologies-for-social-inclusion

Liebig, P., & Ramamurti, P. V. (2018). Living arrangements and social support for older adults in India. In *Handbook of Asian aging* (pp. 237–260). Routledge., https://www.taylorfrancis.com/chapters/edit/10.4324/9781315224503-10/living-arrangements-social-support-older-adults-india-phoebe-liebig-ramamurti DOI: 10.4324/9781315224503-10

Liew, S. L., Hussin, S. R., & Abdullah, N. H. (2021). Attributes of Senior-Friendly Tourism Destinations for Current and Future Senior Tourists: An Importance-Performance Analysis Approach. *SAGE Open*, 11(1), 2158244021998658. Advance online publication. DOI: 10.1177/2158244021998658

Li, J., & Wang, Q. (2022). Religiosity and health among Chinese older adults: A meta-analytic review. *Ageing and Society*, 42(2), 271–305. DOI: 10.1017/S0144686X20000835

Li, L., Liu, J., Zhang, Z., & Xu, H. (2014). Late-life depression in rural China: Do village infrastructure and availability of community resources matter? *International Journal of Geriatric Psychiatry*, 30(7), 729–736. DOI: 10.1002/gps.4217 PMID: 25333218

Lim, C. C. L., Low, C. L. T., Hia, S. B., Thang, L. L., & Thian, A. L. (2019). Generativity: Establishing and nurturing the next generation. *Journal of Intergenerational Relationships*, 17(3), 368–379. DOI: 10.1080/15350770.2019.1617603

Lippi, L., Turco, A., Folli, A., D'Abrosca, F., Curci, C., Mezian, K., Sire, A. D., & Invernizzi, M. (2023). Technological advances and digital solutions to improve quality of life in older adults with chronic obstructive pulmonary disease: A systematic review. *Aging Clinical and Experimental Research*, 35(5), 953–968. DOI: 10.1007/s40520-023-02381-3 PMID: 36952118

Loh, P., Estrella-Luna, N., & Shor, K. (2023). Pandemic Response and Mutual Aid as Climate Resilience: Learning From Community Responses in the Boston Area. *Journal of Climate Resilience & Climate Justice*, 1, 8–19. DOI: 10.1162/crcj_a_00006

London, M. (2011). Lifelong learning: introduction. *The Oxford handbook of life-long learning*, 3-11.

López-Sintas, J., Rojas-DeFrancisco, L., & García-Álvarez, E. (2017). Home-based digital leisure: Doing the same leisure activities, but digital. *Cogent Social Sciences*, 3(1), 1309741. DOI: 10.1080/23311886.2017.1309741

Lorenz, N., Ihle, P., & Breyer, F. (2020). Aging and Health Care Expenditures: A Non-Parametric Approach. SSRN *Electronic Journal*. DOI: 10.2139/ssrn.3576293

Loretto, W., Duncan, C., & White, P. (2000). Ageism and employment: Controversies, ambiguities and younger people's perceptions. *Ageing and Society*, 20(3), 279–302. DOI: 10.1017/S0144686X00007741

Lu, X., Yao, Y., & Jin, Y. (2022). Digital exclusion and functional dependence in older people: Findings from five longitudinal cohort studies. *EClinicalMedicine*, 54, 101708. DOI: 10.1016/j.eclinm.2022.101708 PMID: 36353265

Lythreatis, S., El-Kassar, A.-N., & Singh, S. K. (2022). The digital divide: A review and future research agenda. *Technological Forecasting and Social Change*, 175(6), 121359. DOI: 10.1016/j.techfore.2021.121359

Maj-Waśniowska, K., Wałęga, A., & Wałęga, G. (2018). Silver Economy, Poverty and Social Exclusion in the European Union Countries. *Proceedings of the 10th Economics & Finance Conference,* Rome, 341–353. DOI: 10.20472/EFC.2018.010.023

Manfred, E. (2021, July 21). *More Seniors Achieve Digital Equity*. Seniorplanet. https://seniorplanet.org/news/2021/07/21/seniors-achieve-digital-equity/

Mareš, J., Cígler, H., & Vachková, E. (2016). Czech version of opqol-35 questionnaire: The evaluation of the psychometric properties. *Health and Quality of Life Outcomes*, 14(1), 93. Advance online publication. DOI: 10.1186/s12955-016-0494-7 PMID: 27317441

Marken, D. M., & Howard, J. B. (2014). Grandparents raising grandchildren: The influence of a late-life transition on occupational engagement. *Physical & Occupational Therapy in Geriatrics*, 32(4), 381–396. DOI: 10.3109/02703181.2014.965376

Marston, H. R., Genoe, R., Freeman, S., Kulczycki, C., & Musselwhite, C. (2019). Older Adults' Perceptions of ICT: Main Findings from the Technology In Later Life (TILL) Study. 27

Ma, Y., Xiang, Q., Yan, C., Liao, H., & Wang, J. (2022). Poverty Vulnerability and Health Risk Action Path of Families of Rural Elderly With Chronic Diseases: Empirical Analysis of 1,852 Families in Central and Western China. *Frontiers in Public Health*, 10, 776901. Advance online publication. DOI: 10.3389/fpubh.2022.776901 PMID: 35237547

McCrea, J. M., & Smith, T. B. (2014). Types and models of intergenerational programs. In *Intergenerational programs* (pp. 81–93). Taylor & Francis., https://www.taylorfrancis.com/chapters/edit/10.4324/9781315783451-7/types-models-intergenerational-programs-james-mccrea-thomas-smith

McDonnell, S. (2021, February 22). *Meet and Make Friends Online*. Seniorplanet. https://seniorplanet.org/meet-and-make-friends-online/

Mebane, M. E., & Pezzuti, L. (2020). Intergenerational solidarity in triads of adult grandchild, parent, and grandparent: The positive view of elders, positive expectations towards the future and young-elders divide. *Educational Gerontology*, 46(9), 512–524. DOI: 10.1080/03601277.2020.1785672

Melchiorre, M., D'Amen, B., Lamura, G., & Socci, M. (2022). Health emergencies, falls, and use of communication technologies by older people with functional and social frailty: Aging in place in deprived areas of Italy. *International Journal of Environmental Research and Public Health*, 19(22), 14775. DOI: 10.3390/ijerph192214775 PMID: 36429499

Merom, D., Gebel, K., Fahey, P., Astell-Burt, T., Voukelatos, A., Rissel, C., & Sherrington, C. (2015). Neighborhood walkability, fear and risk of falling and response to walking promotion: The easy steps to health 12-month randomized controlled trial. *Preventive Medicine Reports*, 2, 704–710. DOI: 10.1016/j.pmedr.2015.08.011 PMID: 26844140

Merriam and Kee (2014). *Promoting Community Wellbeing: The Case for Lifelong Learning for Older Adults*.

Merriam, S. B., & Bierema, L. L. (2014). *Adult learning: Linking theory and practice*. Jossey-Bass.

Merriam, S. B., & Kee, Y. (2014). Promoting community wellbeing: The case for lifelong learning for older adults. *Adult Education Quarterly*, 64(2), 128–144. DOI: 10.1177/0741713613513633

Michel, J. P., & Sadana, R. (2017). "Healthy aging" concepts and measures. *Journal of the American Medical Directors Association*, 18(6), 460–464. DOI: 10.1016/j.jamda.2017.03.008 PMID: 28479271

Mihaly Csikszentmihalyi, (1990). "Flow: The Psychology of Optimal Experience"

Ministry of Social and Family Development, Republic of Singapore. 2022. Ageing Families in Singapore, 2010–2020. Insight Series Paper 01/2022.

Minkler, M., & Fuller-Thomson, E. (1999). The health of grandparents raising grandchildren: Results of a national study. *American Journal of Public Health*, 89(9), 1384–1389. DOI: 10.2105/AJPH.89.9.1384 PMID: 10474557

Miraç, Ö. Y., & Acar, M. (2015). *Türkiye Sosyal Hizmet Birikiminde Yaşlılık: Bibliographic Bir Değerlendirme (1950-2013)* (1st ed.). Açılımkitap Publications.

Miskelly, F. G. (2001). Assistive technology in elderly care. *Age and Ageing*, 30(6), 455–458. DOI: 10.1093/ageing/30.6.455 PMID: 11742772

Mitzner, T. L., Boron, J. B., Fausset, C. B., Adams, A. E., Charness, N., Czaja, S. J., Dijkstra, K., Fisk, A. D., Rogers, W. A., & Sharit, J. (2010). Older adults talk technology: Technology usage and attitudes. *Computers in Human Behavior*, 26(6), 1710–1721. DOI: 10.1016/j.chb.2010.06.020 PMID: 20967133

Mohamad, Z., Nee, A., Yang, F., Rehman, M., & Yin, Y. (2019). *Achieving community happiness through affordable eco-friendly smart houses.* Kne Social Sciences., DOI: 10.18502/kss.v3i21.5021

Mohan, R., Saleem, F., Voderhobli, K., & Sheikh-Akbari, A. (2024). Ensuring Sustainable Digital Inclusion among the Elderly: A Comprehensive Analysis. *Sustainability (Basel)*, 16(17), 7485. DOI: 10.3390/su16177485

Mohd, S., Senadjki, A., & Mansor, N. (2018). Trend of Poverty among Elderly: Evidence from Household Income Surveys. *Journal of Poverty*, 22(2), 89–107. DOI: 10.1080/10875549.2016.1186779

Molzahn, A., Skevington, S. M., Kalfoss, M., & Makaroff, K. S. (2010). The importance of facets of quality of life to older adults: An international investigation. *Quality of Life Research: An International Journal of Quality of Life Aspects of Treatment, Care and Rehabilitation*, 19(2), 293–298. DOI: 10.1007/s11136-009-9579-7 PMID: 20063124

Moon, J. S., & Mikami, H. (2007). Difference in subjective well-being between ethnic Korean and Japanese elderly residents in an urban community in Japan. *Geriatrics & Gerontology International*, 7(4), 371–379. DOI: 10.1111/j.1447-0594.2007.00427.x

Morais, D. M. D. C. B., Faria, C. M. G. M., & Fernandes, L. P. N. S. (2019). Intergenerational caregiving: The role of attachment and mental representation of caregiving in filial anxiety of middle-aged children. *Journal of Intergenerational Relationships*, 17(4), 468–487. DOI: 10.1080/15350770.2019.1596187

Morris, T. H. (2019). Adaptivity through self-directed learning to meet the challenges of our ever-changing world. *Adult Learning*, 30(2), 56–66. DOI: 10.1177/1045159518814486

Moscone, F., & Tosetti, E. (2010). Health expenditure and income in the United States. *Health Economics*, 19(12), 1385–1403. DOI: 10.1002/hec.1552 PMID: 19842092

Mubarak, F., & Suomi, R. (2022). Elderly Forgotten? Digital Exclusion in the Information Age and the Rising Grey Digital Divide. *Inquiry*, 59(1), 004695802210962. DOI: 10.1177/00469580221096272 PMID: 35471138

Muramatsu, N., Žefran, M., Stiehl, E., & Cornwell, T. (2024). AI-based technology in home-based care in aging societies: challenges and opportunities. *Handbook of Artificial Intelligence at Work*, 166-190. DOI: 10.4337/9781800889972.00017

Murayama, Y., Ohba, H., Yasunaga, M., Nonaka, K., Takeuchi, R., Nishi, M., Sakuma, N., Uchida, H., Shinkai, S., & Fujiwara, Y. (2015). The effect of intergenerational programs on the mental health of elderly adults. *Aging & Mental Health*, 19(4), 306–314. DOI: 10.1080/13607863.2014.933309 PMID: 25010219

Murciano-Hueso, A., Martín-García, A. V., & Cardoso, A. P. (2022). Technology and quality of life of older people in times of COVID: A qualitative study on their changed digital profile. *International Journal of Environmental Research and Public Health*, 19(16), 10459. DOI: 10.3390/ijerph191610459 PMID: 36012093

Murray, V., & Holliday, R. (1981). Increased error frequency of DNA polymerases from senescent human fibroblasts. *Journal of Molecular Biology*, 146(1), 55–76. DOI: 10.1016/0022-2836(81)90366-1 PMID: 7265228

Nagarajan, N. R., & Sixsmith, A. (2023). Policy initiatives to address the challenges of an older population in the workforce. *Ageing International*, 48(1), 41–77. DOI: 10.1007/s12126-021-09442-w PMID: 34465930

Narayan, P. K., & Narayan, S. (2008). The role of permanent and transitory shocks in explaining international health expenditures. *Health Economics*, 17(10), 1171–1186. DOI: 10.1002/hec.1316 PMID: 18076005

Nash, S. (2020, June 4). *The pandemic has accelerated the need to close the digital divide for older adults. Stanford Center on Longevity*. https://longevity.stanford.edu/the-pandemic-has-accelerated-the-need-to-close-the-digital-divide-for-older-adults

National Council on Aging. (2015). *National Council on Aging (NCOA)*. NCOA. https://www.ncoa.org/

Netuveli, G., & Blane, D. (2008). Quality of life in older ages. *British Medical Bulletin*, 85(1), 113–126. DOI: 10.1093/bmb/ldn003 PMID: 18281376

Neumark, D., & Song, J. (2011). *Do Stronger Age Discrimination Laws Make Social Security Reforms More Effective?* DOI: 10.3386/w17467

Neves, B. B., Waycott, J., & Malta, S. (2018). Old and afraid of new communication technologies? Reconceptualising and contesting the "age-based digital divide.". *Journal of Sociology (Melbourne, Vic.)*, 54(2), 236–248. DOI: 10.1177/1440783318766119

Newhouse, J. P. (1977). Medical care expenditure: A cross-national survey. *The Journal of Human Resources*, 12(1), 115–125. DOI: 10.2307/145602 PMID: 404354

Ng, C. T. C., & James, S. (2013). "Directive approach" for Chinese clients receiving psychotherapy: Is that really a priority? *Frontiers in Psychology*, 4, 49. DOI: 10.3389/fpsyg.2013.00049 PMID: 23408043

Ng, S., Lim, X., Hsu, H., & Chou, C. (2022). Age-friendliness of city, loneliness and depression moderated by internet use during the covid-19 pandemic. *Health Promotion International*, 38(3), daac040. Advance online publication. DOI: 10.1093/heapro/daac040 PMID: 35437585

Nguyen, A. (2020). *Digital Inclusion*. Handbook of Social Inclusion, 1–15. DOI: 10.1007/978-3-030-48277-0_14-1

Nguyen, C., Leanos, S., Natsuaki, M. N., Rebok, G. W., & Wu, R. (2020). Adaptation for growth via learning new skills as a means to long-term functional independence in older adulthood: Insights from emerging adulthood. *The Gerontologist*, 60(1), 4–11. PMID: 30321326

Niazi, A. R. K., Mubeen, M., Niazi, M. H. K., & Asnan, C. M. (2020). Generation gap is a difference i Generation Gap in Pakistan: Antecedents and Effects. *The Dialogue*, 15(4), 64–75. https://journals.qurtuba.edu.pk/ojs/index.php/thedialogue/article/view/222

Nishijima, M., Ivanauskas, T. M., & Sarti, F. M. (2017). Evolution and determinants of digital divide in Brazil (2005–2013). *Telecommunications Policy*, 41(1), 12–24. DOI: 10.1016/j.telpol.2016.10.004

Nojomi, M., Goharinezhad, S., Saraei, R., Goharinejad, S., Ramezani, G., & Aalaa, M. (2023). Exploring the attitudes of general medical students toward older adult's care in a lower middle-income country: Implications for medical education. *BMC Medical Education*, 23(1), 649. Advance online publication. DOI: 10.1186/s12909-023-04626-1 PMID: 37684593

Noone, C., McSharry, J., Smalle, M., Burns, A., Dwan, K., Devane, D., & Morrissey, E. C. (2020). Video calls for reducing social isolation and loneliness in older people: A rapid review. *Cochrane Database of Systematic Reviews*, 5(5). Advance online publication. DOI: 10.1002/14651858.CD013632 PMID: 32441330

Nyamweya, N. K. (2017). Healthcare expenditure and economic growth: The kenyan case (1970- 2016).

NYU Tandon School of Engineering. (2021, February 24). *Impact of online communities*. ScienceDaily. https://www.sciencedaily.com/releases/2021/02/210224120312.htm

O'Loughlin, K., Loh, V., & Kendig, H. (2017). Carer characteristics and health, wellbeing and employment outcomes of older Australian baby boomers. *Journal of cross-cultural gerontology, 32*, 339-356. doi: , R. P. (2022). *The Grandparent Vocation: Wisdom, Legacies, and Spiritual Growth*. Rowman & Littlefield. https://www.google.co.in/books/edition/The_Grandparent_Vocation/xdKUEAAAQBAJ?hl=en&gbpv=1&dq=As+part+of+the+%E2%80%9Cgrandparent%E2%80%9D+generation+within+the+family,+individuals+still+can+be+helpful+to+their+growth+of+spring+and+serve+as+source+of+wisdom,+guidance+and+support.+However,+a+major+shift+has+taken+place.+&pg=PR9&printsec=frontcoverDOI: 10.1007/s10823-017-9321-Olson

O'Toole, M. (2021, August 23). *Leveraging eCommerce Adoption by Seniors Post-Pandemic*. Clarkston Consulting. https://clarkstonconsulting.com/insights/ecommerce-adoption-by-seniors/

OECD Pensions at a Glance (2023), https://www.oecd.org/en/publications/pensions-at-a-glance- 2023_678055dd-en.html, (Accessed: 08.10.2024).

OECD. (2023). *Pension at a Glance 2023*. https://www.oecd.org/en/publications/pensions-at-a-glance-2023_678055dd-en.html

OECD. (2024). *OECD Data Explorer.* https://data-explorer.oecd.org/vis?fs[0]= Topic%2C1%7CSociety%23SOC%23%7CInequality%23SOC_INE%23&pg=0&fc =Topic&bp=true&snb=2&df[ds]=dsDisseminateFinalDMZ&df[id]=DSD_WISE _IDD%40DF_IDD&df[ag]=OECD.WISE.INE&df[vs]=1.0&pd=2010%2C&dq= .A.PR_INC_DISP%2BINC_DISP_GINI...Y_GT65%2B_T.METH2012.D_CUR.& to[TIME_PERIOD]=false&ly[cl]=TIME_PERIOD&ly[rs]=COMBINED_UNIT _MEASURE&ly[rw]=REF_AREA%2CAGE%2CCOMBINED_MEASURE& vw=tb

Öksüzokyar, M. M., Eryiğit, S. Ç., Düzen, K. Ö., Mergen, B. E., Sökmen, Ü. N., & Öğüt, S. (2016). Causes and effects of biological aging. Mehmet Akif Ersoy University Journal of Health Sciences Institute, 4(1).

Orenstein, G. A., & Lewis, L. (2022). Eriksons stages of psychosocial development. In *StatPearls* [Internet]. StatPearls Publishing.

Orimo, H., Ito, H., Suzuki, T., Araki, A., Hosoi, T., & Sawabe, M. (2006). Reviewing the definition of "elderly". *Geriatrics & Gerontology International*, 6(3), 149–158. DOI: 10.1111/j.1447-0594.2006.00341.x PMID: 16521795

Our World In Data based on Lindert (1994), OECD (1993), OECD Stat - processed by Our World in Data. "public_health_expenditure_pc_gdp" [dataset]. Our World In Data based on, Lindert (1994), OECD (1993), OECD Stat [original data], (Accessed: 12.10.2024).

Park, J. M. (2012). Equity of Access to Primary Care Among Older Adults in Incheon, South Korea. *Asia-Pacific Journal of Public Health*, 24(6), 953–960. DOI: 10.1177/1010539511409392 PMID: 21653609

Park, S., Kim, Y., Kwon, O., & Lee, J. (2023). Influence of consumer innovativeness and cosmetic selection attributes on purchase intention of eco-friendly cosmetics. *The Journal of Cosmetic Medicine*, 7(1), 29–37. DOI: 10.25056/JCM.2023.7.1.29

Parson, C., & Hick, S. (2008). *Moving from the Digital Divide to Digital Inclusion.* Currents: New Scholarship in the Human Services.7. https://www.semanticscholar .org/paper/Moving-from-the-Digital-Divide-to-Digital-Inclusion-Parsons-Hick/ 332768fe9553feabfa7032b9415f98f66d4c39d3

Pascual-Saez, M., Cantarero-Prieto, D., & Castañeda, D. (2017). Public health expenditure, GDP and the elderly population: A comparative study. *International Journal of Social Economics*, 44(10), 1390–1400. DOI: 10.1108/IJSE-03-2016-0106

Payne, G., Laporte, A., Deber, R., & Coyte, P. C. (2007). Counting backward to health care's future: Using time-to-death modeling to identify changes in end-of-life morbidity and the impact of aging on health care expenditures. *The Milbank Quarterly*, 85(2), 213–257. DOI: 10.1111/j.1468-0009.2007.00485.x PMID: 17517114

Peek, S., Luijkx, K., Vrijhoef, H., Nieboer, M., Aarts, S., Voort, C., & Wouters, E. (2017). Origins and consequences of technology acquirement by independent-living seniors: Towards an integrative model. *BMC Geriatrics*, 17(1), 189. Advance online publication. DOI: 10.1186/s12877-017-0582-5 PMID: 28830444

Pérez-Escolar, M., & Canet, F. (2022). Research on vulnerable people and digital inclusion: Toward a consolidated taxonomical framework. *Universal Access in the Information Society*, 22(22), 1059–1072. Advance online publication. DOI: 10.1007/s10209-022-00867-x PMID: 35125988

Perrault, S. (2021). *Towards Inclusive Design of Mobile Privacy and Security for Older Adults* (Doctoral dissertation, Singapore University of Technology and Design).

Peters, R., Ee, N., Ward, S. A., Kenning, G., Radford, K., Goldwater, M., Dodge, H. H., Lewis, E., Xu, Y., Kundrna, G., Hamilton, M., Peters, J., Anstey, K. J., Lautenschlager, N. T., Fitzgerald, A., & Rockwood, K. (2021). Intergenerational programmes bringing together community dwelling non-familial older adults and children: A systematic review. *Archives of Gerontology and Geriatrics*, 94, 104356. DOI: 10.1016/j.archger.2021.104356 PMID: 33567363

Petner-Arrey, J., Howell-Moneta, A., & Lysaght, R. (2016). Facilitating employment opportunities for adults with an intellectual and developmental disability through parents and social networks. *Disability and Rehabilitation*, 38(8), 789–795. DOI: 10.3109/09638288.2015.1061605 PMID: 26114628

Piabuo, S. M., & Tieguhong, J. C. (2017). Health expenditure and economic growth-a review of the literature and an analysis between the economic community for central African states (CEMAC) and selected African countries. *Health Economics Review*, 7(1), 23. DOI: 10.1186/s13561-017-0159-1 PMID: 28593509

Piaget, J. (1976). Piaget's theory.

Polonsky, W. H., & Hessler, D. (2013). What are the quality of life-related benefits and losses associated with real-time continuous glucose monitoring? A survey of current users. *Diabetes Technology & Therapeutics*, 15(4), 295–301. DOI: 10.1089/dia.2012.0298 PMID: 23427866

Promoting social integration through social inclusion - 2021 Report | Division for Inclusive Social Development (DISD). (2021). Un.org. https://social.desa.un.org/publications/promoting-social-integration-through-social-inclusion-2021-report

Pruchno, R. (1999). Raising grandchildren: The experiences of black and white grandmothers. *The Gerontologist*, 39(2), 209–221. DOI: 10.1093/geront/39.2.209 PMID: 10224717

Qassem, T. (2015). Emerging technologies for dementia patient monitoring. *Advanced Technological Solutions for E-Health and Dementia Patient Monitoring*, 62-104. DOI: 10.4018/978-1-4666-7481-3.ch004

Quinn, J. F. (2002). Changing Retirement Trends and Their. *Policies for an aging society*, 293.

Rainer, S. (2014). Social participation and social engagement of elderly people. *Procedia: Social and Behavioral Sciences*, 116, 780–785. DOI: 10.1016/j.sbspro.2014.01.297

Rasi-Heikkinen, P., & Doh, M.Päivi Rasi-Heikkinen. (2023). Older Adults and Digital Inclusion. *Educational Gerontology*, 49(5), 345–347. DOI: 10.1080/03601277.2023.2205743

Rawas, S. (2024). ChatGPT: Empowering lifelong learning in the digital age of higher education. *Education and Information Technologies*, 29(6), 6895–6908. DOI: 10.1007/s10639-023-12114-8

Reis da Silva Tiago. (2024j) The Value of Emotional Intelligence in Midwifery: Enhancing Care and Outcomes for Mothers and Infants through Sustainable Development Goals and Leadership. Journal of Womens Healthcare & Midwifery Research. SRC/JWHMR-133. Link: https://www.onlinescientificresearch.com/articles/the-value-of-emotional-intelligence-in-midwifery-enhancing-care-and-outcomes-for-mothers-and-infants-through-sustainable-developme.pdf

Reis da Silva, T. H (2024e). Oncology and Cancer Medicine: Understanding the complexities in Older Patients. Biomed J Sci & Tech Res 55(3)-2024. DOI: DOI: 10.26717/BJSTR.2024.55.008720

Reis da Silva. Tiago Horta (2024d). Death and Its Significance in Nursing Practice. Palliat Med Care Int J. 2024; 4(3): 555640. DOI: https://juniperpublishers.com/pmcij/pdf/PMCIJ.MS.ID.555640.pdf

Reis da Silva, T. (2024c). The Evolution of Nursing for Older Adult: A Historical Perspective. Associative J Health Sci. 3(3). *AJHS*, 000561, 2024. DOI: 10.31031/AJHS.2024.03.000561

Reis da Silva, T. (2024g). Can supplementing vitamin B12 improve mental health outcomes?: A literature review. *British Journal of Community Nursing*, 29(3), 137–146. DOI: 10.12968/bjcn.2024.29.3.137 PMID: 38421889

Reis da Silva, T. H. (2023a). Moving and Handling in the Community. *British Journal of Community Nursing*, 28(8), 369. DOI: 10.12968/bjcn.2023.28.8.369 PMID: 37527217

Reis da Silva, T. H. (2023b). Aging in place: Aging at home and in the community. *British Journal of Community Nursing*, 28(5), 213–214. DOI: 10.12968/bjcn.2023.28.5.213 PMID: 37130715

Reis da Silva, T. H. (2023c). Falls assessment and prevention in the nursing home and community. *British Journal of Community Nursing*, 28(2), 68–72. DOI: 10.12968/bjcn.2023.28.2.68 PMID: 36735363

Reis da Silva, T. H. (2024a). Falls prevention in older people and the role of nursing. *British Journal of Community Nursing*, 29(7), 335–339. DOI: 10.12968/bjcn.2024.0005 PMID: 38963269

Reis da Silva, T. H. (2024b). Loneliness in older adults. *British Journal of Community Nursing*, 29(2), 60–66. DOI: 10.12968/bjcn.2024.29.2.60 PMID: 38300245

Reis da Silva, T. H. (2024f). Understanding body fluid balance, dehydration and intravenous fluid therapy. *Emergency Nurse*. Advance online publication. DOI: 10.7748/en.2024.e2201 PMID: 38978385

Reis da Silva, T. H. (2024h). Chronic kidney disease in older adults: Nursing implications for community nurses. *Journal of Kidney Care*, 9(4), 174–179. DOI: 10.12968/jokc.2024.9.4.174

Reis da Silva, T. H. (2024i). Pharmacokinetics in older people: An overview of prescribing practice. *Journal of Prescribing Practice*, 6(8), 2–9. DOI: 10.12968/jprp.2024.6.9.374

Reis da Silva, T. H., & Mitchell, A. (2024a). Integrating Digital Transformation in Nursing Education: Best Practices and Challenges in Curriculum Development. In Lytras, M., Serban, A. C., Alkhaldi, A., Malik, S., & Aldosemani, T. (Eds.), *Digital Transformation in Higher Education, Part B Cases, Examples and Good Practices*. Emerald Publishing Limited.

Reis da Silva, T. H., & Rodrigues, E. C. P. (2023). Body Image Related Discrimination. In Leal Filho, W., Azul, A. M., Brandli, L., Lange Salvia, A., Özuyar, P. G., & Wall, T. (Eds.), *Reduced Inequalities. Encyclopedia of the UN Sustainable Development Goals*. Springer., DOI: 10.1007/978-3-319-71060-0_61-1

Reisdorf, B., & Rhinesmith, C. (2020). Digital Inclusion as a Core Component of Social Inclusion. *Social Inclusion (Lisboa)*, 8(2), 132–137. https://www.researchgate .net/publication/341383220_Digital_Inclusion_as_a_Core_Component_of_Social _Inclusion/citation/download. DOI: 10.17645/si.v8i2.3184

Rejeski, W. J., & Mihalko, S. L. (2001). Physical activity and quality of life in older adults. *The Journals of Gerontology. Series A, Biological Sciences and Medical Sciences*, 56(suppl_2), 23–35. DOI: 10.1093/gerona/56.suppl_2.23 PMID: 11730235

Reynolds, C. F. III, Jeste, D. V., Sachdev, P. S., & Blazer, D. G. (2022). Mental health care for older adults: Recent advances and new directions in clinical practice and research. *World Psychiatry; Official Journal of the World Psychiatric Association (WPA)*, 21(3), 336–363. DOI: 10.1002/wps.20996 PMID: 36073714

Richardson, V. E., & Barusch, A. S. (2005). *Gerontological practice for the twenty-first century: A social work perspective*. Columbia University Press., https:// www.google.co.in/books/edition/Gerontological_Practice_for_the_Twenty_f/ OsWQ2U0HoBkC?hl=en&gbpv=1&dq=Thus+the+greater+the+number+of+ role+resources+with+which+individual+enter+old+age+the+better+off+they+ will+be+adjusting+to+the+demoralizing+effects+of+role+exits+(Blau,+1973). &pg=PR7&printsec=frontcover

Richeson, J. A., & Shelton, J. N. (2006). A social psychological perspective on the stigmatization of older adults. *When I'm, 64*, 174-208.

Rights of Older People. (2021, August 24). In www.hrw.org. https://www.hrw.org/ news/2021/08/24/russia-insufficient-home-services-older-people

Rodrigues, N., Han, C., Su, Y., Klainin-Yobas, P., & Wu, V. (2021). Psychological impacts and online interventions of social isolation amongst older adults during covid-19 pandemic: A scoping review. *Journal of Advanced Nursing*, 78(3), 609–644. DOI: 10.1111/jan.15063 PMID: 34625997

Rowe, J. W., & Kahn, R. L. (1998). *Successful aging*. Dell/Random House.

Russell, C. (2024). *The aging experience*. Taylor & Francis., DOI: 10.4324/9781032683720

Ryan, A. K., & Willits, F. K. (2007). Family ties, physical health, and psychological well-being. *Journal of Aging and Health*, 19(6), 907–920. DOI: 10.1177/0898264307308340 PMID: 18165288

Ryan, R. M., & Deci, E. L. (2000). Self-Determination Theory and the Facilitation of Intrinsic Motivation, Social Development, and Well-Being. *The American Psychologist*, 55(1), 68–78. DOI: 10.1037/0003-066X.55.1.68 PMID: 11392867

Sağın, A., & Karasaç, F. (2018). The Effect of Health Expenditures on Economic Growth in Oecd Economies. *Kirklareli University Journal of Faculty of Economics and Administrative Sciences*, 7(1), 72–86.

Sampson, D. (2008). The experience of grandparents raising grandchildren: A phenomenological study. https://digitalscholarship.unlv.edu/rtds/2429/

Sánchez-Rico, A., Garel, P., Notarangelo, I., Quintana, M., Hernández, G., Asteriadis, S., Popa, M., Vretos, N., Solachidis, V., Burgos, M., & Girault, A. (2017). ICT services for life improvement for the elderly. In *Harnessing the Power of Technology to Improve Lives* (pp. 600–605). IOS Press.

Sanderson, W. C., & Scherbov, S. (2015). Are We Overly Dependent on Conventional Dependency Ratios? *Population and Development Review*, 41(4), 687–708. DOI: 10.1111/j.1728-4457.2015.00091.x

Sanz, I., & Velázquez, F. J. (2007). The role of ageing in the growth of government and social welfare spending in the OECD. *European Journal of Political Economy*, 23(4), 917–931. DOI: 10.1016/j.ejpoleco.2007.01.003

Scheckler, S. (2020). Housing, affordability, and community-based aging. *Innovation in Aging*, 4(Supplement_1), 690–691. DOI: 10.1093/geroni/igaa057.2415

Schneiders, M. L., Phou, M., Tum, V., Kelley, M., Parker, M., & Turner, C. (2021). Grandparent caregiving in Cambodian skip-generation households: Roles and impact on child nutrition. *Maternal and Child Nutrition*, 17(S1), e13169. DOI: 10.1111/mcn.13169 PMID: 34241960

Schultz, D. H., Gansemer, A., Allgood, K., Gentz, M., Secilmis, L., Deldar, Z., Savage, C. R., & Ghazi Saidi, L. (2024, August 7). Second language learning in older adults modulates Stroop task performance and brain activation. *Frontiers in Aging Neuroscience*, 16, 1398015. DOI: 10.3389/fnagi.2024.1398015 PMID: 39170898

Scotté, F., Bossi, P., Carola, E., Cudennec, T., Dielenseger, P., Gomes, F., Knox, S., & Strasser, F. (2018). Addressing the quality of life needs of older patients with cancer: A SIOG consensus paper and practical guide. *Annals of Oncology : Official Journal of the European Society for Medical Oncology*, 29(8), 1718–1726. DOI: 10.1093/annonc/mdy228 PMID: 30010772

Scott, M. (2021). Planning for age-friendly cities. *Planning Theory & Practice*, 22(3), 457–492. DOI: 10.1080/14649357.2021.1930423

Seifert, A., Cotten, S. R., & Xie, B. (2020). A Double Burden of Exclusion? Digital and Social Exclusion of Older Adults in Times of COVID-19. *The Journals of Gerontology. Series B, Psychological Sciences and Social Sciences*, 76(3), e99–e103. Advance online publication. DOI: 10.1093/geronb/gbaa098 PMID: 32672332

Semrush. (2024). *Distribution of internet users worldwide as of February 2024, by age group* [Review of Distribution of internet users worldwide as of February 2024, by age group]. In Statista. https://www.statista.com/statistics/272365/age-distribution-of-internet-users-worldwide/

Sen, P. (2016). Anyone for Social Security Reform? SSRN *Electronic Journal*. DOI: 10.2139/ssrn.2844652

Sen, K., Prybutok, G., & Prybutok, V. (2022). The use of digital technology for social wellbeing reduces social isolation in older adults: A systematic review. *SSM - Population Health*, 17(101020), 101020. DOI: 10.1016/j.ssmph.2021.101020 PMID: 35024424

Settles, B. H., Zhao, J., Mancini, K. D., Rich, A., Pierre, S., & Oduor, A. (2009). Grandparents caring for their grandchildren: Emerging roles and exchanges in global perspectives. *Journal of Comparative Family Studies*, 40(5), 827–848. DOI: 10.3138/jcfs.40.5.827

Sharit, J., & Czaja, S. J. (2017). Technology and work: Implications for older workers and organizations. *Innovation in Aging*, 1(suppl_1), 1026–1026. DOI: 10.1093/geroni/igx004.3735

Sharma, K. (2008) a quarterly journal devoted to research on ageing Vol. 22, No. 2,. *Book Reviews,* 256, 262.

Shiwani, T., Relton, S., Evans, R., Kale, A., Heaven, A., Clegg, A., Abuzour, A., Alderman, J., Anand, A., Bhanu, C., Bunn, J., Collins, J., Cutillo, L., Hall, M., Keevil, V., Mitchell, L., Ogliari, G., Penfold, R., van Oppen, J., & Todd, O. (2023). New Horizons in artificial intelligence in the healthcare of older people. *Age and Ageing*, 52(12), afad219. Advance online publication. DOI: 10.1093/ageing/afad219 PMID: 38124256

Shubham, S., & Joshi, A. K. (2021). *Challenges and opportunities in social care of elderly in urban India*. Ageing. DOI: 10.1007/978-981-16-5827-3_19

Silver, M. P. (2014). Socio-economic status over the lifecourse and internet use in older adulthood. *Ageing and Society*, 34(6), 1019–1034. DOI: 10.1017/S0144686X12001420

Silverstein, M., Giarrusso, R., & Bengtson, V. L. (2003). Grandparents and grandchildren in family systems. Global aging and challenges to families, 75-102. https://www.google.co.in/books/edition/Global_Aging_and_Challenges_to_Families/AnMIEQAAQBAJ?hl=en&gbpv=1&dq=Transitioning+from+joint+to+nuclear+family+systems+has+widened+the+gap+between+grandparents+and+grandchildren.+&pg=PA75&printsec=frontcover

Simpson, M., Oetzel, J., Wilson, Y., Nock, S., Johnston, K., & Reddy, R. (2022). Codesigning a culture-centered age-friendly community for Māori Kaumātua: Cultural principles and practices. *The Journals of Gerontology. Series B, Psychological Sciences and Social Sciences*, 77(12), 2265–2275. DOI: 10.1093/geronb/gbac092 PMID: 35796864

Sixsmith, A., Horst, B. R., Simeonov, D., & Mihailidis, A. (2022). Older people's use of digital technology during the COVID-19 pandemic. *Bulletin of Science, Technology & Society*, 42(1-2), 19–24. DOI: 10.1177/02704676221094731 PMID: 38603230

Social Security Institutions Budget Statistics. (2023). https://muhasebat.hmb.gov.tr/sosyal- guvenlik-kurumlari-butce-istatistikleri, (Accessed: 11.10.2024).

Sokolec, J. (2016). The meaning of "place" to older adults. *Clinical Social Work Journal*, 44(2), 160–169. DOI: 10.1007/s10615-015-0545-2

Soósová, M. (2016). Determinants of quality of life in the elderly. *Central European Journal of Nursing and Midwifery*, 7(3), 484–493. DOI: 10.15452/CEJNM.2016.07.0019

Spulber, D. (2019). Coping and resilience in life-long learning and ageing: New challenges. *Geopolitical. Social Security and Freedom Journal*, 2(1), 93–103. DOI: 10.2478/gssfj-2019-0009

Srinivasan, S. (2015). Situation of Older People: A Comparative Study of Countries in the SAARC Region. Perpustakaan Negara Malaysia Cataloging-in Publication Data, The 2nd International Social Work Conference 2015 – Celebrating Diversity in One World, Proceeding: ISBN 978-967-394-244-2.

Srinivasan, S. (2015). The Elderly Inmates in the Indian Prisons – A Psychosocial Perspective, Perpustakaan Negara Malaysia Cataloging-in Publication Data, the 2nd International Social Work Conference 2015 – Celebrating Diversity in One World, Proceeding: ISBN 978-967-394-244-2.

Srinivasan, S. (2023). Situation of Elderly Person with TB: A Comparative Study of Countries in the SAARC Region. International Journal for Multidisciplinary Research (IJFMR), E-ISSN: 2582-2160, IJFMR23057862, Volume 5, Issue 5, September-October 2023.10.28.SJIF Impact Factor(2023) is 8.224 & ISI:1.188, Journal DOI:DOI: 10.36713/epra2013

Srinivasan, S. Ilango (2021). Health Problem Faced by Elderly Inmates in Central Prisons in India, A Quarterly International Multilateral Thamizh Journal, Modern Thamizh Research, Arts and Humanities, Vol 28, No 7, ISSN: 2121-984X, Raja Publication, UGC Care Listed (Group – I).

Srinivasan, S. Ilango (2021). Mental Health Problems faced by Aged Inmates due to Overcrowding of Central Prison in Tamil Nadu, A Quarterly International Multilateral Thamizh Journal, Modern Thamizh Research, Arts and Humanities, Vol 28, No 7, ISSN: 2121-984X, Raja Publication, UGC Care Listed (Group – I).

Srinivasan, S., Ilango (2013). Work Problems Faced by Aged Construction Workers in Thanjavur District, Tamil Nadu. SLAP Journal of Social Science ISSN-0975 9999

Srinivasan, S., & Rajavel, N. (2025). A Study of the Psychological Well-Being of Tamil Nadu Prison Inmates With Special Reference of AI. In *AI Technologies and Advancements for Psychological Well-Being and Healthcare* (pp. 219–254). IGI Global., DOI: 10.4018/979-8-3693-9158-7.ch009

Statista, (2022). Annual number of adult social care homes in England from 2009 to 2019, Statistia.

Staying the Course on Reforms: Progress Amidst Challenges (2024, october 17) In *World Bank Group*. https://www.worldbank.org/en/news/press-release/2024/10/17/nigeria-staying-the-course-on-reforms-progress-amidst-challenges#:~:text=%E2%80%9CGDP%20is%20projected%20to%20grow,naira%20and%20increased%20gasoline%20prices

Steels, S. (2015). Key characteristics of age-friendly cities and communities: A review. *Cities (London, England)*, 47, 45–52. DOI: 10.1016/j.cities.2015.02.004

Stefanacci, G. R. (n.d.). Overview of Healthy Ageing [Review of Overview of Healthy Ageing]. *MSD Manual*. https://www.mdpi.com/2071-1050/16/17/7485

Sudarmathy, S., & Kannan, M. (2019). Quality of Life of Senior Citizens Residing at the Home for Aged.

Sung, P., Chia, A., Chan, A., & Malhotra, R. (2023, May 11). Reciprocal Relationship Between Lifelong Learning and Volunteering Among Older Adults. *The Journals of Gerontology. Series B, Psychological Sciences and Social Sciences*, 78(5), 902–912. DOI: 10.1093/geronb/gbad003 PMID: 36626304

Sun, Q., Lou, V. W., Dai, A., To, C., & Wong, S. Y. (2019). The effectiveness of the young–old link and growth intergenerational program in reducing age stereotypes. *Research on Social Work Practice*, 29(5), 519–528. DOI: 10.1177/1049731518767319

Sun, X., Yan, W., Zhou, H., Wang, Z., Zhang, X., Huang, S., & Li, L. (2020). Internet use and need for digital health technology among the elderly: A cross-sectional survey in China. *BMC Public Health*, 20(1), 1–8. DOI: 10.1186/s12889-020-09448-0 PMID: 32917171

Tamakoshi, T., & Hamori, S. (2015). Health-care expenditure, GDP and share of the elderly in Japan: A panel cointegration analysis. *Applied Economics Letters*, 22(9), 725–729. DOI: 10.1080/13504851.2014.972540

Tanlamai, U., Jaikengkit, A., Jarutach, T., Rajkulchai, S., & Ritbumroong, T. (2022). Use of daily posture and activity tracking to assess sedentary behavior, toss-and-turns, and sleep duration of independently living Thai seniors. *Health Informatics Journal*, 28(1), 146045822110702. DOI: 10.1177/14604582211070214 PMID: 35220815

Tannou, T., Lihoreau, T., Couture, M., Giroux, S., Wang, R. H., Spalla, G., Zarshenas, S., Roy, M. G., Aboujaoude, A., Yaddaden, A., Morin, L., & Bier, N. (2023). Is research on 'smart living environments' based on unobtrusive technologies for older adults going in circles? Evidence from an umbrella review. *Ageing Research Reviews*, 84, 101830. DOI: 10.1016/j.arr.2022.101830 PMID: 36565962

Tannou, T., Lihoreau, T., Gagnon-Roy, M., Grondin, M., & Bier, N. (2022). Effectiveness of smart living environments to support older adults to age in place in their community: An umbrella review protocol. *BMJ Open*, 12(1), e054235. DOI: 10.1136/bmjopen-2021-054235 PMID: 35078843

Thang, L. L. (2011). Promoting intergenerational understanding between the young and old: the case of Singapore. In UN report of the expert group meeting in Qatar (pp. 8-9). https://www.un.org/esa/socdev/family/docs/egm11/EGM_Expert_Paper_Theng_Leng_Leng.pdf

The National Council on Aging. (2023, July 06). Www.ncoa.org. https://www.ncoa.org/article/how-older-adults-can-improve-their-personal-cyber-security/

Thomas, P. A., Liu, H., & Umberson, D. (2017). Family relationships and well-being. *Innovation in Aging*, 1(3), igx025. Advance online publication. DOI: 10.1093/geroni/igx025 PMID: 29795792

Thomson, C. (2024, May 29). Generational AI: Digital inclusion for aging populations. Atlantic Council. https://www.atlanticcouncil.org/in-depth-research-reports/report/generational-ai-digital-inclusion-for-aging-populations/

Toda, H. Y., & Yamamoto, T. (1995). Statistical inference in vector autoregressions with possibly integrated processes. *Journal of Econometrics*, 66(1-2), 225–250. DOI: 10.1016/0304-4076(94)01616-8

Tolkien, J. R. R. (2004). *The Return of the King: Being the third part of The Lord of the Rings*. HarperCollins Publisher.

Tomczyk, Ł., Mascia, M. L., Gierszewski, D., & Walker, C. (2023). Barriers to digital inclusion among older people: A intergenerational reflection on the need to develop digital competences for the group with the highest level of digital exclusion. Innoeduca. *International Journal of Technology and Educational Innovation*, 9(1), 5–26. DOI: 10.24310/innoeduca.2023.v9i1.16433

Torku, A., Chan, A., & Yung, E. (2020). Age-friendly cities and communities: A review and future directions. *Aging and Society*, 41(10), 2242–2279. DOI: 10.1017/S0144686X20000239

Torku, A., Chan, A., & Yung, E. (2020). Implementation of age-friendly initiatives in smart cities: Probing the barriers through a systematic review. *Built Environment Project and Asset Management*, 11(3), 412–426. DOI: 10.1108/BEPAM-01-2020-0008

Tornstam, L. (2005). *Gerotranscendence: A developmental theory of positive aging*. Springer.

Treleaven, E., & Ngin, C. (2021). When parents are not present: Decision-making dynamics for young children's health and illness in migrant-sending households in rural Cambodia. *Social Science & Medicine*, 287, 114327. DOI: 10.1016/j.socscimed.2021.114327 PMID: 34509896

Uhlenberg, P. (2000). Why Study Age Integration? *The Gerontologist*, 40, 276–281. DOI: 10.1093/geront/40.3.276 PMID: 10853513

UN. World Population Prospects (2024) - processed by Our World in Data. "Median age, medium projection - UN WPP" [dataset]. United Nations, "World Population Prospects" [original data], (Accessed: 09.10.2024).

UN. World Population Prospects (2024) - processed by Our World in Data. "Population,ages 0-14 - UN WPP" [dataset]. United Nations, "World Population Prospects" [original data], (Accessed: 09.10.2024).

UN. World Population Prospects (2024). - processed by Our World in Data. "Population, ages 0- 14, ages 15-64, ages 65+ - UN WPP" [dataset]. United Nations, "World Population Prospects" [original data], (Accessed: 09.10.2024).

UNECE. (2021). Ageing in the digital era policy policy brief challenging context. https://unece.org/sites/default/files/2021-07/PB26-ECE-WG.1-38_0.pdf

UNESCAP. (2016) Long-Term for Older Persons in India. SDD-SPPS Project Working Papers Series: Long-Term Care for older persons in Asia and the Pacific. https://www.unescap.org/sites/default/files/SDD%20Working%20Paper%20Ageing %20Long%20Term%20Care%20India%20v1-2.pdf

UNESCO. (2022). *5th global report on adult learning and education. Citizenship education: Empowering adults for change.* UNESCO Institute for Lifelong Learning. Hamburg: UIL.

United Nations Department of Economic and Social Affairs, Population Division (2020). World Population Ageing 2020 Highlights: Living arrangements of older persons (ST/ESA/SER.A/451).

United Nations. (2023). *World Social Report 2023: Leaving No One Behind in an Ageing World.* https://desapublications.un.org/publications/world-social-report-2023 -leaving-no-one-behind-ageing-world

United Nations. (2024). *Population Division: World Population Prospects 2024, Online Edition.* https://population.un.org/wpp/Download/Standard/Population/

Vávrová, S., Recmanová, A., Kowaliková, I., Gojová, A., &Vaňharová, A. (2019). Using ICT in social work focused on e-exclusion groups. *European Proceedings of Social and Behavioral Sciences.* DOI: 10.15405/epsbs.2019.11.35

Venkateswarlu, V. (2008). *Problems of Rural Aged: A Sociological Perspective.* Gyan Publishing House.

Vera-Sanso, P. (2023). Will the SDGs and the UN Decade of Healthy Ageing Leave Older People Behind? *Progress in Development Studies*, 23(4), 391–407. DOI: 10.1177/14649934231193808

Vidovićová, L. (2018). New roles for older people. *Journal of Population Ageing*, 11(1), 1–6. DOI: 10.1007/s12062-017-9217-z

Vitman, A., Iecovich, E., & Alfasi, N. (2014, April). Ageism and Social Integration of Older Adults in Their Neighborhoods in Israel. [Ageism and Social Integration of Older Adults in Their Neighborhoods in Israel | The Gerontologist | Oxford Academic ] [oup.com]. *The Gerontologist*, 54(2), 177–189. DOI: 10.1093/geront/gnt008 PMID: 23463803

Vygotsky, L. (2018). Lev Vygotsky. *La psicología en la Revolución Rusa. Colombia: Ediciones desde abajo.*

Wade-Benzoni, K. A., Sondak, H., & Galinsky, A. D. (2010). Leaving a Legacy: Intergenerational Allocations of Benefits and Burdens. *Business Ethics Quarterly*, 20(1), 7–34. DOI: 10.5840/beq20102013

Waite, L., & Das, A. (2010). Families, social life, and well-being at older ages. *Demography*, 47(Suppl 1), S87–S109. DOI: 10.1353/dem.2010.0009 PMID: 21302422

Wallbaum, T., Matviienko, A., Ananthanarayan, S., Olsson, T., Heuten, W., & Boll, S. C. (2018, April). Supporting communication between grandparents and grandchildren through tangible storytelling systems. In *Proceedings of the 2018 CHI Conference on Human Factors in Computing Systems* (pp. 1-12). DOI: 10.1145/3173574.3174124

Wanasphitaksakul, S. (2009). Factors influencing concern about death and dying, coping with death and dying, and satisfaction with life among elderly Thai and Chinese. https://repository.au.edu/server/api/core/bitstreams/05971af4-54de-4866-bcb1-d9e5d80505a7/content

Wang, L., Liang, J., & Wang, B. (2024). Population aging and sustainable economic development: An analysis based on the role of green finance. *Finance Research Letters*, 70, 106239. DOI: 10.1016/j.frl.2024.106239

Wang, L., & Tang, Y. (2023). Impacts of intergenerational caregiving on grandparents' health: Implications for SDG-3. *Economic Analysis and Policy*, 79, 584–598. DOI: 10.1016/j.eap.2023.06.015

Warner, M., & Zhang, X. (2023). Representative bureaucracy, age-friendly planning, and the role of gender, public engagement, and professional management. *Administration & Society*, 55(9), 1738–1757. DOI: 10.1177/00953997231183000

Watson, J. (2023). Skipped Generation Parenting: A Program to Enhance the Grandparent Caregiver Experience (Doctoral dissertation, John F. Kennedy University).

Weber, J. A., & Waldrop, D. P. (2000). Grandparents raising grandchildren: Families in transition. *Journal of Gerontological Social Work*, 33(2), 27–46. DOI: 10.1300/J083v33n02_03

Weismann, A. (1891). The duration of life. In Poulton, E. B., Schonland, S., & Shipley, A. E. (Eds.), *Essays on Heredity and Kindred Subjects* (2nd ed., pp. 163–256). Oxford University Press.

Wernher, I., & Lipsky, M. S. (2015). Psychological theories of aging. *Disease-a-Month*, 61(11), 480–488. DOI: 10.1016/j.disamonth.2015.09.004 PMID: 26603197

Wetzel, M., & Hank, K. (2020). Grandparents' relationship to grandchildren in the transition to adulthood. *Journal of Family Issues*, 41(10), 1885–1904. DOI: 10.1177/0192513X19894355

What is Russia like for older people? (n.d.). In *The Bearr Trust*.https://bearr.org/regional-news/what-is-russia-like-for-older-people/#:~:text=for%20older%20workers.-,Society%20valued%20older%20people.,vulnerable%20sectors%20of%20the%20population

Whitley, D. M., Kelley, S. J., & Sipe, T. A. (2001). Grandmothers raising grandchildren: Are they at increased risk of health problems? *Health & Social Work*, 26(2), 105–114. DOI: 10.1093/hsw/26.2.105 PMID: 11378995

WHO. (World Health Organization), (2020). Decade of Healthy Ageing 2020-2030. Geneva: WHO.

Wolf, M. A., & Brady, E. M. (2010). Adult and continuing education for an aging society. In Kasworm, C. E., Rose, A. D., & Ross-Gordon, J. M. (Eds.), *The handbook of adult and continuing education* (2010 edition, pp. 369–378). Sage.

Wolinsky, F., Jones, M., & Dotson, M. (2020). Does visual speed of processing training improve health-related quality of life in assisted and independent living communities?: A randomized controlled trial. *Innovation in Aging*, 4(4), igaa029. Advance online publication. DOI: 10.1093/geroni/igaa029 PMID: 32964141

Wong, J. S., & Hsieh, N. (2019). Functional status, cognition, and social relationships in dyadic perspective. The Journals of Gerontology: Series B, 74(4), 703-714. DOI: 10.1093/geronb/gbx024

Wong, E. L., Lau, J. Y., & Yeoh, E. K. (2018). Thinking intergenerationally: Intergenerational solidarity, health and active aging in Hong Kong: Policy. *Journal of Intergenerational Relationships*, 16(4), 478–492. DOI: 10.1080/15350770.2018.1489328

Worldbank Indicators. (2024). Economic Indicators, https://databank.worldbank.org/indicator/NY.GDP.PCAP.CD/1ff4a498/Popular-Indicators, (Accessed: 11.10.2024).

Wright, R., Gamaldo, A., & Lee, A. (2022). Neighborhood quality as it relates to health and well-being in older African Americans. *Innovation in Aging*, 6(Supplement_1), 113–114. DOI: 10.1093/geroni/igac059.452

Wrigley, H. S., Richer, E., Martinson, K., Kubo, H., & Strawn, J. (2003). The language of opportunity: Expanding employment prospects for adults with limited English skills.

Xu, H. (2019). Physical and mental health of Chinese grandparents caring for grandchildren and great-grandparents. *Social Science & Medicine*, 229, 106–116. DOI: 10.1016/j.socscimed.2018.05.047 PMID: 29866373

Xu, L., Chi, I., & Wu, S. (2018). Grandparent–grandchild relationships in Chinese immigrant families in Los Angeles: Roles of acculturation and the middle generation. *Gerontology & Geriatric Medicine*, 4, 2333721418778196. DOI: 10.1177/2333721418778196 PMID: 30035201

Yaa Boakye-Adjei, N. (2020). *FSI Briefs Covid-19: Boon and bane for digital payments and financial inclusion*. https://www.bis.org/fsi/fsibriefs9.pdf

Yamada, K., Murotani, K., Mano, M., Lim, Y., & Yoshimatsu, J. (2023). Age-friendly approach is necessary to prevent depopulation: Resident architectural designers and constructors' evaluation of the age-friendliness of Japanese municipalities. *International Journal of Environmental Research and Public Health*, 20(17), 6626. DOI: 10.3390/ijerph20176626 PMID: 37681766

Yang, Z., Norton, E. C., & Stearns, S. C. (2003). Longevity and Health Care Expenditures: The Real Reasons Older People Spend More. *The Journals of Gerontology. Series B, Psychological Sciences and Social Sciences*, 58(1), S2–S10. DOI: 10.1093/geronb/58.1.S2 PMID: 12496303

Yeh, I. L., Wong, S. Y. X., Safaruan, L. S. B., Kang, Y. Q., Wong, M. S., & Wilson, I. M. (2022). Development and Implementation of an Intergenerational Bonding Program in a Co-Located Model: A Case Study in Singapore. *Social Sciences (Basel, Switzerland)*, 11(12), 557. DOI: 10.3390/socsci11120557

Yerli, G. (2017). Characteristics Of Ageing Period And Social Works For The Elderly. *Journal Of International Social Research*, 10(52).

Ying, L., Lai, M., & Hwa, L. (2021). Modelling age-friendly environment for social connectedness: A cross-sectional study. *F1000 Research*, 10, 955. DOI: 10.12688/f1000research.73032.1 PMID: 35035892

Yu, C. (2024, April 12). *Will AI be a Boon to an Aging Society*. Repec.org. https://econpapers.repec.org/paper/osfthesis/a8suh.htm

Yu, J., Ma, G., & Wang, S. (2021). Do age-friendly rural communities affect quality of life? a comparison of perceptions from middle-aged and older adults in China. *International Journal of Environmental Research and Public Health*, 18(14), 7283. DOI: 10.3390/ijerph18147283 PMID: 34299736

Zamarro, G. (2020). Family labor participation and child care decisions: The role of grannies. *SERIEs*, 11(3), 287–312. DOI: 10.1007/s13209-020-00213-5

Zeng, Y., Xu, W., Luo, B., & Fang, Y. (2020). *Study on the Demand and Utilization of Health Services for the Poor Elderly in China*. DOI: 10.21203/rs.3.rs-46192/v1

Zeng, Y., Xu, W., & Tao, X. (2022). What factors are associated with utilisation of health services for the poor elderly? Evidence from a nationally representative longitudinal survey in China. *BMJ Open*, 12(6), e059758. DOI: 10.1136/bmjopen-2021-059758 PMID: 35760535

Zhang, M., You, S., Zhang, L., Zhang, H., & Wang, Y. (2023). Dynamic Analysis of the Effects of Aging on China's Sustainable Economic Growth. *Sustainability (Basel)*, 15(6), 5076. DOI: 10.3390/su15065076

Zhang, Y., Wang, J., Zu, Y., & Hu, Q. (2021). Attitudes of Chinese college students toward aging and living independently in the context of China's modernization: A qualitative study. *Frontiers in Psychology*, 12, 609736. Advance online publication. DOI: 10.3389/fpsyg.2021.609736 PMID: 34135797

Zhou, J., Mao, W., Lee, Y., & Chi, I. (2017). The impact of caring for grandchildren on grandparents' physical health outcomes: The role of intergenerational support. Research on Aging, 39(5), 612-634. doi:s10.1177/0164027515623332

Zhu, Y., Collins, A., Xu, Z., Sardana, D., & Cavusgil, S. T. (2021). Achieving aging well through senior entrepreneurship: A three-country empirical study. *Small Business Economics*, 59(2), 665–689. DOI: 10.1007/s11187-021-00564-8

Zijdeman, (2015);Riley (2005) - with minor processing by Our World in Data. "Life expectancy at birth - Various sources - period tables" [dataset]. Human Mortality Database, "Human Mortality Database"; United Nations, "World Population Prospects 2022"; United Nations, "World Population Prospects"; Zijdeman et al., "Life Expectancy at birth 2"; James C. Riley, "Estimates of Regional and Global Life Expectancy, 1800-2001", (Accessed: 09.10.2024).

Zuiderveen, A., Ivey, C., Dordan, S., & Leiras, C. (2016). Encouraging occupation: A systematic review of the use of life review and reminiscence therapy for the treatment of depressive symptoms in older adults. *Occupational Therapy in Mental Health*, 32(3), 281–298. DOI: 10.1080/0164212X.2016.1145090

Zunzunegui, M. V., Alvarado, B. E., Del Ser, T., & Otero, A. (2003). Social networks, social integration, and social engagement determine cognitive decline in community-dwelling Spanish older adults—. *Journal of Gerontology*, 58B(2), S93–S100. DOI: 10.1093/geronb/58.2.S93 PMID: 12646598

Zweifel, P., Felder, S., & Meiers, M. (1999). Ageing of population and health care expenditure: A red herring? *Health Economics*, 8(6), 485–496. DOI: 10.1002/(SICI)1099-1050(199909)8:6<485::AID-HEC461>3.0.CO;2-4 PMID: 10544314

Зиганшина, Л., Yudina, E., Talipova, L., Sharafutdinova, G., & Khairullin, R. (2020). Smart and age-friendly cities in russia: An exploratory study of attitudes, perceptions, quality of life and health information needs. *International Journal of Environmental Research and Public Health*, 17(24), 9212. DOI: 10.3390/ijerph17249212 PMID: 33317150

# About the Contributors

**Ali Gökhan Gölçek** is a Dr of Department of Public Finance at Niğde Ömer Halisdemir University, Türkiye. His scholarly interests pertain to poverty, energy policy, public finance policy, health economics, history of economics, and international political economy. He completed his PhD in Public Finance at Pamukkale University in 2022. Gölçek has published numerous articles and book chapters.

\*\*\*

**Akanksha** is a renowned psychiatrist and an expert in providing consultation on mental, behavioral, and sexual problems to patients. She specializes in the treatment of depression, anxiety, obsessive-compulsive disorder (OCD), bipolar disorder, schizophrenia, addictions, childhood, and geriatric mental health disorders, as well as neurological disorders. She is focused on a well-rounded, holistic approach to treating patients through medications, active listening, and recommending talk-centered counseling programs. She is also a member of the International Association of Sexual Medicine Practitioners (Modern Medicine) and has completed a course on addiction treatment training from AIIMS. She is also involved in administrative work and mental health awareness camps for better healthcare delivery of psychiatry services.

**Hamza** is an Assistant Professor in the Department of Clinical Psychology; she has qualified national level NTA-NET thrice and GATE in Psychology. She has presented several research papers at various national and international conferences and seminars. Her interest areas are psychosocial management of mood disorders, primary headaches (migraine, tension-type headaches), and neurodevelopmental disorders (ASD & ADHD).

**Salma Afroj** is currently pursuing a Ph.D. in the Department of Linguistics at Aligarh Muslim University. Her research interests are centered on applied linguistics, with a particular emphasis on translation, stylistics, and English language teaching. Salma distinguished herself academically by securing the 1st rank in her graduation from the Department of Linguistics at Aligarh Muslim University in 2017, an achievement for which she was awarded a Gold Medal. She has also qualified the UGC NET exam conducted by UGC, India. In addition to her academic achievements, Salma has actively contributed to the field through her presentations at various international and national conferences

**Deoshree Akhouri** working as a Professor (Clinical psychology) in the Department of Psychiatry, Faculty of Medicine, AMU, Aligarh. She has completed her M.Phil (Medical & Clinical Psychology) from Ranchi Institute of Neuro - Psychiatry & Allied Sciences (RINPAS), Kanke, Ranchi (Jharkhand) and done her PhD from Ranchi University. Prof. Akhouri is registered as Clinical Psychologist from Rehabilitation Council of India (CRR A13965). She has participated and presented various research papers related to psychiatric patients at National and International conferences, seminars & workshops. She has published more than 70 research papers in various National & International Journals. Additionally she has published more than 10 Articles in Souvenir, Newsletter (Indian Epilepsy Association, Ranchi Chapter, Ranchi, Jharkhand) and Newspapers. Her areas of interests are psychotherapy, mindfulness meditation, psycho-diagnostic and psychometric in Various Psychiatric Conditions and Forensic Psychology. She is also interested in hypnotherapy and stress management for adolescents & adults.

**Tabassum Bashir** is a respected Clinical Psychologist affiliated with the Psychiatry Department at J. N. Medical College and Hospital, Aligarh Muslim University (AMU). Specializing in multidisciplinary research on biopsychosocial phenomena, Bashir has made notable contributions to the field of Clinical Psychology over the past five years. Her expertise includes the management and treatment of mental disorders, leveraging a range of research methodologies to enhance patient care and therapeutic practices. Bashir focuses on exploring innovative treatment modalities and advancing research methods to improve patient outcomes. Her work reflects a strong commitment to integrating clinical practice with cutting-edge research, aiming to advance mental health care. Bashir has presented her research at numerous national and international conferences, and her scholarly work is well-regarded in the academic community. She has authored several research articles and book chapters published in esteemed journals and conference proceedings. Beyond their academic pursuits, she is dedicated to conducting community outreach programs for the awareness of mental health related disorders and wellbeing.

**Bilal Göde** is a Dr of Department of Public Finance at Pamukkale University, Turkey. His scholarly interests water economics, gerontological economics, public finance policy and international political economy. He completed his PhD in Public Finance at Pamukkale University in 2023.

**Tiago Horta Reis da Silva** is a Lecturer in Nursing Education (AEP) at King's College London, with a range of qualifications including BSc in Nursing, BSc in Traditional Chinese Medicine, MSc in Emotional Intelligence, Counselling and NLP, a Master of Business Administration, and MSc in Traditional Chinese Medicine. He has experience in other Higher Education Institutions and NHS and is a member of the Adult Nursing department, assisting with the running, development, and administration of BSc and MSc programmes. He also assists with teaching other modules' content and assists with interviews and assessment matters for other courses. Tiago is a Senior Fellow in Higher Education, a Fellow of the Royal Society of Medicine, and a Fellow for Faculty Nursing and Midwifery at the Royal College of Southern Ireland.

**J.O. Jeryda Gnanajane Eljo** is a Professor and Head in the Department of Social Work at Bharathidasan University, Tiruchirappalli. With over 27 years of teaching experience and 24 years of research expertise, she specializes in areas such as child and adolescent mental health, school mental health, and medical & psychiatric social work. She has guided numerous PhD and MPhil scholars and has published extensively in national and international journals. Dr. Jeryda has also been actively involved in various academic and social initiatives.

**Kalim Ahmad Khan** is an Assistant Professor of Law at Government Law College, Ujjain, Madhya Pradesh, India. He has successfully qualified for the UGC NET and JRF examinations conducted by the University Grants Commission (UGC). Mr. Khan is known for his academic excellence and strong oratory skills, and he is actively involved in community outreach and awareness programs. Mr. Khan's areas of specialization include Criminal Law, Civil Law, Constitutional Law, and Family Law. His scholarly contributions are reflected in numerous articles published in prestigious law journals and through presentations at both national and international conferences. With a profound commitment to legal education and research, Mr. Khan continues to make significant contributions to the field, leveraging his expertise and academic endeavors to advance legal scholarship and practice.

**Lakshmi R. Nair** is currently working as an Assistant Professor in the Department of English and Cultural Studies, Christ (Deemed To Be University), Bangalore. She specializes in Resistance Studies in her higher research. The title of her Doctoral research is: "Transformative Resistance through Creativity Revolution and Literary Resistance through Narrative Agency in Selected Works." She was teaching at St. Teresa's College Ernakulam affiliated to Mahatma Gandhi University. She completed her under-graduation in St. Teresa's College Ernakulam and post-graduation in UC College, Aluva. She has published several papers.

**Priya S. Dev** is currently an ICSSR Doctoral Scholar at the Department of Social Work, Bharathidasan University, Tiruchirappalli. She has four years of experience as an Assistant Professor in the Postgraduate Department of Social Work at Kuriakose Elias College, Kottayam, Kerala, before pursuing her PhD. She holds a Master's degree in Social Work with First Rank and Proficiency Prize from St. Berchmans College (2014-2016), specializing in Medical and Psychiatric Social Work. Additionally, she served as MG University Question Bank in-charge and Chief Examiner for "Abnormal & Social Psychology." Ms. Priya is actively involved in research, having published in reputed journals and presented papers at national seminars. Her research interests include children, women and Gerontological social work with a focus on counselling and welfare initiatives.

**Srinivasan S.** is an accomplished Assistant Professor (Research) in the Department of Humanities and Social Science at Graphic Era (Deemed to be University), Dehradun. He has previously contributed as Guest Faculty (Social Work) at Bharathidasan University, Tiruchirappalli, Tamil Nadu, where he served for two years. Mr. Srinivasan holds a Master of Philosophy degree from the Central University of Pondicherry, Pondicherry, India. His academic journey is marked by the publication of numerous research papers that cover a broad spectrum of subjects. His expertise spans across various areas including migration, ageing, women's and children's issues, public health issues, Tuberculosis, correctional administration, public policy, gender issues, artificial intelligence, and machine learning. Mr. Srinivasan's diverse research interests reflect his commitment to addressing complex social issues through an interdisciplinary lens, making significant contributions to both the academic and practical realms of social science.

**Pallav Vishnu** is an esteemed Associate Professor (Psycholinguistics) in the Department of Linguistics at Aligarh Muslim University. He holds an MA in Linguistics and a PhD in Linguistics, complemented by a Postgraduate Diploma in Journalism and Mass Communication (PGDJMC). Dr. Vishnu is distinguished as a Gold Medalist in his MA Linguistics program, reflecting his academic excellence. His contributions to the field of linguistics have been recognized with four prestigious awards from the India Friendship Forum, New Delhi, honoring his outstanding services and research. Dr. Vishnu has an extensive publication record, with 170 articles featured in both national and international journals. Additionally, he has authored nine books with prominent Indian publishing companies.

# Index

www.ingramcontent.com/pod-product-compliance
Ingram Content Group UK Ltd.
Pitfield, Milton Keynes, MK11 3LW, UK
UKHW010808200125
453967UK00007B/29